THE RUTLAND ROAD

— Rutland Railway

THE RUTLAND ROAD

SECOND
EDITION

by Jim Shaughnessy

To Bud Cushman —
Enjoy your ride on the Rutland —
Jim Shaughnessy

SYRACUSE UNIVERSITY PRESS

First Syracuse University Press Edition 1997

97 98 99 00 01 02   6 5 4 3 2 1

Second edition originally published in 1981 by Howell-North Books.

The paper used in this publication meets the minimum requirements of
American National Standard for Information Sciences—Permanence of Paper
for Printed Library Materials, ANSI Z39.48-1984. ∞™

Library of Congress Cataloging-in-Publication Data

Shaughnessy, Jim.
The Rutland Road / Jim Shaughnessy. — 2nd ed.
p.   cm.
Includes bibliographical references and index.
ISBN 0-8156-0469-6 (cloth : alk. paper). — ISBN 0-8156-0456-4
(pbk. : alk. paper)
1. Rutland Railway Corporation—History.   I. Title.
HE2791.R973S5   1997
385' . 06'5743—dc21   96-51169

To the late HAROLD W. ZENGER, *whose deep dedication and meticulous research provided the basics for this work. His love for the Rutland and Vermont was deep and strong. It is unfortunate indeed that fate deprived him of seeing the completion of the work he had begun so capably.*

— *William D. Middleton*

Acknowledgments

The work of preparing a volume of this size is unbelievable. It takes many people, scattered all over, to supply the thought, fact and illustration. I am indebted to all of these generous friends for their interest and participation.

The launching of this endeavor is credited entirely to Harold W. Zenger, who originally started the project, but suddenly and unfortunately passed away early in 1962. He gathered great quantities of historical facts and anecdotes. His deep interest is reflected in the content of the material.

I want to thank David W. Messer for his extensive editorial assistance and Donald S. Mac-Naughton and my wife, Carol, for their copy reading and advice. My mother, Mrs. James A. Shaughnessy, handled all the transcription.

The photos and illustrations distinguish a work of this type from an average archival reference to a living review of the past. I am especially pleased that Dr. Phil Hastings, native of Vermont, one time resident of Burlington, and friend of long duration was able to add his great record of the Rutland during its glory days of steam.

All the following photographers, collectors and owners of rare prints have contributed greatly to this record as well. Without them it would be lean indeed: Bob Adams, Association of American Railroads; Ed. Bond, E. H. Brown, Charles Castner-L&N Ry., Richard L. Church, Robert F. Collins, Richard Costello, Gordon Cutler, Claude Dern, Lawrence Doherty, Charles E. Fisher-Ry. & Locomotive Historical Society; Donald W. Furler, F. Stewart Graham, Al Gayer, Paul Green, Ken Gypsom, Ray Haseltine, Fred Hewitt, Frances Kingsley, Robert Lank, Marjorie Ludlow, James R. MacFarlane, O. K. McKnight, Manchester Historical Society, William D. Middleton, E. L. Modeler, John E. Pickett, R. S. Ritchie, Donald S. Robinson, Rutland *Herald* — Ken Wild, Fred Sankoff, Shelburne Museum — David Webster, Howard Towsley, Vermont Historical Society — Richard Wood and S. S. Worthen.

Finally, Frank C. Dodge, of the Industrial Photo Service, for his technical advice and assistance in making the numerous photo copies.

My sincere gratitude and appreciation to all.

JIM SHAUGHNESSY

Troy, New York
1964

The southbound *Green Mountain Flyer* rolls into Rouses Point, New York, station from Montreal and Canadian National trackage behind mountain type 92. In the distance can be seen the dining car of D&H's Montreal–New York counterpart *The Laurentian* crossing the diamond on the Rutland's line west to Ogdensburg on its daily southbound journey.—*John Pickett.*

Contents

Early railroad plans for connecting the Atlantic seaboard
with the Great Lakes and the St. Lawrence ⚹ ⚹ ⚹ Differ-
ences between Follett and Paine ⚹ ⚹ ⚹ Chartering of the
Champlain & Connecticut and the Vermont Central ⚹ ⚹ ⚹
Fight between the two roads for financing ⚹ ⚹ ⚹ Infil-
tration of "spies" into each other's organizations ⚹ ⚹ ⚹
Construction of the Champlain & Connecticut ⚹ ⚹ ⚹ Re-
organization of Champlain & Connecticut into Rutland &
Burlington Company ⚹ ⚹ ⚹ The race for the mail contract
⚹ ⚹ ⚹ Opening of the line and attendant festivities ⚹ ⚹ ⚹
First schedules ⚹ ⚹ ⚹ Connections with other roads

Refusal of Vermont Central to connect at Burlington ⚹ ⚹ ⚹
Vermont Central's connection with Vermont & Canada at
Essex Junction, blocking the Rutland from a northern connection ⚹ ⚹ ⚹ Entry of the Smiths in Vermont Central-
Rutland fight ⚹ ⚹ ⚹ Desperate plight of the Rutland for
line-haul business ⚹ ⚹ ⚹ Court actions ⚹ ⚹ ⚹ Vermont Central finally cooperates, but direct northern connection for
the Rutland still far in the future.

Reorganization of the Rutland and Burlington into the Rutland Railroad Company ⚹ ⚹ ⚹ Eastern and western connections ⚹ ⚹ ⚹ Connections with the new London Northern
⚹ ⚹ ⚹ Rutland threats to the Vermont Central's dominance
of northern connections ⚹ ⚹ ⚹ Leasing of the Rutland by
the Vermont Central.

Recession and financial troubles for the Vermont Central.
⚹ ⚹ ⚹ Connections to New York City ⚹ ⚹ ⚹ More financial
troubles ⚹ ⚹ ⚹ Reorganization of the Vermont Central into
the Central Vermont Railroad ⚹ ⚹ ⚹ D & H interest in the
Rutland ⚹ ⚹ ⚹ Lease renewed ⚹ ⚹ ⚹ Still more financial
troubles ⚹ ⚹ ⚹ Vermont Central control crumbles ⚹ ⚹ ⚹
Delaware & Hudson stuck with the Rutland ⚹ ⚹ ⚹ Charles
Clement takes over.

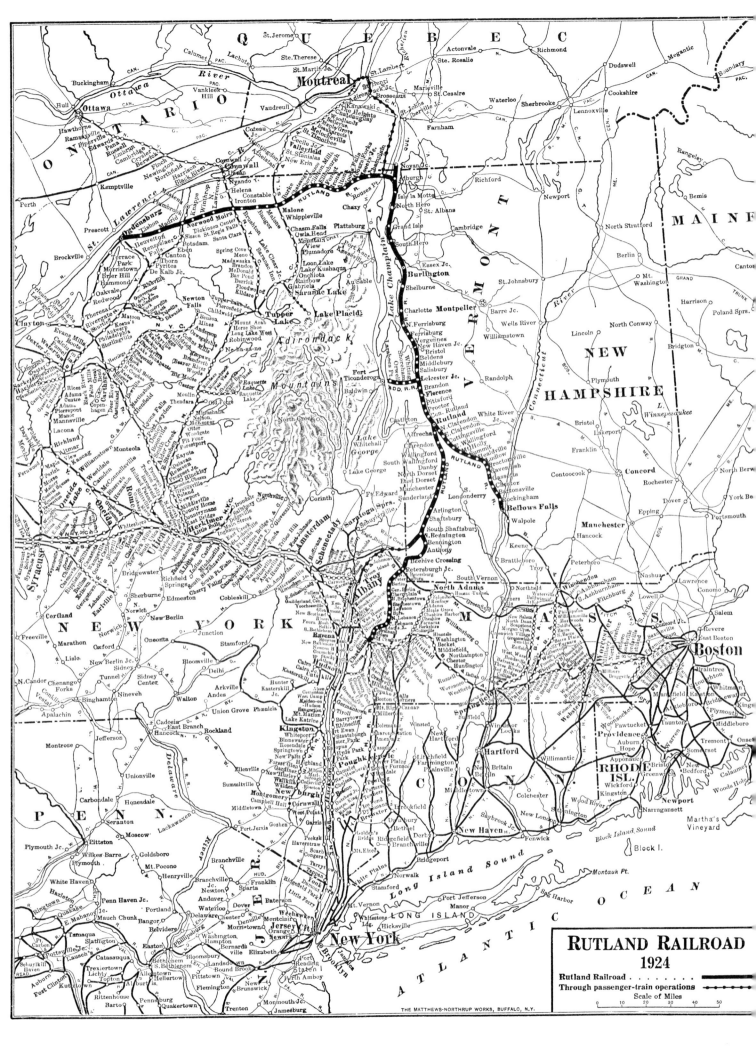

RUTLAND RAILROAD
1924

Rutland Railroad . . . .
Through passenger-train operations
Scale of Miles

THE MATTHEWS-NORTHRUP WORKS, BUFFALO, N.Y.

Chapter 1

Burlington-Boston or Bust

"The enterprise in which we are engaged, gentlemen, is one of great interest and importance not only to us, its stockholders, and the immediate region through which the road passes, but to the whole state of Vermont, to Boston, to all New England and New York. A country fertile in the productions of agriculture, and rich in minerals to an unparalleled extent is penetrated by this road and rendered accessible at all seasons of the year. By it the markets of the Atlantic are brought to our doors, and over it the trade and travel of the mighty West and Canada will find their outlet to all our great cities and towns."

Timothy Follett of Burlington, Vermont, was speaking, delivering his report as president to the first annual meeting of the stockholders of the Rutland & Burlington Railroad. It was not difficult for those present in the room to become infected by Follett's glowing optimism for on that January 12, 1848, the little city of Burlington was an isolated island in the vast frozen wasteland that stretched almost from the Atlantic shore to the Great Lakes. Walled off from the markets of Massachusetts and southern New England by the high escarpments of the Green Mountains, the trade of the Champlain valley was at most a seasonal thing, flourishing from May to November and dropping to a trickle with the first deep snows of winter. To the west of Lake Champlain, northern New Yorkers were even more isolated.

Transportation, or the lack of it, had been a major problem ever since the first great influx of set-tlers following the War of 1812. The land was good along the valleys. The forested slopes would yield all the prime timber that could be cut, if it could reach the markets. Iron and marble lay in the hills for the taking, but the taking was a slow, laborious, and costly process. What trade there was in the Champlain valley was oriented to the accessible markets of Montreal and Quebec, a trade route altered somewhat when the opening of the Great Northern Canal between Whitehall and Troy began to siphon the riches of the valley down toward the Hudson and New York. But the magic promise of the Boston market beckoned. The Great Lakes trade was burgeoning, and the challenge was to join the two from the St. Lawrence River port of Ogdensburg across northern New York by the easy grades north of the Adirondacks, across the foot of Lake Champlain, and then somehow over the spine of Vermont to the Connecticut River valley.

The last was the challenge that stalled every plan for a grand canal through the 1820s, and there were many of them, inspired by the Great Northern and the "big ditch", the Erie. The most feasible of the canal surveys indicated that at least three hundred locks would be necessary to navigate Vermont, a situation to give pause even to the most dedicated canal promoter. It appeared that this promising land was doomed to lie in loneliness while progress passed it by along the Hudson and the Mohawk Rivers. The canal fever stayed alive, but the centers of capital exhibited an almost complete indifference. Financiers in the seaboard cities were gradually becoming intrigued by a revolutionary new mode of transportation, that of moving goods and people swiftly and smoothly over roads of iron, *rail*roads.

The more progressive businessmen of Vermont were quick to abandon the canal idea. Here was transportation that could conquer the Green Mountain barrier without locks. What's more, it could run all the year 'round! The railroad virus flared with a warmth that the canal fever could never attain. Travellers from Boston could talk of nothing else but the marvels of the railroads; they became the consuming topic of conversation in a thousand general stores, and desire began to shape into decision.

In 1831 the village of Rutland, Vermont went railroad-crazy with a series of mass meetings proposing lines to lead off in all directions. Completely land-locked, the community suffered more than the Champlain valley towns from the restrictions of its primitive roads, and before the year was out it had chartered the first railroad in Vermont, to build west to the head of Lake Champlain and the Great Northern Canal in New York State. Rutlanders had their charter, but no money. The charter gathered dust for a decade.

The progressive citizens farther north were not idle. A year earlier they had fought their way through a howling February storm to gather in their first railroad "convention" in the capital village of Montpelier. Few of them had actually seen a railroad. Some of them had, perhaps, only the fuzziest notions about the appearance and performance of a "locomotive engine". But most of them were sophisticates who had traveled to Boston and Philadelphia, perhaps even to Charleston where a colossus of a railroad was planning an operation extending nearly a hundred miles out into the countryside. Key leaders in the railroad movement began to emerge from the days of meeting and argument: Charles Paine of Northfield, holder of vast lands, banker, mill owner; George Parish of Ogdensburg, easily the wealthiest man in northern New York, but perhaps more famous as the winner of the beauteous Ameriga Vespucci diamond from John VanBuren in a classic poker game a few years before; and Timothy Follett, merchant and steamboat operator from Burlington.

The subject at hand was a project that staggered all imagination — a railroad to extend all the way

Charles Paine was founder of the Vermont Central Railway and bitter rival of Timothy Follett, governor of Vermont, 1841-43. — *Vermont Historical Society.*

from Ogdensburg on the St. Lawrence River to the port city of Boston, a four-hundred mile iron pathway to siphon the riches of the lakes to the greatest seaport in New England. At the time, a scant 25 miles of railroad trackage was in operation in the entire United States. It was an intriguing idea, the connection of the vast navigable system of lakes and rivers, reaching into the heartland of the continent, with the young country's major seaport. The Boston financiers present were impressed, but not to the point of pledging cash to so farfetched a dream. Undaunted, the convention adjourned to the State Capitol across the street to ram a resolution through the Assembly asking the state's congressional delegation to use its influence in requesting the federal government to finance a survey of the road.

There the matter rested; Washington evidenced no enthusiasm for the requested survey. A few local railroad meetings were held at various points in Vermont and northern New York. Though the subject of a railroad aroused considerable interest through the Green Mountain country for a year or so, the mechanical monster was still too new, too untried, to warrant the gambling of many hard-earned Yankee dollars. The overwhelming majority of cautious Vermonters and northern New Yorkers were perfectly willing to let others experiment with this revolutionary new mode of transportation. After all, they had a good system of corduroy and dirt roads, and there were always the dependable lakes and rivers for eight months of the year.

There was a brief flurry of excitement in 1837 when a Boston group proposed the construction of a completely covered railroad through the mountains — a dream that would have denuded a sizeable swath through the forested hills — but that commendable idea fortunately died quickly. In those days before the invention of spark arresters for locomotive stacks, the passage of the first train would probably have set off the longest fire the world had ever seen.

A decade had passed while they cogitated on the matter, years which saw spidery lines of track reach out from the seacoast westward and the pioneer Mohawk & Hudson linked to a series of little lines across the breadth of New York State. To the discerning men of Vermont it became all too obvious that a surging new economy, a new pattern of prosperity, was developing rapidly along these new railroad lines. A new sense of urgency developed in Vermont and spread like wildfire. If the northern region was not to be caught in an economic backwash, it must replace its slow and costly methods of transportation with rails of iron. Besides, reports being circulated indicated that there might be some handsome profits in a railroad venture, and no Yankee worthy of the name could turn down an opportunity to make an honest dollar.

The idea of a single trunk line from the St. Lawrence to Boston had been abandoned long before as being too vast an undertaking to be practical. The basic project had now been divided into segments, a series of interconnected railroads, each autonomous, but with operating agreements comprising a through route. The Boston & Lowell and the Fitchburg were building west from the Hub of the Universe, and in New York State, George Parish and his associates were organizing the line to operate as the Northern of New York from Og-

densburg to the vicinity of Plattsburgh on Lake Champlain. To the northeast, the Northern of New Hampshire was constructing its tortuous line through the White Mountains.

Vermont cogitated further until 1843 when there was a flurry of activity in the Assembly session. Four roads were chartered in rapid-fire succession, granting the Connecticut & Passumpsic Rivers Railroad the right to build north out of the Connecticut River valley toward Canada, the Vermont & Massachusetts the right to build south from Brattleboro to Fitchburg, and not one but *two* lines to bridge the state from the Connecticut valley to Burlington. For as frequently happens when strong men become involved in the same dream of empire, a deep and widening schism had developed between Charles Paine and Timothy Follett over the most practical route for a trans-Vermont railroad. Each had selfish interests. Paine saw a route north through the White and Onion River valleys, passing through his home town of Northfield, as a golden opportunity to gain a personal fortune. Follett, already established in the steamboat business on Lake Champlain, saw greater possibilities for success in a more southerly route leaving the Connecticut to follow the Williams River north to Mount Holly, then descending through the Otter Creek valley by way of Rutland, and north along the relatively level lands west of the mountains to Burlington. This route would feed more lucrative traffic to his steamers, especially since George Parish was then busily organizing the Northern Rail Road to build from Ogdensburg to Plattsburgh, almost directly across the lake from Burlington. With this proposal he gained the enthusiastic support of the vociferous Rutland contingent.

The proponents of both lines descended on the State Capitol like a swarm of locusts in October of 1843. The hapless legislators were trapped by constituents arguing the merits of one road while threatening defeat at the polls if the other was granted a charter. In desperation they tried to avoid the issue, but there was no escape. On October 23 Senator Ebenezer Briggs of Brandon introduced Senate Bill No. 16, entitled "An Act to incorporate the Champlain and Connecticut River Rail Road Company."

Five days later it was passed, giving the Company "all rights to construct a rail road from some point at Burlington, thence southwardly through the counties of Addison, Rutland and Windsor or Windham, to some point on the west bank of the Connecticut River, as such company shall designate; for the transportation of persons and property by steam or horse power." With a few changes of detail, the Assembly rushed through a similar bill granting a charter to the Vermont Central Rail Road, then hurriedly closed up shop and went home, completely fed up with railroads for one session.

There is evidence, however, that considerable location work had been accomplished before the charter was granted. The Rutland *Herald* of August 20, 1843, reported, "The corps of engineers now surveying a route for the railroad from Rutland to the Connecticut take this method of expressing their thanks to the inhabitants bordering on the route for the generous hospitality evidenced by them, also for the liberal aid in personally assisting them in the work." Enthusiasm was running high; the surveying crews were truly men of distinction as they slowly worked their way across Vermont.

Open warfare broke out immediately. Follett, still oriented closely to lake shipping, immediately seized what he considered an advantage through the acquisition of 65 acres of prime waterfront for a Burlington terminal, even before the stock subscription books were opened. Paine's associates naturally charged collusion and chicanery, but the furor seemed to be more for propaganda purposes than anything else. The really vicious infighting had not yet started.

With the opening of the books for taking of stock subscriptions, agents for both companies set to work in earnest. Hardly a lonely farmhouse in the state escaped the blandishments of one or the other, or both, of the railroad promoters. Both enterprises found support to almost equal degree in the financial marts of Boston. The struggle for funds reached its zenith around Burlington and in the Connecticut River valley, for these were areas to be affected by both railroad propositions, and being the most prosperous sections of the state, they were naturally prime hunting grounds for representatives

RAIL ROAD NOTICE.
———o———

THE COMMISSIONERS appointed by the act of the Legislature incorporating the CHAMPLAIN and CONNECTICUT RIVER RAIL ROAD COMPANY, hereby give notice that Books for subscriptions to the capital stock of said company, will be opened on the 10th day of June next at the following places :—at Follett, Bradley & Co's. Store in Burlington ;—at George T. Hodges Store in Rutland;—at Calvin Townsley & Sons in Brattleboro', and at some place in every town on and contiguous to the line of the road.

Timothy Follett,
John A. Conant,
George T. Hodges,
Luther Daniels,
Calvin Townsley,   } Commissioners.
Samuel Barker,
William Nash,
Ambrose L. Brown,
Henry N. Fullerton,
William Henry.

From the *Burlington Free Press*, May 27, 1845.

of both factions. Slander by the spoken word and the public press attended almost every share of stock subscribed, and whole communities split on the comparative merits of the two railroad routes.

In spite of the vicious vendetta, both propositions gained a reasonable amount of support. For a time, the Follett group seemed to waver, but a quick reorganization and a new charter, granted in November of 1847 and changing the name to the Rutland & Burlington Railroad Company, salved the injured pride of Vermont's second city and swung the balance of financial support in its favor. Moreover, the new charter authorized the company to build a second tap toward the lucrative Lake Champlain shipping through a branch along the banks of Otter Creek west of Vergennes.

While the Rutland & Burlington company was still looking to Lake Champlain, Charles Paine and his associates were busy along the eastern border of the state. An eminent engineer, Samuel M. Felton, had been engaged to make a survey for the Vermont Central, and it became immediately apparent that the most feasible route to Boston would be, for some distance, down the Connecticut valley. Two other roads, the Cheshire, to run the 64 miles between Bellows Falls and Fitchburg, and the fifty-mile Fitchburg Railroad between that city and Boston were essential as eastern connections for both the Rutland & Burlington and the Vermont Central lines. Paine executed a secret pact with the managements of the two roads in 1845, committing them to exclusive interchange with the Vermont Central. In spite of Paine's eminence (he had been Governor of Vermont in 1841 and 1842), the managers of the two smaller roads did not trust him entirely, and soon abrogated their agreements. Paine promptly linked his railroad with the Northern of New Hampshire for an entry into Boston via that road and the Boston & Lowell line.

The Rutland & Burlington managers arranged for the construction of the northern division of the road between Burlington and Brandon in January, 1847. The contractor, possibly on sober second thought, refused to enter a written contract with the company and made no move to start construction. The work on the 51-mile segment was started by a second builder on the first of May, with completion scheduled for late in 1848. Construction started up the other end of the line from Bellows Falls at about the same time, but the contractor on that end soon abandoned the job and it too had to be relet. In June, the directors let the contract for the balance of the line from the summit of Mount Holly north to Brandon, a stretch of 35 miles. Here again the contractors quickly abandoned their portion of the line. Significantly, several of these construction gangs soon appeared on the Vermont Central route a few miles to the north.

James Barrett, a Rutland merchant and avid supporter of the railroad project who was to donate the land for the railroad station in that village, wrote to his son in 1846, "They have arrested a railroad worker near Windsor for trespassing. The Central folks have no right to come below White River. An injunction will be brought immediately before the Supreme Court to see if they have the right in their charter to go all over Vermont." Later in the year, Barrett wrote, "Our railroad is going on finely. Judge Timothy Follett has agreed to give up his business in Burlington and devote his whole time to the Road, and he is to have the whole direction of the business. The road is advertised for proposals for contract until January 1, 1847, from Bellows Falls to Summit and from Burlington

to Brandon, the remaining part to be put under contract as it can be located, Governor Paine's opposition to the same notwithstanding."

In spite of these discouragements and delays, Follett confidently predicted in his first report that "The portion of the road between Burlington and Rutland, and between Bellows Falls and Ludlow — in all over ninety miles — will be in readiness for the cars by the first day of January, 1849, and the remainder at a somewhat later period during the year." Gradually, the grade began to stretch out along the route of the old Green Mountain Turnpike (a road chartered in 1799) from Bellows Falls to Clarendon.

It is of more than passing interest to note that when the contractors began to clear the rocks near Summit (elevation 1511 feet) in preparation for blasting, they were obliged to clean out a small pond or pothole near where the station now stands. The draining of the pond disclosed a bed of mud and silt, and when this was cleared, the skeleton of a mastodon was uncovered. The discovery attracted the attention of many scientists and led to the placing of the skeleton in a Boston museum.

Orders for rails had been placed with a Boston manufacturer on January 14, 1847, but that supplier promptly defaulted, using the "condition of the money market" as an excuse. Follett promptly contracted for 2,000 tons of English rail — enough, at least, to get track work under way. For other metal furnishings, he turned to sources on his own line. By so doing, he also benefited one of his company's directors and supporters.

A limited supply of good quality hematite iron ore exists in the region around Pittsford and Brandon, where primitive smelters were in operation. These provided castings for rail chairs, spikes and other appurtenances for the line, as well as castings for car parts to supply the new works established at Brandon by director John A. Conant. Conant's firm was awarded orders for 190 freight cars, forty gravel cars and eight baggage cars. At the same time, the new railroad contracted with the busy Taunton Locomotive Works for eight passenger locomotives of 18 tons each and four freight engines, each weighing twenty tons.

While the Rutland & Burlington was completing its financial structure and beginning to take shape

Brandon station in 1851 forms a background for Dobbin and his express wagon, apparently driven by a big black dog.

The solemnity of this picture was twofold: one had to remain still for a minute while early photos were made; and Rutland & Burlington No. 15, the CHESTER, had just arrived from its builder in Taunton, Massachusetts this summer's day in 1850.

as an operating railroad, a third giant on the Vermont railroad scene had quietly made his entrance. John Smith was a man of considerable wealth and influence up in Franklin County on the Canadian border, where he operated the bank in the sleepy little lakeside hamlet of St. Albans and owned considerable inland farming property. Canny man that he was, Smith had sat back during the early stages of the railroad controversy, closely watching the struggle between Follett and Paine. He knew that both of the new lines would eventually have to obtain a connection north to Canada and the foot of Lake Champlain. The only feasible route lay through his empire.

When Smith finally moved, his decision had been carefully made. In October of 1845, he received a charter for the Vermont & Canada Railroad and immediately began negotiations with Charles Paine and the Vermont Central. The charter specified that the Vermont & Canada was to build "from some point in the town of Highgate" to an unnamed point of junction with the Vermont Central and Rutland & Burlington lines in Chittendon County. It was probably no accident that the Legislature neglected to clarify the point. That omission placed John Smith squarely in control of the situation, and laid the foundation for a dynasty that was to exercise power over transportation in Vermont for the next half-century.

When the direction of Smith's interest was clearly evident, Follett moved, belatedly to provide for a northerly extension of the Rutland & Burlington route. In the October, 1849 session of the Legislature, he secured an amendment to the road's charter which authorized it to build north of Burlington "to intersect the Vermont & Canada Railroad at the village of St. Albans." This was a move in defense of the Rutland & Burlington. The Vermont & Canada was building down to a junction with the Vermont Central several miles east of Burlington, the terminal city, to create a station that would become storied as one of the most dismal points in American railroading — Essex Junction. By this maneuver, Smith and Paine had set Follett out on the end of a long and shaky limb. In so doing, they had also placed the largest city in Vermont on the stub end of a branch line of their own railroad system!

The granting of the amended charter to the Rutland road came as no surprise to the opposition interests. When it was granted, they had made certain that a clause was inserted which gave the Rutland & Burlington only two years to complete the project, under penalty of revocation. The ink had hardly dried on the governor's signature on the bill before a man named Byron Stevens walked out of Chancery Court with an injunction preventing Follett's road from building the new line. Stevens, holding only five shares of Rutland & Burlington stock, was of course a Vermont Central "plant" in the opposition's camp, one of several deliberately set up to take care of such contingencies. Backed by a battery of good lawyers in the Vermont Central employ, Stevens had no difficulty in delaying the case until the Rutland road's time ran out.

Consternation reigned in the Rutland & Burlington's board. In his report to the stockholders for 1851, Follett was forced to state that the proposition had been abandoned. Director D. E. Smalley of Burlington had headed a valiant fight in the courts to no avail.

The litigation had no effect on the completion of the line south of Burlington. In that city, a new station and four-stall engine house were built, and work was started on wharves and warehouses to take care of the expected lake trade. At Rutland, stone masons were laying up a huge roundhouse for 16 locomotives, a repair shop and a handsome passenger station. At the southern terminal in Bellows Falls, facilities were building to take care of the Cheshire's equipment and passengers in addition to the Rutland & Burlington's. But trouble with various grading and track contractors had erupted again, and in desperation the board of directors placed all the remaining portions of unconstructed line under one contract. The section between Rutland and Ludlow had proved particularly troublesome; the combination of sinkholes and heavy rock cuttings had defeated three contractors before the railroad, in despair, assigned the job to its own chief engineer, William B. Gilbert. Long before the rock cuts at the summit of Mount Holly had been completed, 12,000 tons of rails began arriving at Bellows Falls and Burlington, nearly 7,000 tons arriving at the latter point by water via the Hudson River, the Champlain Canal, and subsequently by lake steamer. Tie material was no problem. Farmers and woodsmen along the route found a bonanza in the apparently insatiable demand for chestnut, oak, and maple lengths.

On April 15, 1849, workmen for the firm of Eastman & Page swarmed onto the raw grade at Bellows Falls, at Vergennes, and at Burlington. Teams moved creaking wagons along the cuts and fills, lengthening a trail of dropped ties that were quickly swung into position and spaced, ready between the string of sixty-pound rails that would soon be spiked into position. The junction switch connection with the Cheshire Railroad was mauled into place at Bellows Falls and Rutland & Burlington No. 9, the RUTLAND, rolled onto home iron. No. 5, the MIDDLEBURY, was eased ashore at Burlington a few days later. With these two engines moving materials in a steady stream to the construction sites, work proceeded at an even more rapid pace through the summer months. By early autumn it was apparent that, barring a catastrophe, the Rutland & Burlington would be completed before its scheduled date at the beginning of 1850.

On the strength of the rapid progress of construction, the road put in a bid for a contract to carry the mails. Understandably, the stage line operators protested vehemently against this threatened loss of revenue. They were strong in their contention that natural horses could and would move the United States mail over the Green Mountains faster and safer than the iron variety. The harassed superintendent of the mails finally arranged a race to solve the dilemma, with the contract to go to the winner.

The race was held on one of those golden October days when Vermont is at its best. Henry H. Howe, the Ludlow postmaster, had been placed in charge of the competition which started at the Bellows Falls station. There, a light stage with four fast and rested horses champing at their bits waited beside the track. Alongside, the diminutive RUTLAND, coupled to one car, steamed quietly, pluming a thin haze of acrid wood smoke up into the brilliant sky. Engineer Silar Pierce checked his water gauge for the tenth time as Howe handed a sack of mail onto the stage and another onto the railroad car. The fireboy made a last lubricating check of the cylinders, dropped the stinking

tallow pot back into its bracket, and laid a few more pine billets on the pile within easy reach on the deck. He checked the roaring firebox and noted with satisfaction the feather of steam wafting from the pop valve. Across the way, the stage driver noted these preparations dourly and held the reins a little tighter and higher against the pull of the spirited teams.

Howe walked slowly out into the space between the two vehicles, eyes on the big watch in his hand. His arm raised slowly, held, then flashed down to his side. The stage driver let out a mighty shout, punctuated by the slap of leather as the four horses lunged forward. Two screaming toots from the RUTLAND's whistle sent them into full gallop. Engineer Pierce eased the throttle back and steam rushed into the cylinders with a whoosh. The bright red drivers spun briefly, rods flashing in the morning sun, then bit the iron as Pierce eased off. Sparks rose high in the air as the little Taunton engine began to roll, her exhaust quickening into an urgent staccato rhythm that echoed from hill to brilliant hill in the opalescent morning sunshine. The careening stage was out of sight now, and as the little train rolled out into the countryside, Pierce notched her open. Trackside trees gradually merged into a reeling kaleidoscope of flowing color, punctuated only by the lonely crossings where little knots of open-mouthed farmers stood safely back as the screaming monster hurtled past. Up the line, nervous mothers dragged at little boys who, ears to track, heard and felt the vibration of the pounding drivers. On the RUTLAND, the fireboy struggled to hold his feet as he pitched the three-foot billets into the raging firebox. The supply in the tender was melting with alarming rapidity, and between his stoking the fireman raced back to pile wood forward to a ready position on the deck.

Pierce leaned far out of the rocking cab, opening the throttle wide on the upgrades, easing it only a little on the down. The whistle screamed like a banshee as they roared through Brockway's Mills, Chester and Gassetts. Flanges screamed on the outside iron as they lurched into the big bend at Cavendish. Beyond Ludlow, Pierce whistled imperiously for brakes, and brawny arms strained to "tie her down". Locked wheels screeched to a

smoking stop, and almost before they had ceased turning, a waiting horseman had the mail sack across his saddle, his fast horse in a straight-out gallop up the grade beyond the end of track, laborers scattering like geese before him. Pierce hung limply from the mercifully-still cab window and watched him gallop out of sight.

Three relays of men, with the fastest horses in Vermont, carried the precious sack over the summit to Cuttingsville where engine No. 17, the BELLOWS FALLS, started rolling down the western grade as soon as the last lathered horse pounded into view. She rolled easily until the rider flung the sack aboard, then sharply picked up speed as the full pressure of steam slammed into her cylinders.

From Cuttingsville to Rutland the track drops along the mountainside in a series of short tangents, finally straightening out for a long downgrade run into the Rutland home yard, now waiting with everything in the clear and every switch guarded and lined for the main. The BELLOWS FALLS rammed through like a demented demon, her screaming whistle drowning out the roar of the waiting crowd. At Pittsford and again at Ferrisburg she screeched to a stop while waiting gangs sent wood in a torrent into her tender. At Middlebury she slaked her thirst and blasted out while water still gushed from the feedpipe. Early in the afternoon the valiant little locomotive ground to a halt in front of the new Burlington station and the weary, shaken crew dropped down into a jubilant crowd.

The Rutland & Burlington had won the race, as it proved, by a good two hours.

The jubilation of the weary crews was more than matched by the management. The mail contract was worth $1200 a month, and every cent of revenue was important to the directors. Money was tight, and the company's treasury was becoming alarmingly depleted. But in spite of the carefully guarded official concern, work was pushed rapidly toward completion of the line. All through the ever-colder days of November the steady clank of maul on spike echoed near the summit of Mount Holly, merging in a cacophony of metallic rhythm as the two ends of track drew near to connection in the early weeks of December.

On the bright, sharp morning of December 18, the valiant little MT. HOLLY whistled the train from Boston out of Bellows Falls for Summit. This time, no records were involved; the dignitaries loading the coaches behind would get the gentlest ride Engineer Pierce could give them over the still-unballasted track. The polished little engine puffed and labored under the load, snorting into the grades with an air of restrained, dignified effort. For this was a very special day, the day the Rutland & Burlington became, in truth, a railroad.

Down from the north the 20-ton MIDDLEBURY, fresh from the Taunton works, headed another stockholders' special out of Burlington, proudly deigning to make stops at Vergennes, Middlebury, Rutland and other important towns along the line to add to the human cargo now jamming her six bright coaches. Late in the morning the two trains labored up the opposite slopes of Mount Holly, fighting to defeat the ruling grades on the raw new line. Stops for wood had to be made four times by the train from Bellows Falls. Those who waited near the summit saw a pale blue haze rising above the trees to the east and west, and finally, in the clear cold air, heard the blending beat of the two exhausts. In the rock cut at the summit came sharp whistles for brakes and the shoes ground down on the wheels as waiting brakemen applied their hickory clubs on every platform. The proud new engines halted with pilots almost touching.

Passengers poured from the coaches, rushing forward to greet the people from the other side of the mountain. President Follett bore a bottle of clear Champlain water; from the Boston train came Nathan Rice, a promoter of the road, with a similar bottle of murkier fluid from Massachusetts Bay. With appropriate remarks, duly noted by the now-shivering crowd as having something to do with a milestone in the history of the railroad, the State of Vermont and the Union, the beaver-hatted dignitaries solemnly puddled the two together in the trampled snow between the cowcatchers.

The formal ceremony disposed of, a number of other bottles of varying size, shape and content promptly appeared and were emptied in a slightly slower but infinitely more satisfying manner. The delegation up from Boston displayed commendable alacrity in rolling out a keg of prime rum, bashed

The cut at Summit on the Bellows Falls line.

in the head, and magically produced a supply of tin dippers. Not to be outdone, the group from Burlington added its contribution, Vermont apple cider, to the general libation. Perhaps not as glamorous as the rum imported from the Indies to Boston but with as much, if not more, of the basic ingredient for merrymaking, hard cider has been known to liven up any occasion it has been brought to, church supper or other.

History does not record the duration of the celebration in that frigid rock cut on the top of Mount Holly. It can only be assumed that nobody suffered chilblains and that by the time the kegs had run dry and the last stragglers been helped aboard (some, inevitably, boarding the wrong train in the process) there was universal agreement that this had indeed been one of the most glowing historical events in the history of the state. Between lake and bay water and other potables — mixed with an occasional tear of emotion — it also qualified as one of the wettest.

It took the new railroad a few days to recover from its expansively moist dedication, during which gandy dancers leveled a few of the waves in the new track and L. Bigelow, the assistant superintendent, posted his first timetable:

RUTLAND AND BURLINGTON RAILROAD

Through to Bellows Falls!

Change of Hours!

On and after Monday, December 24, 1849, Trains will leave from Burlington for Boston at 6½ A.M., Sundays excepted, stop an hour at Bellows Falls for dinner, arriving at Boston 5:55 P.M., fare, $6.00; connecting at Walpole with the stage for Brattleboro and thence to New York, also at Groton Junction with Worcester and Nashua, Norwich and Worcester Railroad and Steamers on Long Island Sound, arriving at New York, 5 A.M., next morning, fare $8.80.

Returning leave Boston 7½ A.M. arriving Burlington 6½ P.M. leave New York 4 P.M. arriving at Burlington the next evening in the first train from Boston, connecting at Bellows Falls, both ways, with Sullivan Railroad, to White River Junction and Wells River. Also accommodation train will leave Rutland at 7½ A.M. for Burlington returning at 1½ P.M. arriving at Rutland 5 P.M.

RUTLAND & BURLINGTON RAILROAD.

CHANGE OF HOURS.

On and after Wednesday, June 11, 1851,
Two Trains Daily, to and from Burlington and Boston.

	FIRST TRAIN.	SECOND TRAIN.
Leave Burlington at	8 A. M.	10.45 A. M.
Arrive Bellows Falls at	1 P. M.	3.40 P. M.
" Boston at	6½ P. M.	8.30 P. M.

RETURNING.

Leave Boston at	7.30 A. M.	12.30 P. M.
Bellows Falls	11.45 "	5.00 P. M.
Arrive Burlington at	4.00 P. M.	10.00 P. M.

Way Accommodation leaves Rutland at 6.30 A. M., and arrives at Bellows Falls at 8.45 A. M., and at Boston at 2 o'clock P. M. Returning, leaves Bellows Falls at 1.25 P. M., and arrives at Rutland at 3.45 P. M.

L. BIGELOW,
d& wtf. *Superintendent.*

NORTHERN RAILROAD, N. Y.
OGDENSBURGH & ROUSE'S POINT.

SUMMER ARRANGEMENT.

HEREAFTER, TRAINS WILL RUN AS FOLlows, until further notice :

Leave Rouse's Point at 8 o'clock A. M. & 2 P. M.
Arrive at Ogdensburgh at 1 P. M. & 7½ P. M.
Leave Ogdensburgh at 8 A. M. & 2 P. M.
Arrive at Rouse's Point at 1 P. M. & 7 P. M.

At Ogdensburgh the trains connect with Steamers, for Brockville, Kingston, Sacketts Harbor, Oswego, Toronto, Lewiston, Niagara, Hamilton and the Upper Lakes ; and at Rouse's Point with Steamers for St. John's, Montreal, Plattsburgh, Burlington, Whitehall, Saratoga, Troy, Albany and New York.

At Rouse's Point trains also connect with the trains of the Vermont Central Railroad, running through the heart of New England to Boston ; and it connects, by means of steamers to Burlington, with the Rutland and Burlington Railroad, leading also through the New England states to Boston.

This is the most desirable route for either pleasure or business travel between New England and the Western States ; and it is the most expeditious route from Montreal to Western Canada.

CHARLES L. SCHLATTER,
April 24. d& wtf. *Superintendent.*

From the *Burlington Free Press*, May 1, 1851.

Rutland & Burlington Railroad.

Independence Day!

ODD FELLOWS, MASONS, & SONS OF TEMPERANCE

CELEBRATION!

AT RUTLAND,
JULY 4TH, 1853.

FIRE WORKS IN THE EVENING!!

EXTRA TRAINS

Will be run to Rutland in the morning, and from Rutland in the evening, after the close of the Fire Works, of which due notice will be given.

When tickets are purchased at the Offices, HALF FARE will be received to and from all Stations on the Road.

Full Fare will be exacted in the Cars.

JOHN S. DUNLAP,
Superintendent.

SUPERINTENDENT'S OFFICE,
Rutland, June 20, 1853.

This poster advertises one of the many excursions of the day. — Vermont Historical Society.

All further information, together with tickets can be obtained at the Ticket Office in Burlington, and at the Station Agents on the line.

L. BIGELOW
Asst. Superintendent

Dec. 19, 1849.

The road was well equipped to handle its business when the first through passenger trains rolled over the bumpy sixty-pound rail on that Christmas Eve. In addition to the handsome little MIDDLEBURY, already in service, the RUTLAND, BURLINGTON, and BELLOWS FALLS had rolled onto Rutland iron on June 25, fresh from the Taunton shops. On September 12, the road purchased the VERGENNES and the 23-ton MT. HOLLY from Taunton. On the same day, two 17-ton switchers, the CUTTINGSVILLE and ROCKINGHAM were added to the motive power roster. The Brandon shops had delivered the first rolling stock on orders that included 16 passenger cars, two 72-seat second-class passenger cars, five baggage and two mail cars, 360 eight-wheel box-cars, eighty eight-wheel cattle cars, and 101 eight-wheel platform cars. Later, this impressive order was to be supplemented by the addition of two "saloon cars" and three way cars. The railroad already was using some sixty gravel cars and twenty four-wheel boxcars which were soon scrapped; they had a marked propensity for leaving the rough track at frequent and embarrassing intervals.

The lords of the high iron in those first years of operation were the four passenger conductors: J. Bowtell, Daniel Arms, P. R. Downer and Henry H. Howe, the same Henry Howe who had acted as starter in the mail race two months before. These men were among the most handsomely paid on the Rutland & Burlington line, receiving $54 a month for their services. No trains were operated on Sundays during the first few years; later, a more liberal but still-cautious legislature ruled that con-

ductors would be required to read passages from the Scriptures to unregenerate passengers who insisted on riding trains on Sunday, and a Bible rack was provided in each coach. The road's general passenger agent, William A. Burnett, received $90 a month with the stipulation that he pay his own assistants out of that princely sum. Passenger train brakemen were a little farther down the ladder at $30 per month, but the lowest of all was the unnamed waterboy who was merely listed as receiving fifty cents a day. No money was wasted on wood train crews; Edgar L. Stearns served as both engineer and conductor of that lowly drag, supervising its 12 laborers who pitched and piled the heavy billets at the rate of eighty cents a day.

These high salaries may have been a contributing factor to the mounting worries in the company's executive offices. More likely the deep concern among the brass hats was due to a combination of two indisputable facts: costs of completing the road had proved to be far in excess of the original estimates, and revenues, largely due to the failure of the Vermont & Canada to effect a connection, were far below their original projections, with scant chance of improving.

The COL. MERRILL stands outside Rutland shop after her 1866 rebuilding. Originally built in 1853 by Amoskeag, she proudly carried the name TIMOTHY FOLLETT, founder of the railroad she served.

The waterfront view of Burlington in 1858 shows the Rutland & Burlington's little steamer *Boston* steaming toward Rouses Point, at the left, and a R. & B. train heading south at the extreme right. — *Shelburne Museum.*

Rutland & Burlington No. 18, OTTER CREEK, was built in 1854 by Hinkley. She had 60-inch drivers.

Chapter 2

As the Vermont & Canada and the Vermont Central linked their rails at Essex Junction, the harassed directors of the Rutland & Burlington turned to the lake as a possible salvation. Paine's railroad had flatly refused to make a connection with the Rutland road at Burlington, precluding even the slim chance that an occasional revenue car would be interchanged from the north by this necessarily roundabout route. The Vermont & Canada was throwing a long trestle across the shallow foot of Lake Champlain to connect with the Ogdensburg road and complete what was, in effect, a 275-mile trunk line from Ogdensburg in New York to Windsor on the eastern border of Vermont.

The Rutland & Burlington acquired a little side-wheel steamer, the *Boston*, and a few assorted barges. Hurriedly erecting wharf facilities at Burlington adjacent to the railroad station, and at Rouses Point, it managed to salvage a few passengers and tons of freight from the Vermont & Canada line. But this small satisfaction was tempered by the fact that it was seasonal; when the first heavy freeze came, the road would lose even this small feeder service at the northern end of the line.

There was a little more reason for encouragement near the southern end of the road. March of 1852 saw the completion of a route between Rutland and Troy, N.Y., over the rails of the Rutland & Washington, Troy & Rutland, and Troy & Boston railroads. A year later the Troy & Boston abrogated its agreement with the other two short lines, building eastward to a connection with the Western Vermont Railroad, thus giving the Rutland & Bur-

lington yet another outlet to the south. West of Rutland the Rutland & Whitehall Railroad had been chartered to build west through Castleton and Fair Haven to the head of Lake Champlain, with the provision that should the Saratoga & Washington, a New York corporation, complete its road east of Castleton to Rutland in three years, the Rutland & Whitehall should build only from a junction at the village of Castleton to the western border of the state. The Saratoga & Washington was successful in building its line from Castleton to Rutland and in addition ultimately leased the Rutland & Whitehall.

The Rutland & Burlington proved an exceedingly cooperative neighbor to these roads. Reasonable agreements were made which permitted the other roads to use the Rutland & Burlington's extensive station, yard and roundhouse facilities at Rutland, which had become the leading railroad center in Vermont. Such hospitality was simply good business; through it a considerable flow of passengers and freight passed over the Bellows Falls division to be interchanged at Rutland's humming terminal in the shadow of the huge, ungainly cupola that dominated the teeming roundhouse. The arrangement proved to be a mutually profitable one until the Hoosac tunnel was completed and opened to traffic in 1875. But the Rutland's share of this traffic was only a 52-mile haul over its toughest division. There was little money in short trains and helpers, and it appears that the key railroad in the chain profited less than the others. Revenues were slim; the first full year of operation brought in only $142,609.67 before the payment of any of the railroad's fixed obligations.

Loose grades that had a tendency to slide out from under the rails at the first sign of rain had not been equal to the heavy floods in the spring of 1850, and in addition to a substantial loss of operating revenue the repair crews worked for days making costly repairs to bridges, fill and trackage. Treasurer Samuel Henshaw resigned. The floating debt was mounting faster than the flood waters. In lieu of certificates which were to have been issued as interest on the capital stock of the company, the stockholders reluctantly voted in 1851 to accept script certificates, payable in 1855 at a rate of six percent. In spite of the restricted earnings, the meeting authorized a committee of directors to investigate the possibility of uniting the Cheshire Railroad with the Rutland & Burlington. It was purely a defensive measure. Paine and Smith had made overtures to the Cheshire, it was known, and should the Vermont Central gain control of that short line, the Rutland road's only direct link with the New England railroad network would be in hostile hands.

What these men did not know for a certainty was that their own fiscal troubles of the moment were exceeded by those of Charles Paine and his Vermont Central, trapped in the meshes of an exceedingly strange contract when he leased the Vermont & Canada road. This contract allowed Smith to take over Paine's line should lease payment be defaulted. In 1852, John Smith closed the net he had craftily laid out, and Paine soon disappeared from the railroad scene in Vermont. The change was hardly noticeable to the Rutland & Burlington; if anything the competition intensified as Smith took over complete control of the Central. Rival agents solicited passengers and freight off each other's platforms in Burlington — a procedure which frequently ended in fisticuffs. At about the same time the State Legislature found it expedient to rush through a law fixing stringent penalties for wilfully damaging railroad tracks, rolling stock and other property.

Neither pugilistic agents nor protective legislation could save the Rutland & Burlington from the inexorable pressure of its financial troubles as it brought forth a new stock issue that nobody

wanted to buy, borrowed to meet fixed charges and interest, and floundered ever deeper into a complex morass of debt. It was inevitable that the Rutland & Burlington would slide into receivership only a few weeks after its rival railroad, and fighting Timothy Follett would pass into oblivion with his bitter personal enemy. Harry Bradley, another Burlingtonian, succeeded him in the presidency, but only briefly. As one of his last acts in the presidency, Follett, together with Franklin Haven and Samuel Hooper, executed an issue of $1,500,000 in first-mortgage bonds under an indenture made on February 1, 1851. This sum was promptly augmented by an additional $300,000 when William Raymond Lee took over the presidency following Bradley's single term. In August of 1853 the directors executed a second mortgage, in the amount of $1,200,000, with practically the same provisions for the conveyance of the property that had been given to the first-mortgage bondholders. Most of the mortgage certificates in both instances were purchased by a group of Boston merchants and financiers, railroad investments having quickly lost their allure for thrifty Vermonters.

The Rutland & Burlington defaulted on its interest payments on both the first- and second-mortgage bonds, due February 1, 1854. Lee and his companion trustee under the first mortgage, Samuel Henshaw, promptly demanded delivery of the property — only to find that the board of directors had already surrendered the road to the second-mortgage bondholders through a legally-executed conveyance. All hell broke loose among the directors and creditors of the Rutland & Burlington. On March 12 the treasurer, Peter Harvey, summarily resigned, and exactly one week later Lee arbitrarily handed in his resignation and promptly assumed the presidency of the rival Vermont Central, leaving the affairs of the Rutland & Burlington in utter chaos. After Lee's defection to the enemy camp, Thomas Thatcher was hurriedly elected to his place, but before he could effectively take over the reins the harrassed directorate found it necessary to negotiate a third mortgage, also for $1,200,000, just to keep the tottering railroad alive.

A committee of directors issued the annual report on May 31, 1854. Unlike the earlier reports of the company, this one carried no message of optimism.

It was terse and to the point, stating that:

"It will be seen that the stock account has been somewhat depleted since the last report, sundry shares of forfeited and other stock, which reverted to the company, and were heretofore considered as among the assets, having been extinguished. In view of the existing excitement with regard to over-issues of stock in other railroad corporations, the different stock ledgers of this company have been examined by a gentleman familiar with stock accounts.

"The Directors have received from the trustees no official information of the road's business. It is proper also to state in this connection, that the directors found themselves unable to comply with the vote of the stockholders, authorizing an investigation of the accounts of the company. An investigating committee was nominated by the gentlemen appointed by the stockholders for that purpose, who signified their willingness to engage in the duty, provided the expense of the investigation could be met — a contingency for which our treasury is wholly unprepared."

The railroad was too poor to sweep the cobwebs from its own tangled affairs!

Things had reached a sorry state indeed. During 1855, a solitary mixed train fumbled its way over the Bellows Falls division, creeping down from Rutland in the morning, dispiritedly shuffling a few cars around in the afternoon, and shuffling back over the mountain in the evening. The height of ignominy was reached when, in the fall of that year, a sheriff's sale in Bellows Falls brought only $22 for 22,000 shares of Rutland & Burlington stock, knocked down to William Henry, a Bellows Falls banker, his fellow townsmen, Attorney Jabez D. Bridgeman, and Peyton R. Chandler, superintendent of the Vermont Valley road. On the $22 investment, these three were elected directors of the Rutland & Burlington company.

By September of 1855 the battle between the first- and second-mortgage bondholders was in Chancery Court. Attorneys for each group of creditors and the railroad engaged in a complicated and exhausting battle through the month, with Ellis Gray Loring of Boston the plaintiff

Rutland & Burlington R. R.

On & after Monday Dec. 4, 1854, Trains will run as follows:

TRAINS MOVING SOUTH.					TRAINS MOVING NORTH.			
	Accomm. Train.	Mail Train.	Accomm. Train.			Accomm. Train.	Mail Train.	Accom. Train.
LEAVE	A. M.	A. M.	P. M.	A. M.	LEAVE	A. M.	P. M.	P. M.
Burlington,	....	8.45	6.00	....	Bellows Falls,	....	12.05	5.40
Shelburne,	....	9.03	6.17	....	Rockingham,	....	12.18	5.55
Charlotte,	....	9.18	6.31	....	Bartonsville,	....	12.29	6.08
No. Ferrisburgh,	....	9.26	6.40	....	Chester,	....	12.40	6.18
Ferrisburgh,	....	9.34	....	....	Gassetts,	....	12.52	6.30
Vergennes,	....	9.40	6.54	....	Duttonsville,	....	1.02	6.43
New Haven,	....	9.53	7.07	....	Proctorsville,	....	1.08	6.47
Brooksville,	....	....	....	....	Ludlow,	....	1.19	6.57
Middlebury,	....	10.13	7.27	....	Healdville,	....	1.35	7.12
Salisbury,	....	10.28	7.42	....	Summit,	....	1.41	7.17
Whiting,	....	10.40	7.54	....	Mount Holly,	....	1.48	7.24
Brandon,	....	10.52	8.06	....	East Wallingford,	....	1.56	7.31
Pittsford,	....	11.07	8.21	....	Cuttingsville,	....	2.05	7.40
Sutherland Falls,	....	11.16	8.30	....	Clarendon,	....	2.14	7.49
Center Rutland,	....	....	....	....	North Clarendon,	....	....	7.55
Rutland,	6.00	Ar. 11.26 Le. 11.42	....	Ar. 8.45	Rutland,	6.00	Ar. 2.30 Le.	Ar. 8.05
No. Clarendon,	6.07	11.47	....	....	Center Rutland,	....	....	....
Clarendon,	6.16	11.56	....	....	Sutherland Falls,	6.14	3.15	....
Cuttingsville,	6.25	12.05	....	....	Pittsford,	6.23	3.23	....
East Wallingford,	6.34	12.14	....	....	Brandon,	6.40	3.38	....
Mount Holly,	6.41	12.21	....	....	Whiting,	6.51	3.49	....
Summit,	6.48	12.28	....	....	Salisbury,	7.03	4.01	....
Healdville,	6.52	12.32	....	....	Middlebury,	7.16	4.16	....
Ludlow,	7.07	12.47	....	....	Brooksville,	....	....	....
Proctorsville,	7.17	12.57	....	....	New Haven,	7.35	4.36	....
Duttonsville,	7.21	1.02	....	....	Vergennes,	7.45	4.49	....
Gassetts,	7.34	1.15	....	....	Ferrisburgh,	....	....	....
Chester,	7.46	1.27	....	....	No. Ferrisburgh,	7.59	5.02	....
Bartonsville,	7.57	1.38	....	....	Charlotte,	8.07	5.10	....
Rockingham,	8.10	1.51	....	....	Shelburne,	8.20	5.23	....
Bellows Falls,	Ar. 8.25	Ar. 2.05	....	....	Burlington,	Ar. 8.34	Ar. 5.40	....

Trains leave Bellows Falls,

Via Cheshire Road, for Fitchburgh, Groton Junction, Nashua, Concord, N. H., Lowell Lawrence, Boston, Worcester, Providence and New York. Also via Vt. Valley Railroads for Springfield, Hartford, New Haven and New York; and via Sullivan Railroads for Windsor, Montpelier, St. Johnsbury and the White Mountains.

Trains leave Rutland,

Via Western Vermont, Troy & Boston, Rutland & Washington and Albany Northern, Saratoga & Washington, and Saratoga & Schenectady Railroads, for Troy Albany, Saratoga Springs, Schenectady, Niagara Falls, Buffalo and the West.

Trains leave Burlington,

Via Vermont Central, Vt. & Canada and Champlain and St. Lawrence R. Roads, for Montpelier, Rouse's Point, Montreal and Ogdensburgh.

E. A. CHAPIN Sup't.

Rutland, Dec. 1, 1854.

— Collection of Gordon Cutler.

for the first-mortgage bondholders, and James Cheever and William Minott, Jr., also Bostonians, cast in the unhappy role of defendants. As the case progressed, it became increasingly evident to all parties that the litigation, if it was permitted to run its course, would be costly and long — probably so lengthy that the litigants would be arguing over a corporate corpse. At the suggestion of the Court, the two factions got together in Boston and finally managed to reach an agreement. Since the second-mortgage group was in active control of the railroad and had demonstrated some ability in its operation, it was agreed that they would continue, with the proviso that twice yearly the net earnings of the road would be apportioned to meet the interest on the first-mortgage bonds, if possible.

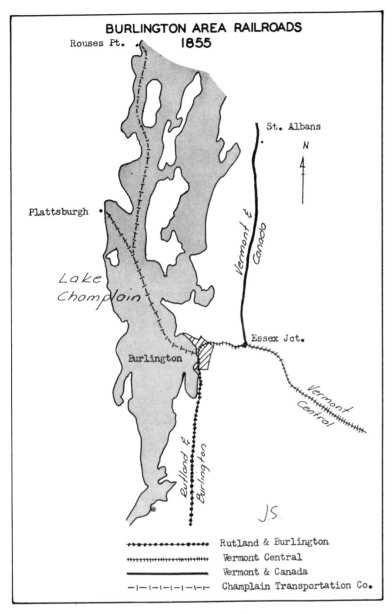

BURLINGTON AREA RAILROADS
1855

Rouses Pt.

St. Albans

N

Plattsburgh

Vermont & Canada

Lake Champlain

Essex Jct.

Burlington

Vermont Central

Rutland & Burlington

J.S.

•••••••••••••• Rutland & Burlington
╫╫╫╫╫╫╫╫╫╫╫ Vermont Central
╼╼╼╼╼╼╼╼ Vermont & Canada
─┤─┤─┤─┤─┤─┤─ Champlain Transportation Co.

Any amount remaining after this division would be credited to the second-mortgage bondholders and, should some miracle produce a flood of profitable business, a division would be made among the holders of third-mortgage certificates. The first-mortgage trustees would have a lien on all property in the hands of the second-mortgage trustees, and all future property that should accrue to the railroad under their management. The agreement was ratified before the court on October 3, 1855.

The agreement served to cool the tempers of the litigants for a time, though it was to spawn some unorthodox accounting procedures and was to do little for the preservation or improvement of the

troubled but potentially fine little railroad. The operating superintendent, E. A. Chapin, was sentenced to creeping defeat in his Herculean efforts to keep the road's rolling stock, built by the amateurs at Brandon, from falling apart, and the lightly constructed right of way from disintegrating under even the sparse traffic. With the first-mortgage certificate holders adamantly demanding their interest, the second- and third-mortgage holders hovering like vultures in the background, and the Vermont Central interest using every device to throttle the road completely, his was a hopeless and thankless job. With gross earnings of less than a quarter-million dollars a year, a fixed indebtedness of nearly five million at seven percent, and an ever-increasing floating debt of over one and one-half million, there was little prospect that he would be able to improve the operating conditions.

The board of directors did renew the fight for a junction with the Vermont & Canada at Burlington, and with the Vermont Central, which was continuing to use every expedient against the Rutland line, even at its own expense in lost traffic. In these efforts the Rutland & Burlington gained the vociferous and wholehearted support of a disgusted public and, finally the backing of the state's railroad commissioner, George P. Marsh. In a special report to the General Assembly at its October session in 1858, Marsh stated:

"The change to which passengers by the Central railroad to and from Burlington, and places connected with Burlington by steamboat or railroad, are subject at Essex Junction, is a matter of universal dissatisfaction. It is true that the Vermont & Canada road and the Central railroad south of Essex are run as one road, but it is too notorious to be disputed that the original object of forming the connection was to control the travel and transport to and from points north of Essex and secure to the Central a preference in business. No such advantage was contemplated by the Legislature, and the associated companies ought not to be permitted to embarrass and annoy travelers who prefer to take the Rutland & Burlington route, and thus deprive the public of rights impliedly secured to it by the charter of the companies. So far as the convenience of the Vermont & Canada railroad is concerned, it is sufficient to say that by the charter of the company, it was required to form a connection with the Rutland & Burlington road within thirteen years of the date of its incorporation, which was in October, 1845. No such connection has been formed. For eight years passengers from the west have been subject to annoyance. To expose them longer to this inconvenience would be to allow the company to take advantage of its own wrong."

From the beginning, the Vermont Central had studiously scheduled its trains in and out of Burlington at times that made any sort of reasonable connection with the trains of the Rutland & Burlington a virtual impossibility. Despite the fact that Burlington was the largest city in Vermont and a prime source of traffic, through cars were routed only over the Vermont & Canada out of Essex Junction, with all Burlington passengers forced to change to a local at that dismal depot. The Rutland line's morning train north left that city at the witching hour of 5:45 A.M. and with several stops reached Burlington at 8:45, not a bad running time for 52 miles at mid-point in the nineteenth century. But the Central road promptly scheduled its shuttle train east out of Burlington for 7:30, possibly on the assumption that its hardy passengers would prefer to rise an hour earlier for the seven-mile ride so that they could bask an extra hour in the salubrious atmosphere of Essex Junction while waiting for a connection. Conversely it exercised extreme care to make certain that no train arrived in Burlington until the Rutland train had pulled out. Infuriated passengers charged that, on occasion, the Central's shuttle train would back away from the city if it was observed that the Rutland train was still waiting!

No. 1.
TRAINS LEAVE RUTLAND,
NORTH, 6.00 A. M., 3.15 P. M. | EAST, 5.00 A. M., 12.00 M.

North—Rutland & Burlington R.

Ms	ARRIVE	Frs.	1 A.M.	2 P.M.
2	Center Rutland.	10	....	....
6	Sutherland Falls	15	6 15	3 30
10	Pittsford	30	6 25	3 40
17	Brandon	50	6 40	3 56
22	Whiting	65	6 55	4 11
27	Salisbury	80	7 05	4 21
33	Middlebury	1 00	7 22	4 37
37	Brooksville	1 10	....	....
41	New Haven	1 20	7 45	4 58
46	Vergennes	1 35	8 00	5 12
48	Ferrisburgh	1 40	....	....
52	N. Ferrisburgh	1 50	8 12	5 25
56	Charlotte	1 65	8 22	5 35
61	Shelburn	1 80	8 37	5 49
67	Burlington	2 00	8 55	6 05
107	Montpelier			8 20
99	St. Albans		11 29	7 51
128	Rouse's Point		12 42	9 05
			P.M.	A.M.
167	Montreal		4 00	9 00
241	Ogdensburgh		8 00	11 00

East—Rutland & Burlington R.R.

Ms	ARRIVE	Frs.	1 A.M.	2 P.M.
3	North Clarendon	10	....	....
6	Clarendon	20	....	12 17
9	Cuttingsville	30	5 50	12 28
13	E. Wallingford	40	....	12 39
15	Mount Holly	50	....	12 47
18	Summit	55	6 40	12 55
19	Healdville	60	....	1 00
25	Ludlow	75	7 10	1 16
28	Proctorsville	85	7 27	1 25
30	Cavendish	90	....	1 30
34	Gassetts	1 05	7 55	1 43
39	Chester	1 20	8 25	1 56
43	Bartonsville	1 30	8 45	2 06
47	Rockingham	1 40	....	....
53	Bellows Falls	1 60	9 30	2 30
57	Walpole	1 80	....	2 41
63	Westmoreland	1 95	....	2 56
75	Keene	2 30	....	3 23
81	Marlboro	2 55	....	3 43
85	Troy, N. H.	2 65	....	3 52
90	Fitzwilliam	2 85	....	4 05
99	Winchendon	3 15	....	4 25
107	S. Ashburnham	3 35	....	4 45
113	Westminster Ms.	3 50	....	....
117	Fitchburg	3 70	....	5 12
121	Leomister	3 85	....	5 22
132	Groton	4 15	....	5 45
142	So. Acton	4 45	....	6 13
147	Concord	4 60	....	6 30
157	Waltham	4 75	....	6 57
167	Boston	4 75	....	7 30
143	Worcester	4 55	....	7 00
159	Lowell	4 65	....	6 30
58	Westminster Vt.	1 80	....	2 50
68	Putney	2 15	....	3 17
72	Dummerston	2 25	....	3 27
77	Brattleboro	2 40	....	3 40
87	South Vernon	2 75	....	4 05
101	Greenfield	3 25	....	4 33
109	South Deerfield	3 55	....	4 56
116	Hatfield	3 80	....	5 15
120	Northampton	3 90	....	5 30
129	Holyoke	4 20	....	5 54
134	Cabotville	4 35	....	6 10
137	Springfield	4 45	....	6 20
163	Hartford	5 20	....	7 20
199	New Haven	6 20	....	8 45
275	N. Y., via Con.R.	6 50	....	11 50
79	Windsor	2 45	2 00	7 00
93	W. R. Junction	2 95	2 30	....
133	Wells River	4 35	4 00	....
154	St. Johnsbury	5 05	4 55	....
153	Littleton	5 20	5 00	....

RUTLAND, February 1, 1858.

J. M. BAGLEY, RECEIVER.

TRAINS LEAVE RUTLAND,
RUTLAND & WASHINGTON RAILROAD, 6.00 A. M. AND 1.00 P. M.
WESTERN VERMONT RAILROAD, 6.00 A. M. AND 3.00 P. M.
SARATOGA & WHITEHALL RAILROAD, 6.00 A. M. AND 1.00 P. M.

Via Rutland & Washington R. R.

Ms	ARRIVE	Frs.	1	2
			A. M.	P. M.
2	Center Rutland	...	6 05	1 05
4	West Rutland	...	6 10	1 10
11	Castleton	40	6 30	1 30
18	Poultney	70	6 50	1 50
24	Middle Granville	95	7 08	2 08
26	Granville	1 00	7 13	2 13
29	Pawlet	1 15	7 23	2 23
36	Rupert	1 40	7 45	2 45
38	West Rupert	1 50	7 52	2 52
44	Salem	1 60	8 10	3 10
51	Shushan	1 70	8 25	3 25
56	Cambridge	1 80	8 38	3 38
62	Eagle Bridge	1 85	8 54	3 54
85	Troy	2 50	10 15	5 00
95	Albany	2 60	10 55	5 45
235	New York	5 50	6 28	10 50
			P. M.	
112	Schenectady	2 50	1 00	7 20
190	Utica	4 10	4 05	11 08
204	Rome	4 40	4 55	11 50
			A. M.	
243	Syracuse	5 15	6 20	1 40
269	Auburn	5 65	7 40	8 15
324	Rochester	6 75	9 40	8 15
393	Buffalo	8 15	12 00	8 15
398	S. Bridge	8 15	12 20	9 00

Via Western Vermont R. R.

Ms	ARRIVE	Frs.	1	2
			A. M.	P. M.
6	Clarendon	20	6 12	3 18
9	Wallingford	30	6 20	3 32
13	S. Wallingford	40	6 30	3 48
18	Danby	55	6 42	4 13
22	North Dorset	65	6 52	4 26
25	East Dorset	75	7 00	4 47
30	Manchester	90	7 15	5 00
36	Sunderland	1 10	7 29	5 45
39	Arlington	1 20	7 39	6 02
44	Shaftsbury	1 35	7 51	6 28
49	S. Shaftsbury	1 45	8 06	6 49

Via Western Vermont R. R.

Ms	ARRIVE	Frs.	1	2
			A. M.	P. M.
52	N. Bennington	1 55	8 15	7 00
54	State Line	1 65	8 30	....
84	Troy	1 50	10 10	....
			P. M.	
90	East Albany	1 60	1 00	....
234	New York	4 50	6 28	....
105	Schenectady	1 75	1 00	....
183	Utica	3 85	4 05	....
197	Rome	3 65	4 55	....
236	Syracuse	4 40	6 20	....
262	Auburn	4 90	7 40	....
317	Rochester	6 00	9 40	....
386	Buffalo	7 40	12 00	....
391	S. Bridge	7 40	12 20	....

Via Saratoga & Whitehall R. R.

Ms	ARRIVE	Frs.	1	2
			A. M.	P. M.
14	Hydeville	55	6 40	3 38
16	Fair Haven	60	6 46	3 44
25	Whitehall	95	7 15	4 10
31	Comstocks	1 20	7 35	4 29
35	Fort Ann	1 35	7 48	4 42
39	Smith's Basin	1 50	7 59	4 52
47	Fort Edward	1 85	8 21	5 14
48	Moreau	1 85	8 26	5 19
53	Gansevoorts	2 00	8 41	5 33
63	Saratoga	2 25	9 13	6 00
85	Schenectady	2 50	11 00	7 20
95	Troy	2 50	11 00	....
101	Albany	2 60	11 52	....
			P. M.	
245	New York	5 50	10 50	....
163	Utica	4 10	4 05	11 08
177	Rome	4 40	4 55	11 50
216	Syracuse	5 15	6 20	1 40
242	Auburn	5 65	7 40	8 15
297	Rochester	6 75	9 40	5 35
			A. M.	
366	Buffalo	8 15	12 00	8 15
371	S. Bridge	8 15	12 20	9 00

Commissioner Marsh, properly irritated at these shenanigans, laid out a connecting schedule for the two roads and recommended to the Legislature that it be enforced, closing his angry report with, "The Commissioner does not think that the jealousies naturally existing, being rival routes should be allowed to prejudice interests so important as the unrestricted intercourse between the citizens of Eastern and Western Vermont, or between them and any other sections of the Union."

The opposition railroads, callous as they were in many ways, could not stand against the rising, bitter tide of public and governmental anger. More realistic schedules were instituted, and with extreme reluctance the Vermont & Canada began to lay down a rickety line to connect with the Rutland & Burlington at the latter city, but only after the Legislature threatened to take a direct hand in the matter. It is not known whether or not apoplexy caused by this turn of events resulted in heavy-handed old John Smith's death in 1858, but his demise made little difference. His heirs, J. Gregory and Worthington Smith, had been well-schooled in their father's methods of railroad operation and his standards of business ethics. The connection with the Rutland & Burlington was completed in 1860, but the Vermont & Canada immediately began to find myriad excuses for not running regular trains over the ramshackle track it had installed. Only after another tongue-lashing by the commissioner and further threats from the Legislature was regular service instituted into Burlington.

☆ ☆ ☆

The net operating earnings of the Rutland & Burlington demonstrated small and gradual improvement during the years preceding the Civil War, largely, as it proved, through deferred maintenance. The second-mortgage trustees were hard pressed to meet the insistent demands of the first-mortgage bondholders, who adamantly insisted on their interest payments at the expense of the property. The desperate managers were even forced to the expedient, highly questionable in accounting circles, of charging the cost of four critically-needed new locomotives to "repairs of engines and rolling stock". Mainline track gradually became a vast obstacle course over which crews negotiated clanking, leaking engines hauling strings of fugitives from the jammed bad order tracks. The rotting platforms at the scabrous stations became a menace to passengers even before they boarded the sway-backed, reeling cars. Except for one year, 1863 in which Daniel Smalley, their counsel from Burlington, held office, the presidency rested in Boston, where offices had been established.

With the absentee owners exhibiting no deep concern for the railroad beyond the scheduled interest payments, the Rutland & Burlington company was desperately in need of strong leadership — a man of dedication who would devote his utmost energies to the solution of its multiple problems. In the Rutland & Burlington's case, the man was John B. Page.

Page had served on the board of directors for a time when, in 1863, he was named trustee for the second-mortgage bondholders, along with a Brandon man, Edwin A. Birchard. Just as the railroad teetered on the brink of complete collapse, the ultimate responsibility for the road had finally come back to Vermont. John Page was easily the most substantial and influential man in southern Vermont, with more than a passing academic interest in the fortunes of the railroad. As president of the Howe Scale Company in Rutland, he was the line's largest single shipper. As a heavy investor in its mortgage bonds, he had a personal financial stake. As Treasurer of the State of Vermont, in which the railroad was a vital artery of communication and commerce, he had a public duty. In truth, John Page's fortunes were irrevocably tied to those of the Rutland & Burlington Railroad.

Albert S. Catlin, a Boston merchant, succeeded Smalley in the presidency until 1867, but it soon became evident that Page was exerting tremendous influence in the affairs of the line. Under his pressure, indolent and incompetent personnel were weeded out; some of them, it was indicated, were in league with the rival Vermont Central. He fought the first-mortgage bondholders on their own ground in Chancery Court to stem the leeching of the road's lifeblood before it literally fell apart. Most of all, to western Vermont and the railroad he demonstrated a brand of competent, confident leadership that soon filtered down to lift the faith of the most humble gandy dancer.

In less than ten years a basically good railroad had come apart; nine locomotives lay useless at Rutland for want of repair, while those still in operation were mostly patched-up hulks. A true bad order car was one that could not be moved over the road under any circumstances — and sidings at Rutland were jammed with them. Slow orders were standard operating procedure, and even the bravest trainmen went out on their runs in fear. The rest simply quit and went back to the farm or moved to other roads. Passengers embarked with a high sense of adventure — and they generally experienced it. The heaviest blow of all fell in 1863, when the Rutland & Burlington's connecting lines served notice that they would not accept its

cars unless they had been repaired. To quote one such notice, "Many are old and not safe to run, and trains and men are in constant danger from this cause." Because of the condition of the railroad's trackage, its frequent wrecks, and the almost total absence of any car maintenance, several of these connecting roads also refused to deliver their cars at junction points, forcing added costs and delays on the hard-pressed Rutland line, which then had laboriously to transfer the manifests to its own battered sway-backed cars.

The first of many gloomy clouds were indeed casting their ominous shadows across the Rutland road's once proud line.

RUTLAND & BURLINGTON RAIL ROAD---TIME TABLE No. 2.

FOR THE GOVERNMENT AND INFORMATION OF EMPLOYEES ONLY.

TAKES EFFECT MONDAY, MAY 7, 1860.

TRAINS MOVING SOUTH.

LEAVE	1 Way Passgr	2 Mail Passenger	3 Express Passenger	4 Night Express	5 Through Freight	6 Through Freight	7	8	9	10
	A. M.	A. M	A. M	P. M	A. M	A. M.				
•Burlington,.		8.45	10.45	8.55	4.00					
•Shelburn,		9.02	10.56	9.13	4.35					
•Charlotte,		9.16	11.07	9.28	5.00					
•N. Ferrisburg,		9.25	11.11	9.39	5.15					
•Ferrisburg,										
s Vergennes,		9.40	11.23	9.52	5.45					
•New Haven,		9.54	11.33	10.10	6.10					
•Brooksville,										
sMiddlebury		10.17	11 48	10.35	6.57					
•Salisbury,		10.34	11.59	10.50	7.27					
sWhiting,		10.46	12.07	11.04	7.50					
sBrandon,		11.00	12.18	11.20	8.20					
•Pittsford,		11.20	12.31	11.38	8.53					
•Suth'd Falls,		11.30	12.38	11.50	9.17					
•Cen. Rutland,										
Rutland,	5.25	A.11 45 / L.12.15	12.49	12.05	A .9.45 / L 11.10	4.15				
•N. Clarendon,										
•Clarendon,	5.42	12.32			11.42					
•Cuttingsville,	5.52	12.42			12.05	5.10				
•E. Wallingf'd	6.02	12 50			12.27					
•Mt. Holly,	6.11	12.58			12.45					
•Summit,	6.18	1.05			A. 1.00 / L. 1.10	A. 6.10 / L. 6.23				
•Healdville	6.22	1.10								
sLudlow,	6.37	1.26			1.45	7.00				
sProctorsville,	6.47	1.35			2.02	7.20				
•Cavendish,	6.51	1.39			2.13	7.30				
sGassetts,	7.06	1.52			2.37	7.50				
sChester,	7.19	2.05			3.03	8.12				
•Bartonsvile,	7.30	2.16			3.30	8.30				
•Rockingham										
Bellows Falls,	7.55	2.40			4 20	9.15				

TRAINS MOVING NORTH.

LEAVE	11 Way Pass'n'r	12 Mail Passenger	13 Way Pass'n'r	14 Night Express	15 Express Freight	16 Freight Through	17 Local Freight	18
	A. M.	P. M	P. M	P. M	P. M.	P. M	A. M.	
Bellows Falls,		12.30	5.30		8.30		5.25	
•Rockingham								
•Bartonsville,		12.55	5.50					
s Chester		1.07	6.05		9.37		6.35	
•Gassetts,		1.20	6.21		10.02		7.06	
•Cavendish,		1.31	6.34				7.30	
•Proctorsville,		1.35	6.40		10.32		7.40	
sLudlow,		1.45	6.50		10.50		8.00	
•Healdville,		2.00	7.04					
•Summit,		2.05	7.08		11.30		8.45	
•Mt. Holly,		2.13	7.16				8.54	
•E. Wallingf'd		2.22	7.24		11.52		9.08	
•Cuttingsville,		2.32	7.33		12.09		9.22	
•Clarendon,		2.42	7.43		12.30		9.42	
•N. Clarendon,								
Rutland,	6.15	A.3.00 / L.3.40	8.00	2.20	1.00	1.45	10.10	
• Cen. Rutland								
•Suth'd Falls,	6.30	3.52		2.32		2.14		
•Pittsford,	6.40	4.00		2.40		2.35		
sBrandon,	7.00	4.15		2.54		3.08		
sWhiting,	7.15	4.26		3.06		3.38		
•Salisbury,	7.27	4.35		3.16		4.00		
sMiddlebury	7.45	4.50		3.32		A. 4.35 / L. 4.55		
•Brooksville								
•New Haven,	8.07	5.07		3 50		5.36		
s Vergennes,	8.23	5.18		4.02		6.03		
•Ferrisburg,								
•N. Ferrisburg,	8.37	5.27		4.13		6.27		
•Charlotte,	8.47	5.35		4.23		6.47		
•Shelburn,	9.02	5.47		4.35		7.15		
Burlington,	9.20	6.00		4.50		7.45		

SPECIAL RULES.

* Trains should meet and pass at stations marked with full face figures.
• Denotes Trains do not stop unless signalled or to leave passengers. sDenotes all Trains and Extra Engines stop. No Train or Engine following a Passenger Train will leave any station until 5 minutes after Pass'r Train has left Train No. 3 will have the right to the road against No. 11. Train No. 11 will keep out of the way of No. 3. Train No. 12 will have the right to the road against No. 2 and No. 3. Trains No 2 and No 3 will keep out of the way of No. 12. Train No. 4 will have the right to the road against No 14. No. 14 will keep out of the way of No 4. Tuesday's Castle Train will run on time of train No 3. Train No. 14 will have the right to the road to Burlington until 5.30 A. M., after that time it will keep out of the way of all regular trains. Train No 14 will not run on Monday.

Train No. 3 stops only at Vergennes, Middlebury, and Brandon. Train No 12 will not stop at Cen. Rutland nor Sutherland Falls and between Middlebury and Burlington stop only at Vergennes. All trains must run at reduced rate of speed and without working steam over the Bridge at Ferrisburgh and Brooksville When trains are delayed Conductors having the right to the road will leave each station as much behind their regular time, until the expected train is passed as they were required to wait at the station appointed for passing. In all cases subject to 40th Rule Station Agents will see that rules 150 and 162 are complied with At 5.00 A. M. the right to road ceases of any train of the previous day and after that hour such Train will keep out of the way of a regular Trains.

RUTLAND, MAY 4th, 1860.

E. A. CHAPIN, Sup't.

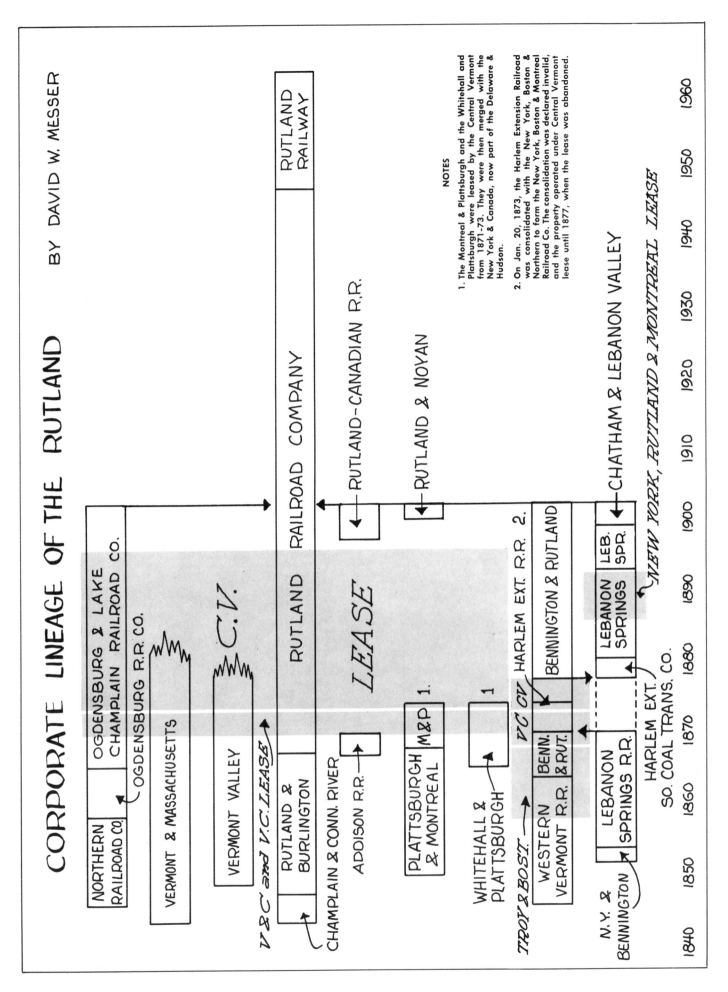

CORPORATE LINEAGE OF THE RUTLAND
BY DAVID W. MESSER

NOTES

1. The Montreal & Plattsburgh and the Whitehall and Plattsburgh were leased by the Central Vermont from 1871-73. They were then merged with the New York & Canada, now part of the Delaware & Hudson.

2. On Jan. 20, 1873, the Harlem Extension Railroad was consolidated with the New York, Boston & Northern to form the New York, Boston & Montreal Railroad Co. The consolidation was declared invalid, and the property operated under Central Vermont lease until 1877, when the lease was abandoned.

Chapter 3

∽◌∽◌∽◌∽◌∽◌∽◌∽ *The Hunted Traps the Hunter*

Drastic measures were called for if the ailing company, its corporate pulse beating only feebly, was to be brought to a semblance of robust economic health. The new management, with Trustee Page providing the impetus, quickly devoted itself to the most pressing rehabilitation of the line. The most salvageable cars were refurbished in the Rutland shops, the shops at Brandon having been closed in 1861, and parts were scraped up to repair the aging motive power. Track crews were pooled and sent out on the worst parts of the road to replace rotted ties, spike down and realign the loose and battered rail, and repair the eroded grade.

That these simple items of maintenance were long overdue was evidenced by the fact that the total value of the company's capital stock had shrunk to a negligible $834,000 when Page assumed the trusteeship under demands from the first mortgagees that the whole shebang be junked or sold, alternatives that the beleaguered directors could not conscientiously permit. Page and Birchard, as second-mortgage trustees, found themselves immediately embattled on several fronts: the almost hopeless fight against advanced deterioration, the need to replace discouraged and incompetent personnel, the necessity of holding off the financial buzzards who would pick the road's carcass clean, and the continued hostile pressures of the Vermont Central clan. Their labors were immensely complicated by the multitude of legal actions that dragged on in the state's Chancery and Supreme Courts.

In spite of these difficulties, the Rutland & Burlington Railroad Company, as such, passed out of existence on July 9, 1867, and the Rutland Railroad Company was born by decree of Chancery Court. With the exception of the certificates represented by Thomas Cheever and W. T. Hart (first-mortgage bondholders who had seized certain railroad properties at Burlington) most of the outstanding mortgage bonds were converted into preferred and common stocks in the new company. The case of Cheever and Hart was continued until 1870 when a decision of the Supreme Court rendered a verdict in their favor, requiring the railroad to pay their interests and court costs amounting to a total of $989,000.

As the new company emerged from the ashes of the old Rutland & Burlington, John Page was elected to the presidency and another Rutland man, Joel M. Haven, assumed the post of treasurer. Birchard was named to a seat on the board of directors of the new company. The capitalization of the Rutland Railroad had been set at $3,000,000. A small amount of new stock was peddled to supplement the exchanged mortgage bonds and the managers found their credit improved enough to float another modest mortgage or two.

Business had improved gradually during the Civil War years, and the railroad, far removed from the fighting, had little to cope with but high prices, complaints when some purchases of new equipment had been conveniently charged to the "maintenance of motive power and rolling stock," and one casualty when a drunken trooper from the First Vermont Cavalry fell off the roof of a coach and

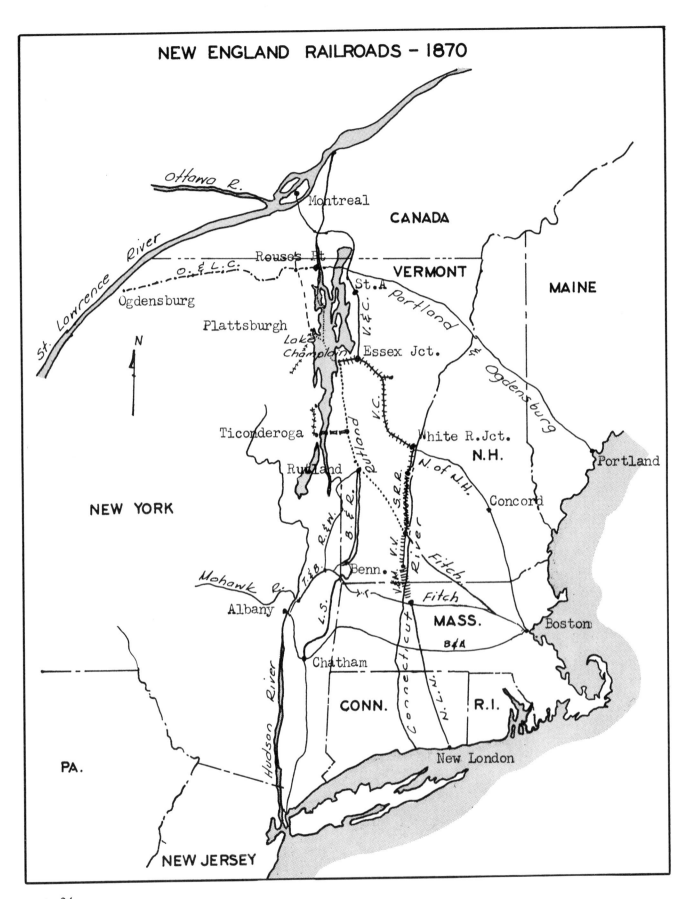

NEW ENGLAND RAILROADS - 1870

landed on his head with no damage to the Rutland yard, but with permanent and fatal damage to himself. Despite these and other minor diversions, the managers entered the task of refurbishing the line with vigor. Orders went out for new motive power, sleek new coaches and head-end cars, and sturdy new boxcars. Stations blossomed out in new paint, and their rotted platforms were replaced with firm planking, considerably enhancing the safety of passengers before they boarded the cars.

The basic ills remained. The new Rutland was still a railroad that for all practical purposes ran from "nowhere to nowhere." Cooperation by the Vermont & Canada was given with much reluctance; the Vermont Central offered none at all. The Rutland still needed dependable interchange agreements to insure a reasonable flow of business over its rails.

A basic plan of action was in the making even while the road was undergoing reorganization. Smith had cut the cross-lake traffic on the *Boston* to a trickle by the simple expedient of concluding a traffic agreement with the Ogdensburg line which permitted transfer of freight to the Rutland's boat only at a punitive rate differential. Page's plans now turned to the south and east, relegating the line north of Rutland to a status little better than that of an elongated branch. To the east, interchange of traffic with the Cheshire Railroad at Bellows Falls afforded a route to Boston. Looking to the south, Page and Birchard, while still trustees, had in 1865 leased, in their own names, the Vermont Valley line south from Bellows Falls, an action that was later to bring them into considerable controversy. At the time, it was a popular and well-conceived action which did no harm to Page's successful campaign for Governor of Vermont two years later, the same year he emerged as president of the railroad.

The immediate eastern connection thus assured, the Rutland forces turned to the west and effected a favorable agreement with the Rensselaer & Saratoga. The spa at Saratoga Springs was then approaching its zenith as a mecca for the wealthy and fashionable, and in itself would provide considerable passenger business. Moreover, it afforded a good connection with the lines stretching along the Mohawk valley toward the rich, opening West,

John B. Page was Governor of Vermont, 1867-1869, and president of Rutland Railroad, 1868-1883. — *Vermont Historical Society.*

and with the pending completion of the Albany & Susquehanna, a potentially fine source of revenue freight from the anthracite fields of Pennsylvania. Bitter opposition to this move erupted from the Western Vermont Railroad and the Troy & Boston, which was then driving iron east toward the Hoosac and saw in the Rensselaer & Saratoga agreement a heavy diversion of traffic. (Even as late as 1960, when the Hoosac Tunnel was made single track, high wide loads that were limited by clearances took this longer route through Rutland to New England.) The two railroads, the Western Vermont and the Troy & Boston, carefully fanned ill feeling against the Rutland & Burlington, culminating in a meeting held at Manchester on October 6, 1865, which documented a memorial to the Vermont General Assembly outlining the "Late Hostile Measures of the Managers of the Rutland & Burlington Railroad Against the Western Vermont Railroad and the Public."

In a detailed rebuttal, Page and Birchard pointed out that the foreclosed bonds of the Western Vermont had passed into the hands of the Troy & Boston at a fraction of their face value and that, in effect, the leased line, now reorganized as the Bennington & Rutland, was a Troy & Boston property. Furthermore, traffic which seemed of such momentary concern to the short line would be routed over the parent road as soon as the Hoosac tunnel was drilled through. In a closing shot Page stated, "This very respectable (Manchester) committee and the good people along the line of the Western Vermont road, and the present proprietor of that road have meantime the satisfaction of knowing that the Troy & Boston is bound to run the road for some fifteen months longer, paying the stipulated rent, and that the less its track is worn by a through business in which these people have no share or interest, the more valuable will be the property both to its owner and the public when the Troy & Boston Company shall be obliged to restore it. Whenever that day shall come, and the Bennington & Rutland road shall fall under the care and management of a Vermont interest, your memorialists indulge the hope that such arrangements may be made between all these great interests as shall be mutually satisfactory, and be at the same time satisfactory to the public — an arrangement which we see no difficulty in effecting, and which we will gladly favor."

Though their reasoning in regard to the welfare of the little line may have been obscure, especially to the proprietors of the road, their vague promises for the future were merely a smoke screen. The Rutland's plans lay in other directions. Page's prime adversary was in the north. He had no intention of encumbering the Rutland road with a southerly appendage it did not need.

The arrangement with the Rensselaer & Saratoga proved a reasonably productive one for both railroads and contributed in no small measure to the effective reorganization of the Rutland company. To the casual observer there followed a period of relative quiet on the Vermont Central front, although intense activity was taking place behind the scenes. The only visible matters of note were that one of the recurrent floods struck in the spring of 1869, costing the Rutland a quarter-million dollars, and a couple of passenger trains staged a cornfield meet in the deep cut on Mount Holly, which the road settled with "gratuities" amounting to $50,000. By this time the Rutland had built up enough financial stability to weather these incidents with a minimum of distress.

Lightning struck, not twice but three times, in 1870. On September 26, the Rutland leased a seemingly remote section of the Whitehall & Plattsburgh, 17 winding miles along the western shore of Lake Champlain from Ticonderoga to Port Henry, tapping the rich iron deposits in the hills west of the latter village and serving the blast furnaces beside the lake. The transaction seems to have aroused little interest in Vermont, save to cause some speculation on the sagacity of the Rutland managers. Even this speculative gossip had died down by December 1. On that date the Rutland also leased the 21-mile portion of the Vermont & Massachusetts from Brattleboro south to Grout's Corners (now Millers Falls) gaining controlled trackage to the New London Northern line, the principal feeder to Connecticut and the Long Island Sound.

St. Albans began to get nervous. Things were happening on the Rutland which did not look good for the Vermont Central.

A second jarring announcement came exactly one week later, when the Rutland took over the Addison Railroad's franchise and announced that it would immediately begin construction on the 15-mile line west from Leicester Junction to Ticonderoga. The shallow, broad portion of Lake Champlain would be bridged, the center section being constructed on a barge to permit opening for the passage of steamers. This novel arrangement was to be used for many years, in spite of its predilection for dumping cars, and on one occasion a whole train, into the lake. Crude as the arrangement was, it enabled a connection with the Whitehall & Plattsburgh and the good potential tonnage of Port Henry iron. The Addison road opened for business on December 1, 1871, operating under lease to the Rutland.

Before the first spike had been driven in the Addison road, however, the third blow was struck in the north. The Whitehall & Plattsburgh had built from the Canadian border south as it built north from Whitehall, intending to join the two segments as work progressed, a process that proved to be extremely difficult. Before 1870 the company had

The Geo. B. Chase, built in 1870 by Taunton, poses with Rutland lettering. This was changed during the period of lease by the Vermont Central.

Rutland stock certificates were signed by President John B. Page. — *Collection of J. R. McFarlane.*

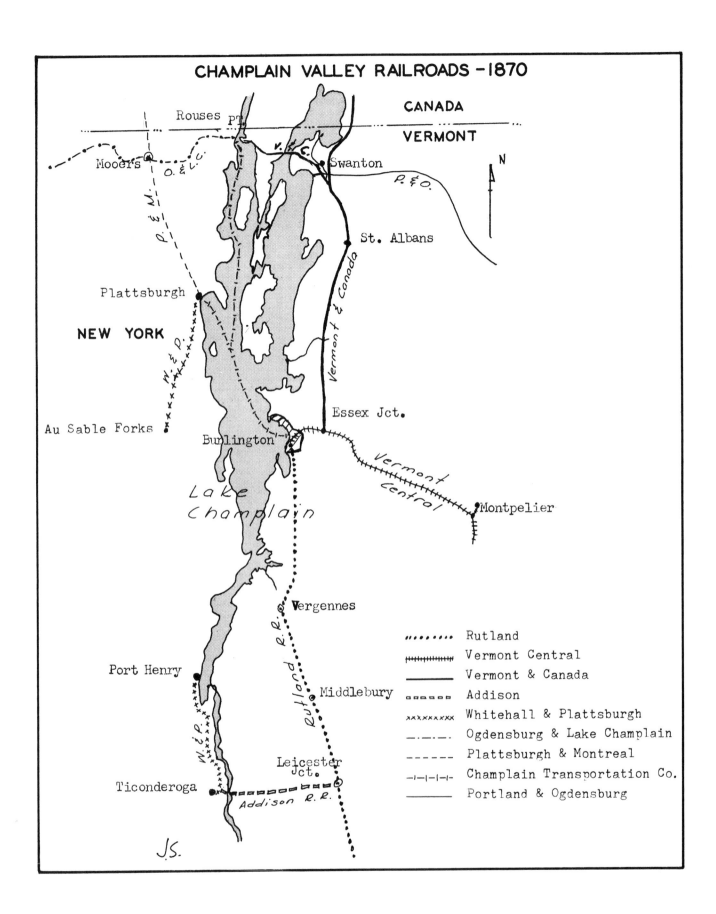

CHAMPLAIN VALLEY RAILROADS – 1870

CANADA

Rouses Pt.

VERMONT

N

Mooers

O. & L.C.

Swanton

P. & O.

P. & M.

St. Albans

Plattsburgh

NEW YORK

Vermont & Canada

Essex Jct.

Au Sable Forks

Burlington

Vermont Central

Montpelier

Lake Champlain

W. & P.

Vergennes

P. & O.

Rutland R.R.

Port Henry

Middlebury

W. & P.

Leicester Jct.

Ticonderoga

Addison R.R.

.... Rutland
ᴴᴴᴴᴴᴴᴴ Vermont Central
──────── Vermont & Canada
▭ ▭ ▭ ▭ Addison
xxxxxxxx Whitehall & Plattsburgh
_._._._. Ogdensburg & Lake Champlain
─ ─ ─ ─ Plattsburgh & Montreal
─ı─ı─ı─ Champlain Transportation Co.
──────── Portland & Ogdensburg

JS.

page 28

become afflicted with an illness that seemed peculiar to railroad projects of the period, acute financial embarrassment. On May 1, 1869, the Whitehall & Plattsburgh leased its northern division to the Montreal & Plattsburgh Railroad Company, a new corporation which, strangely, listed an unexplainably large number of Vermont names on its stock records, including John B. Page. The road cleanly bisected the Ogdensburg road at Mooers Junction, some 11 miles west of Rouses Point.

On June 23, 1870, the Whitehall & Plattsburgh company announced that negotiations were being opened with John B. Page for the construction of the middle section of the road, and John B. Page promptly and ostentatiously sent a crew of surveyors, bearing transits, to prowl the eastern Adirondacks. At almost the same time, he emerged as the controlling interest in the Rutland & Whitehall railroad, which ran west out of Rutland to a connection around the head of Lake Champlain with the lower severed half of the New York state line.

Though the Vermont Central command was staggering under the combined impact of these developments, there was one more to come. In 1867, the Rutland & Burlington had bought heavily into the Champlain Transportation Company to effect the operation of the little *Boston,* relinquishing control of the steamship company two years later when the Vermont Central's agreement with the Ogdensburg line squeezed the profit out of it. Now, suddenly, the Rutland railroad was back in the steamboat business. In the spring of 1868, a large and handsome 1100 ton steamer, the *Oakes Ames,* named for a Massachusetts congressman and railroad investor who was later to be branded as one of the Credit Mobilier ring, slapped its huge paddles into the placid Champlain water and thereafter churned incessantly on the shuttle run between Plattsburgh and the trackside docks at Burlington. The steamer was operated by the Champlain Transportation Company, and the Rutland Railroad had once again become deeply interested. The big sidewheeler could carry cars or package freight on her large main deck, and passengers rode in luxury on the deck above.

The busy ship commuted across the lake night and day, churning it to a froth with her 19-mile-an-hour speed, unheard of until then. A thousand cars

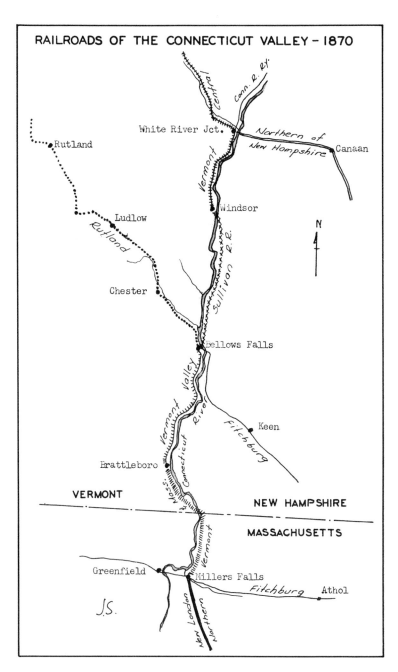

RAILROADS OF THE CONNECTICUT VALLEY — 1870

a month crossed the lake to Rutland tracks via this water passage, to the extreme annoyance of the Smiths, who had so carefully engineered the favorable traffic agreement between the Vermont Central and the Ogdensburg road. The rapid construction of the Montreal & Plattsburgh to its southern terminal, with a junction with the Ogdensburg at Mooers (11 miles west of Rouses Point and therefore not affected by the agreement) had, to a large degree, by-passed the carefully planned Vermont Central traffic blockade. Moreover, the Ogdens-

Lake steamer *Oakes Ames* was built in 1868 by the Champlain Transportation Company when all attempts failed to exchange traffic between the Rutland and its archrival, the Vermont Central. This craft, 258 feet long and 34 feet wide, carried railroad cars on her maindeck and passengers above. She plied the lake between Burlington and Plattsburgh at a fast 19 knots. The steamer transferred as many as 1100 cars a month when leased to the railroad, but ceased when the Vermont Central took over the Rutland in 1870. She had herself been instrumental in forging this move.

Vermont Valley No. 3, WESTMINSTER, in this rare photo was a classic 4-4-0 built by Rogers in 1851. Note whistle on extension high above boiler.—*Collection of Robert Adams.*

RUTLAND, VT. VALLEY, MONTREAL & PLATTSBURGH AND W. & PLATTSBURGH R. R'DS---TIME TABLE NO. 29.

FOR THE GOVERNMENT AND INFORMATION OF EMPLOYES ONLY

TAKES EFFECT MONDAY. MAY 9th. 1870.

TRAINS MOVING SOUTH.

Miles between stations	LEAVE	1 Mail.	2 Express.	3 Night Express.	4 Mixed Train.	5 F. & w. Exps. Ft.	6 Local Freight.	7 Mondays Cattle.	8 Mixed Train.	9 Local Freight.	10 Freight.
		A. M.	A. M.	P. M.	A. M.		P. M.	A. M.	P. M.	A. M.	A. M.
	Burlington	8.15	10.15	10.00				5.00	3.35	6.00	
6.5	Shelburne	9.03	10.25	10.16				5.25	4.00	6.57	
5.3	Charlotte	9.16	10.36	10.30				5.56	4.00	7.09	
4.1	North Ferrisburg	9.27	10.44	10.42				6.20	4.10	7.33	
3.3	Ferrisburg	9.37		10.52					4.55	7.55	
1.8	Vergennes	9.42	10.55	10.56				7.05	5.04	8.05	
5.2	New Haven	9.56	11.03	11.10				7.45	5.24	8.44	
4.5	Brooksville										
3.7	Middlebury	10.18	11.18	11.31				8.38	5.58	9.35	
6.4	Salisbury	10.35	11.29	11.47				9.14		10.14	
4.5	Whiting	10.46	11.37	12.00				9.37	6.47	10.40	
5.6	Brandon	11.01	11.46	12.15				10.08	7.08	11.40	
4	Pittsford Quarry										
2.6	Pittsford	11.19	11.58	12.34				10.44	7.34	1.08	
3.6	Sutherland Falls	11.28	12.04	12.44				11.04	7.47	1.33	
4.6	Center Rutland										
1.5	Rutland	A.11.45 L.12.20	12.15	1.00 L.1.30	4.50	10.00	10.20	A11.35 L.11.40	8.10	A.2.10 L.5.40	
3	North Clarendon										
3.4	Clarendon	12.35		1.45	5.13	10.36	10.54	1.15		6.07	
3.5	Cuttingsville	12.45		1.55	5.25	10.46	11.12	1.35		6.23	
3.1	East Wallingford	12.52		2.03	5.33	11.07	11.28	1.55		6.36	
2.7	Mount Holly	12.59		2.09	5.44	11.26	11.43	2.10		6.49	
2.6	Summit	1.05		2.15	5.54	11.55	11.55	2.24		7.00	
1.5	Healdville	1.09		2.19	6.00	11.58	12.13	2.30		7.05	
5.5	Ludlow	1.22		2.33	6.18	12.24	2.59		7.30		
3.4	Proctorsville	1.31		2.41	6.30	12.41	3.16		7.45		
1.5	Cavendish	1.35		2.45	6.35	12.48	1.41	3.26		7.50	
4.5	Gassetts	1.46		2.56	6.50	1.14	2.07	3.48		8.07	
4.4	Chester	1.57		3.07	7.05	1.33	2.34	4.11		8.26	
4	Bartonsville	2.07		3.16	7.19	1.53	2.56	4.32		8.43	
4.1	Rockingham										
5.3	Bellows Falls	A.2.30 L.2.35		3.40	A.7.40 L.7.55	2.40	A.3.50 PM L.4.00 AM	5.20		9.20	8.25
4	Westminster	2.46		3.48	8.05		4.16				8.45
8	East Putney	3.05		4.06	8.24		4.48				9.26
5	Putney	3.14		4.12	8.30		5.00				9.41
4	Dummerston	3.23		4.20	8.39		5.16				10.01
5	Brattleboro	3.35		4.30	8.50		5.35				10.25
		P. M.	P. M.	A. M.	A. M.	A. M.	A. M.	P. M.	P. M.	P. M.	

TRAINS MOVING NORTH.

LEAVE	11 Mail.	12 Day Express.	13 Night Express.	14 Mixed Train.	15 Mixed Train.	16 Local Freight.	17 Local Freight.	18 Freight.	19 F. & W. Exp. Ft.	20 Freight.
	A. M.	P. M.	P. M.	A. M.	P. M.	A. M.	A. M.	A. M.	A. M.	A. M.
Brattleboro	10.45		9.15	4.14	2.00					6.00
Dummerston	10.56		9.25	4.52	2.25					6.23
Putney	11.05		9.35	5.09	2.45					6.37
East Putney	11.13		9.42	5.09	3.00					6.50
Westminster	11.30		10.00	5.30	3.45					7.24
Bellows Falls	A.11.40 L.11.45		A.10.10 L.10.20	5.40 5.45	A.4.05 L.5.00 AM			9.00	1.50	7.40
Rockingham										
Bartonsville	12.09		10.45	6.19	5.55			9.50	5.30	
Chester	12.19		10.55	6.35	6.20			10.11	5.59	
Gassetts	12.30		11.06	6.52	6.48			10.34	6.10	
Cavendish	12.41		11.19	7.09	7.17			10.57		
Proctorsville	12.45		11.23	7.15	7.25			11.05	6.49	
Ludlow	12.55		11.32	7.20	7.45			11.23	6.58	
Healdville	1.07		11.46	7.50				8.16	11.52	7.25
Summit	1.15		11.50	7.55				8.25	12.00	7.32
Mount Holly	1.22		11.58	8.04				8.40	12.13	7.42
East Wallingford	1.30		12.04	8.14				8.55	12.25	7.55
Cuttingsville	1.40		12.13	8.25			9.10		12.40	8.12
Clarendon	1.51		12.23	8.37			9.28		1.10	8.29
North Clarendon										
Rutland	A.2.10 L.2.20	5.30	12.40 L.1.30	9.00	5.40	10.00	12.15	1.45	9.00	
Center Rutland										
Sutherland Falls	2.34	5.44	1.44		6.00	12.50				
Pittsford	2.41	5.53	1.53		6.00					
Pittsford Quarry										
Brandon	2.56	6.07	2.06		6.35	2.03				
Whiting	3.09	6.19	2.19		6.52	2.42				
Salisbury	3.19	6.30	2.29		7.08	3.14				
Middlebury	3.34	6.44	2.43		7.28	4.10				
Brooksville										
New Haven	3.51	7.01	3.01	7.55		5.12				
Vergennes	4.04	7.13	3.12	8.12	6.00					
Ferrisburg	4.07	7.17	3.17	8.17	6.10					
North Ferrisburg	4.15	7.25	3.25	8.29	6.29					
Charlotte	4.25	7.34	3.34	8.43	6.50					
Shelburne	4.36	7.45	3.45	9.00	7.17					
Burlington	4.50	8.00	4.00	9.23	7.50					
	P. M.	P. M.	A. M.	P. M.	A. M.	A. M.	P. M.	P. M.	A. M.	A. M.

SPECIAL RULES.

1. Trains should meet and pass at stations marked with full face figures.
2. No Engine following a Passenger Train will leave any station until five minutes after Passenger Train has left.
3. All Trains and Extra Engines stop at stations printed in large type,—DO NOT STOP at other stations unless signalized or to leave Passengers.
4. Train No. 1 will have the right to the road against Train No. 11. Trains 1 and 3 will have the right to the road against train No. 13.
5. Train No. 7 will have the right to the road against all other freight trains, and against No. 14 until 7 o'clock p. m.
6. Train No. 1 does not stop at North Clarendon.
7. Train No. 4 will have the right to road against No. 19.
8. Train No. 9 and 19 are Mixed Trains between Rutland and Bellows Falls.
9. Freight and Cattle Trains will in all cases wait for Passenger Trains, and be kept entirely out of their way, never leaving a station without full time per Time Table, to arrive at the next station before the time of the Passenger Train.
10. All trains must run at a reduced rate of speed, not exceeding six miles per hour, and without working steam over the bridge at Brooksville.
11. All trains must run at a reduced rate of speed, not exceeding eight miles per hour, past the stations at Whiting and Proctorsville.
12. When trains are delayed conductors having the right to the road will leave each station as much behind their regular time until the expected train is passed, as they were required to wait at the station appointed for passing. In all cases subject to Rule 49.
13. Station Agents will see that rules 159 and 162 are complied with.
14. At 5.30 a. m. the right to the road ceases of all trains of the previous day, and after that time such trains will keep out the way of all regular trains.
15. On Sunday morning Train No. 3 will stop at Rutland, proceeding to destination Monday mornings.
16. Train No. 13 will run through to Burlington Sunday mornings, and will not be run Monday mornings.
Train No. 2 will stop only at Vergennes, Middlebury and Brandon.
Irregular trains will keep out of the way of all regular trains.
Trains Nos. 12 and 13, north of Rutland, will stop only at Brandon, Middlebury and Vergennes, except to take or leave through passengers.
Train No. 5 will run Sunday nights, and not Saturday nights.

CHAMPLAIN DIVISION.

MONTREAL & PLATTSBURGH RAIL ROAD.

TRAINS MOVING SOUTH.

LEAVE.	1 Mail.	2 Night Express.	3 Mixed Train.	4 Freight.
	A. M.	P. M.	A. M.	P. M.
Province Line	7.40	6.10		4.30
2.6 Mooer's Junction	7.47	6.16	10.30	4.43
.5 Mooer's Village				
4.7 Sciota	7.59	6.32	11.19	5.25
5.9 Chazy	8.14	6.47	11.19	5.25
5. Beekmantown	8.25	7.00	11.41	6.00
4.3 Plattsburgh	8.35	7.20	12.00	6.20
	A. M.	P. M.	A. M.	P. M.

TRAINS MOVING NORTH.

LEAVE.	5 Morning Express.	6 Mail.	7 Freight.	8 Mixed Train.
	A. M.	P. M.	A. M.	P. M.
Plattsburgh	6.00	6.50	8.00	2.10
Beekmantown	6.10	7.05	8.20	2.29
Chazy	6.23	7.18	8.46	2.51
Sciota	6.38	7.37	9.14	3.16
Mooer's Village				
Mooer's Junction		7.54	9.35	3.40
Province Line	7.15		9.46	
	A. M.	P. M.	A. M.	P. M.

WHITEHALL & PLATTSBURGH RAIL ROAD.

TRAINS MOVING SOUTH.

LEAVE	1 Mail.	2 Mixed.	3	4
	A. M.	P. M.		
Plattsburgh	8.40	2.00		
5 Salmon River	8.54	2.34		
8 Lapham's Mills	9.05	2.56		
10 Peru	9.00	2.45		
14 Harkness	9.22	3.04		
17 Ferrona	9.31	3.16		
20 Ausable River	9.40	3.30		
	A. M.	P. M.		

TRAINS MOVING NORTH.

LEAVE	5 Mail.	6 Mixed.	7	8
	P. M.	A. M.		
Ausable River	1.00	11.00		
Ferrona	1.09	11.13		
Harkness	1.18	11.27		
Peru	1.31	11.46		
Lapham's Mills	1.36	11.54		
Salmon River	1.45	12.07		
Plattsburgh	5.00	12.30		
	P. M.	P. M.		

Train No. 6 will have right to the Road against No. 2 until 7.20 P. M., after which time No. 6 must keep out of the way of No. 2.

The standard time for trains on Champlain Division, will be the clock at Plattsburgh.

All trains will run at a reduced rate of speed over the Bridge at Plattsburgh and without working steam.

Passenger Trains having the right of Road must not leave any Station or Side Track, where, by the Time Table, it should pass a Train, till FIVE minutes after its time, per Time Table, and this five minutes, allowed for safety, must operate at every succeeding Station until the expected Train is passed. Freight and Mixed Trains must keep off time of Passenger Trains.

Observe carefully Rules relative to speed over Bridges, approaching and leaving Stations and Yards.

RAILROAD OFFICE, RUTLAND, VT., May 6th, 1870.

TUTTLE & CO., PRINTERS, RUTLAND, VT.

GEO. A. MERRILL, Gen'l Supt.

Looking south from the River Street overpass in Rutland, the Howe Scale Company is between the Bellows Falls line, left, and the Bennington line, right. To the right of the old ball signal is a Rutland & Washington train as well as that road's turntable and woodshed.

The home yard in Rutland was a busy place in the good old days. A double-headed freight with 4-4-0 No. 16, the ROCKINGHAM, leading awaits departure for Bellows Falls over Mount Holly. Track to the right leading up to the covered train shed is the Rutland & Washington's line up from Troy. The huge dome on the completely circular roundhouse covers the internal turntable.

The J. M. HAVEN was the Rutland's only home-built loco-motive. A proud, derby-hatted engineer poses with oil can poised, by the engine outside the shop building in Rutland, shortly after her completion in 1870.

Old No. 203 was built by Taunton in 1867 and originally named BENSLIDE. She didn't look like much, but she puffed around Rutland, switching cars and posing for pictures with her proud crew, until the turn of the century. — *Collection of Gordon Cutler.*

burg managers suddenly awoke to the fact that, under changing circumstances, it might be foolhardy to be too closely aligned with one of the corporate combatants.

As the sequence of events progressed, nervousness changed to complete consternation in the offices of the Vermont Central Railroad. In a matter of a few years the situation of dominance that it had enjoyed in much of the State of Vermont and across a wide band of New York's fertile North Country had deteriorated badly. Now it faced a major threat. Page's announced intention of building a second trunk line around Lake Champlain posed a trying problem, since the Smith interests prevented him from effectively connecting with Canada and northern New York by a rail route across its foot. By itself, the *Oakes Ames* had been at the worst a seasonal threat, tapping the northern railroad traffic during only seven or eight months of a year. But now, if Page intended to connect

The Vermont & Massachusetts Railroad was leased by John Page for the Rutland in December 1870. Here V. & M.

No. 3, built by Hinkley in 1849, poses with three ornate cars just north of Brattleboro.

the Whitehall & Plattsburgh with the Montreal & Plattsburgh, the Rutland would be in as good, if not a better, competitive position than the Vermont Central route. During all the year it could tap the Ogdensburg traffic at Mooers Junction, supplementing this during the warm months with the ferry service across the lake. With the Addison Railroad connection at Ticonderoga, traffic could be shifted across to Rutland rails at Leicester Junction; if it became too heavy, it could be shifted down to the Rutland & Whitehall line. Moreover, the completion of the through line would place Rutland interests in a position to divert from the Vermont Central much traffic from Canada and the Great Lakes destined for New York and southern New England.

J. Gregory Smith was in frequent and heated conference with his directors. Word filtered back to St. Albans that Page's surveying crews were actually running lines west of the lake—an action that held little encouragement for a favorable Vermont Central solution to the problem. As the meaning of events of the past months suddenly became apparent, crafty old Gregory realized he had finally met his match. There was only one solution, "If you can't lick 'em, join 'em!" Emissaries were dispatched from St. Albans to Rutland.

"Would the Rutland railroad consider being leased to the Vermont Central?" It would.

An offer was made. Too low. Another team of surveyors went into the field.

A few days later, a second offer was tendered to Page. Still too low. Rumor had it that the Whitehall & Plattsburgh was ready to negotiate for a right of way north of Port Henry.

Just before Christmas of 1870, a reluctant Santa Claus in the guise of J. Gregory Smith journeyed south to Rutland with an early, albeit a very substantial gift in the form of a final offer. Ex-Governor Smith stated his terms to Governor Page, who heard them graciously and allowed that he would take the matter up with his board of directors, and, if they approved, lay it before the Chancery Court just to make it legal. The two men parted with mutual felicitations for the holidays. It may be

assumed that Mr. Smith's hand may have been a little bit forced by the venerable Mr. Page.

Page was jubilant. The offer was one which would handily take both him and the Rutland out of a situation which, if his calculated risk had failed, would have plunged the road into another financial abyss. Smith's offer called for payment of a lump sum of $376,000 for rental of the Rutland alone for the first year, with total payments over a twenty-year period aggregating $7,144,000. In addition, Page had unloaded the *Oakes Ames* on the Vermont Central at a rental of $10,000 a year. Under the terms of the contract, the Vermont Central was also committed to take over the leases of the subsidiary lines that had been acquired by the Rutland directly, and by sundry Rutland stockholders, in the interest of the company.

The surveying crews in New York State promptly disappeared.

The board of directors met at the Boston office of the Rutland, 13 Kilby Street, on December 31, 1870. It was unanimously voted that "The president of this company be directed, and he is hereby authorized, to execute in its name and behalf, a contract or lease of their railroad and property, in connection with other roads and lines, as well as to sell and transfer the supplies, fuel, lumber, contracts and interests in said contracts named, to the managers of the Vermont Central and Vermont & Canada Railroads . . ." Not a voice dissented, nor was much time wasted in discussion. It was easily the best deal the Rutland Railroad Company had ever made. It may also be assumed that the august managerial body breathed a collective sigh of relief.

The total gross earnings of the road for the seven years prior to the lease had amounted to only slightly more than $6,000,000; the rental schedule worked out with the Vermont Central represented a much better net return than the Rutland's managers could hope to produce by operating the road themselves!

The lease was quickly approved by the Court, and all the leased roads were duly notified that, retroactive to December 30, 1870, they were essentially the properties of the Vermont Central.

The N. L. Davis, No. 24, is pictured outside the shops in Rutland. The gleaming new paint and Central Vermont lettering were placed on her shortly after C. V. leased the Rutland in 1870. The Taunton works built her for the Rutland & Burlington in 1868. — *Collection of Robert Adams.*

Three Burlington boys, securely hatted, play in Battery Park in 1870. In the background is the old covered train shed, the Champlain Transportation Company's wharves, and Shelburne Bay in the distance.

Chapter 4

Mr. Smith Takes the Throttle

The Smiths of the Vermont Central, either by design or in defense, now controlled the largest railroad in New England and the seventh largest in the entire United States, with more than nine hundred miles of trackage and control of two steamship lines — one connecting the New London terminus with the port of New York and the other running out of Ogdensburg to the western Great Lakes, an important link in Gregory Smith's dream of an integrated transportation system spanning the continent.

Gregory had been well-schooled by his astute father; his career ascended like a rocket. Already he had served as Governor of Vermont, almost a prerequisite for railroad presidents in that state, and now he devoted his full energies to the expansion of the system. He had assumed control of the Montreal & Vermont, a 23-mile road from St. Albans to St. Johns, along the Richelieu River where it connected with the Grand Trunk line for the Canadian metropolis. During his tenure as Governor, he had also leased the little Sullivan Railroad, gaining control of trackage south to Bellows Falls. These and other minor acquisitions had, by 1865, placed J. Gregory Smith in a position of dominance over the railroads of Vermont.

It was this situation that John Page and the resurgent Rutland threatened in the years following the Civil War. The Vermont Central, through the Vermont & Canada, had enjoyed the lion's share of all transportation business to the north and west through the St. Albans gateway and the trestle across Champlain to the Ogdensburg road. Page's rapid acquisitions and the threat of a diversionary route via his Whitehall & Plattsburgh could, if completed, effectively cut off much Canadian and lake traffic from the Smith-controlled lines. After the launching of the *Oakes Ames*, Gregory Smith leased the Ogdensburg & Lake Champlain in March of 1870 as a purely defensive measure, assuming that only direct control could prevent a debacle west of the lake. That move was only partially successful; many shippers were demanding transit via the Rutland-controlled Plattsburgh & Montreal and the lake route. Moreover, Boston interests had placed him in the presidency of the far-away Northern Pacific, a position he was to hold until Jay Cooke took over that line, and the threatening Rutland was doing little to enhance his dream of a transcontinental route embracing the Northern Pacific and the Vermont Central with, of course, J. Gregory Smith as president.

It became readily apparent that the only alternative was to take over the Rutland and its appendages. The parent road had little value to the Vermont Central except as a feeder and the fact that it conceivably could be used as a link for a direct line into New York. Of greater importance were the leased lines, the Vermont Valley and the Vermont & Massachusetts, acquired by John Page for the Rutland, since the previous arrangements with the Northern of New Hampshire, providing access to Boston, were proving to be something less than satisfactory. (The Vermont Valley, running from Bellows Falls to Brattleboro was leased in May 1865, and the Vermont & Massachusetts from Brattleboro to Grout's Corners in December, 1870.) Smith did not like the terms imposed by the Rut-

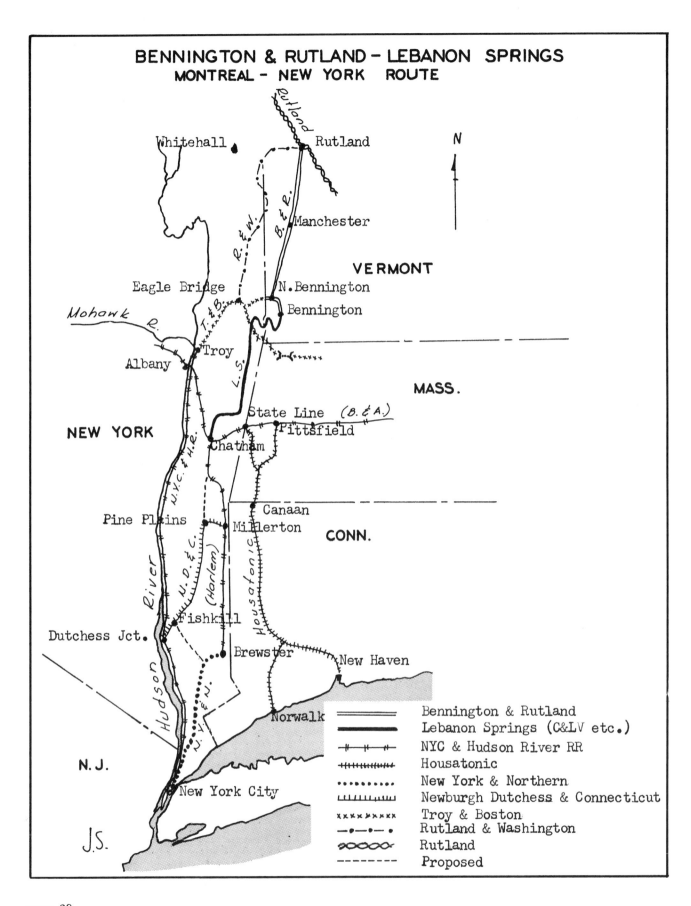

BENNINGTON & RUTLAND – LEBANON SPRINGS
MONTREAL – NEW YORK ROUTE

N

Whitehall

Rutland

Rutland

Manchester

VERMONT

Eagle Bridge

N. Bennington

Bennington

Mohawk R.

R. & W.

B. & R.

T. & B.

Troy

Albany

L. S.

MASS.

State Line (B. & A.)

NEW YORK

Pittsfield

Chatham

Canaan

Pine Plains

Millerton

CONN.

N.Y.C. & H.R.R.

N.D. & C.

(Harlem)

Housatonic

River

Fishkill

Dutchess Jct.

Brewster

New Haven

Hudson

N.Y. & N.

Norwalk

N.J.

New York City

J.S.

	Bennington & Rutland
	Lebanon Springs (C&LV etc.)
	NYC & Hudson River RR
	Housatonic
	New York & Northern
	Newburgh Dutchess & Connecticut
	Troy & Boston
	Rutland & Washington
	Rutland
	Proposed

land management, but there was a better than even chance, on the basis of the much-improved earnings of the Rutland line, that it could pay its way and possibly even prove to be a profitable adjunct to the Vermont Central system. But most important, a lease of the Rutland would remove a threat that was hanging like a sword over the future of his own railroad system, the alternate route on the west side of Lake Champlain. It was with extreme reluctance and some misgiving that he capitulated and signed as the year 1870 drew to an end.

The acquisition of the Rutland-controlled Vermont Valley and Vermont & Massachusetts now gave the Vermont Central management an entry it had long coveted to the New London Northern's line that had been completed to connect with the Vermont & Massachusetts for a water route via Long Island Sound to New York City. In due time the acquisition of this road was to be for the long range benefit of the Vermont Central. The Ocean-to-Lakes bridge system had finally become a reality under the single control of the Vermont Central, though under somewhat different circumstances than had been originally conceived, and with considerable change in the location of the eastern terminal.

Almost immediately it became evident that the Vermont Central had gotten the short end of the deal with the Rutland. Apparently the Central's management had not taken enough time to analyze the situation, a procedure that would have revealed the faulty reasoning that lay in the assumption that the Rutland's earnings would remain consistently high under Central control. Much of the Rutland's improved revenues resulted from the operation of the *Oakes Ames* (included in the lease at $10,000 per year) which would be superfluous to the Vermont Central. Moreover, much of the traffic handled over Rutland rails to Burlington was originally diverted from the Central's tracks. Now, much of this would be rerouted via the Central, cutting into the Rutland's earnings. Governor Page had neatly worked Governor Smith into a trap.

The Central hardly had time to absorb the Rutland properties when, in 1873, the inevitable postwar recession settled on the land. Already hard-

J. Gregory Smith, president of the Vermont Central, was Governor of Vermont from 1863 to 1865. — *Vermont Historical Society.*

pressed to meet the exorbitant rentals, the Smith line defaulted on its rent, and by mid-1875, was more than a quarter-million dollars in arrears. Gregory Smith, driven by the insistence of the Rutland's directors that he "pay up," lashed out with charges of falsity, chicanery and collusion against Page and his associates.

In an effort to lighten the financial burden acquired with the Rutland and its leased lines, Smith now sought to unload those that would be of no value to him. As his directors convened early in 1873 he notified them that negotiations were pending at the time for the surrender by the Vermont Central and Vermont & Canada of the leases of the Whitehall & Plattsburgh and Montreal & Plattsburgh railroads, and the steamer *Oakes Ames* and their assignment to the New York & Canada Railroad (later absorbed by the Delaware & Hudson). March 1, 1873, saw the Delaware & Hudson Canal Company pick up the offered leases on behalf of New York & Canada Railroad.

With Smith's present financial problems and his Boston–Great Lakes route assured, even the completion of this line on the west side of the lake by the Pennsylvania coal-hauling Delaware & Hudson would be of little concern.

Meanwhile the Vermont Central managers had made a real effort to utilize the Rutland line to good advantage as part of a through route from New York to Montreal. They leased the Harlem Extension Railroad, south from Rutland, a consolidation of the old Western Vermont (Bennington & Rutland) and Lebanon Springs roads. In connection with a 128-mile patchwork of short lines east of the Hudson, this offered a through route to New York City, though a rough and tortuous one in comparison to the straight and level high-speed track of the New York Central & Hudson River. Out of this combination came a rather nebulous operating company, largely financed by New York City interests, called the New York, Boston & Montreal Railroad Company. The arrangement lasted less than five years. In order to maintain fast schedules, the line had to give its passengers one of the most hair-raising rides in the East, over two hundred miles of rough track and sharp reverse curves, before they hit the relatively long tangents and easy grades of the Rutland line north to Burlington.

Despite the attempt to establish fast passenger service between Montreal and New York via the Rutland, and a second route to New York by way of New London, there was no solution for the Vermont Central's financial troubles. Page and the

This poster, displayed in Manchester, Vermont, introduced through service to the West in 1875 via *The White Mountain Express* and Rutland Division connections of the Central Vermont.

The TIMOTHY FOLLETT was renumbered as No. 213 Central Vermont, Rutland Division, after the 1870 lease. Here she poses in the rock cut at Summit. Near this spot mastadon bones were unearthed during construction in 1849.

Rutland directors went into the courts to force payment; the stockholders of the Vermont & Canada, far from profiting from their acquisition of the Vermont Central, now found it a millstone around their necks relentlessly dragging them into insolvency. The top-heavy Vermont Central structure, now encompassing ownership or leases of twelve companies, threatened to tumble into inefficiency and insolvency. J. Gregory Smith was finding the president's chair up in St. Albans an extremely hot seat.

His bitter charges of chicanery against the directors of the Rutland Railroad were actually in defense of his personal judgment for the Rutland's earnings and operating reports had been a matter of open record for his inspection before he negotiated the lease. Adding to his troubles, charges of mismanagement and diversion of company funds were leveled against him, his brother, Worthington Smith and Joseph Clark who was a heavy stockholder in the railroad and a partner with the Smiths in many related enterprises.

As the Vermont Central reorganized into the Central Vermont Railroad Company in 1873, J. Gregory Smith shrewdly weathered the transition and remained as president. He was not hampered greatly in his activities by the trustees appointed by Chancery Court; they were all picked friends. The troublesome court action to force rental payments, brought against the Central Vermont by the Rutland, was finally compromised in February 1875, with a modified lease that reduced the fees somewhat, but still called for considerably more than the Central Vermont wanted or was able to pay. Smith would have been happy to give up the lease completely, but the Rutland and the Ogdensburg & Lake Champlain had petitioned the court not to have their leases set aside, and at the same

Below and on the following two pages is reproduced an 1872 Vermont Central system timetable. It shows all of that company's acquired lines, including those of the Rutland interests. — *Collection of J. R. McFarlane.*

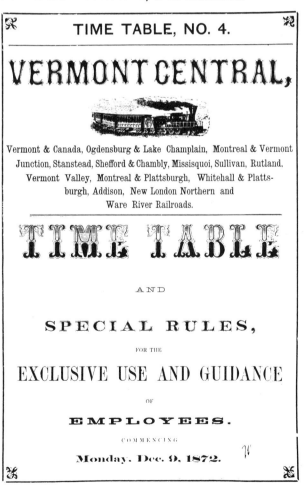

TRAINS MOVING WEST.
Western Division.

Dist.	STATIONS.	No. 2 THROUGH FREIGHT.	No. 4 MAIL.	No. 6 WAY FREIGHT.	No. 8 FREIGHT.	No. 10 THROUGH FREIGHT.	No. 12 ACCOMMODATION.	No. 14 EXPRESS.	No. 16 THROUGH FREIGHT.	No. 18	No. 20	No. 22	No. 24
		A. M.	A. M.	A. M.	A. M.	P. M.	P. M.	P. M.	P. M.	P. M.			
6,2	St. Albans	3.40	6.45		6.10	12.00	7.20						
6 2	Swanton June.	4.10	7.00		6.45	12.45	12.18	7.35					
9,1	Swanton	{4.30/5.10	7.08		{7.00/7.10	1.00	12.38	7.41					
16,4	AlburghSprings	5.48	7.24		7.50	1.35	12.44	8.00					
20,3	Alburgh	6.10	7.32		8.15	1.55	12.55	8.10					
2,2	West Alburgh	6.20	7.38		8.30	2.08	1.00	8.15					
23,9	Rouse's Point	{6.35/6.55	7.45		{8.45/9.00	{2.20/2.30	{1.10/1.20	8.25					
28,4	Champlain	7.20	7.55		9.22	3.00	1.40	8.36					
31,4	Perry's Mills	7.40	8.03		9.42	3.18	1.55	8.45					
35,6	Mooers	{8.10/8.15	8.15		{10.10/10.30	3.45	2.14	8.57					
39,1	Centerville	8.32	8.2		{10.55/11.10	4.05	2.30	9.06					
41,6	Wood's Falls	8.45	8.28		11.24	4.20	2.40	9.14					
44,6	Altona	9.02	8.35		{11.40/12.00	{4.40/4.50	2.55	9.23					
46,9	Irona	9.12	8.40		12.12	5.05	3.05	9.30					
49,7	Forest	{9.28/9.50	8.48		12.30	5.22	3.18	9.38					
51,7	Dannemora	10.06	8.53		12.41	5.35	3.30	9.44					
52,7	Ellenburgh	10.12	8.5		{12.50/1.0	5.42	3.34	9.47					
1,37,7	Brandy Brook	{10.20/11.05	8.57		1.26	5.49	3.38	9.50					
58,7	Clinton Mills	11.30	9.09		{2.00/2.10	6.20	{4.00/4.05	10.04					
61,2	Cherubusco	11.45	9.15		2.25	{6.35/6.45	4.15	10.10					
68,7	Chateaugay	12.20	9.34		{3.15/3.35	7.30	4.38	10.32					
73,2	Burke	12.45	9.47		4.05	8.00	4.52	10.39					
80,7	Malone	{1.20/1.25	{10.06/10.11	6.45	{2.00/2.10	{8.45/8.50	{5.13/5.20	{11.10/11.15					
86,7	Bangor	1.56	10.26	7.20/8.00	2.25	9.25	6.35	11.26					
92,4	Brush's Mills	2.25	10.4	{8.35/8.45	{10.00/10.10	5.52	11.40						
91,9	Moira	2.40	10.46	9.00/9.10	10.25	6.00	11.45						
100,7	Lawrence	3.15	11.00	{9.45/10.00	11.00	6.15	12.00						
106,1	Brasher Falls	3.50	11.15	{10.35/10.45	11.35	6.31	12.18						
111,2	Knapps	{4.35/4.45	11.35	11.20	{12.25/12.35	6.52	12.35						
117,2	Potsdam	5.00	11.42	{11.35/11.55	12.50	7.00	12.42						
121,7	Madrid	5.47	12.03	{12.10/12.40	1.40	7.25	1.04						
133,2	Lisbon	{6.35/6.45	12.25	{2.00/2.20	{2.25/2.30	7.50	1.24						
141,9	Ogdensburgh	7.30	12.45	3.13	3.10	8.10	1.45						
		A. M.	A. M.	P. M.	P. M.	P. M.	P. M.	P. M.	P. M.				

For Crossing Stations, see Page 3.

No. 14 Train does not stop at Perry's Mills, Woods Falls, Irona, Forest, Brandy Brook, Clinton Mills, Cherubusco, Burke, Knapps and Lisbon.

No. 1 Train does not stop at Brandy Brook.

West of Swanton Junction, Trains moving East, take precedence of Train moving West.

Harlem Extension Division.—Trains going North & West.

Miles	STATIONS	No. 6A MIXT.	No. 14 MONTREAL EXPRESS.	No. 2 N.Y. EXPRESS.	No. 4 MAIL.	No. 6 MIXED.	No. 16 SUNDAY MAIL.	No. 24 NEW YORK EXPRESS.	No. 26 MAIL.	No. 28 FREIGHT.	No. 30 FREIGHT.	No. 32 PASSENGER.	No. 34 NEW YORK EXPRESS.
		A. M.	A. M.	P. M.	P. M.	P. M.	P. M.	P. M.	A. M.	A. M.	P. M.	P. M.	A. M.
6,2	Chatham 4 Cor's.	8.20			3.55								
6,2	Chatham	8.50		4.20									
8,8	Rider's Mills	9.05		4.30									
11,4	Brainards	9.20		4.40									
13,7	West Lebanon	9.30		4.49									
16,7	Lebanon C. ntre	{9.55/10.05		5.00									
17,7	New Leb'non	10.05		5.05									
19,0	L-banon Springs	10.12		5.11									
21,4	St-phentown	{10.35/10.40		5.33									
27,0	So St-phentown	11.00		5.45									
28,7	Coal Switch	11.20											
30,7	So. Berlin	11.30		6.00									
32,3	Center Berlin	{11.45/11.55		6.05									
35,0	Berlin	12.17		6.20									
39,2	Petersburgh	12.46		6.38									
44,1	N. Petersburgh	{12.50/1.00		7.03									
45,9	T.& B JUNC	1.34		7.08									
51,2	East Hoosick	{2.10/3.15		7.30	8.00								
58,2	Bennington	{3.35/3.15	9.15	10.50	8.00	7.50	8.05	1.20					
62,2	No Bennington	3.55	9.30	11.05			8.05	1.24	10.10	1.00	4.45	12.10	
64,2	State Line	3.40	9.50	1.14					10.23	1.15	4.50	12.14	
62,2	No. Bennington	3.55	9.45	11.10									
64,2	So. Shaftsbury	4.25	9.50	1.14									
69,2	Shaftsbury	4.50/5.00	10.02	11.26									
74,2	Arlington	{5.55/6.05	10.14	11.40									
77,2	Sunderland	6.18	10.22	11.50									
83,2	Manchester	{6.35/6.45	10.35	12.05									
85,2	Barnumville	7.05	10.40	12.10									
88,2	East Dorset	{7.30/7.40	10.47	12.20									
91,2	North Dorset	8.10	10.55	12.30									
95,2	Danby & M. Tabr.	{8.35/11.25	11.04	12.40									
100,2	So. Wallingford	8.55	11.15	12.55									
104,2	Wallingford	9.30/11.30	11.25/11.30	1.05									
107,2	Clarendon	9.30	11.35	1.15									
113,2	Rutland	9.30	11.55	1.30									
		a. m.	a. m.	p. m.	p. m.	p. m.	a. m.	p. m.	a. m.	p. m.	p. m.	p. m.	a. m.

Trains Moving South.—Rutland Division.

☞ For Crossing Stations, see page No. 14. ☜

Dist. S to S	STATIONS.	No. 1 Passenger A.M.	No. 3 Mixed A.M.	No. 7 Through Freight A.M.	No. 9 Way Freight A.M.	No. 11 Mail A.M.	No. 13 New York Express A.M.	No. 17 Freight	No. 21 Express P.M.	No. 23 Mixed P.M.	No. 25 Express P.M.	No. 29 Mail P.M.	No. 31 Night Express P.M.	No. 33
	Essex Junction	5.20					9.35	6.00	1.00		6.00		8.35	
5.0	Winooski	5.35				7.55	9.30	{6.25 {6.35	1.15		6.15		8.50	
3.0	Burlington, Ar.	5.45	No. 3 Mixed A.M.		8.55	8.00	10.00	6.53	1.25		6.25		9.00	
	Burlington, Lv.			2.45						2.20			9.10	
14.5	Shelburn			3.30	9.54	8.25	10.20			2.47			9.30	
19.8	Charlotte			{4.05 {4.15	{10.27 {10.35	8.42	10.33			3.10			9.46	
23.9	No. Ferrisburg			4.46	{11.00 {11.10	8.55	10.43			3.29			10.00	
27.2	Ferrisburg			5.06	11.30	9.05	10.52			3.42			10.10	
29.0	Vergennes			{5.10 {5.25	{11.40 {12.10	9.10	10.57			3.50			10.15	
31.2	New Haven			5.35	{12.30 {12.40	9.25	11.09			{4.10 {4.20			10.32	
35.7	Brooksville			6.22	1.18	9.40	11.20			4.40			10.47	
42.4	Middlebury			{6.45 {7.15	{1.40 {2.10	{9.50 {10.10	11.30			4.48			11.00	
48.8	Salisbury			7.57	2.48	10.10	11.46			5.25			11.20	
53.3	Leicester June.			{8.25 {8.35	{3.15 {3.30	10.25	12.08			{5.45 {5.55	5.45		11.35	
58.9	Brandon			{9.05 {9.20	{4.05 {4.40	10.42	12.10			6.15	6.20		11.52	
62.9	Pittsford Quar'y.													
65.5	Pittsford			{10.00 {10.05		11.03	12.27		6.10		{7.05 {7.10		12.14	
69.1	Sutherla'd Falls.			10.28		11.13	12.35		6.52		7.26		12.22	
73.7	Center Rutland.			11.00		11.28	12.45	E. & W. P.M. 6.30	7.10		7.34		12.35	
75.2	Rutland			{11.10 {12.35	6.40	{11.32 {12.10	12.50	E. & W. Way Freight A.M. 10.00	12.00	7.15	5.00	8.05	{12.40 {12.50	
78.2	No. Clarendon.			12.52		12.17	1.00	10.18	10.18				1.00	
81.6	Clarendon.			1.11		12.24	1.08	10.38	10.38		5.52		1.10	
85.1	Cuttingsville.			{1.30 {1.56		12.33		11.00	11.00		5.50		1.20	
88.2	E. Wallingford.			2.15		12.43		{11.15 {11.20	{11.15 {11.20		6.05		1.30	
90.9	Mount Holly.			2.30		12.49		11.26	12.05		6.18		1.38	
93.5	Summit.			{5.55 {6.00	{2.48 {2.53	12.56		11.50	{12.20 {12.25		6.30		1.45	
95.0	Healdville.			6.05	3.02	1.00	12.35	11.59	12.35		6.37		1.50	
100.5	Ludlow.			6.20	3.35	1.15	1.05	{12.30 {12.40	1.30		{7.05 {7.10		2.05	
103.9	Proctorsville.			6.30	3.55	1.23	1.30	1.00	2.05		7.26		2.15	
105.4	Cavendish.			6.35	4.04	1.28	1.50	1.10	2.30		7.34		2.20	
109.9	Gassets.			6.48	4.31	1.40		1.36	3.00		7.55		2.32	
114.3	Chester.			{4.55 {5.10	7.00	1.50	2.00	2.00	3.10		8.17		2.45	
118.3	Bartonsville.			5.45	7.10	2.00	2.22	2.22	{4.20 {4.25		8.35		2.58	
122.1	Rockingham.			6.05	7.21	2.12	2.46	2.46	4.55		8.35		3.10	
127.7	Bellows Falls.			6.30	{7.35 {7.00	2.25	3.15	3.15	5.30		9.20		3.25	

Remls carefully Crossing of trains and Special Rules. Your attention is particularly called to Special Rule No. 27.

No. 31 train will run through to Bellows Falls Sunday morning.

No. 18 and 16 trains will not stop at Rockingham, No. Clarendon, Brooksville and Ferrisburgh, except to leave passengers, unless flagged.

No. 18 train will stop only at Pittsford, Brandon, Middlebury, Vergennes, Burlington and Winooski, except to leave passengers coming on Rutland road, via Castleton.

Trains Moving North.

	STATIONS.	No. 2 Mail A.M.	No. 4 Mixed P.M.
	Plattsburgh.	6.00	3.30
2.6	Beekmantown.	6.16	3.48
3.1	Chazy.	6.38	4.10
7.2	Sciota.	7.00	4.36
12.7	Mooer's Village.		
18.7	Mooer's Junctin.	7.23	5.00
22.0	Province Line.	7.30	

Trains Moving South.

	STATIONS.	No. 1 Mixed A.M.	No. 3 Mail P.M.
	Province Line.		
2.6	Mooer's Junctin.	10.20	5.55
3.1	Mooers Village.		
7.2	Sciota.	10.50	
12.7	Chazy.	11.16	6.10
18.7	Beekmantown.	11.40	6.25
22.0	Plattsburgh.	12.00	6.45

For signals at Mooer's Junction, see page 3.

All trains must run at a reduced rate of speed over the bridge at Plattsburgh.

NORTHERN DIVISION OF WHITEHALL & PLATTSBURGH RAILROAD.

Trains Moving North.

	STATIONS.	No. 2 Mixed A.M.	No. 4 Pass. P.M.
	Ausable.	9.00	5.00
3.0	Ferrona.	9.20	5.15
3.0	Harkness.	9.38	5.30
4.0	Peru.	10.00	5.50
2.0	Lapham's Mills.	10.12	6.00
3.0	Salmon River.	10.36	6.15
5.0	Plattsburgh.	11.00	6.30

Trains Moving South.

	STATIONS.	No. 1 Pass. A.M.	No. 3 Mixed P.M.
	Plattsburgh.	7.00	2.15
5.0	Salmon River.	7.25	2.45
8.0	Lapham's Mills.	7.40	3.05
10.0	Peru.	7.50	3.20
14.0	Harkness.	8.10	3.45
17.0	Ferrona.	8.25	4.05
20.0	Ausable.	8.40	4.20

SOUTHERN DIVISION OF WHITEHALL & PLATTSBURGH AND ADDISON RAILROADS.

Trains Moving North.

	STATIONS.	No. 2 Mixed A.M.	No. 4 Pass. P.M.
	Leicester June.	6.20	5.55
3.2	Whiting.	6.40	6.05
3.2	Shoreham.	7.00	6.23
2.5	Orwell.	7.15	6.38
5.7	Larabees Point.	7.46	6.45
1.0	Ticonderoga.	8.10	6.57
8.6	Crown Point.	9.00	7.15
8.8	Port Henry.	9.20	7.27

Trains Moving South.

	STATIONS.	No. 1 Pass. A.M.	No. 3 Mixed P.M.
	Port Henry.	8.35	2.00
8.8	Crown Point.	9.00	2.50
8.6	Ticonderoga.	9.20	3.40
1.0	Larabees Point.	9.30	4.00
5.7	Orwell.	9.45	4.15
2.5	Shoreham.	10.05	4.30
3.2	Whiting.	10.20	5.30
3.2	Leicester June.		

Crossing Stations for Trains going North.

No. 2.—Crown Point, meet 1.

No. 4.—Leicester Junction, meet 3.

Crossing Stations for Trains going South.

No. 1.—Crown Point, meet 2.

No. 3.—Leicester Junction, meet 4.

☞ A Red Flag by day, or a Red Light by night, placed over the Draw at Ticonderoga, indicates that the Draw is open.

This Central Vermont time-table map shows the Rutland as a division of Mr. Smith's company. — *Collection of J. R. McFarlane.*

time announced a plan to join together in one system if they were — a proposal that was calculated to give the Central Vermont a bad case of chills. To complicate matters further, there was evidence that the fast-growing Delaware & Hudson was casting covetous eyes on both the Rutland and the Ogdensburg roads.

Under these and other pressures, an agreement was reached which lumped the earnings of the Rutland and Addison roads with those of the Central Vermont and Vermont & Canada. Slightly more than 36 percent of this total was allocated to the Rutland and its subsidiary Addison Railroad Company. After that, the Central Vermont company retained 75 percent of this sum as its operating fee, with the balance going into the coffers of the leased company as net earnings. Though not the best possible arrangement for the Central Vermont, it had sufficient merit to last until the expiration of the lease in 1890, after which the Central Vermont reluctantly renewed it as a protective measure against a new threat that had arisen — the Delaware & Hudson.

For the first time in the history of Vermont railroading, the presidents of the Rutland and the Central Vermont found themselves aligned together against a common enemy. For Page it was a losing battle. Outvoted by the board of directors in 1883, he retired from the presidency of the Rutland after fifteen stormy years — years that had seen the transition of the road from practically a hopeless ruin to a relatively well-run line.

Charles Clement, the son of Percival W. Clement, a prominent Rutland banker, followed Page in the presidency. The elder Clement had been purchasing Rutland stock as it became available in the early 80s, but chose to remain in the background for the present. Some of the shares purchased were in a "deal" with Rutland treasurer J. M. Haven and were of questionable validity.

The Delaware & Hudson was just completing its line on the west side of Lake Champlain and was in firm control of the connecting lines west out of Rutland. In 1887 they became particularly interested in the Rutland and actually acquired enough stock to give them control of the line. It was now apparent that the Delaware & Hudson had definite

Poster. — *Collection of J. R. McFarlane*

EXCURSION RATES
AND
Special Trains
— TO THE —
STATE FAIR

SEE A MAN DROP FROM THE CLOUDS!
One Mile high, with a Mammoth Umbrella as his sole companion and support.

Friday, September 6, 1889,
HOWARD PARK, BURLINGTON.

THE
CENTRAL VERMONT R. R.
WILL SELL ROUND TRIP TICKETS TO
HOWARD PARK, (BURLINGTON,) AND RETURN,
AS FOLLOWS FROM

Shelburne	$ .25	Proctor	$1.25
Charlotte	.45	Centre Rutland	1.25
North Ferrisburgh	.50	Rutland	1.25
Ferrisburgh	.55	East Clarendon	1.40
Vergennes	.55	Cuttingsville	1.50
New Haven	.65	East Wallingford	1.50
Middlebury	.75	Mount Holly	1.50
Salisbury	.80	Healdville	1.50
Leicester Junction	.80	Ludlow	1.50
Whiting	.85	Proctorsville	1.60
Shoreham	.95	Cavendish	1.60
Orwell	1.00	Gassetts	1.75
Ticonderoga	1.00	Chester	1.75
Brandon	1.00	Bartonville	1.75
Pittsford	1.15	Bellows Falls	1.75

The N. L. DAVIS is pictured in Rutland after being converted to coal while still under control of the Central Vermont in 1888.

The afternoon train down from Burlington pauses at the station in Brandon in 1889, while the engineer oils around and Aunt Liz rides to town in a surrey with the fringe on top. The N. L. DAVIS heads the train.

intentions to reach out into northern New England.

When the Central Vermont's lease expired in 1890, it lay within the Delaware & Hudson's power to terminate it and take the Rutland over as an appendage. But President Robert M. Olyphant of the Delaware & Hudson was not completely satisfied with the prospects for the Green Mountain line; the strong Delaware & Hudson company felt no necessity to burden itself with direct management of the line as long as the Central Vermont was willing to continue a guaranteed profit to insure its own protection in the Vermont market. The Rutland's new president, Charles Clement, and the Delaware & Hudson-controlled board of directors promptly renewed the lease to the Central Vermont, this time for 99 years.

A rental of $345,000 per year, somewhat lower than the previous lease of $376,000 per year, was to be paid, and this amount was increased $25,000 a year as new equipment and other permanent improvements were made by the Rutland management during the next three years. As a precautionary measure, the Rutland interests insisted that the rent be paid monthly in *gold*. A $3,500,000 mortgage was put on the Rutland to pay off two previous mortgages and to pay for the new equipment.

Depression struck the nation again in 1894 and Olyphant's decision not to take over the Rutland Railroad was fully vindicated; even under the reduced rental arrangement, the Central Vermont found it a heavy drain on the reduced resources of the lessees. There was no comfort in the knowledge that these enforced payments were largely passing into the credit of the Delaware & Hudson. By March of 1896 the situation had reached a critical stage. The Central Vermont was forced into receivership, and notified President Clement that it was abrogating its lease. All the rent installments had been promptly paid thus far, but no more could be expected.

Naturally, the Rutland's managers took exception to this. Why should they assume the work and worry of running their own road when it was profitably leased to the Central? Again the railroads went to court. President E. C. Smith, (son of J. Gregory who took over in 1891 upon his father's death), and his party junketed down from St. Al-

The N. L. Davis just made it to solid trestle as the collapsing Rouses Point structure gave way under her train in 1871.

bans by special train for the hearing on May 6. Clement introduced accounts and evidence showing that for the previous five years, the Rutland's losses had averaged less than $7,000 per year. Apparently he was unable to convince the court that this justified retention of the lease by the Central Vermont, and the court ruled that Clement had to take his railroad back whether he wanted it or not. He took possession on May 7, 1896. Perhaps the fact that Clement had not yet gotten around to serving as Governor of Vermont may have had something to do with it — his turn was still a few years in the future.

Word was promptly relayed to President Olyphant of the Delaware & Hudson, who the following month told a meeting of his board of managers that the Rutland would undoubtedly be unable to meet its obligations and that to protect its heavy investment, the Delaware & Hudson would be forced to advance cash to the now-orphaned Rutland company. The authorization was given with reluctance; only days before Olyphant had been forced to borrow $450,000 for the use of his own company.

The Delaware & Hudson nursed the Rutland along for two years. By 1898 it had had enough. On October 22, the Honorable Percival W. Clement, the President's father and a prominent stockholder already, entered a contract with the Delaware & Hudson to take over the company's 30,000 shares of preferred and 10,000 shares of common stock in the Rutland.

Forty years of vicious fighting between the railroad giants of Vermont had ended for all time.

American type No. 233 was built by Schenectady in 1891 as Adirondack & St. Lawrence No. 12. She waits with a sister at the engine house in Rutland, 1899.

The ETHAN ALLEN was built for the Rutland & Burlington by Hinkley in 1854. The Central Vermont lettering shown here appeared on all Rutland power during the period of Mr. Smith's lease.

Old Rutland & Burlington LAKE DUNMORE poses on the banks of the Connecticut River at Bellows Falls after bringing a train down from Rutland in 1889. This engine which carries Central Vermont, Rutland Division, No. 215 was built by Hinkley in 1854.—*Collection of Robert Adams.*

No. 50 was an 0-4-0 built by American in 1891 as Adirondack & St. Lawrence No. 1. It was used as a switcher in Bellows Falls until sold to the Hoisting Machine Company in 1917. — *Collection of Robert Adams.*

The night of April 6, 1888, near Rockingham, the *Night Express*, up from Bellows Falls and pulled by Engine No. 21, the NATHAN RICE, hit a section of roadbed softened by a plugged culvert and the spring runoff. The engine was wrecked, its crew killed, the baggage car burned, and the coach overturned. Miraculously the sleeper remained on the rails, un-.ruffled and unharmed. In the clean-up operation Engine No. 3, the PETER BUTLER prepares, with the aid of a rather dubious looking combination of chains, ropes, and pulleys, to pull the coach back up the bank. The patchwork trestle spans a section of embankment which slid out under pressure of backed-up rain water. — *Collection of Robert Adams.*

The J. BURDETT, built by Taunton in 1869, waits on the turntable in Rutland, bedecked to pull her master mechanic namesake's funeral train to Arlington in 1896.

Numerous sidewalk superintendents watch a wrecking crew of the Central Vermont, Rutland Division, as it unscrambles the pieces of two woodburners in front of the Ludlow depot in 1885. Northbound night train No. 6 with 4-4-0 LAKE DUNMORE ahead, stopped at the station and was smacked by a runaway freight headed by the H. F. CHAMBERLAIN. — *Collection of Robert Adams.*

MAP OF THE
Ogdensburg & Lake Champlain RAILROAD
AND ITS CONNECTIONS.

Map as of May 17, 1880. — *Railway & Locomotive Historical Society.*

Chapter 5

"The Old and Late Coming"

(The Ogdensburg & Lake Champlain)

While the Rutland & Burlington and its rival Vermont Central were building up to the east shore of Champlain, another line that was destined to loom large in the histories of both roads was laying down iron toward the west side of the same lake.

For many years, the thriving little city of Ogdensburg on the shore of the St. Lawrence River had served as the foot of navigation on the Great Lakes. Vicious rapids on down the mighty river, however, precluded easy passage of the small sailing vessels of the day. Before the advent of the iron horse, a good network of turnpikes and corduroy roads radiating south and east from the town provided the most direct arteries to the valley towns and east to the steamers of Lake Champlain. During the shipping season, heavy freight wagons plodded back and forth between Ogdensburg and Plattsburgh, their sweating teams and steady oxen taking well over a week for each round trip. It was, in fact, a jolting two-day journey even by fast stage.

Small wonder that railroad fever hit early and hard in the valley, with the projection of a rail line from the St. Lawrence to the port of Plattsburgh. Hardly had the proposal been made before some sagacious engineer took a close look at the mountain grades east of that latter city and persuaded the projectors of the line to reconsider. Charters being somewhat flexible instruments at the time, the eastern terminus was changed to Rouses Point, to the considerable dismay and disgust of the good burghers to the south. But the decision was a wise one. Rouses Point could be

reached with relatively easy grades, yet it afforded the needed connection with the Champlain boats. Above all, it was a road more suited to the limited capabilities of mid-century motive power.

The Northern Ogdensburg line was opened for business in 1850, after twenty-one years of conjecture, conference, and finally construction. The die was cast at a meeting in Montpelier as early as 1830, when a group of enterprising Vermonters and northern New Yorkers met on a howling February night in the very birth period of railroad transportation, to discuss the dream of a rail system that would permit travel from the Great Lakes to Boston town in the unbelievably short time of thirty-five hours!

Such fantastic speed was hard to conceive, especially by some of the old heads who had journeyed in stages, bundled to the ears, for three days to reach the Montpelier meeting. But progress prevailed over native caution, and a month later another well-attended meeting took place in Ogdensburg. The idea grew slowly, and it was nearly a full year before Malone, midway on the proposed line, was host to another "railroad convention". After that the plan languished while farther downstate the Mohawk & Hudson and the Rensselaer & Saratoga pushed their shaky rails out to experiment into the unknown.

Nearly a decade and a half later the cautious North countrymen concluded that there might be a future in the railroad business, and took steps to incorporate the Northern Railroad.

It was capitalized at $2,000,000 in shares of $50 par value, and the New York State Legislature

CONDENSED THROUGH TIME-TABLES FROM WESTERN CITIES TO EASTERN POINTS.

Chicago to the EAST via Grand Trunk.

Lv Chicago	9.00a	9.10p
Ar Detroit	6.30p	7.46a
Lv Detroit	7.00	8.00
" Toronto	7.12a	6.52p
" Brockville	4.00p	8.40
Ar Prescott	4.30	8.40
" Ogdensburg	5.30	6.30

Chicago to the East via Lake Shore & Michigan So. R.R.

Lv Chicago, L. S. & M. S.	5.15a	
" Cleveland	7.30a	
" Buffalo, N. Y. Central	2.10	
" Rochester	5.15	
" Rochester, R. W. & O.	8.15	
Ar Watertown	11.30	
" Norwood, connect with O. & L. C. R.R.	2.40	

Chicago to the EAST via Detroit, Buffalo or Suspension Bridge, Syracuse & Watertown.

Lv Chicago, M. C.	5.15
Ar Detroit	3.35
Lv Detroit, via Gt. Western	4.00
" Detroit, via Canada So.	4.00
Ar S. Bridge, Gt. W.estern	1.15
" Buffalo, Canada So.	1.30
Lv S. Bridge, N.Y. Central	2.00
" Buffalo, "	2.10
" Rochester, "	5.15
" Syracuse, "	8.15
Ar Watertown, "	11.30
" Norwood, connect with O. & L. C. R.R.	2.40

Passengers arriving at Ogdensburg or Norwood as above make close connection with the Ogdensburg & Lake Champlain R.R. as follows:

For White Mountains and Portland.

Lv Ogdensburg	2.00a
" Norwood	2.50
" Roue's Point	6.05
" St. Albans	7.15
" Wells River	9.35
" Burlington	11.00
Ar Fabyan's	1.45p
" Crawford's	2.00
" North Conway	3.30
" Portland	6.00

For BOSTON and Intermediate Points, via Burlington, Bellows Falls and Fitchburg.

Lv Ogdensburg	2.00a
" Norwood	2.50
" Roue's Point	6.05
" St. Alban	10.05
" Burlington	11.12
" Rutland	1.30p
" Bellows Falls	3.35
" Fitchburg	8.15
Ar Boston	10.00

For Saratoga, Albany and New York.

Lv Ogdensburg	2.00a	12.45p
" Norwood	2.50	1.38
" Roue's Point	6.05	5.10
" Plattsburg	10.05	6.25
" Saratoga	3.12	11.20
" Troy	4.40	12.35a
" Albany	4.10	12.45
Ar New York	10.10	6.45

For BOSTON and Intermediate Points, via White River Jc.

Lv Ogdensburg	2.00a
" Norwood	2.50
" Roue's Point	6.05
" St. Albans	10.05
" White River Junc.	2.00
" Concord	4.33
" Manchester	5.10
" Nashua	5.45
" Lowell	6.15
Ar Boston	7.15

PULLMAN PALACE CARS run between Syracuse and Fabyans without change.

PULLMAN PALACE CARS run between Ogdensburg and St. Albans and St. Albans and Boston.

People's Line of Steamers (Drew and St. John) leaving Albany at 8.15 p.m. daily, except Sunday, arriving in New York at 7.00 a.m.

Or Albany Day Line Steamer, leaving Albany at 8.30 a.m. daily, except Sunday, making landings on Hudson River, and arriving in New York at 6 p.m.

Or Citizens' Line Steamers from Troy, leaving Troy at 7.45 p.m., arriving in New York at 7.00 a.m.

Rail Tickets are accepted on either of the boat lines between Albany or Troy and New York.

Passengers desiring to stop over at Saratoga or Albany can resume their journey on the

---

OGDENSBURG & LAKE CHAMPLAIN RAILROAD

THROUGH TIME-TABLE FROM OGDENSBURG to the WHITE MOUNTAINS And PORTLAND (via Montpelier).

MS	STATIONS	Express	Mail	Mixed
	Lve Ogdensburg	2.00 a.m.	12.45 p.m.	6.10 p.m.
	Madrid	2.35	1.22	7.30
	Norwood	2.50	1.38	8.05
	Brasher	3.13	2.01	8.63
	Laurence	3.25	2.13	9.20
	Moira	3.37	2.25	9.45
	Brushton	3.43	2.1	10.00
	Malone	4.08	2.57	11.00
	Chateaugay	4.33	3.23	
	Ellenburgh	5.06	4.00	
	Irona	5.17	4.15	
	Altona	5.22	4.20	
	Moore's Forks	5.33	4.33	
	Moore's Junc	5.41	4.42	
	Champlain	5.56	5.00	
0	Arr Rouse's Point	6.05	5.10	
0	Lve Rouse's Point	6.05		
4	" Alburgh	6.17		
	" Alburgh Springs	6.27		
15	" Swanton	6.45		
18	" Swanton Junc	6.52		
24	Arr St. Albans	7.05		
	Lve St. Albans	7.15	8.45	
13	" Milton	7.43	9.15	
33	Arr Essex June	8.06	9.46	
33	" Burlington	8.30	10.10	
35	Lve Burlington	7.35	9.15	
	" Essex Junction	8.05	9.40	
34	" Richmond	8.29	10.06	
47	" Waterbury	8.67	10.37	
62	" Middlesex	9.09	10.50	
57	" Montpelier Junc	9.20	11.00	
58	Arr Montpelier	9.25	11.10	
0	Lve Montpelier, M.&W.R.R.	9.25		
28	Arr Wells River	11.00		
0	Lve Wells River, B. C. & M.	11.00		
36	Arr Wing Road	12.20 p.m.		
	Lve Wing Road	12.25		
6	" Bethlehem	12.40		
4	" Twin Mountain	1.02		
12	" Fabyan's	1.45		
17	" Crawford's	2.00		
28	" Bemis	2.35		
38	" Upper Bartlett	3.00		
38	" Glen Station	3.15		
44	" North Conway	3.30	5.55	
45	" Fryeburg	3.55		
73	" Baldwin	4.40		
87	" Sebago Lake	5.15		
104	Arr Portland	6.00		

(Central Vermont R.R.)

CONNECTIONS— (1) With Grand Trunk, Rome, Watertown and Ogdensburg R.Rds., Utica & Black River R.R., N.E.T. Line steamers for Toronto and Chicago, Royal Mail Steamers, Steamer "Stranger" for Alexandria Bay. (2) With R. W. & O. R.R. (3) With G. T. Ry. Central Vermont and Delaware & Hudson Ry.

PULLMAN SLEEPING CARS RUN BETWEEN SYRACUSE and the WHITE MOUNTAINS.

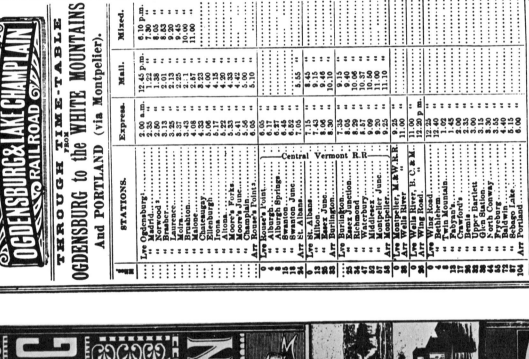

OGDENSBURG AND LAKE CHAMPLAIN RAIL ROAD BETWEEN THE EAST & WEST

Loring S. Richardson, GENERAL TICKET AGENT.

RAND AVERY & CO. BOSTON

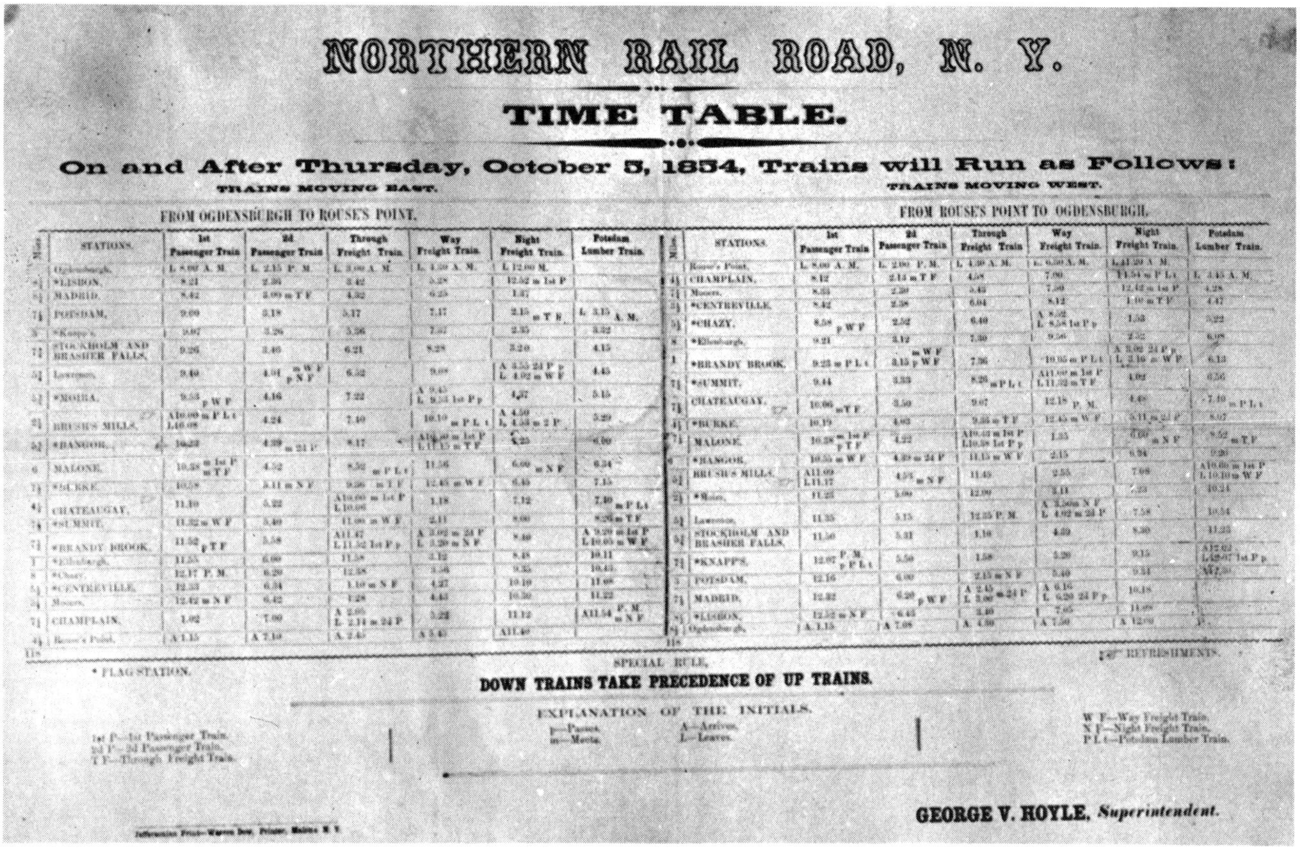

NORTHERN RAIL ROAD, N. Y.

TIME TABLE.

On and After Thursday, October 5, 1854, Trains will Run as Follows:

TRAINS MOVING EAST.

FROM OGDENSBURGH TO ROUSE'S POINT.

Miles	STATIONS.	1st Passenger Train	2d Passenger Train	Through Freight Train	Way Freight Train	Night Freight Train	Potsdam Lumber Train
	Ogdensburgh,	L. 8.00 A. M.	L. 2.15 P. M.	L. 3.00 A. M.	L. 4.30 A. M.	L. 12.00 M.	
4¾	*LISBON,	8.21	2.36	3.42	5.28	12.52 m 1st P	
6¼	MADRID,	8.42	3.00 m T F	4.32	6.25	1.37	
7½	POTSDAM,	9.00	3.18	5.17	7.17	2.15 m T F	L. 3.15 A. M.
3	*Knapp's,	9.07	3.26	5.36	7.37	2.35	3.32
7½	STOCKHOLM AND BRASHER FALLS,	9.26	3.46	6.21	8.28	3.20	4.15
5¾	Lawrence,	9.40	4.01 m W F p N F	6.52	9.08	A. 4.55 2d P p L. 4.02 m W F	4.45
5½	*MOIRA,	9.53 p W F	4.16	7.22	A. 9.45 L. 9.53 1st P p	4.27	5.15
2¾	BRUSH'S MILLS,	A10.00 m P L t L10.08	4.24	7.40	10.10 m P L t	A. 4.50 L. 4.53 m 2 P	5.29
5½	*BANGOR,	10.23	4.39 m 2d P	8.17	A10.[illegible] m 1st P L11.15 m T F	5.25	6.00
6	MALONE,	10.38 m 1st P m T F	4.52	8.52 m P L t	11.56	6.00 m N F	6.34
7½	*BURKE,	10.58	5.11 m N F	9.36 m T F	12.45 m W F	6.45	7.15
4½	CHATEAUGAY,	11.10	5.22	A10.00 m 1st P L10.06	1.18	7.12	7.40 m P L t
7⅛	*SUMMIT,	11.32 m W F	5.40	11.00 m W F	2.11	8.00	8.26 m T F
7½	*BRANDY BROOK,	11.52 p T F	5.58	A11.47 L.11.52 1st P p	A. 3.02 m 2d P L. 3.20 m N F	8.40	A. 9.20 m 1st P L10.05 m W F
1	*Ellenburgh,	11.55	6.00	11.58	3.32	8.48	10.11
8	*Chazy,	12.17 P. M.	6.20	12.38	3.56	9.35	10.45
5¼	*CENTREVILLE,	12.33	6.34	1.10 m N F	4.27	10.10	11.08
3¾	Mooers,	12.42 m N F	6.42	1.28	4.45	10.30	11.22
7½	CHAMPLAIN,	1.02	7.00	A. 2.05 L. 2.14 m 2d P	5.22	11.12	A11.54 P. M. m N F
4¾	Rouse's Point,	A 1.15	A 7.10	A. 2.45	A 5.45	A11.40	
118							

TRAINS MOVING WEST.

FROM ROUSE'S POINT TO OGDENSBURGH.

Miles	STATIONS.	1st Passenger Train	2d Passenger Train	Through Freight Train	Way Freight Train	Night Freight Train	Potsdam Lumber Train
	Rouse's Point,	L. 8.00 A. M.	L. 2.00 P. M.	L. 4.30 A. M.	L. 6.30 A. M.	L.11.20 A. M.	
4¾	CHAMPLAIN,	8.12	2.13 m T F	4.58	7.00	11.54 m P L t	L. 3.45 A. M.
7½	Mooers,	8.33	2.30	5.45	7.30	12.42 m 1st P	4.28
3¾	*CENTREVILLE,	8.42	2.38	6.04	8.12	1.00 m T F	4.47
5¼	*CHAZY,	8.58 p W F	2.52	6.40	A. 8.52 L. 8.58 1st P p	1.53	5.22
8	*Ellenburgh,	9.21	3.12	7.30	9.56	2.52	6.08
1	*BRANDY BROOK,	9.23 m P L t	3.15 m W F p W F	7.36	10.05 m P L t	A. 3.02 2d P p L. 3.16 m W F	6.13
7½	*SUMMIT,	9.44	3.33	8.20 m P L t	A11.00 m 1st P L.11.32 m T F	4.02	6.56
7⅛	CHATEAUGAY,	10.06 m T F	3.50	9.07	12.18 P. M.	4.48	7.40 m P L t
4½	*BURKE,	10.19	4.03	9.35 m T F	12.45 m W F	5.11 m 2d P	8.07
7½	MALONE,	10.38 m 1st P p T F	4.22	A10.43 m 1st P L10.58 1st P p	1.35	6.00 m N F	8.52 m T F
6	*BANGOR,	10.55 m W F	4.39 m 2d P	11.15 m W F	2.15	6.34	9.20
5½	BRUSH'S MILLS,	A11.09 L.11.17	4.57 m N F	11.45	2.55	7.08	A10.00 m 1st P L.10.10 m W F
2¾	*Moira,	11.23	5.00	12.00	3.11	7.23	10.24
5½	Lawrence,	11.35	5.15	12.35 P. M.	A. 3.50 m N F L. 4.02 m 2d P	7.58	10.54
5¾	STOCKHOLM AND BRASHER FALLS,	11.50	5.31	1.10	4.33	8.30	11.25
7½	*KNAPP'S,	12.07 P. M. p P L t	5.50	1.58	5.20	9.15	A12.02 L.12.07 1st P p
3	POTSDAM,	12.16	6.00	2.15 m N F	5.40	9.31	A12.30
7½	MADRID,	12.32	6.20 p W F	A. 2.45 L. 3.00 m 2d P	A. 6.16 L. 6.20 2d P p	10.18	
6¼	*LISBON,	12.52 m N F	6.45	3.40	7.05	11.00	
4¾	Ogdensburgh,	A. 1.15	A 7.08	A. 4.30	A 7.50	A 12.00	
118							

* FLAG STATION.

REFRESHMENTS.

SPECIAL RULE,

DOWN TRAINS TAKE PRECEDENCE OF UP TRAINS.

EXPLANATION OF THE INITIALS.

1st P—1st Passenger Train.
2d P—2d Passenger Train.
T F—Through Freight Train.

p—Passes.
m—Meets.

A—Arrives.
L—Leaves.

W F—Way Freight Train.
N F—Night Freight Train.
P L t—Potsdam Lumber Train.

GEORGE V. HOYLE, *Superintendent.*

Collection of Lawrence Doherty.

authorized S. C. Wead of Malone and Joseph Barnes and David Judson of Ogdensburg to distribute the stock and take subscriptions after May 14, 1845. A month later the organizational meeting was held in Ogdensburg, and George Parish, one of the North Country's outstanding and wealthiest citizens, was elected president. However, Parish stepped down from his high office in a matter of months, and a Boston financier, T. P. Chandler, stepped in, no doubt with an assist from Charles Paine, who appeared prominently in the first board of directors.

Things began to happen with the advent of Chandler at the helm. Engineers under the direction of James Hayward ran out their survey lines, and promptly recommended the Rouses Point route. A retired Army Engineer, Col. Charles L. Schlatter, began to marshal construction materials, no small problem in itself in that remote region. Ties and stringers were to be had for the cutting, but rails, spikes, and rolling stock had to be shipped in from outside.

Early in March of 1848, shovels bit into the still-frozen earth at both ends of the line. Driving his crews from daylight to dusk, Schlatter's men raised the grade rapidly, his trackmen spiking iron down to the hemlock ties as fast as the graders could level it off. Work progressed so rapidly that barely six months later a little 4-4-0 the CHATEAUGAY, and its single wooden-benched car were shuttling regularly between Rouses Point and Centreville, 16 miles to the west. By autumn of 1849, runs were making the round trip to Ellenburgh over thirty miles of newly-laid iron. By June of 1850, forty-five miles of line were in operation to Chateaugay and two month later to the headquarters town of Malone. On September 30, 1850, steel met steel a few miles west of town and the first train of resplendent, bright yellow coaches rocked over the new track to a whistle-tooting, toast-drinking, celebration at Ogdensburg. Engineer John Scharier was a proud man indeed as he rolled the sleek new CHATEAUGAY to a stop beside the red brick station.

O. & L. C. DEER *(top)*, built in 1850 by Kirk Locomotive Company at their Cambridgeport works, is shown by the stone roundhouse at Malone. The ST. LAWRENCE *(above)*, O. & L. C. No. 22, was built by Hinkley & Drury, 1849. It was unusual in its tapered boiler, capped tapered stack, and large-windowed cab.

Some of the boys from the Northern Railroad's busy shop in Malone pose behind a string of car wheels, 1855. — *Collection of Lawrence Doherty.*

All morning long people had been pouring into Ogdensburg for the "great railroad celebration" and by train time thousands jammed the erstwhile pasture that modern technology had transformed into a busy railroad terminal.

Far in the distance, a faint haze of wood smoke spurted above the trees, matched by a faint chuffing, followed by a long faint whistle blast. A cannon boomed from the crest of the hill, as train No. 1 rolled into town, and Ogdensburg let go with a whoop that lasted into the early hours, long after the speeches had died away.

The directors of the Northern did not stop with the laying of track — they expected great things from this new artery of commerce between Boston and the Lakes. Their optimism was evidenced by their plan to lay rails well on one side of the embankment, in anticipation of the second track that they were certain would soon be laid to accommodate the expected traffic.

Ship terminal facilities were a must as well, and 4,000 feet of dockage went in adjacent to the Ogdensburg yard. A commodious grain elevator, with 42 bins to hold 12 tons of wheat each, was framed up beside the deep channel that would accommodate the big lakers. A nine-stall roundhouse and a huge wooden freight shed rose opposite the station. At Malone, a gray stone shop was built to service the road's high-stepping 4-4-0's.

The road brought a burst of prosperity to the North Country. For the first time, the relative isolation of this rich and vast section of New York State was broken, and markets for the produce of the lush farming country were within reach. It is reported that land prices in the terminal city of Ogdensburg jumped five-fold with the first whistle blast.

The railroad, progenitor of this prosperity, unfortunately did not share in it. For a short time, it literally ran from nowhere to nowhere; the Potsdam & Watertown road, affording a rail connection west, was still in the future, while to the east the Vermont railroad vendettas and the powerful Champlain shipowners at first blocked construction of a rail connection with eastern lines. Traffic was seasonal, subject to the whims of northern winters that locked the Ogdensburg harbor with ice late in autumn and held it with an iron grasp until spring. Four months of the year, traffic over the line amounted to only a thin dribble, easily accommodated by one mixed train fighting through the snowdrifts.

Old John Smith of the Vermont & Canada, however, was quick to see the Northern as the final link in his Boston-to-the-lakes rail network. The Vermont & Canada had only to throw a bridge across the lake and build a short stretch of track west from East Alburg to effect the connection. The Northern could see itself benefiting from the access to the Boston market, and a charter for such a bridge was sought by each road in their respective states.

Vermont was quick to grant a charter to the Vermont & Canada — John Smith never did seem to have much trouble in getting what he wanted from the Legislature. For the Northern, it was another story.

New York City interests also saw the advantage the construction of such a bridge would be to Boston business. A bitter fight ensued in the New York Legislature, during which the New York bloc contended that such a bridge would impede navigation on the lake and would render approach impossible to a United States fort, located just north of the proposed location on the international border. This plus the steamship operators on the lake resulted in the denial of the first request. The railroads sought the right to go through Canada but were blocked there as well.

William A. Wheeler, a state senator from Malone, and later Vice President of the United States, succeeded in lining up the anti-New York City forces, along with groups seeking special favors from the Legislature. The reluctant lawmakers finally granted the charter late in 1849.

The New York interests still thought they had the situation in hand by demanding that three hundred feet of the lake be left open for navigation. By this clause they sought to stump the efforts of the builders. They thought that no workable method for such a bridge could be devised and that eventually the northern New York commerce would make it necessary to build a line down the west side of the lake and connect with the lines leading to New York.

page 57

The ingenious "Floating Bridge" across Lake Champlain to Rouses Point, N. Y. is shown during construction in 1851. — *Vermont Historical Society.*

These city folks hadn't appreciated the Yankee ingenuity of Henry R. Campbell, the Vermont & Canada's master bridge builder, and Charles L. Schlatter of the Northern. They devised an ingenious system by which a 301-foot barge would be placed in the middle of the 5290-foot structure that could be swung aside whenever lake traffic warranted. A boiler and steam winch were placed on the barge, and a system of chains was rigged through blocks that would allow the whole unit to be swung out at right angles in a couple of minutes.

The barge with the track across it and three-fifths of the trestle were built by the Vermont & Canada, the remainder by the Northern. The total structure cost $60,000, of which $20,000 went into the floating section and its equipment.

The first train, pulled by the little locomotive OTTAWA of the Northern, crossed into Vermont in January, 1852. In the consist were several refrigerator cars of butter for Boston.

The Northern was certainly a line for creating firsts, in its own North country as well as in the entire country. Not only did the line have the first *floating* railroad bridge, but was the first to build and operate an "Icebox on wheels".

The road took a regular boxcar, and in its Ogdensburg car shop put another wall, floor, and roof inside and filled the space between with sawdust for insulation. On July 1, 1851, the car carried eight tons of butter to Boston, and after paying all the freight charges the farmers had $800 more than the butter would have sold for locally. That, in 1851, was enough to take men's breath away.

The butter cars were an immediate success, and in all about fifty of them were built. Until the bridge was completed the next year, these, as well as all other cars were ferried to Vermont at Rouses Point.

Overnight the "butter train" became famous. The Northern put on a special that ran from Ogdensburg on each Monday, picking up its "reefers" all along the 118 miles to Rouses Point. These shipments reached Boston early Wednesday morning in perfect condition. For years Monday was "butter day" as well as washday along the Northern Railroad. At all the principal butter stations, the buyers attended, sampled the product, agreed on prices, and paid cash.

Results were far-reaching. The railroad prospered famously; Boston got fresh butter, and this led to a falling off of the city's East India spice trade. In 1851 one of the principal uses for spices was to make rancid butter palatable. By the summer of 1853 the value of dairy farms along the Northern Railroad had almost exactly doubled.

The Northern was also quick to realize that its geographical location, at the lower end of the entire Great Lakes system, could be exploited for great traffic potential. In March of 1853 it organized the Northern Transportation Corporation, a wholly-owned subsidiary of the Northern Railroad. Waterfront property was acquired in Chicago, and dockage and grain handling facilities were constructed there and at Ogdensburg. The first year of operations the boats handled 20,000 tons of merchandise west and 30,000 tons eastward using the Welland Canal and the Great Lakes.

This company also ferried freight cars from Ogdensburg to Prescott in Canada on a boat called the *Transit*. Here connection was made with the Canadian Pacific Railroad. This car ferry operation, again constituted another first of its kind on international waters.

Reorganizations were early and frequent; some said they occurred with greater regularity than on-time arrivals. At the first sign of a shower, the loosely-piled right of way, mostly an elongated heap of porous earth and sand, exhibited a marked tendency to wash out. The hemlock ties disintegrated with alarming rapidity, and the iron rails wore down all out of proportion to the light traffic.

The Northern's creditors foreclosed, and on January 1, 1858, a reorganized company called the Ogdensburg Railroad emerged. The company retained this identity until June 10, 1864, when, still another reorganization made it the Ogdensburg & Lake Champlain.

The ship operation, too, was changed in 1858 to the Ogdensburg Transportation Company. The old wooden steamers, the *W. L. Frost, Jacob W. Pierce, A. H. Church, W. J. Averill, A. Haskell* and the *W. A. Short*, were gradually replaced by new steel vessels named *Bennington, Burlington, Brandon, Manchester, Rutland* and *Arlington* which, of course, reflected the Rutland Railroad's later influence in the whole operation. The car ferry operation was reorganized in 1888, when the Canadian Pacific became more interested in the interchange across the river, and the name was

Jonas Wilder was father of the railroad refrigerator car. While acting as representative of Vermont Central in Rouses Point he proposed insulating boxcars to foster the butter trade to Boston. The Northern Railroad built eight cars to his specifications. — *Vermont Historical Society*.

changed to "The Canadian Pacific Transportation Company".

The Civil War was only a recent memory when the Ogdensburg & Lake Champlain Railway, far from the scenes of the major action, found itself involved in a war of its own.

Late in March of 1866 a greatly increased number of strange passengers began riding the trains, all ticketed to Malone. Matching the influx of passenger traffic was an unaccountable movement of freight, all billed to Edward G. Mannix at Malone. Long wooden boxes labeled "Machinery" slid out of the freight cars onto the platform; finally entire carloads arrived. Probably strangest of all for the curious people of Malone to understand was the fact that these bearded newcomers, now in numbers that would do justice to a small army, were unloading Mannix's wooden crates.

In June speculation gave way to certainty, and panic gripped northern New York: The Fenians were on the move!

The unique station at Malone featured a covered train shed between the twin tower-like structures housing offices and waiting room. Great activity greets the arrival of the three-car train from Ogdensburg in the 1910 picture *(above)*. Apparently the Model T had not yet reached the taxi stand in this upper New York city. Consolidation No. 27 *(below)* flies white Extra flags as it heads west into the shed. — *Lawrence Doherty.*

The Fenian Society, an outgrowth of the Irish Revolutionary Brotherhood, had been established less than two decades before, with the avowed purpose of freeing Ireland from British domination by armed force. Thousands of Irishmen had received training in the Union Army and many had found no jobs upon discharge. In the midst of seething unrest, the Fenian leaders decided that a move toward freeing Ireland from the British could be made by attacking Canada.

By mid-June 2500 men were encamped on the fairgrounds commanded by Col. Edward G. Mannix, now of the Fenian Army. The ruffians virtually took over the town, commandeering what they could not buy and stealing what they could not commandeer.

Canada, understandably, was somewhat concerned. A Canadian gunboat sailed up and down the river just off the Ogdensburg & Lake Champlain terminal at Ogdensburg to prevent any "D-day" invasion from taking place there.

General George G. Meade, famed commander of the Union forces at Gettysburg, was ordered to the area with instructions to break the threat to international peace. The Ogdensburg & Lake Champlain rolled trains of federal troops in, and on June 9, 1866, the Fenian Army was dispersed and its leaders arrested. The railway collected many fares from the disgruntled Sons of the Old Sod going home — this time paid for by the government.

The Irish have never been noted for giving up a firmly-planted idea easily, and the Fenian plan had not been destroyed, only temporarily delayed. Again the call went out in the spring of 1870. Once again the yellow coaches were filled with bearded Irishmen, this time going to a large pasture on the banks of Trout River, just east of Malone. The general staff, however, sacrificed the dubious pleasures of camp life to establish headquarters in the bar of the Flanagan Hotel in Malone. Again General Meade and a thousand troops were ordered back to Malone, but too late.

Under cover of darkness on May 26, the Fenian Army moved straight north for the border and Montreal. Just across the line, near Huntingdon, over a thousand Canadian militiamen were waiting. The next day they advanced and met the first Fenian volley which somehow seemed to do noth-

ing but clip a few leaves from the maple trees. The Canadians still advanced. Evidently Colonel Mannix of Malone and his Fenian general staff were better versed in intrigue than discipline; their company of lodge hall patriots never fired again.

History does not record who got back to Malone first, the officers or the men. It does describe the retreat, however, as one of the greatest marathon running events in the North Country's history, and the local citizens gathered enough discarded rifles to threaten the entire deer population for a long time to come.

Once again, and for the last time, the railway did a land-office business moving the disbanded Fenian Army and the federal troops out to southbound connections, scheduling special trains for the purpose.

The Ogdensburg & Lake Champlain, its war history behind it, settled back into the routine business of shuttling people and produce across the top of New York State. With the completion of the Potsdam & Watertown line and its prompt absorption into the Rome, Watertown & Ogdensburg company and the bridging of the lake at Rouses Point for a connection with the Vermont Central, the O&LC was no longer completely isolated and a larger volume of interchange began to come its way. In November, 1875, the New York & Canada finished construction from Whitehall north along the west shore of Champlain to Rouses Point to complete the Delaware & Hudson's trunk line. The result was that substantial tonnage of coal from the anthracite fields of Pennsylvania found its way to the Ogdensburg line via Rouses Point.

The line won early passenger acceptance, in spite of the fact that winter passengers for Canadian points had to travel across the frozen St. Lawrence by sleigh to make a connection with the Grand Trunk at Prescott, opposite Ogdensburg. Unfortunately, little of this was long-haul business; the average ticket cost a dollar and five cents. But in spite of meager territory, short hauls and poor connections, traffic in this department rose to 153,412 annual revenue passengers by 1870.

In the ensuing years the Vermont Central, now under the leadership of J. Gregory Smith (John's son), had become a dominant factor in New Eng-

An American of classic proportions stands proudly on the "armstrong" turntable outside the stone roundhouse at Malone, 1910. Consolidation No. 2064 with Fox tender trucks, an old St. Lawrence & Adirondack veteran, still has the marker light on her tank used on the return trip from a pusher assignment up to the top of the hill at Cherubusco, 20 miles east.

American No. 866 grinds to a halt in Lisbon, as the mailman moves toward the spot where the mail car stops on its daily morning run to Rouses Point, winter, 1909.

Malone is deep in a north country winter as 4-4-0 No. 865, an old Bennington & Rutland engine, with a snow plow pilot and plenty of the white stuff on her running gear pulls out of the station with the local for Rouses Point. — *Lawrence Doherty.*

Warm weather seems to have made jackets superfluous for these people at Cherubusco station to meet 4-4-0 No. 796, on its afternoon run across the top of New York state to Rouses Point, 1903. — *Collection of O. K. McKnight.*

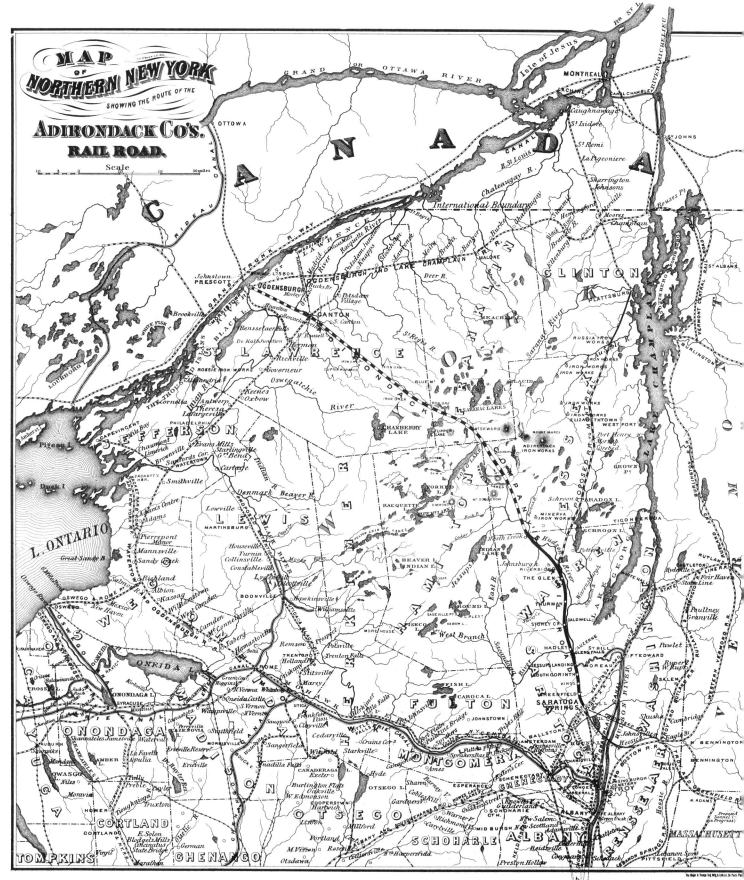

This 1856 map clearly shows all roads in the Rutland area and to the West at that time.

page 64

land rail transportation. Gregory had things pretty much to himself, save for a pesty gentleman named John B. Page down in Rutland. His father before him had the Boston-Great Lakes vision and Gregory was no different. Actually he had no problem with the connection west as it was, but John Page controlled the Montreal & Plattsburgh Railroad which crossed and interchanged with the Ogdensburg & Lake Champlain at Mooers Junction. Page was becoming a bigger railroad magnate than J. Gregory Smith cared to allow.

It was entirely possible for Page to build a connection between the Montreal & Plattsburgh south to the Whitehall & Plattsburgh where he had a connection via the Addison Railroad, which the Rutland leased, to the main line of the Rutland and on to Boston. Such a move in conjunction with an agreement with the Ogdensburg & Lake Champlain by Page could cut the Vermont Central out of much or all of the Boston traffic. Page was already getting more than Smith wanted him to via the car ferry *Oakes Ames*, steaming across Lake Champlain to Burlington where the Rutland's northern terminus was located.

Business on the O&LC wasn't so good that its management wouldn't listen to any propositions that would net them a bigger return from their 118 miles of line. Smith made them an offer to lease the line. They pointed out that Mr. Page might be interested too, and they would ponder the move. J. Gregory, no fool by a long shot, saw the picture.

Smith then made an offer of over $8.5 million for a 20 year term, $348,620 a year for the first three years, $415,390 for the next and $446,160 a year for the balance of the lease. The O&LC management were no fools either. On March 1, 1870, they signed, and J. Gregory Smith had himself a railroad to the St. Lawrence River.

Acquisition of this line gave the Vermont Central managers an important link in their dreams of a Great Lakes-to-ocean transportation system with a branch to the southeast, via the New London Northern Ry. to a terminal on the shore of Long Island Sound.

With the organization of a shipping line from New London to New York, only the western link remained to be completed to give the line control

This 1875 poster, advertising *The White Mountain Express* was issued by the Central Vermont, when the O. & L. C. was a part of that system. — *Collection of J. R. McFarlane.*

over a route spanning nearly half the continent. The answer, of course, was the Ogdensburg Transportation Company owned by the O&LC, which boasted six "propellers" operating out of the terminal beside the St. Lawrence, through the Welland Canal, and on to the Company's own docks and warehouse facilities in Chicago.

Better days came to the Ogdensburg line under the Vermont Central as the result of these combined moves, and traffic balanced out in a two-way flow. Total tonnage, only 38,837 in 1871, climbed steadily to a half-million tons in 1888, and nearly a million tons in 1890, with grain and coal shipments accounting for nearly half the volume and lumber traffic a large portion of the balance.

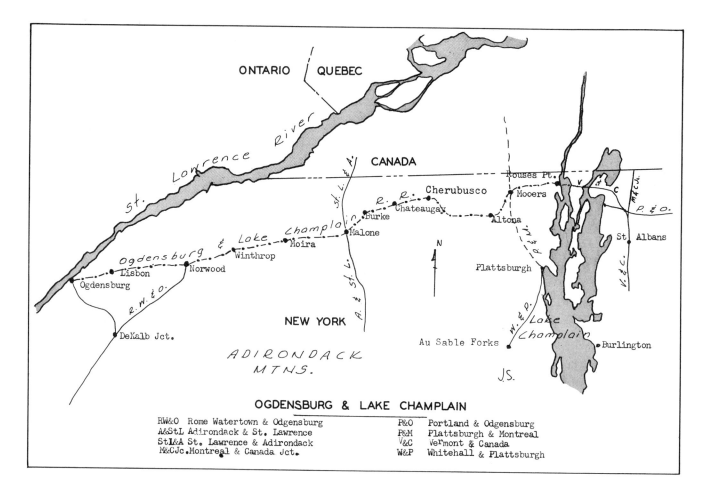

OGDENSBURG & LAKE CHAMPLAIN

RW&O	Rome Watertown & Odgensburg	P&O	Portland & Odgensburg
A&StL	Adirondack & St. Lawrence	P&M	Plattsburgh & Montreal
StL&A	St. Lawrence & Adirondack	V&C	Vermont & Canada
M&CJc.	Montreal & Canada Jct.	W&P	Whitehall & Plattsburgh

For a few years a name train, the *White Mountain Express,* burnished a part of the Ogdensburg & Lake Champlain's track with its luxurious Wagner sleeping and parlor cars. This interline string of varnish operated on a fast schedule, for its day, over the line of the Rome, Watertown & Ogdensburg, the Ogdensburg & Lake Champlain, the Vermont Central, The Boston & Lowell and the Portland & Ogdensburg, making the run from Niagara Falls to Portland in twenty-three hours and fifty minutes eastbound, and three hours longer in the opposite direction. This was fast time over a single track in 1886!

The schedule took advantage of the stop at Norwood on the eastbound run; passengers had a few minutes for breakfast if they wished to leave the cars at 6:30 A.M. while the O&LC crew took over from the RW&O men for the hour and a half run into Rouses Point. Considering the condition of the Ogdensburg line's rails, which were comparable to most of the other trackage on the inter-

line route, it is small wonder that the *White Mountain Express* established no records for adherence to either tracks or schedule. In spite of the rough roadbed that must have provided a truly spirited ride, the *Express* was well-patronized, and the Ogdensburg frequently double-headed the eleven-car consist of baggage car, smoker and nine sleepers.

The completion of the Rome, Watertown & Ogdensburg into Niagara Falls brought far more lucrative business than just the *White Mountain Express* to the Ogdensburg & Lake Champlain. President Charles Parsons of the Rome, Watertown & Ogdensburg was locked in a bitter struggle with the Vanderbilts, whose line almost paralleled the Parsons trackage across the western half of New York State. Parsons slashed freight rates on through shipments, while cannily upping local rates to help compensate the loss. He willingly sacrificed his on-line shippers in favor of the through-haul business, and the interchange between the line of the four-leafed clover and the Ogdensburg & Lake Champlain at Ogdensburg and Norwood became a very healthy one indeed, so much so that between 1887 and 1892 the Ogdensburg & Lake Champlain freight tonnage jumped from 582,000 to 1,090,000 tons. The Ogdensburg line increased its roster from 28 to 34 engines, ten of them heavy moguls, to handle the increased flood of traffic.

This new-found prosperity was short-lived and was doomed even before it had reached its peak. In mid-March of 1891, the Rome, Watertown & Ogdensburg capitulated in the rate war and was leased to its hated rival. The end effects on the Ogdensburg road were slow to become evident; like the swirling waters of a creeping flood they crept up slowly to devour the road. With the western connection in the hands of the New York Central & Hudson River, the Vanderbilt line had little reason to divert through traffic from its magnificent main line over the roundabout Watertown route to deliver it to the O&LC. The flood of interchange traffic at Norwood dwindled to a trickle; the once-proud *White Mountain Express* lingered a while and finally dropped from the timecard.

The climax came in a brief note in the *Railroad Gazette* of March 4, 1898:

"Judge Coxe of the United States Court at Utica, N. Y., February 14, issued a decree of foreclosure and sale of this road, and William H. Comstock of Utica was appointed to conduct the sale, which will take place at Utica at some day and hour to be fixed by the master. The upset price is fixed at $1,000,000 and bidders must deposit $100,000 cash or certified check. It was leased in perpetuity by the Central Vermont, June 1, 1886, but the interest on the bonds has been defaulted since April 1, 1896."

The collapse of the Vermont Central's empire, piled onto the loss of the RW&O's bridge line trade, was more than the frail financial structure could stand. Once more, the Ogdensburg & Lake Champlain was up for grabs, as was the Rutland, another cast-off of the Vermont Central's once great system.

Charles Parsons, the driving force behind the Rome, Watertown & Ogdensburg road had been

The unique mushroom-like water tank was a lonely sentinel at the crest of the big grade on the O. & L. C. division near Cherubusco, N. Y.

named receiver of the O&LC. A bid of $2,500,000 for the road was made by Charles R. Batt, president of the National Security Bank of Boston, together with William Lummis of New York, representing the first mortgage bondholders. A protest filed by the luckless holders of income bonds was overridden, and the road was transferred to the Parsons group on June 1, 1898.

At one time Parsons had toyed seriously with the thought of adding the Ogdensburg & Lake Champlain to the Rome Watertown & Ogdensburg system, giving the Four Leaf Clover Route, a nickname arising from the RW&O herald, trackage all across New York State. Such a move would have been a windfall for the Vermont roads, but it never materialized. Parsons turned his attention instead to the New York, Ontario & Western, interchanging at Oswego for entry into the New York metropolitan area. Though the arrangement did relatively little harm to the isolated O&LC, it did nothing to help it.

The following year the purchasing committee deeded the property to the railroad corporation, and the Ogdensburg was once again tottering on its own feet. Rutland money lost no time in moving in on the now-free line, and the roster of officers reported in 1899 was comprised entirely of Rutland men.

The Ogdensburg's corporate freedom was mercifully brief. Without a strong interline connection the Ogdensburg could not have survived for long, so the only remaining alternative was to join with the other orphan of economic storm, the Rutland. September 27, 1901, saw the signing of the papers by Rutland President Percival W. Clement.

Both motive power and rolling stock were depleted, and what remained was in poor condition, some units so bad that the new owners destroyed them as unsafe to operate. With dwindling interchange on grain from the Rome, Watertown & Ogdensburg, the frame elevator at Norwood was ripped down. But the Rutland men were ambitious and thorough. Better maintenance was immediately instituted on both equipment and right of way. Good management and better times brought a respectable increase in both passenger traffic and freight tonnage. A through Ogdensburg-Boston sleeping car was put in service and enjoyed good patronage for many years.

Only once more was the line to fall into alien hands when the Vanderbilt group moved in on the Rutland and its holdings. For a time, the O&LC boasted a board of directors that read like a Who's Who of financial titans, with Chauncey Depew, J. P. Morgan, William Rockefeller and no less than two Vanderbilts, William K. and Frederick W., along with a Vanderbilt son-in-law, Dr. William Seward Webb.

With the coming of the gasoline age, passenger traffic dwindled rapidly, and by the advent of World War II, the Ogdensburg line's passenger service consisted of one mixed train each way daily. In the mid-forties, that too quietly disappeared.

Meanwhile, the Rutland had breathed new energy into the Ogdensburg line. The Rutland Transit Company, a reorganization of the earlier Ogdensburg Transit line, sent its little freighters plying back and forth between Chicago and the end of track with energy and dispatch. Only the Panama Canal Act of 1915, which would terminate railroad ownership of a competing form of transportation, was to end this valuable service, leaving the Ogdensburg once again the virtual stub end of the line.

When the Rutland gained its corporate freedom for the last time, the old Ogdensburg line had lost its identity in the Green Mountain Gateway.

The stone roundhouse at Malone looked like the headquarters of "The Untouchables" in this 1936 photo. Built by the Northern Rail Road of New York in 1852, the old building has withstood the years well.—*Lawrence Doherty.*

The John C. Pratt
(A Jewel of Yesteryear)

The steam locomotives of bygone days were delicate little machines of only 25 tons or so. They were more like watches, made of brass and polished iron, than their modern day counterparts which are black and brutish. Take the Ogdensburg & Lake Champlain's John C. Pratt, built in the Taunton works in the Bay state in April of 1868 as an example. It was the builder's 431st locomotive, had 60″ drivers powered by 12″x 24″ cylinders, and weighed only 62,500 pounds.

She was named for a Boston gentleman who had generously loaned money for the building of the road when even native New Yorkers were uncertain of the future of railroads, or were selfishly afraid of the competition they would cause. John C. Pratt served on the railroad's board of directors from the beginning and rose to the presidency of the line in July, 1865, three years before the arrival of this Taunton-built namesake.

Soon after her delivery she was assigned to Train Number 3, the *Ogdensburg Express*, under the capable guidance of Engineer Hiram Weeks. A hogger of the old school, Weeks probably thought more of his locomotive than he did of his wife and kept the 4-4-0 in immaculate condition. In addition to the frequently swept reed mat that graced the cab floor, he carried a heavy quilt which would be draped over the side of the tender to protect the paint from a carelessly thrown log during the loading of wood. "Old Hiram," as he was called, would descend from his cab at all stops to stand guard, ready to take the head off any unsuspecting patron who might dare to rub an admiring hand over the polished brass cylinders or waxed wood trim of his pet engine.

Weeks had just cause for his pride—the Pratt was a thing of beauty. From her highly polished and waxed oak cowcatcher to the gold leaf lettering on her black enamel tender she glittered in a rainbow of color.

The big oil-burning headlight was polished black iron with gold leaf trim and had hand painted inserts that would be illuminated at night when the lamp was lighted. It rested on a platform supported by a delicately scrolled brass bracket. Below, on the fluted boiler front, a large brass number plate carried the numeral 4 and the road's name in a circle around it.

Highly polished brass was everywhere, on the boilerbands, the running boards, piping, railings, sand and steam domes, whistle and bell, headlight and cylinders, even the rivets and joints on her great black stack. Of particular interest were the big flag stanchions that stood at either end of the pilot beam. In the absence of flags, two brass balls with giant spread-winged eagles, 18″ across, rode the breeze. Another eagle perched atop the bell.

The cab was oak, varnished and rubbed to a soft sheen. The roof was gray, while the interior was white with bright green seat boxes and trim. The fine striping and "John C. Pratt" on the sides were 24k gold leaf.

The driving rods were inset with mahogany, and both were polished to a gloss. The boiler water injector pump, just ahead of the first driver, looked like a string of brass sausages held vertically and only operated while the locomotive was moving. Old timers tell of jacking up the engine and running the wheels to pump water into the boiler when stuck in winter drifts.

Her highly decorated tender carried little more than 3000 gallons of water and about three cords of wood. There were certainly no long range capabilities in her day.

Efficiency wasn't the goal in the old days anyway. Each engine was a tailored job, built more to the whim of a master mechanic than to a definite set of specifications. With each shopping they would be lovingly pampered and decorated. The enginemen themselves would invest hours in cleaning and polishing to have the most outstanding machine on their road, or any other. Competition was keen between rival roads at connecting points.

What would we give today, to go down to the depot and see the likes of the Pratt roll into town?

Freight No. 9, for Norwood and New York Central connection to the west, was often so long as to require a helper engine or two. Since the shaky old trestle across the northern tip of Lake Champlain was restricted against double heading, 2-8-2 No. 32 has to pull her heavy load alone from Alburgh, Vermont, to Rouses Point, New York. There, after crossing the Delaware & Hudson main line, she rejoins helper 2-8-0 No. 26, which crossed the bridge alone ahead of the train, and starts accelerating for the west. — *Philip R. Hastings.*

The two engines begin to hit the grade *(above)* as they near Champlain, four miles west of Rouses Point, and each fireman responds by bailing in the "real estate" as the pressure gauges begin to drop on the hard-working engines. As they pound past the station at Mooers *(below)* they have 25 more miles of climb before they reach the summit at Cherubusco, almost 1300 feet above Lake Champlain. — *Philip R. Hastings.*

The grade gets heavier as engines No. 32 and 26 pull the Norwood bound freight across the west branch of the Great Chazy River west of Mooers Forks. This picture and the four on the preceding pages were taken during the Rutland's last year of steam, in July 1949. — *Philip R. Hastings.*

Milk train No. 7 eases away from Rouses Point station as the fireman waits to acknowledge the clear signal to cross the D. & H. main line just ahead. Ten-wheeler No. 72 will easily take the grade for the next 36 miles west to Cherubusco with its light train of empty milk reefers. — *Jim Shaughnessy.*

The Malone shop was a busy place from its beginning in 1850 until the great depression of the 1930's. This 1929 scene is only a memory, since all activity was moved to a consolidated operation at Rutland. — *Lawrence Doherty.*

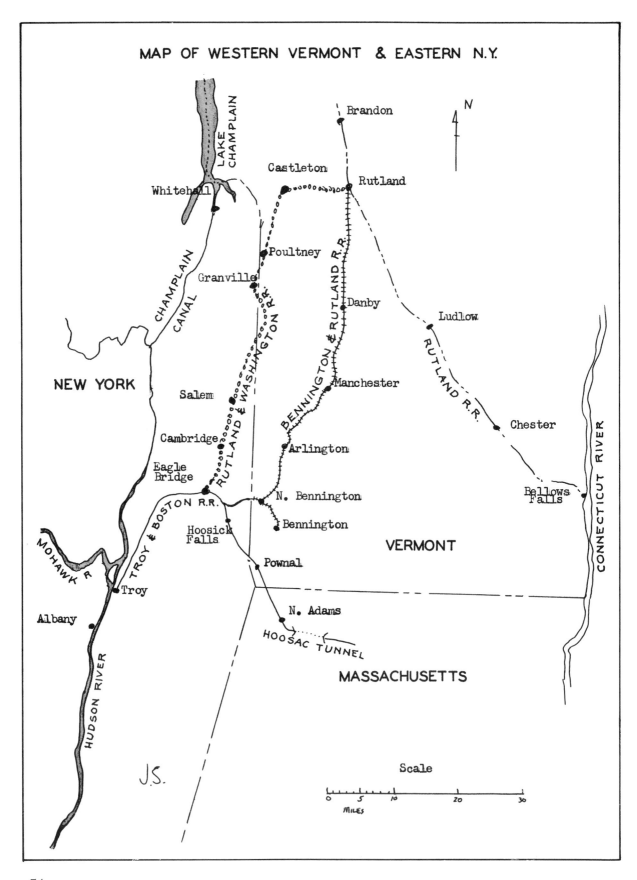

MAP OF WESTERN VERMONT & EASTERN N.Y.

N

Brandon

LAKE CHAMPLAIN

Castleton

Rutland

Whitehall

CHAMPLAIN CANAL

Poultney

Granville

RUTLAND & WASHINGTON R.R.

BENNINGTON & RUTLAND R.R.

Danby

Ludlow

NEW YORK

Salem

RUTLAND R.R.

Manchester

Chester

Cambridge

Arlington

Eagle
Bridge

TROY & BOSTON R.R.

N. Bennington

CONNECTICUT RIVER

Bellows
Falls

Hoosick
Falls

Bennington

VERMONT

MOHAWK R.

Pownal

Troy

Albany

N. Adams

HOOSAC TUNNEL

HUDSON RIVER

MASSACHUSETTS

J.S.

Scale

0   5   10   20   30
MILES

page 74

Chapter 6

Branching Out

The release by the Delaware & Hudson of its stock in the Rutland Railroad came as a windfall to its President Percival W. Clement. Blocked by the Page forces in the stockholders' skirmish of 1883, he had been quietly building for a fresh assault by picking up occasionally available small blocks of Rutland shares. Olyphant's decision to get out of the Rutland could not have been better timed, and for the Clement interests, more gratuitous. Straining his personal resources and borrowing heavily from his friends, Clement scraped together enough to take over the Delaware & Hudson's Rutland stock in 1898. These holdings, plus support from a minority of the stockholders, were enough to swing control of the company, and best of all, the origin of this additional stock and its validity were beyond challenge.

Firmly in control, the new managers began to improve the Rutland line, which, considering the tribulations of the Central Vermont during its period of proprietorship, was returned in reasonably good condition, though the 29 locomotives to come back under the Rutland herald were showing unmistakable signs of age and hard wear. Some of these had been outshopped by Taunton as early as 1850 for the original Rutland & Burlington company and now, weak and wheezing, were destined for the scrap heap as soon as they could be replaced. Old No. 24, the N. L. DAVIS, and No. 32, the J. M. HAVEN, their proud youth long in the distant past, led the parade to the torch in 1900. They were replaced the following year by a brace of Americans, weighing almost twice as much, which arrived in company with two big ten-

wheelers fresh from the Schenectady works. The names were gone from the cab panels of the old engines, buried under coats of paint and the wear of decades of faithful service. The Central Vermont had renumbered the lot in its 200 series, and these numbers remained as the fleet returned to home ownership.

The master mechanic at Rutland set about a final effort to keep the fleet rolling until new engines could be delivered to take over the heaviest service, although Clement's plans did not include replacement of old motive power with new engines. The Rutland's resources were promptly directed toward the realization of a forty-year-old-dream — the extension north of Burlington. Now there were no obstacles save those of Nature, though the ghost of old John Smith may have been screaming silently. His fighting son, J. Gregory, had already joined him, and his grandson, Edward, who had stepped into the presidency of the Central Vermont, now in receivership, inherited few of their aggressive attributes. Besides, times had changed. No longer could the high-handed tactics of past generations restrain competition. The Interstate Commerce Commission had been established in 1887, and the state's Board of Railroad Commissioners had exhibited almost complete impartiality for an even longer period. Like their creaking old engines, the days of the giants were numbered.

By 1899, the Rutland Railroad had consolidated its position and was ready to move. Some new money had come into the corporation, and the mighty resources of the New York Central were

Percival W. Clement, president of Rutland R.R. 1889-1902, Governor of Vermont 1919-1921. — *Vermont Historical Society.*

represented on the board of directors by Dr. W. Seward Webb and George Bird. Percival Clement had replaced his son in the president's chair the year before, and another son, Wallace C. Clement, had come into the directorate. Only one other Vermonter, John W. Stewart of Middlebury, served on the board, the other six members representing Boston and New York interests. The dream of St. Lawrence-to-Boston traffic was still alive; now it was augmented by the additional lure of lucrative business between Canada and New York City.

When the Central Vermont cast the Ogdensburg & Lake Champlain road adrift to fend for itself, the little North Country pike found swimming alone very difficult indeed, although it was managing to show a very modest surplus after reorganization. Like the Rutland, it needed attention and a bit of modernizing; some of the battered old rail remaining in its 118 miles of line was dangerously

light, though the majority of its mileage was laid with reasonably good eighty-pound steel. Its motive power, on the average, was newer and better than the Rutland's; it had augmented or replaced its older engines during the Nineties with a number of handsome, powerful Baldwin Moguls, a trio of Rhode Island ten-wheelers, and, in 1897, three more heavy Consolidations from the Schenectady Locomotive Works. Still in service were four home-made engines, products of the Malone shops in the Civil War years. In all, 26 locomotives of varying vintage and ancestry and about a thousand cars of all types and conditions comprised the rolling stock. Another asset of doubtful value was the subsidiary Ogdensburg Transit Company, the remnant of the Central Vermont's Great Lakes fleet, then dropping over the brink of bankruptcy.

The northern New York property was inviting to the Rutland managers, as it had been a magnet for Rutland executives from the very first. Now, in almost simultaneous moves, it bought control of the Ogdensburg & Lake Champlain and chartered the Rutland & Canadian Railroad. The Ogdensburg control came high, with the Green Mountain route laying out $4,400,000 in January, 1899, for preferred and common stocks and an additional $3,700,000 for first mortgage bonds. On the latter, the Rutland company added its guarantee and promptly resold all but $200,000 worth. In addition, the Rutland purchased the $1,000,000 capitalization of the Ogdensburg Transit Company, forming the Rutland Transit Company. The O&LC was finally absorbed into the Rutland on September 27, 1901.

The Rutland & Canadian project, the necessary link between Burlington and the Ogdensburg line's terminus at Rouses Point, was organized by a combine of interests from Burlington and Rutland. No longer would the Rutland Railroad's managers rely on the old Vermont & Canada line to bridge the gap. The initial capital stock issue of $1,500,000 was retained in its entirety by the Rutland Railroad, and an issue of $1,100,000 in fifty-year, four percent, first mortgage bonds was executed. Long before the Ogdensburg & Lake Champlain deal was consummated, and a year before a Rutland-controlled board of directors was named in 1899, mauls were clanging on spikes north of Burlington over the new grade of the Rutland & Canadian. The line was completed and leased in 1899, and consolidated into the Rutland in January, 1901.

The planners of this new extension had no intention of competing with the Central Vermont along the slim territory north of Burlington. Taking the most direct route, they struck bravely out into the lake west of Malletts Bay, stretching a marble-rip-rapped causeway for three miles across to South Hero Island, then heading straight north along South Hero, Grand Isle and North Hero for the village of Alburgh and the final crossing of Champlain to the Ogdensburg road. The forty miles of new rail went down in one year.

From Alburg Junction another spur line, the 3.5 mile Rutland & Noyan Railroad turned north to the border and Canadian-built connections.

The dream of a half-century was finally a reality. The Rutland now controlled 278 miles of main line. In combination with the friendly Fitchburg (now in control of all lines east of Bellows Falls), it formed a trunk route of 392 miles from the lakes at Ogdensburg to tidewater at Boston. In connection with the Ogdensburg Transit Company's little steamers, the combination route reached all the way to Chicago and Duluth. But now the original dream had taken an additional direction; the influence of the Delaware & Hudson and the growing interest of the New York Central system in the affairs of the Rutland drew it like a magnet toward the great metropolis to the south.

The Bennington & Rutland Railroad, a second incarnation of the original Western Vermont (turned loose to fend for itself by the Troy & Boston after the opening of the Hoosac tunnel made it useless) offered a direct route south out of Rutland. This 57-mile pike was no stranger to integration with the Rutland Railroad; in 1867 John Page as President of the Rutland and J. Gregory Smith as President of the Central Vermont had exhibited rare trust and cooperation by jointly leasing the road in their own names — and likely, to their own profit. On the very day these two men effected the lease, January 16, the Bennington & Rutland filed suit against the Troy & Boston line, charging breach of contract in failing to maintain the road, and claiming $200,000 damages against the Troy & Boston managers.

Collection of James R. McFarlane.

Even while the attorneys were arguing in court, contention of a much more violent nature was in the making in the little North Bennington yard, where a brace of Troy & Boston locomotives, the I. V. BAKER, and the R. P. HART, shuffled peaceably about their business, making up a drag for the afternoon run down to Troy. Suddenly the sheriff of Bennington County swung up the gangway of first one and then the other, served a writ of attachment on the engineer, and then posted a deputy in the cab as the crew was ordered out. (A statute on the lawbooks of Vermont at the time allowed the plaintiff to attach any property of the defendant without prior notice.)

To make doubly certain that no Troy & Boston equipment would be moved out of the yard, switches were closed against the engines and padlocked. The two kettles simmered in the dull January noon while their erstwhile crews hightailed it to the nearest telegrapher to flash the word down to Troy. There was no simmering there; things erupted to a full boil as a fast road engine was hooked onto an idle coach which soon took on a full manifest of brawny Irish trackmen equipped with pick handles and hickory brake clubs, plus a hurriedly-called pair of off-duty engineers.

The militant special blasted out of Troy just after noon, scorching the rails up the Hoosick River valley while Trainmaster John L. Wellington braced himself in the rocking coach and bawled his orders to his impromptu commandos. These muscular worthies were ready, hands gripped on their hardwood weapons as the boss laid out his strategy. As the train rocketed through Eagle Bridge they began to deploy toward doors and platforms; a few pried up windows to avoid delay in getting into action. As they approached the scene, the engineer shut off to prevent stack exhausts from revealing their arrival. The train drifted into town as quietly as the guest of honor at a shotgun wedding.

Suddenly the pastoral quiet was shattered by one stentorian blast on the whistle. Brake shoes slammed down hard against squealing wheels as a howling horde spilled out on the right of way, racing like a swarm of demented banshees down on the impounded locomotives. The two luckless deputies sprang up from the padded seats in the cabs as ruddy, whiskered faces surged up the gangways over the tenders and over the running boards.

It wasn't even a good fight; as the deputies sailed ungracefully out on the cinders, the engineers swung into their accustomed seats and cracked the throttles. There was still enough pressure on the boilers to move, and each cab was crowded with strong and willing firemen. There was no time to file or break the binding chains at the turnouts; already men were running toward the yards from town. Drivers slid and caught as sand poured down. The I. V. BAKER split the switch and rolled out on the high iron, with the HART on her tail. In those few seconds of wild confusion, Wellington's raiders had even found time to tie a baggage car and a coach to her tender! Ahead, the little train up from Troy had already roared out of sight, running in reverse with the coach reeling dangerously for the New York state line. By the time the three engines pounded into White Creek and safety, they were almost running tandem, draped with whooping, elated Irishmen.

Back in Vermont, a disgruntled sheriff and his men listened meekly as railroad officials voiced opinions on the raid in terms that paled the blue haze of wood smoke that still lingered over the hills.

There still remained two Troy & Boston trains in Vermont. The D. T. VAIL headed a train in Manchester, and the WALLOOMSAC had a passenger train in Rutland. The sheriff and his posse commandeered the HILAND HALL, a Bennington and Rutland engine just in from Bennington on a wood train, and raced up to Manchester. There the VAIL's crew was unaware of the battle that had just taken place in North Bennington and were easily taken over.

With the VAIL captured, they were off in a matter of seconds to Rutland where the WALLOOMSAC lay waiting. Somehow a telegraph dispatch alerted the Troy & Boston crew in Rutland, and the engine and cars fled into New York State via the Rutland & Washington, leaving behind a puzzled group of passengers covered with wood ashes.

Down in the corner of the state below Bennington, at Pownal, the GENERAL WOOL had been seized with the train from North Adams at the same time the engines were grabbed in North Bennington. While the sheriff and his men were

"War" erupted between Bennington & Rutland and Troy & Boston in 1867, when deputies of the Bennington County sheriff seized some T. & B. engines. Trainmaster Wellington's men descended on the R. P. Hart to evict the bewildered deputy. — *Ken Gypson.*

The General Wool was impounded at Pownal on its way back to Troy with a train from North Adams, Massachusetts. Later, as will be seen on the next page, Wellington and his men captured it back and ran it home to safety from attachment.

Vermont sheriff's men try in vain to catch the WOOL as she blasts out of Pownal toward the York State line and safety. — *Ken Gypson.*

The HILAND HALL, built by Mason, 1866, was commandeered by the sheriff and his deputies who ran her up to Manchester, then on to Rutland. The beautifully painted and polished 4-4-0's boiler feed pump is being lubricated near the Bennington engine house.

Troy & Boston's WALLOOMSAC escaped the clutches of the sheriff by fleeing Rutland for the legal safety of New York State via Rutland & Washington rails during the B. & R.-T. & B. "war".

racing to Rutland, Wellington and his raiders were about to attack again.

After making it across the state line at White Creek, the three engines moved on down to Hoosick Junction, where the BAKER and the HART continued on to Troy, far away from danger. Wellington and his men then went east, through Hoosick Falls and North Petersburg, and crossed the state line toward Pownal. They eased to a stop just out of town, deciding on different tactics from the brash, noisy arrival North Bennington had witnessed earlier in the afternoon.

Several huskies, including Trainmaster Wellington and an engineer, slipped along the lengthening shadows toward the GENERAL WOOL simmering by the station. As the luck of the Irish would have it, the two deputies, thinking the situation pretty well in hand, had gone up the street to a little restaurant for supper.

Before the sheriff's men knew what happened the WOOL was blasting out of town with Wellington and a crew of muscular gandy dancers stoking wood into the firebox. By the time the deputies reached the station platform, the engine was fading into a haze of wood smoke as it headed west for the state line.

The wires between Troy, Bennington and Rutland had been sputtering acrimony all night. The next morning the sheriff of Bennington County armed himself and his deputies with John Doe warrants for the arrest of any Troy & Boston employee who should, perchance, wander across the state line. Later in the day, the Troy & Boston managers served notice that no more cars would be delivered or accepted from the Bennington & Rutland. To all purposes, this left Bennington at the long end of nowhere as far as rail transportation was concerned — a situation that caused little joy in that historic little community. In retaliation, every Troy & Boston car remaining on the system was promptly moved into Rutland and shunted onto a storage track.

There matters stood for a month while lawyers argued and the good citizens of Bennington fumed and the merchants of Troy wrung their hands over the lost business. Page and Smith made some overtures toward a truce with the Troy & Boston managers, at first meeting only a cold silence and then a flat "No!" Traffic over the Bennington & Rutland dropped to a thin trickle; one by one the railroad's slim roster of light Baldwin and Rogers 4-4-0's cooled their boilers on sidings safely away from the state line, until finally a single locomotive shuffled up and down doing the work of the road.

This desperate state of affairs could not be permitted to continue. The only alternative to bankruptcy was to find a new connection to the south.

There was one possibility in this direction: the faltering little Lebanon Springs Railroad had poked a few miles of wavering iron north of Chatham in the direction of Bennington before it ran out of funds. The charter was there; all that was needed was money. This the Vermont interests provided (with an assist from the Vanderbilts, who owned the New York & Harlem south of Chatham), ramming the revitalized little railroad through to a junction with the Bennington & Rutland. On completion, the two lines were promptly merged — on January 1, 1870 — into the Harlem Extension Railroad, with 114 miles of track extending from Chatham Four Corners to Rutland. The Troy & Boston road promptly capitulated, but too late. By prolonging the battle, it had lost the war and was not to regain the traffic south of Bennington for nearly a century, and then as a Boston & Maine route granting trackage rights to the Rutland.

This, then, was the beginning of the checkered career of the "corkscrew" line that was to become the Chatham division of the growing Rutland system.

In a series of transactions, coming with machine gun rapidity during the summer and fall of 1900, the Clements acquired for the Rutland all the properties involved in the Chatham route, thus adding another 114 miles of track, complete with heavy grades and 263 curves, to its route mileage. The final deal in the chain of events was an agreement of consolidation with the stockholders of the Chatham & Lebanon Valley Railroad Company, the last of a series of reorganizations. Two shares of C&LV stock were exchanged for one of Rutland preferred. It was largely a formality, for Percival Clement signed the agreements as President of both companies on November 1, 1901.

The Rutland now embraced nearly five hundred miles of trackage running the length of Vermont and tapping into New York State at two places. But it was still essentially a rural railroad, nowhere reaching a city of any major importance in the commercial or industrial structure of the Northeast. Outside of a handful of quarries and factories centered around Rutland and Burlington, no substantial individual shippers of tonnage freight originated traffic on its lines. It did serve as a bridge line between east and west, north and south, but in every direction it met stiff competition for this business, generally from better built and more economically operable railroads. In extending the system out to include the wobbly Chatham line Percival Clement sowed the seeds of eventual destruction for his control of the Rutland Railroad.

☆　　　☆　　　☆

THE BENNINGTON & RUTLAND RAILROAD

A charter dated November 5, 1845, to build a line from Rutland to North Bennington was given to the newly-formed Western Vermont Railroad. This company would then build west two miles to the New York state line at White Creek for a connection with the Troy & Boston.

It wasn't until May of 1852 that the first scheduled service came to the picturesque 55 mile valley line. In 1854, a branch was extended to the north side of Main Street in Bennington, four miles to the south. Later the Lebanon Springs Railroad would make a connection here to realize the dream of entering New York City.

The Western Vermont operated normally until it encountered financial trouble late in 1857. The mortgage trustees took over and proposed a lease to the Troy & Boston Railroad. This line would be a vital link for the east-west Troy & Boston until their Hoosac Tunnel was completed. The Berkshires, now pierced by the famous five mile bore, had been a formidable obstacle to rail builders of those days. The Troy & Boston and the Western Vermont completed a through route to Boston from New York and the west. Traffic out of Boston went up over the Cheshire to Bellows Falls, over Mount Holly on the Rutland & Burlington to Rutland and then down the west side of the Berkshires. Thus a through route was formed, though many miles longer than the latter-day direct line through the Hoosac.

The mortgage holders had no trouble leasing the property to the Troy & Boston and the new managers took over November 1, 1857.

A Troy & Boston subsidiary company, the Troy & Bennington Railroad, extended from Hoosick Junction to White Creek on the state line to make the connection to the new route around the mountains. This was the only outlet on the south end of the Western Vermont, and was the largest single factor in maintaining traffic down from Rutland.

By the time the Troy & Boston lease expired on January 15, 1867, the Western Vermont corporate structure was reorganized and became the Bennington & Rutland.

In 1866 the Bennington & Rutland bought four new locomotives, three from Baldwin and one from Mason. Apparently the Bennington & Rutland had no intention of renewing the lease held by the Troy & Boston, but planned to operate the line once again for themselves.

Instead it was leased on the following January 16, the day after the Troy & Boston's agreement expired, to John B. Page and J. Gregory Smith. This indeed was a strange pair to be doing business together, as they themselves were presidents of railroads that were bitter enemies. In three years they would all be one big family, although perhaps not the happiest.

It was at this point that actual violence and a long series of legal actions were brought against the Troy & Boston by T. W. Park, the Bennington & Rutland's principal owner, resulting in the so-called "Railroad War".

Although there appeared to be some question as to the actual method employed, the Bennington & Rutland was completely within its rights. It seemed that almost any method was justified in dealing with a company that had the questionable reputation the Troy & Boston enjoyed at the time. Newspaper accounts charge that an agent of the Troy & Boston, working in North Bennington at the time, sold out to Mr. Park and arranged to have the equipment where it could be easily seized.

In retaliation the Troy & Boston gave notice that they would no longer operate the Troy & Bennington, therefore very effectively shutting off all traffic to Bennington from the south. The Troy & Boston the previous year had agreed with the Rensselaer & Saratoga to divert all its Rutland traffic over that line, entirely within New York State. They probably anticipated that the lease of the Bennington & Rutland would not be renewed, and took this step to force the Vermont line into bankruptcy and eventually to buy it on the Troy & Boston's own terms.

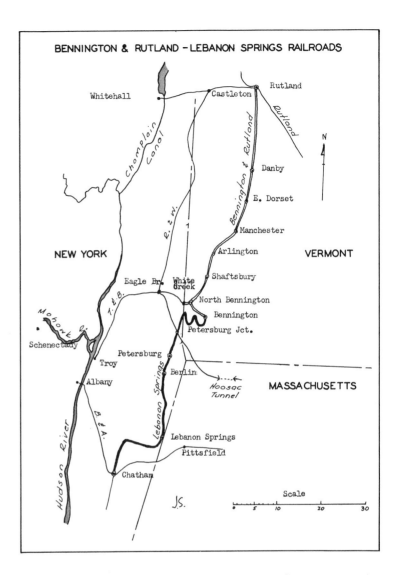

BENNINGTON & RUTLAND – LEBANON SPRINGS RAILROADS

All attempts to negotiate after the "War" were ignored, and finally rejected completely by the Troy & Boston management. The loss was keenly felt both in Troy and the southwestern part of Vermont.

The Bennington & Rutland was now faced with the prospect of drying up way out on the end of the vine. The only solution seemed to lie to the south and with the little Lebanon Springs road. This little line had been partially completed but at the moment was dormant for lack of funds. If this line could be completed, rails would reach Chatham and connect with the New York & Harlem line to New York and the Boston & Albany both east and west. The prospect of such metropolis was all that the Bennington investor needed and the line was rushed to completion in 1869. It

Unissued B.&R. stock certificate. — *Collection of J. R. McFarlane.*

Rutland No. 171 was Bennington & Rutland No. 12 before coming to the Rutland when the B.&R. was purchased in 1901. Built by Alco, 1884, she stands at North Bennington, 1904, with crew and odd caboose.

page 84

Bennington & Rutland's H. W. SPAFFORD looked like this in 1900. Originally built by Brooks, 1873, and named the M. S. COLBURN, she was rebuilt, 1882, by Taunton and then renamed. — *Collection of F. Stewart Graham.*

Bennington & Rutland No. 10 pushes a group of Sunday picnickers up the Bennington & Glastenbury Railroad on flatcars with benches built on them. This little line ran five miles east from Bennington to the resort of Woodford Hollow. Later it was electrified with open trolley cars. — *Collection of F. Hewett.*

was immediately leased to the Bennington & Rutland and in February of 1870 both roads were consolidated as the Harlem Extension Railroad. This combination was leased in turn to the newly formed and short-lived New York, Boston & Montreal Railroad. Finally, on December 1, 1873, the whole works was leased by J. Gregory Smith and integrated into his nine-hundred mile Vermont Central empire.

In the meantime the Troy & Boston realized that nothing was being gained and relented on its traffic blockade into Bennington — but by now the route to Chatham had become far more important to the Bennington & Rutland.

The Vermont Central canceled the lease in 1877 when its own fiscal problems began to mount and the Bennington & Rutland's own managers took over once again. The reorganized Bennington & Rutland ran its railroad until its capital stock was purchased by Rutland President Percival W. Clement in February of 1900, and lost its identity for all times in the Chatham division of the Rutland.

☆   ☆   ☆

THE LEBANON SPRINGS RAILROAD

The Lebanon Springs Railroad has a background considerably longer and more diversified than its 57 miles of track. Its record of participation in various combinations and ownerships far exceeds that found in most roads ten times its size.

A charter was granted to the New York & Bennington Railroad on October 13, 1851, to build from the New York & Harlem at Chatham north to the state line near Bennington. The Vermont & New York, chartered in Vermont, would build the six miles down to the state line from Bennington.

Before construction even started, a new company, The Lebanon Springs Railroad formed in March of 1852, purchased the New York & Bennington. The line was completed to Lebanon Springs but lack of funds prevented completion all the way to Bennington. The completed section north from Chatham operated mostly to accommodate New York vacationers who would come to the mineral springs at Lebanon Springs by way of the New York & Harlem line to Chatham.

When the Bennington & Rutland had its war with the Troy & Boston, interest in completing the Lebanon Springs line to connect Bennington with New York City immediately became apparent. T. W. Park, majority owner in the Bennington & Rutland, hoped to persuade Commodore Vanderbilt of the New York & Harlem to put up a million dollars and complete the project. The Commodore might agree that this line would give him a direct Montreal-New York route, and one reaching the prosperous Lebanon Valley communities as well. This line, connecting Vanderbilt's Harlem Division with existing track to the north, was much shorter than his own line to Canada through Utica and the Adirondacks.

Vanderbilt was skeptical and said the line would have grass growing on it in three generations. Park, with the help of Bennington interests, got the capital on his own. The line was rushed to completion in 1869, giving him his southern outlet without the aid of his rival, the Troy & Boston.

Vanderbilt was interested in the line, but not to the tune of a million dollars. Bennington people were wealthy, but it has always been assumed that the Commodore had his interests forwarded by the Bennington financiers so he himself would not be directly connected with the project and have his great wealth exploited — no one would admit it directly.

On the first day in January of 1870 the Bennington & Rutland and the Lebanon Springs Railroad were consolidated into the Harlem Extension Railroad.

When J. Gregory Smith took over the Rutland he leased the Harlem Extension Railroad and with the aid of New York capital formed the New York, Boston & Montreal Railroad in December of 1872.

This New York, Boston & Montreal Railroad was an operating company which planned a new New York-Montreal route, using the projected New York & Boston, the existing Dutchess & Columbia, the projected Pine Plains & Albany, along with the Harlem Extension, Rutland, and Vermont & Canada. If anyone could do it, J. Gregory would be the one, considering his railroad dealings and the vast empire he had already built.

The arrangement only lasted a few years. The curved route could not compete with the lines newly opened in the Hudson and Champlain valleys where greater speed and less time were the rule.

In mid-1877 the Central Vermont, its own financial problems mounting, got out and the properties reverted to the original owners. The section in Vermont, except the portion from Bennington to the state line, once again became the Bennington & Rutland.

The Harlem Extension South Coal Transportation Company was formed to run the New York state section. Soon they sank in the morass of debt only to be sold to the bondholders who formed the New York, Rutland & Montreal Railroad Company. This company had been chartered in 1883 to consolidate the Lebanon Springs with the Bennington & Rutland. Apparently things were so confused by this time the lawyers couldn't find which end was which and the union never took place.

The New York, Rutland & Montreal operated on a shoestring until it went broke in mid-1893. The bondholders now formed still another corporation, the Lebanon Springs Railroad, the second company to use this name.

By July of 1896 the shaky track was declared unfit for operation by the New York Board of Railroad Commissioners, but was put back into operation after a minimum of repairs in December 1897. The second Lebanon Springs Railroad fared no better than the first and was sold under foreclosure in the fall of 1899 to the Chatham & Lebanon Valley Railroad Company.

The Rutland Railroad was branching out considerably now and it immediately leased the Chatham & Lebanon Valley, finally buying it outright in June, 1901.

The Rutland had about the best luck of anyone running the "corkscrew" division. For years it routed a New York-bound milk train down the valley to Chatham with cars that had come all the way from Ogdensburg. There was little business on the line, and in 1931 passenger service was removed.

By 1953 the "corkscrew" division had had it. The Rutland applied for and received permission to abandon the 57 miles down the valley from Bennington to Chatham.

Late in the afternoon of August 7, the last rail was removed in Bennington, thus ending the career of the Lebanon Springs Railroad with its countless consolidations, mergers, reorganizations and tribulations. Commodore Vanderbilt had said it wouldn't last a hundred years.

Everybody in the Chatham engine terminal got into the act when the photographer focused on Lebanon Springs Railroad 4-4-0 No. 2, built by Baldwin, 1890.

Old Chatham & Lebanon Valley No. 6, later Rutland No. 797, under New York Central control, ran off the Stephentown turntable while Hostler Bill Dillion was busy pulling on his overalls.

C.&L.V. No. 5, beautifully painted and polished, is shown at Bennington, 1899. She was built, 1883, by the Brooks Works, later becoming Rutland No. 78. — *Collection of F. Stewart Graham.*

The engineer and fireman of Chatham & Lebanon Valley No. 5 eye a barrel of cabbage on the platform of Center Berlin station as they wait for head-end business to be completed on their Chatham-bound local run.

The train crew patiently waits for the photographer to finish his business before backing Chatham & Lebanon Valley No. 3 with the two-car *Stephentown Limited* down to Chatham station, 1898.

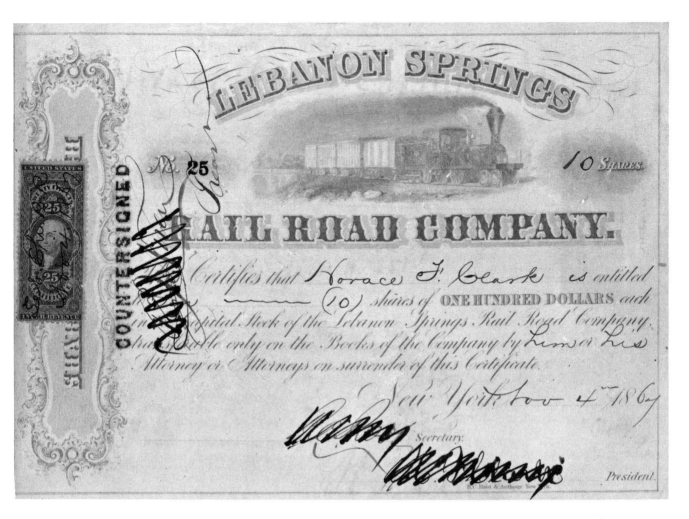

The "Corkscrew" branch was afflicted with many washouts. Here is Steam Shovel No. 477 at work in a gravel pit at Center Berlin, loading fill to repair track after one of them.

American Type No. 65 was built by St. Albans shop of the Central Vermont for the Rutland, during the lease. She ran her tall stack through Caboose No. 30 at Pittsford, in 1903, was scrapped in 1909.

The train crew and two gentlemen patrons admire a little girl in her Sunday best, while the New York, Rutland & Montreal train takes on water at Cherryplain, New York.

This ornate old covered station in Burlington was replaced by a new building, 1916. — *Collection of James R. Mc-Farlane.*

Rutland's red brick passenger station had green lawns and awning-shaded windows, 1900.

The Bristol Railroad, opened 1890, ran from Bristol 7.5 miles east to connect with the Rutland at New Haven, Vermont, just above Middlebury. Bristol No. 1, sporting a huge back-up light, gleams with polish, even to her tall little stack, as she stands in Bristol station, ready for her short run.

The neat little Rhode Island-built 0-4-4T appears somewhat less shiny, and her hopper has been altered in this later picture *(below)*, but her bell still perches jauntily atop her sand dome. She was to be replaced by a gas buggy before the final demise of the line in the 1930's.

Surprise awaited the Rutland-bound *Flyer* at Ludlow, 1905, when it met a car of pulpwood racing down from Mount Holly. The wild car got away from a local freight crew switching up the line at Summit.

Many cars were loaded at the Vermont Marble Company's finishing plant, Proctor, 1900, with Rutland's main line to the right.

"You are there," riding the coal pile of 2-8-0 No. 28 as she crosses the narrow, marble-protected, three-mile-long fill between Colchester Point and South Hero Island, across Lake Champlain with Milk Train No. 87 for Alburgh, June 1950, near the end of steam operation. The color light signal protects trains as they approach the manually operated drawbridge at Allen's Point just ahead. — *Philip R. Hastings.*

The aerial view drawing of Bennington, 1887 *(overleaf)*, shows two Bennington & Rutland trains, one coming from the north and the other easing down the hill past the Battle Monument, from the Chatham line. — *Collection of H. R. Towsley.*

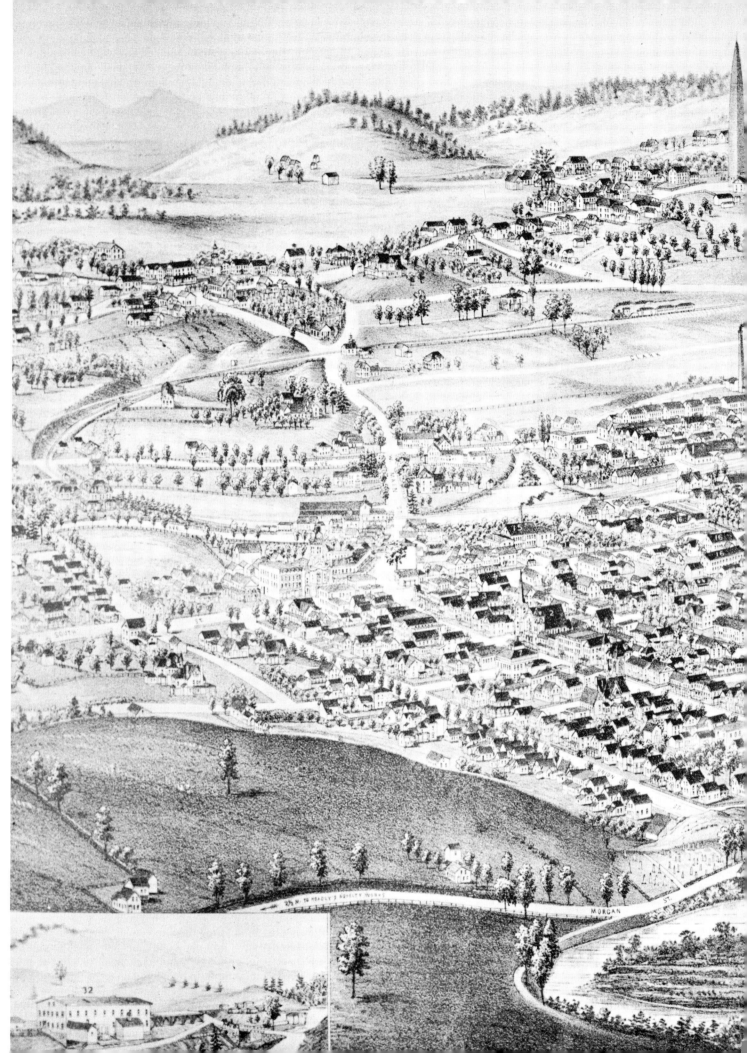

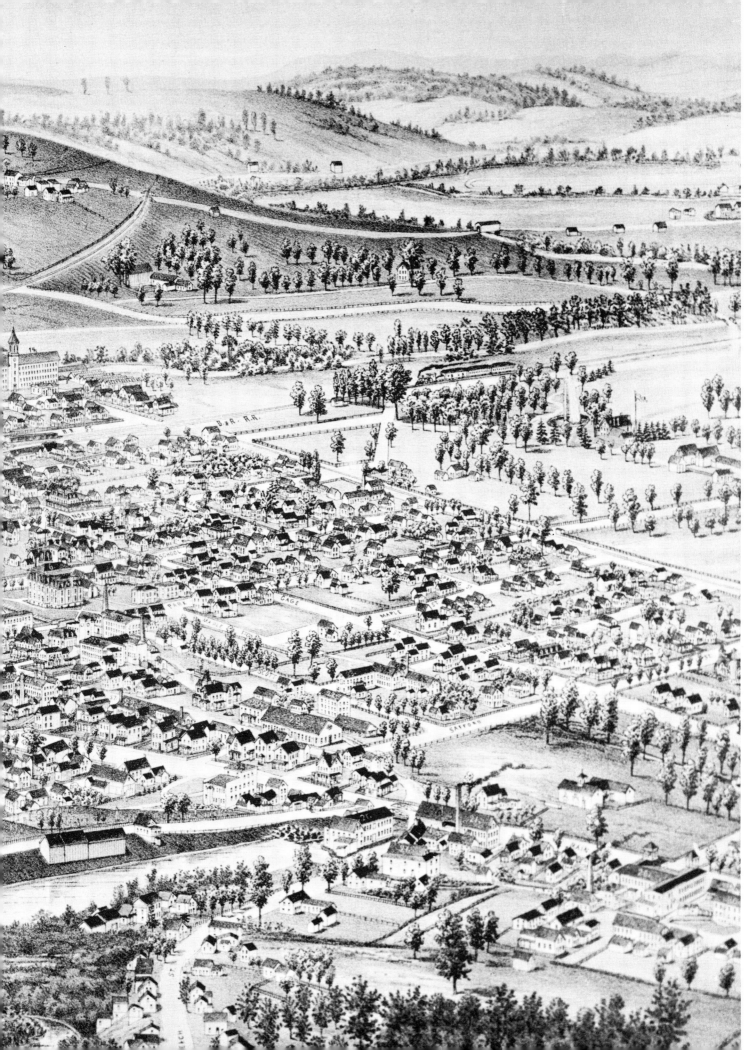

One of the most striking of the many scenic highlights of the Rutland's geography was its route across the northern end of Lake Champlain, hopping from island to island. The longest stretch of open water was between the Vermont mainland and South Hero Island. This causeway *(above)* was over three miles long. Northbound milk train No. 87 is seen from Allen Point in this 1949 photo against a backdrop of New York's Adirondacks, with Pacific No. 80 at the head.

Malone-bound Milk Train No. 7 *(right)* approaches the Rouses Point end of the mile-long trestle crossing Richelieu Bay. Engine No. 73, a 4-6-0, is easing her eight cars toward the New York shore observing the ten miles per hour speed limit imposed on the bridge used jointly by the Rutland and the Central Vermont.

The Rouses Point drawbridge *(page opposite)* is seen from the last coach of westbound Milk Train No. 7 in this 1950 picture. Rutland used the right hand pair of the gauntlet tracks on this bridge she shared with Central Vermont. — *Three pictures, Philip R. Hastings.*

page 98

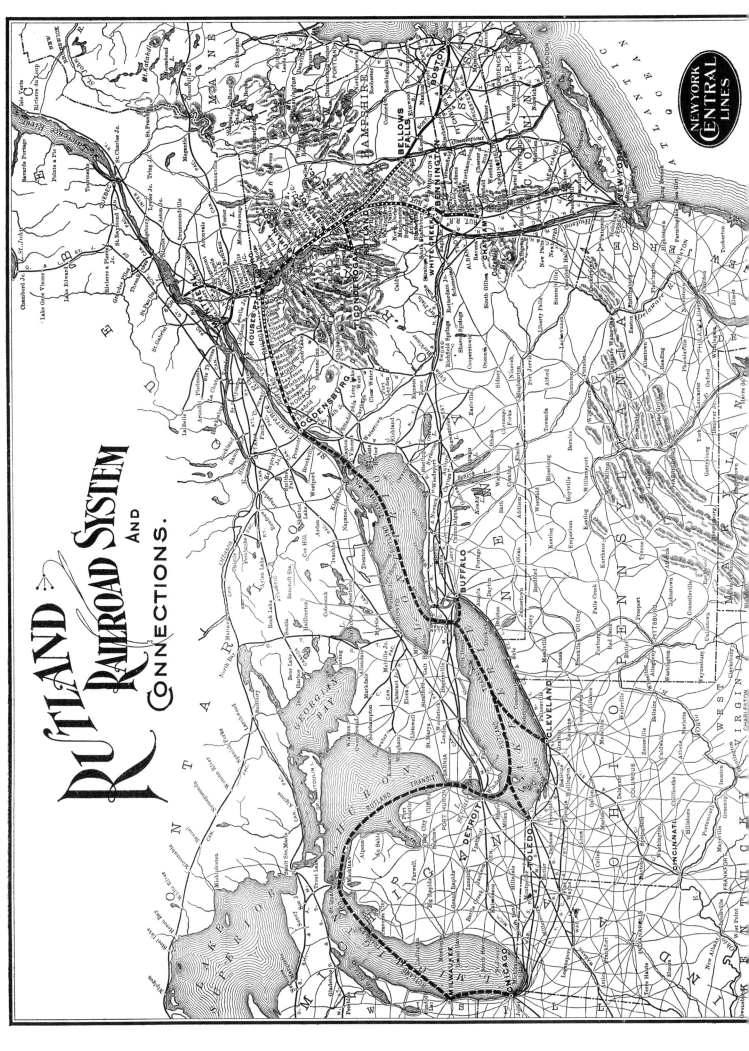

Chapter 7

Your Move, Mr. Vanderbilt

As troubles mounted for the now-inflated Rutland system, an eastern giant was once again flexing its corporate muscles. The great New York Central system had consolidated its control over many smaller railroads, and in the last decade of the Nineteenth Century was looking for new fields to conquer. The Vanderbilt dynasty was approaching its zenith as a power in the field of American transportation. With the control of the busy New York Central & Hudson River Railroad and heavy interests in other lines, it held a key route east of Chicago.

One of the heirs-apparent in the family was a physician-turned-railroader, Dr. William Seward Webb, son-in-law of William H. Vanderbilt. His interest in railroading prompted him to abandon his lucrative medical practice early in the 1880s to turn his full attention to the preservation and expansion of the family interests. Being somewhat of a character, yet endowed with driving ambition, he assumed the presidency of the family-owned Wagner Palace Car Company in 1883 and did a creditable job in that capacity. But Seward Webb had other goals; his two driving ambitions above all others were to operate his own railroad and to gain the honor and prestige that went with the governorship of the state. If events in New York were anything like those in Vermont, this was not at all impossible.

In the latter part of the Nineteenth Century, the remote lakes of the central Adirondack Mountains in northern New York were becoming a center for the vast summer estates and hunting lodges of New York's very rich — including Dr. Webb, who

had a de luxe establishment on the Fulton chain of lakes. At the same time, the New York Central was looking enviously north toward Montreal, a city that was served primarily by the Delaware & Hudson, the Rome, Watertown & Ogdensburg in conjunction with the Ogdensburg & Lake Champlain line, and the New England roads from the east. In 1891 Webb came forward with a proposition that appeared to make sense at the time: build north from the Central's trunk, open up the vast potential resort region of the central Adirondacks, and then continue on to Montreal to provide a company-controlled feeder to the Canadian metropolis. With the family blessing, he organized the Mohawk & Malone Railroad Company, taking over the narrow gauge Herkimer, Newport & Poland for a few miles north of the Mohawk River. This was widened to standard gauge, and then construction crews struck off into the mountain wilderness to the northeast.

Simultaneously, a related company, the St. Lawrence & Adirondack, began to lay track south from Malone where the Webb line would intersect the Ogdensburg & Lake Champlain. Two items of construction on this line are worthy of comment: Dr. Webb had a handsome private station built for his use and that of his friends on his estate, Ne-Ha-Sa-Ne Park, and he had an inspection engine built to his order. Named for the Webb estate, the little Ne-Ha-Sa-Ne was a thing of beauty from her polished rims to the top of the solid mahogany observation cab. Imported carpeting covered the narrow observation decks along each side of the slim boiler and six luxuriously upholstered chairs

Dr. William Seward Webb, president of Rutland Railroad, 1902-1905, was son-in-law of William H. Vanderbilt, railroad enthusiast, and every inch the turn-of-the-century gentleman. — *Courtesy of the Webb Family.*

graced the interior. A white-coated steward was assigned to her regular crew. In this handsome engine, Webb delighted to entertain his friends as she steamed majestically through the Adirondack wilderness.

In his driving political ambition, Dr. Webb had engaged heavily in good works and undertakings that would bring him into the public eye. But New York would have nothing of him as a gubernatorial prospect; perhaps his personal extravagances created a reverse impression, and the stench from the Erie manipulations of a few years before still lingered, detracting from any railroad executive as a prospect for a position of public trust. The rising tide of unionism was directing its fire against the railroad interests, and the Vanderbilts were being widely caricatured in the best (or worst) traditions of vicious yellow journalism in the widely-read labor press. As a more than willing candidate, William Seward Webb was just too hot

to be accepted by the political overlords of New York in spite of the fact that his nomination would automatically bring with it vast financial backing.

Thwarted in the Empire State, Webb turned his attention to the Green Mountain State, from which his ancestors had sprung. Almost traditionally, railroad presidents in Vermont had become governors; therefore, if a man had a driving desire to be governor of Vermont, he simply had to become a railroad president. The New York Central & Hudson River had started to pave the way; a considerable financial interest in the Rutland Railroad had accrued to the New York Company and its proprietors through stock in the Chatham & Lebanon Valley when that unfortunate road was absorbed by the Rutland. Besides, Rutland stock was now depressed to the point where it might prove to be a good investment, and a second string to the Montreal bow would provide a through route bypassing the Delaware & Hudson line between Canada and New York City. That little coal hauler was threatening to become too powerful a factor in northeastern transportation, anyway. The New York Central & Hudson River and some of its individual stockholders, including Dr. Webb proceeded to buy heavily into the Rutland.

The Clements became aware of the movement early, and stock in the Rutland Railroad became suddenly rather difficult to obtain — but not so difficult as to be impossible. Rutland shares began to appreciate in price, and at their peak, Percival Clement was dribbling out a few shares at a time at $105! Seward Webb's driving ambition to be governor proved to be an extremely profitable one for the Clement interests, and for many years not too bad a deal for the New York Central as well. Once again the Rutland Railroad had passed out of local control.

On May 1, 1902, Percival W. Clement turned the reins of the Rutland over to the newly elected president, Dr. W. Seward Webb, and retired from active management of the railroad. After nearly two stormy decades, the era of the Clements had come to an end.

Webb, secure in his backing, settled quickly into his new job and set out with a vengeance to become Vermont's first citizen. The handsome estate and private station in the Adirondack

Shelburne station, south of Burlington, was unusual in its beautiful park-like grounds. The station itself was leased by the railroad from Dr. Webb whose fabulous mansion was on the shore of Lake Champlain, nearby. His private car, *Ellsmere*, is shown partly inside the shelter adjoining the baggage shed across the tracks from the station. — *Shelburne Museum.*

This luxuriously appointed locomotive, Ne-Ha-Sa-Ne, was built, 1900, by Schenectady. Dr. Webb used it as an inspection engine, named it after his estate in the Adirondacks, and brought it with him when he came to the Rutland.

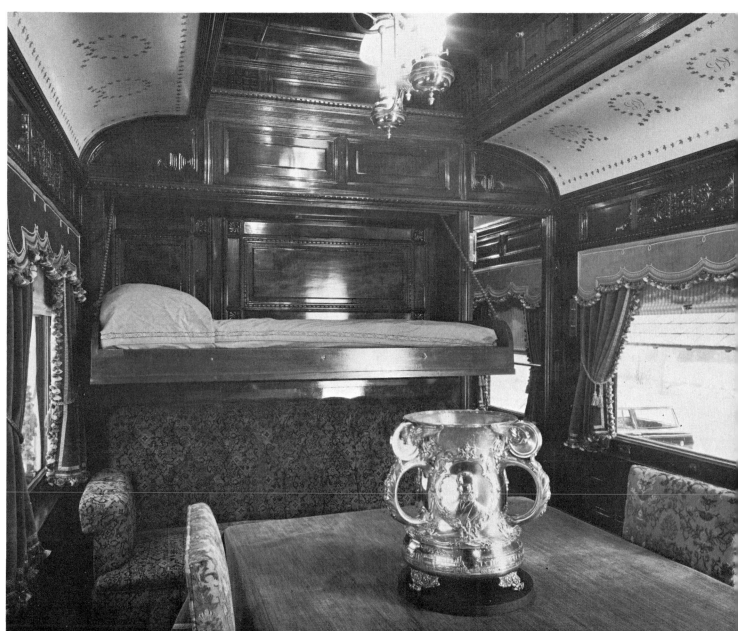

Of the many rich and ornate private cars associated with the Rutland, none was a finer example of the carbuilder's expertise in the 1890's than *Grand Isle*, today one of the beautifully maintained exhibits at Shelburne Museum, adjacent to the Rutland tracks at Shelburne, south of Burlington. *Grand Isle*, like *Ellsmere* and Lila Vanderbilt Webb's *Mariquita*, was made by Wagner Palace Car Company. This one was built, 1898, as a gift from Dr. Webb, then president of Wagner, to Governor Smith of Vermont. Eventually this car became property of the Central Vermont and was used as a business car by that carrier. Many years afterwards when the days of private cars on any extensive scale were over and when the railroads of Vermont were themselves in decline, *Grand Isle* was acquired by J. Watson Webb, son of Dr. Webb and president of Shelburne Museum. Although its decor had sadly deteriorated over the decades, the museum restored it to what must be a close approximation of its former glory, including the magnificently carved berth fronts, the carbuilder's special pride. On these pages are shown various detailed views of *Grand Isle* as she exists today at Shelburne, a monument to the glories of railroading and its nabobs at the turn of the century. — *Four photographs: Shelburne Museum.*

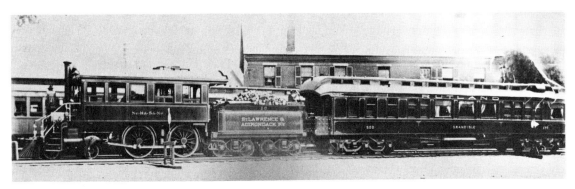

Ne-Ha-Sa-Ne sometimes pulled private cars well worthy of her elegance. Outside the old two-story station at Bellows Falls and still sporting St. Lawrence & Adirondack lettering, for Dr. Webb's old line in New York State, she stands with private car No. 500, glamorous *Grand Isle*.

Crossing the Boston & Maine at Petersburgh Junction, she hauls private car No. 99 down the "Corkscrew Division" for Chatham. The ornate spiral stairways hint at the opulence of her solid mahogany cab. — *Top: Collection of F. Stewart Graham.*

wilderness were forgotten; he set up another palatial summer home on the shore of Lake Champlain at Shelburne, just south of Burlington. But his elegant toy, Ne-Ha-Sa-Ne, he could bring with him, and did. Repainted now in handsome dark green, with the Rutland herald imposed in resplendent gold letters on her immaculate tender, she cruised the rails for many years. Finally, like an aged and discarded mistress, she was relegated to a lonesome twilight life, shuffling in dingy disregard around the back tracks of Rutland.

Absolute control of the Rutland came to the New York Central interests in 1904. As the year drew to a close, the Central owned $4,704,100 of the $9,057,600 worth of capital stock outstanding,

enough to use the Rutland Railroad as it would, and never another dollar's worth would it buy.

Dr. Webb's political star rose no higher in Vermont than it did in New York. Though they are friendly people, Vermonters have a marked distaste for being "used", and here was a man who patently intended to influence them to further his own ambitions. But in all fairness it must be stated that under his management and that of several of his successors, the Rutland Railroad enjoyed many good years under the wing of the New York Central.

Webb's advent on the Rutland was marked by a general refurbishment of the railroad, as usual long overdue. The best power on the line was the

Double Daily Service with Modern Pullman Buffet Parlor and Sleeping Cars between

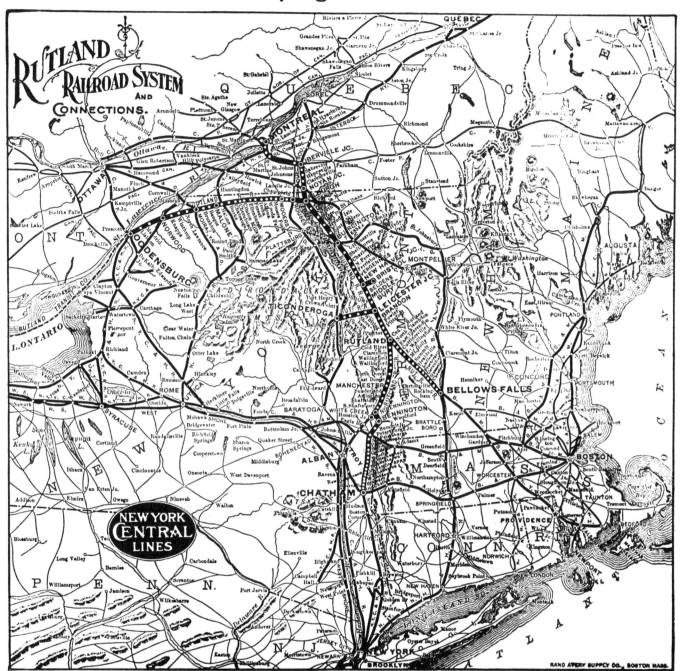

Boston and Montreal via the Bellows Falls Gateway
THE SHORT LINE

Rutland's finest years were during the period when New York Central owned a controlling interest, and both names appeared on timetables and cars. — *Collection of J. R. MacFarlane.*

This 1906 view shows Mogul No. 1890 drifting into Alburg yard with a freight from Burlington over the recently completed line up through the islands.

The *Green Mountain Flyer*, hauled southbound by 4-6-0 No. 2078, stops at Alburg for customs inspection. Passenger operations were in full glory when this 1914 picture was taken. Bewildering is the vagrant "h" which may or may not appear at the end of the names of the various "burgs" in Rutland Railroad territory, as they are inconsistently printed in maps, timetables, and pictures. — *Collection of Gordon Cutler.*

engines obtained through the Ogdensburg & Lake Champlain acquisition. By this time the Rutland's roster had developed a collection of locomotives of varying origin, age, model and condition, gathered from the Ogdensburg road, the Chatham & Lebanon Valley, the Bennington & Rutland, and even a few discards from the New York Central and the St. Lawrence & Adirondack. It appears that the latter were rushed over to the Rutland line to enable the aged and inadequate "home guard" power to cope with the influx of business now being routed over the Green Mountain road by the parent Central.

Orders went out to the Schenectady works for 29 new engines, mostly ten-wheelers, and these handsome dual purpose engines began to roll on the Rutland during 1902, just as over a third of the original roster taken back from the Central Vermont a few years before reached a state of final collapse and headed for the scrap yard. In 1901, the company executed a mortgage of $495,000 for new equipment and the following year another mortgage of $1,500,000.

In addition to the locomotives, the road's rolling stock of all kinds was in bad condition and needed repair and replacement. Hundreds of ancient boxcars and a few creaking, outworn coaches were slated for destruction. The latter had no place in the new management's design for a spanking new passenger service north to Montreal.

In its report for the year ending June 30, 1906, the railroad had posted over forty million passenger-miles for a profit just short of $350,000, while freight earnings turned in a net of $495,000. The company served a number of private car lines including the Red, White and Blue, Canadian Southern, Erie Dispatch and others, rolling them on a percentage basis. The United States Government paid in $80,648 for the transportation of the mails. The Rutland Transit Company (a reincarnation of the old Ogdensburg Transit line) routed cargo through Ogdensburg for much of the year. Though the Central may have appeared to be competing with itself through its ownership in the parent railroad, the Transit line served its purpose in keeping the Rome, Watertown & Ogdensburg on its knees, and it helped to keep the Erie and other

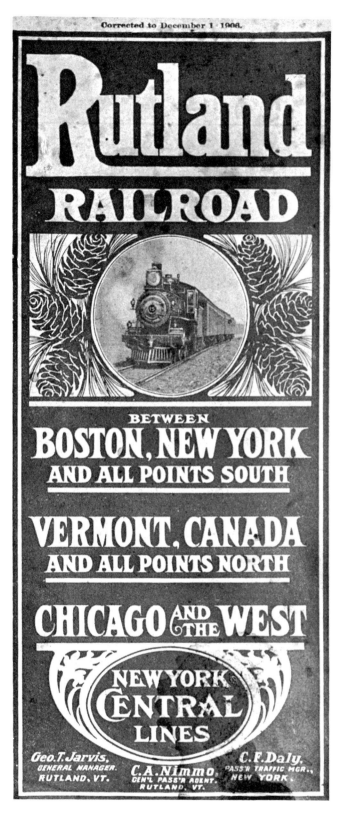

Collection of J. R. MacFarlane.

Rutland R.R.

LOCAL TIME-TABLES
OGDENSBURG DIVISION

	READ DOWN.			STATIONS.	Miles from Alburgh	READ UP.			
225 Freig't	257 Mixed	265 Ex-press	251 Ex-press			264 Ex-press	259 Ex-press	250 Pas-senger	224 Freig't
	P.M.	P.M.	A.M.			A.M.	P.M.	P.M.	P.M.
	7.30	7.55	6.40	Lv ....Alburgh....Ar	0	Ar 10.20	8.40		7.00
	7.35	8.10	6.20	" ..Rouses Point.. Lv	4	Lv 10.05	8.35		6.55
	7.50	8.13	6.31	" .Rouses Pt. Jct.	4	10.00	8.30		6.30
	8.00	8.26	6.43	" ...Champlain...	8	9.49	8.10		6.00
	8.50	8.43	6.48	" ..Moore's Jct..	17	9.35	8.01		5.42
	8.56	8.49	6.55	" .Mooer's Forks.	22	9.28	7.56		5.32
	9.36	8.53	7.01	" ..Woods Falls..	26	9.22	7.52		5.07
	10.00	9.00	7.09	" ....Altona....	32	9.15	7.46		4.55
	10.15	9.05	7.16	" ..Ellenburg L..	42	9.11	7.36		4.18
	11.20	9.11	7.25	" ..Clarence'v'l..	49	9.06	7.31		4.06
	11.45	9.17	7.32	" ..Ellenburgh..	53	9.01	7.27		
	12.00	9.30	7.44	" ..Clinton Mills..	59	8.49	7.21	3.30	
	4.50	9.35	7.50	" ..Alburgh Cr..	71	8.45	7.10	3.00	
	5.06	9.50	8.07	" ..Chateaugay..	78	8.30	7.01	2.45	
	5.16	10.00	8.20	" ....Burke....	80	8.28	6.48	2.28	
	5.28	10.12	8.32	" ...Malone Jct...	87	8.04	6.48	2.15	
	5.43	10.15	8.36	" ....Malone....	94	7.50	6.51	1.40	
	5.57	10.25	8.48	" ...Bangor...	97	7.33	6.51	1.30	
		10.42	9.06	" ....Moira....		7.22	6.34		
		10.54	9.18	" ..No. Lawrence..	75	7.19	6.27	1.10	
		11.04	9.31	" ...Winthrop...	86	7.09	6.16	12.50	
		11.18	9.45	" ...Knapps...	94	6.54	5.59	12.25	
		11.25	9.51	" ..Norwood..	97	6.47	5.48	12.15	
		11.41	10.07	" ...Madrid...	106	6.32	5.45	11.25	
		12.00	10.25	" ...Lisbon...	113	6.16	4.29	11.05	
		12.20	10.46	Ar .Ogdensburg. Lv	122	6.00	4.10	10.46	
	P.M.	P.M.	A.M.			A.M.	P.M.	P.M.	P.M.

"Does not carry baggage" (224/250 column)
"Does not carry baggage" (225/257 column)

CHATHAM DIVISION

READ DOWN.		STATIONS.	Miles from Bennington	READ UP.	
6 Mail	4 Ex-press			1 Mail	3 Mixed
A.M.	A.M.			P.M.	P.M.
6.50	8.15	Lv ..Bennington.. Ar	0	10.46	6.15
6.20	8.30	" ...Summit... Lv	4	10.34	6.15
6.30	9.00	Ar .Pet'rsn'g Jct. Ar	8	10.16	5.35
6.35	9.16	" .Pet'rsn'g Jct. Lv	12	10.10	5.05
6.47	9.30	" .N. Petersburgh.	18	10.00	4.45
7.00	9.35	" ..Petersburgh..	23	9.36	4.25
7.10	10.11	" ...Berlin...	23	9.29	4.10
7.15	10.21	" .Cent'e Berlin.	27	9.27	3.57
7.30	10.31	" .South Berlin.	31	9.07	3.30
7.40	10.48	" .S. Stephentown.	33	9.01	3.07
7.50	11.04	" ..Lebanon Sp'gs.	35	8.53	2.41
7.56	11.29	" ..New Lebanon..	40	8.49	2.20
8.04	11.34	" .Centre Lebanon.	41	8.43	2.00
8.11	11.43	" .Adams Crossing.	49	8.37	
8.23	12.08	" ...Brainard...	51	8.27	
8.30	12.16	" ...Rayville...		8.23	
8.40	12.30	" ..Old Chatham..	61	8.16	
1.00	1.40	Ar ...Chatham... Lv		7.23	
P.M.	P.M.			A.M.	P.M.

ADDISON BRANCH

READ DOWN.		STATIONS.	Miles	READ UP.	
456 Mixed	454 Mixed			457 Mixed	455 Mixed
P.M.	A.M.			P.M.	P.M.
2.35	8.35	Lv .Ticonderoga. Ar	0	12.40	6.50
2.46	8.40	" .LaHarpe's Point.	1	12.25	6.40
3.05	9.21	" ...Orwell...	7	12.05	6.20
3.15	9.49	" ..Shoreham..	9	11.55	6.10
3.30	9.56	" ...Whiting...	12	11.45	5.55
3.45		Ar .Leicester Jct. Lv	16	11.35	5.40
P.M.	A.M.			P.M.	P.M.

Rutland R.R.

LOCAL TIME-TABLES
MONTREAL TO BELLOWS FALLS AND BENNINGTON
GOING SOUTH

Mls. from Montreal	STATIONS.	162 Pas-senger	48 Pas-senger	54 Mail	64 G. Mt. Flyer	56 Mail	22 Mixed	160 Pas-senger	50 Pas-senger	52 Ex-press
		P.M.	A.M.	A.M.	A.M.	P.M.	A.M.	P.M.	P.M.	P.M.
0	Lv ..Montreal..			11.00	8.50					7.10
5	" ..Montreal Jc..			11.05	9.00					7.20
30	" ..St. Johns..			11.25	9.35		6.25			8.02
35	" ..Iberville Jc..			11.25	9.40		6.15			8.13
38	" ..Barnston..			11.35	9.53		6.50			8.25
42	" ..Henryville..			11.53	10.02		7.16			8.34
49	" ..Clarence'v'l..			12.09	10.15		8.20			8.45
53	" ..Nolan Jct..			12.24	10.30					9.20
68	" ..Alburgh..			12.42	10.57	4.00			8.30	9.30
71	" ..Grand Isle..			12.52	11.10	4.12			8.42	9.42
78	" ..North Hero..				11.18	4.23			9.00	9.49
82	" ..South Hero..				12.06	4.43			9.10	10.20
96	" ..Shelburne..			8.30		5.15			9.20	
103	" ..Charlotte..			8.43	12.29	5.04			9.30	
108	" ..Burlington..			9.00	12.37	5.15			9.35	11.16
112	" ..N. Ferris'b'g..			9.20		5.44			9.46	
115	" ..Ferrisburg..			9.50		6.04			10.17	
122	" ..N. Haven Jc..			9.51		6.12			10.27	12.10
128	Lv .Bus'L.B.RR. Ar					6.15			10.40	12.20
	" ...Bristol... Lv									
130	Lv ..Rutland.. Ar			10.56	1.50	6.20	6.30	10.50	12.20	
137	" ..Cold River..			11.00		6.25	6.40	10.57	12.45	
139	" ..Clarendon..			11.09	2.04	6.31	7.15	11.05	5.10	12.30
144	" ..E. Walling'd..			11.12		6.35	7.35	11.18	5.25	1.60
147	" ..Leicest'r Jc..			11.25	2.16	6.45	8.26	11.24	5.40	
153	" ..Danby..			11.41	2.37	7.18	9.35	11.34		1.01
163	" ..Brandon..			11.53		7.32	10.38	12.12		
164	" ..Pittsford..			12.04	2.51	7.40	12.15	12.15	1.25	
162	" ..Proctor..			12.09		7.50	1.10	1.10		
163	Ar ..CtrRutland.. Lv	8.08		12.24	3.10	7.55	1.30	1.30		1.60
	Lv ...Rutland...			10.45	1.50	6.20	6.30	10.50		2.00
166	" ...Belders...	7.46	6.30	11.00		6.30	6.40			2.00
169	" ..Middlebury..	7.58	6.40	11.11		6.50	7.15			
172	" ..Salisbury..	8.02	6.55	11.12	2.04	6.58	7.35			2.10
181	" ..Sudbury..	8.12		11.28	2.16	6.54	8.26			2.30
189	" ..East Dorset..			11.53	2.37	7.18	9.35			1.87
194	" ..Manchester..	6.15		12.09		7.32	10.38			2.46
201	" ..Sunderland..	6.21		12.12		7.40				
204	" ..Arlington..	6.39		12.15	2.51	7.50				
209	" ..Shaftsbury..	6.46		12.16						3.16
214	" ..S. Shaftsb'y..	6.50		12.24	3.04					
220	Lv ..Bennington.. Ar	7.00		12.13	3.12					
223	" ..Bennington..	7.15								
216	Lv .N. Ben'gton. Ar	6.46		12.35	2.45	8.10		3.45	5.10	
218	" ..White Creek..	7.04		12.45	2.45	8.00		3.55	5.25	
223	Ar .Hoosick Jct. Lv	8.15		1.00	3.35			4.30	5.40	
		P.M.	A.M.	A.M.	A.M.	P.M.	A.M.	P.M.	P.M.	P.M.

Rutland R.R.

LOCAL TIME-TABLES
BELLOWS FALLS AND BENNINGTON TO MONTREAL
GOING NORTH

Mls. from B.F.	STATIONS.	161 Pas-senger	121 Mixed	57 Pas-senger	53 Mail	65 G. Mt. Flyer	807 Pas-senger	59 Pas-senger	51 Ex-press
		A.M.	A.M.	A.M.	NOON	P.M.	A.M.	P.M.	P.M.
0	Lv ..Bellows Falls..	6.06	6.30		12.00	3.05		6.46	11.30
4	" ..Rockingham..	6.15	6.45		12.21			6.55	11.44
10	" ..Chester..	6.34	7.10		12.31			7.10	12.06
14	" ..Gassetts..	6.44	7.36		12.40			7.20	12.10
24	" ..Proctorsville..	6.64	7.55		12.49		3.26	7.30	12.26
34	" ...Ludlow...	6.57	8.00		1.00		3.42	7.37	12.31
38	" ..Healdville..	7.05	8.16		1.02	3.43		7.42	12.40
44	" ..Summit..	7.16	8.35		1.15	3.48		7.52	12.44
51	" ..Mount Holly..	7.20	8.40	8.16	1.15			8.01	1.00
53	" ..East Wallingford..	7.36	9.04	8.28	1.21			8.10	1.16
57	" ..Cuttingsville..	7.36	9.16	8.49	1.31	3.00		8.20	12.36
62	" ..E. Clar'ndon..	7.46	9.30	8.37	1.36	2.45		8.30	12.16
66	" ..No. Clarendon..	7.53	9.44	8.49	1.43			8.38	1.44
68	Ar ...Rutland...	8.00	10.00	9.00	1.50	3.10		8.45	1.66
0	Lv .Hoosick Junction.	P.M.		8.16	11.10		A.M.	6.20	
4	" ..White Creek..	1.45		8.28	11.21	3.30	6.55	6.28	
7	Ar .No. Bennington. Ar	2.10		8.45	11.25	2.45	7.04	6.38	
	Lv .No. Bennington. Lv	2.15			11.40		7.20	6.48	
0	Lv ..Bennington..	1.55		8.37			7.30	6.55	
3	" ..So. Shaftsbury..	2.15		8.49			7.35		
9	" ..Shaftsbury..	2.35		9.04		c 3.30	7.45	7.16	
11	" ..Arlington..	4.30		9.07			8.00	7.27	
18	" ..Sunderland..	4.30		9.16			8.07		
24	" ..East Dorset..	5.30		9.42		c 3.53	8.15	7.48	
34	" ..North Dorset..	5.45		9.53			8.12	8.12	
42	" ...Danby...	6.54		10.03			8.30	8.30	
48	" ..So. Wallingford..	7.15		10.08		c 4.05	8.36	9.14	
51	" ..Wallingford..	7.30		10.12			8.50	9.30	
57	" ..Clarendon..			10.03			8.54	9.38	
67	Ar ...Rutland...			10.18		4.20	9.00		
66	Lv ...Rutland...	A.M.		10.48	11.10	4.35	A.M.	9.50	9.46
73	" ..Centre Rutland..	35		10.56	11.02		6.00	9.11	9.53
74	" ..Proctor..	2.5		11.02	11.12	4.12	6.09	9.16	10.05
81	" ..Pittsford..			11.13		4.26	6.18	9.25	10.10
94	" ..Brandon..			11.15			6.35	9.35	9.13
100	Ar ..Leicester Jct..	1.45		11.33					
101	" ..Salisbury Jct..	1.55		11.41		4.36			
104	" ..Belden..	1.50		11.47		4.49			
112	" ..New Haven Jct..	2.00		12.01		5.48			
115	Ar .Bristol, B.R.R..					m5.48			
	Lv .Bristol...								
130	Lv ..Vergennes..			12.10					
135	" ..Ferrisburg..			12.14		5.10			
138	" ..Charlotte..			12.29		5.29			
144	Ar ..Burlington..			12.42		4.12			
150	" ..South Hero..								
155	" ..North Hero..								
163	" ..Isle La Motte..								
167	" ..Nolan Junction..								
171	" ..Clarenville..								
174	" ...Alburgh...								
181	" ..Henryville..								
185	" ..Iberville Jct..								
188	" ..St. Johns..								
195	" ..Clarenville..								
204	Ar ..Montreal..								
		A.M.	A.M.	A.M.	A.M.	P.M.	A.M.	P.M.	P.M.

* Daily. † Daily except Sundays. ‡ Sundays only. ¶ Daily except Mondays.

For other references see page 3.

13
12
11

The *Brandon*, built 1910, was one of the Rutland Transit Company's six steel lake ships. Here she is at Ogdensburg with two different letterings of the house name, easing into the dock, and unloading a cargo of grain at the elevator. The lower picture was made in 1914, a year before the Panama Canal act put an end to ship operations.

competing east-west railroads from becoming too much of a threat.

The Rutland had never had it so good as during the first decade of the Twentieth Century. Straining double-headers challenged the grades, the Moguls and the Ten-Wheelers shouting their labored exhausts against the brooding, forested hills, going reluctantly into too-short passing tracks to make way for hot-shot milk runs. Strings of gleaming green coaches headed by immaculate green engines roared between the greatest cities in the U.S. and Canada over Rutland rails, their luxurious tail end Pullmans rocking rhythmically around the many curves, clicking off the profitable miles on the eighty-pound rail.

This was the beginning of the good years. The recession following the war of 1898 was blessedly short-lived. The industrial revolution was in full swing in the East, pouring its golden flood out of mills and mines. In return, the great West sent its mountains of grain east in growing volume, ships following one another to the Ogdensburg docks in quick succession. The railroads were pulsing as never before with the lifeblood of progress, and the Rutland was swept along with the tide of prosperity. More land was purchased at the central division point to expand the overflowing yards. Harried dispatchers scratched their heads over crowded train sheets, jockeying varnish runs and drags and extras over the overworked single track between Rutland and Alburg. There were even rumors that the top brass hats were considering double-tracking the Rutland-Burlington stretch.

By 1906, the company's accounts showed a healthy surplus of well over a million dollars, and its equipment notes were being paid off rapidly. The first two of six new steel vessels were also added to the Rutland Transit Company's fleet. In that same year, and for three more, the railroad paid modest dividends, but the heavy traffic was taking its toll from a road that was physically unequal to the demands; in 1909 and again in 1910 dividends were passed up so that earnings could be applied to the maintenance and improvement of the line.

In 1909 a through milk train was inaugurated running the complete length of the road daily from Ogdensburg to Chatham. Cars would be gathered all across New York, having as many as twenty upon reaching Alburg. More would be picked up down through Vermont since it was not unusual to have forty or more cars follow a double-header into Rutland. A portion would be sent over the hill to Bellows Falls for Boston, but the majority went down to Chatham and turned over to the New York Central for morning delivery in Gotham.

The New Haven road under the direction of C. S. Mellon, by now a power in all of southern New England, was not exactly happy with the course of events to the north. The New York Central, with its lease of the Boston & Albany in 1899, had bisected New England across Massachusetts and now, crowned with some measure of success in its operation of the Rutland, appeared to be looking for new fields to conquer in this corner of the United States. The New York Central, however, was something less than enthusiastic about the New Haven's control of the wandering New York, Ontario & Western. This road roller coastered its way from Weehawken in New Jersey to Oswego harbor on Lake Ontario across southeastern New York with a tap to the anthracite fields of Pennsylvania. Although this meandering mountain pike could hardly be considered a serious threat to the Central's excellent water-level route, the managers of the larger road felt that it might be safer in their protecting hands. The two then began to discuss what amounted to a swap.

The minority stockholders in the Rutland Railroad did not like this one bit. Under the Central's management, their railroad had enjoyed a period of relative prosperity, the only such sustained period in more than fifty years. Their stock holdings were maintaining their market value — a refreshing development — and moreover, real progress was being made in the physical improvement of the road. They were in no mood to relinquish this happy state of affairs without a struggle, and stockholders' committees began to cool their heels in the offices above Grand Central Station with dogged regularity. Vermont shippers also became alarmed, apparently with reason, that the New Haven line could gain control of Vermont's roads to establish a monopoly such as it had done in its own state, to the sorrow of the people it purported to serve.

The Rutland reached its southernmost point at this modest frame station on Park Row, Chatham, N. Y. — *Collection of F. Hewett.*

The southbound local on Chatham branch meets its northbound counterpart at Petersburgh, N. Y. on a 1906 winter's day. The derby-hatted gentleman and his lady, who eye the photographer, do not seem much bothered by the cold.

The protests were only partially effective. Instead of a complete swap, the Central sold half its holdings to the New Haven in February, 1911, and took a half-interest in the New York, Ontario & Western road to complete the deal. In a last-ditch fight, the Rutland's minority group obtained a temporary injunction to stop the transaction, but on May 9, 1912, the modified transfer of stock was granted by the court. The plaintiffs appealed, and the action dragged on for three more years until it was finally dismissed in 1915.

This was the end of a happy era for the Rutland. Along with the end of the effort to keep continued New York Central ownership of the Rutland came a more serious blow, the Panama Canal Act. Through a quirk of Fate, the very situation that the Rutland's militant minority stockholders were attempting to preserve proved to be its undoing. Under the provisions of the Act, the Interstate Commerce law was amended to prohibit railroad ownership or control of an interstate carrier by water that competed against its railroad owner unless it could be proved that the carrier was "operated in the interest of the public and is of advantage to the convenience and commerce of the people."

The Act also granted to the Commission broad powers of determination that have resulted in many of the railroad industry's difficulties to this day.

For the Rutland Railroad, trouble was immediate and serious. Several major railroads stood to benefit if the Vermont line could be forced to divest itself of the ships it controlled in the lake trade to Chicago. The New York Central owned half the stock of the Rutland, and the Rutland controlled the Rutland Transit Company which operated the Great Lakes ships. Therefore, by the Act, the New York Central was in competition with itself, and the attorneys for the Erie, the Pennsylvania, and a half-dozen other east-west carriers were eager to emphasize the point. The New York Central itself did not plead overly hard in the Rutland's defense, it no longer considered the Rutland an invaluable property. In fact it had reduced its interest in the Rutland in favor of the Ontario & Western line, an error in judgment that would take a few years to resolve.

The Interstate Commerce Commission ruled against the Rutland Railroad. The busy ships were no longer to ply their scheduled trips to the port of Ogdensburg, and the busy lakeside tracks gradually rusted, slowly to disappear in a tangle of weeds.

The *Stephentown Flyer* eases down into Brainard over a high trestle and fill running up from Chatham behind the petite No. 793. — *Collection of Robert Lank.*

Passenger business, or any other business for that matter, was never outstanding on the Lebanon Valley line, but a number of patrons detrain from the Stephentown-Chatham local at Lebanon Springs, N. Y. this fine day, 1906. Perhaps one of them will find comfort, if not luxury, in the hay wagon. American No. 793, which hauls the train, pop valve open, into the station was built, 1884, for the Bennington & Rutland as their No. 11, the M. S. COLBURN. She joined the Rutland when the Vermont line entered the New York state market to the south. — *Collection of Robert Lank.*

The depot in Manchester is setting for both these views. 4-4-0 No. 99, at the head of the afternoon local was formerly No. 10 on St. Lawrence & Adirondack. What appears to be Vermont's first radar antenna is nothing more anachronistic in the 1913 scene than a spinning windmill.

Standard Wagons, advertised on the colorful Cincinnati, Hamilton & Dayton boxcar, may or may not have built the buggy and wagon in the station picture. — Both: Manchester Historical Society.

The Rich Lumber Company operated Shay No. 6 on its line up Lye Brook Hollow in the hills east of Manchester station. Operations began in 1913 with two locomotives, but ended in 1919 when the big mill burned.

The Manchester, Dorset, & Granville ("Mud, Dirt, & Gravel") opened in 1904 with a 5.09 mile run between Manchester depot and South Dorset, providing four trips a day between the two towns. Passengers could ride in trim combination coach No. 100, but the railroad's principal income was from hauling marble blocks to be used in such notable edifices as the New York Public Library. The line never reached its projected destination at Granville, N. Y., 23 miles away, and was abandoned in 1918. Locomotive No. 1 was formerly a Rutland engine, built in St. Albans and acquired by Rutland during the Central Vermont lease. — *Top: Collection of T. Tyler; middle: Manchester Historical Society.*

An Erie boxcar, a combine, and a coach follow Engine No. 794 across the Lake Champlain bridge between Ticonderoga, N. Y., and Larabee's Point, Vermont, from the Delaware & Hudson connection at Addison Junction, 1905. — *Collection of Al Gayer*.

Many of the boxcars in busy Rutland yard, 1910, bear the New York Central herald as well as Rutland lettering, indicating the larger road's interest in its Vermont stepchild at the time.

Engine No. 1063 came to the Rutland from N.Y.C. soon after Central's interest in the Vermont line became notice-able. Engineer Chauncey Gould and Fireman William H. Moses, who appear in the cab here, both met their death in the same locomotive a year later at a double road cross-ing north of Petersburgh, spring, 1909.

The shuttle train from North Bennington stands near the tank on the south leg of the "Y" near the ball signal at North Bennington, 1907. No. 1058, built by Central Ver-mont at St. Albans, and the last vestige of CV's influence on the Rutland, was scrapped, May, 1909. Although the engine is still lettered Rutland, name boards on the coaches read New York Central Lines. — *Below: Collection of Howard R. Towsley.*

New piston valved ten-wheeler No. 2048 heads the north-bound *Flyer* at Ludlow. The expressman and his faithful steed await the Boston papers, 1903.

The 2049 looked mighty handsome in front of the Better Farming Special en route from Burlington to Boston, 1910. Practically the whole crew got into the picture as she waited on the Leicester Junction siding for the northbound *Green Mountain Flyer* to pass. — *Above: Collection of F. Hewett; below: Collection of Gordon Cutler.*

A spring freshet, 1903, undercut the roadbed of Chatham branch near North Petersburgh, dumping the local for Bennington, engine and all, into Little Hoosick River.

Somebody goofed on the meet orders. Result was a three-engine pile-up at Rutland fairgrounds, September 11, 1912, involving Engines No. 2039, 869, and 2401.

Those spring rains caused plenty of trouble. This 1908 mess was the result of a water-softened fill giving way under Engine No. 394, dumping her in the ravine with the hog train on top of her. Probably most of the people in nearby Ludlow had bacon for many months to come.

A station agent became deeply engrossed in a card game one day in September, 1912, so train crews were not informed of a meet they were supposed to make. Consequently the milk train and a passenger train met head-on at Soldier's Home crossing, resulting in the forlorn scene (below). No. 2044 appears to be a total loss, but the ten-year-old Manchester-built engine was rebuilt and finally scrapped in 1939.

Four-wheel bobber No. 43 landed jammed up against a tree at Brainard Station on the Chatham line, 1909, when she and a cut of cars got away from the local freight crew when they were switching at Old Chatham, several miles south and a couple of hundred feet higher.

4-4-0 No. 1063, heading the Chatham local, ended up in the Little Hoosick River near North Petersburgh, fall 1909. — *Above: Collection of C. H. Nash. Below: Collection of Paul Green.*

Burlington's big, modern station featured two long platforms with a closed-up passageway connecting the waiting room with the four station tracks. Its all-marble (Vermont, of course) interior was crowned with a resplendent plaster ceiling. This station opened January 23, 1916. Offices of the Central Vermont Power Corporation are now located here.

Chapter 8

Uncle Sam Takes Over

Close on the heels of the Panama Canal Act came another sad chapter, not only in the history of the Rutland but for all American railroads. It was World War I and the threatened breakdown of the nation's rail transportation system, resulting in the institution of the United States Railroad Administration in 1918. Under the strain of war and early official bungling which permitted almost indiscriminate use of government priorities, shippers created a needless car shortage in 1917. To straighten out the mess, President Wilson named William G. McAdoo director of the hurriedly-created government authority, with virtually unlimited powers over the operation of American railroads.

The Federal Control Act authorized the President to pay as just compensation to the railroads, a sum not exceeding the average annual operating income for the three previous years. Federal payments to the Rutland in its contract with the Director General amounted to $1,023,883 in the two years of operation. No dividends were declared, taxes were paid by the government, and the Rutland willingly placed a half million each year in the undivided profits.

The less said about the two-year existence of this official agency the better. It must be admitted that for the relatively short time of its existence, the Administration did manage to move a prodigious amount of war material, but at a terrific cost to the railroads it had seized. When the roads were turned back to their owners in 1920, they were practically wrecked, some previously fine railroads were on the verge of complete physical disintegration. The American railroad system came out of the

conflict bearing almost as many battle scars as the expeditionary forces in Europe.

The Rutland was no exception. Its captive cars had been shunted from hell to back over foreign lines, with none but the most urgent maintenance. A number of its locomotives, a good fleet of motive power by any standards at the beginning of the war for the purposes of a relatively small road, had been battered and worn in service beyond their capacities. It was a sad collection of near useless hulks that finally beat their weary way back to Rutland after the war ended. Two 0-8-0 switchers, Nos. 109 and 110, allotted to the Rutland and built by Alco in Pittsburgh, never reached home rails but worked for the duration in the NYC yards at Buffalo. Six USRA type Mikados, built in Schenectady, came directly to Vermont in 1918 to help the old veterans haul wartime tonnage across New York and through the Green Mountains. The Rutland shops, still plagued by war shortages of men and materials, resignedly began the job of trying to repair what was still repairable.

Upon cessation of the governmental operations in March of 1920 the Transportation Act was passed to help rejuvenate some of the railroads. Half the yearly compensation would be allotted, but for most lines, including the Rutland, this sum would be quickly soaked up by the rundown plant.

In summary, the war period was one of increased traffic accompanied by mounting costs. Some betterments of a permanent nature were made at government expense which no doubt saved later expenditures when they less easily could be afforded.

A Rutland flatcar carries the crated monument at Proctor. The rock was quarried in Vermont Marble Company's Colorado deposits, but was finished at the Proctor plant.

A southbound local on the Chatham branch, hauled by 2-6-0 No. 1881, stops at Petersburgh to unload barrels of soap for the local shirt factory. The sway-backed boxcar suggests the strain placed on railroad equipment by the demands of World War I.

The floating bridge across Lake Champlain between Ticonderoga and Larrabee's Point had a nasty habit of dumping cars into the lake with the least provocation. Here is the twisted floating section with two victims in the icy water. This incident undoubtedly contributed to the 1917 decision to discontinue operations over this span.

Engineer Con Sullivan rode to his death in the cab of ten-wheeler No. 52 on train 165, the northbound *Flyer*, March 14, 1920. A freight ran past an orderboard at Bartonsville, meeting him head-on at the mouth of Williams River, just above Bellows Falls. — *Below: Collection of Robert Adams.*

Despite her many leaks, old No. 44 faithfully brought the afternoon mail up to Burlington each day. Here she stands in Rutland, on a crisp January day, 1921, ready for her departure.

A group of Berlin schoolgirls wait to board the mixed train for Bennington, headed by 2-6-0 No. 1884. Business dropped off after this 1920 scene and trains down the Lebanon Valley discontinued their coaches five years later. — *Below: Collection of F. Hewett.*

Barely had the railroad begun to get back on its feet when the short but sharp recession of 1921 cut into revenues. But more important was a development that was taking place far to the west, in Detroit. Henry Ford's "tin lizzie" began to whip up the summer dust over the narrow, winding roads, and gas pumps blossomed on every main street from Chatham to Ogdensburg. Another upheaval was in the making, and this time the Rutland country was to be left in a lazy backwash.

The great industrial revolution had passed through its long, slow prelude, the war had introduced the second movement in the symphony of progress with a crashing crescendo; now the tempo quickened with an ever faster metallic beat. The American economy took on a wild urgency in its shift from an agricultural to an industrial base.

The Rutland had few factories in the sleepy little villages that dotted its route map. Its people were not for the most part factory hands but small independent farmers, purchasers but not producers of these marvels of the new mechanical age. Without their fully realizing it, the great surge of industrial progress was passing them by in high gear. True, there was still a demand for many of their basic products; car after car of lumber rolled off sidings from one end of the line to the other; solid trains of milk highballed down to the growing industrial cities; good Vermont marble went into bills of lading destined for the rising towers of commerce in a hundred cities — but not in Vermont.

Here and there a narrow strip of macadam covered the dust, creeping like a black snake over this hill and down that valley, freighted with a growing number of jolting, sputtering automobiles. With every mile of improved road, with every Star or Durant or Chevy or Ford that took its place as a gleaming symbol of pride in front of a Vermont home, a passenger deserted the Rutland (except when the weather was bad).

The bridge on the Addison branch which crossed Lake Champlain to connect with the Delaware & Hudson at Ticonderoga was declared unsafe in 1917. This structure had a rather complex moveable floating section similar to the original Rouses Point span but much shorter in overall length. It lay unused for six years while repairs were con-

templated. Finally, in 1923, it was dismantled and a mile of track removed back to Larrabees Point, now the stub end of the branch. With the elimination of the bridge went the memory of how John Page had forced the Vermont Central into its self-protecting lease of the Rutland a half century before.

With the improvement of the roads (largely with tax monies levied on the railroad) there also came an increasing number of trucks, reaching out from town to town in short-haul service. LCL freight began to shrink in proportion to the local passenger business, which passed its peak in 1924. The transportation of milk, however, was assuming ever greater importance during the mid-twenties. Milk was one commodity that Rutland's operating territory produced in quantity, and with a growing market demand and improving prices, the dairy farms of Vermont and Northern New York expanded their production rapidly. By 1923, milk traffic alone brought in over one million dollars a year in revenue, and largely accounted for the Rutland's credit balance of over five million dollars. Solid trains of milk reefers, running on special schedules, roared through the Otter Creek valley into Rutland. There they were quickly split into sections for Boston and New York.

After the period of readjustment following the war, the Rutland managed very well to adjust to changing circumstances. The Interstate Commerce Commission ordered an increase in both freight and passenger rates that more than offset the 25 percent drop in freight business and the 15 percent decline in passenger fares following the war. At the end of 1923 revenues had jumped to $6,695,000 leaving almost a half million for the surplus account. While the operating ratio had dropped from the high of 103, at the end of the war, to 84, it was still uncomfortably high and no dividends were paid.

In the first five years of the 'twenties, hundreds of outworn cars were replaced, and in 1925 three heavy Pacifics were purchased from the Schenectady Locomotive Works for fast, heavy work in milk service, to be supplemented by three more in 1929. These engines were kept busy with the growing white flood of fluid milk, the frequently-scheduled varnish trains, and the special excursions that marked the era. Americans were prospering; they were learning to travel, and like lemmings, were seized on occasion to move en masse in crowded, ancient coaches, clutching their squirming progeny and shoebox lunches.

But the trend of regular passenger travel was changing. The operation of passenger equipment down over the old Lebanon Springs line to Chatham had never been a successful service, even during the earlier short-lived New York, Boston & Montreal experiment. Now, pitifully few passengers embarked on the daily train; frequently its crew enjoyed sole occupancy of the creaking single combine as it shuffled through the sparsely settled valley with an ancient 4-4-0 engine up front.

Early in 1925, the Rutland proposed to abandon the service, which had been losing heavily. Such a howl arose from the people of the valley that the railroad, with considerable reluctance, turned to the bus business as a measure to reduce the deficit on the admittedly inadequate and unpatronized stretch of line. The Rutland Transportation Corporation was chartered in 1925 with a capitalization of $30,000, owned entirely by the railroad and started operation the following year between Bennington and Chatham with a pair of primitive Yellow Coach buses. The daily mixed train disappeared from the timecard, to be replaced by an alternate-day freight. According to company estimates more than $15,000 a year was saved by these changes in service even though the buses themselves lost slightly. But even with these economies, the Chatham line was never an asset to the railroad, and even the bus service was discontinued five years later when its losses became overwhelming.

The Lebanon Springs had been a poverty-stricken railroad from the beginning, with hardly a hamlet of more than 500 people on its line. Its southerly connection, the New York & Harlem, never developed as a major link to the metropolis, and after it was acquired by the New York Central, sank rapidly back to the status of a meandering country branch while the bulk of its through traffic went over to the high iron and fast running of the Hudson River division to Albany and Troy. With the Fitchburg's acquisition of the Troy & Boston line, the Rutland found a friendly and co-

operative connection at White Creek, and increasing tonnage began to move through that interchange and at Petersburgh Junction. The varnish was turned over to the Boston & Maine at White Creek for the run to Troy, and from there to New York as part of a New York Central consist.

The 53-mile Chatham road became a streak of rust, but it would be 27 long years before the Rutland could rid itself completely of this almost useless appendage. Milk train No. 88 used the line until the end but neither dropped nor picked up cars en route. There was negligible on-line business, and what through freight did go south could be rerouted (and eventually was) along with No. 88.

The year of 1926 was a good one by the Rutland's standards, the best in a decade. Net income added up to $565,575 on a gross business of more than $6,750,000. The operating ratio was down to a healthy 81.8 percent. Milk traffic hit another million-dollar year; general freight tonnage held high, and even passenger traffic was declining at a reduced rate. In spite of a few poor years, the Rutland had enjoyed a quarter century of well-being unparalleled in its annals.

From *The People's Railway Guide*, December, 1919.

Rutland Railroad.

MONTREAL, BURLINGTON, RUTLAND & HOOSICK JCT. 7

Ms	Ar 9 28 19 Lv	A.M.	A.M.	P.M.	P.M.	P.M.	P.M.	A.M.	P.M.	P.M.	A.M.	A.M	A.M.
0	Montreal		*8 25			*7 40							
50	Rouses Point		10 02			9 22							
54	Alburgh		10 24		*8 25								
61	Isle La Motte		10f35		f8 35								
66	North Hero		10f45		f8 46								
74	Grand Isle		10f59		f8 58								
78	South Hero		11f05		9 05								
91	Burlington		11 31		9 30	10 41							
91	Burlington	†8 00	11 38	3f45	9 40	10 51	5§10						
98	Shelburne	8 14	11 51	4 00	9 55		5 25						
103	Charlotte	8 23		4 14	10 06		5 37						
107	N. Ferrisb'g	8 32		4 23	10 15		5 45						
111	Ferrisburg	f8 38		4f28	10/22		5f52						
113	Vergennes	8 45	12 16	4 39	10 28		5 58						
118	N. Haven Jct	8 56		4 50	10 38		6f10						
123	Beldens	f9 06		5f00			6 18						
125	Middlebury	9 11	12 38	5 06	10 52		6 25						
132	Salisbury	9 26		5f24	11/06		6f37						
137	Leicester Jct	9 35		5 32	11/14		6 46						
142	Brandon	9 48	1 05	5 44	11 26		6 57						
149	Pittsford	10 01		5 56	11/38		7 10						
153	Proctor	10 10	1 23	6 04	11/47		7 17						
157	Cen. Rutland	10f10		6 11			7/25						
159	Rutland	10 25	1 35	6 15	12 00	12 33	7 30						
159	Rutland	10 35	1 45	6 35	12 45	12 45	7 40						
165	Clarendon	10f48		6 47			7 55						
158	Wallingford	10 56	f2 02	6 55			8 04						
172	S. Wallingf'd	11f05		7f02			8/12						
177	Danby	11 16		7 23			8 21						
181	North Dorset	11f24		7f35			8f29						
184	East Dorset	11 31		7 50			8 38						
190	Manchester	11 44	2 38	8 05	1 38	1 38	8 51						
196	Sunderland	11f55		8 15			9f07						
199	Arlington	12 05	f2 54	8 24			9 12						
204	Shaftsbury	12 15		8 35			9f24						
209	S. Shaftsbury	12 24		8 45			9 35						
211	N. Benningt'n	12 30	3 15	8 50	2 18	2 18	9 40						
214	White Creek												
	Troy	1 45	4 15	9 55	3 20	3 20	1045						
	Albany Ar	2 30	4 55	1027	4 00	4 00	1127						

b Will stop to leave passengers or take passengers on signal for New York from or for Alburgh or points beyond.   c Stops on signal for boat connection.   e Waits five minutes for boat connection.   f Stops Tuesdays and Saturdays.

No. 2075 stands in Rutland, ready to take the passenger train to Troy, just after World War I. Rutland lettering has replaced New York Central Lines on the tank. — *Collection of Gordon Cutler.*

Switcher No. 110, Alco-Pittsburgh-built 0-8-0 worked for New York Central in Buffalo during World War I by order of United States Railroad Administration before coming to Vermont. In due time she finally reached Rutland where she makes up the afternoon freight for Bellows Falls. — *Jim Shaughnessy.*

Windblown ice on Lake Champlain pushed the Rouses Point trestle out of alignment. A westbound, pulled by Mike No. 33, unable to straighten it out, went off into the icy water at 11 p.m., April 2, 1920. There the big 2-8-2 lay out of reach for over a year. It took heavy wreckers from the Delaware & Hudson and the Boston & Maine to lift her clear of the water. To accommodate the cranes in a stable position for the job it was necessary to erect two spur trestles out from the main structure. Water ran from the Mikado's firebox as she was lifted from the lake. A light Rutland crane was able to lift No. 33's tank, lettered with a large U. S., from the water. — *All collection of Gordon Cutler.*

Proctor's usual bucolic peace was brutally shattered November 3, 1927. Weeks of autumn rains had swollen Otter Creek into a rampaging torrent which tore at everything in its way. When floating trees and debris tangled to dam the flow at Proctor's highway bridge, the current took the easiest available course—down the Rutland right-of-way. Here it can be seen overwhelming the freight shed, wrenching the station, undermining the tracks. — *Above: Jim Shaughnessy.*

Chapter 9

Long Meet at Proctor

It was raining as Train No. 88 rumbled out of the Alburg yard one day in 1927. That in itself was nothing of note; it had been raining off and on for nearly a month, reducing the fallen October leaves on the hillsides to a sodden brown mush spread over the saturated earth. They could hold no more, and now this fresh, slashing onslaught ran swiftly down in growing, icy rivulets eating at the loosening gullies, down into bloated, mud-dirtied brooks swelling up to their banks.

Engineer Henry J. LaParle flicked a glance back along his train of dull green milk reefers, rain-glistened now; he could barely see the ancient combine swaying on their tail, rocking gently on the spongy roadbed. He settled on his seat, eyes squinted against the lashing storm that seemed to part like a reluctant wall over the pilot. He reached for the whistle cord automatically before the familiar board slid into view, hooting the two long and two short in plenty of time before the big drivers slammed over the crossing. With visibility nearly zero, it was well to give any driver crazy enough to be out in this storm an extra second or two of time.

The heavy Pacific, No. 81, was a good steamer and Fireman Sam Langill had her almost to the pop; he checked his fire and clambered into the left-hand seat, blinking a little as he adjusted his vision to the spume of driving rain breaking into mist above the smokebox. As they drummed down through the islands and across the long causeway below South Hero, the train seemed to be almost a giant leviathan of the deep, sliding over the surface of the lake in atmosphere almost as liquid as Champlain's depths.

As he shut off to roll into the Burlington yard limit at the requisite twenty miles per hour, LaParle glanced down at the raging Winooski River while the big Pacific rumbled across the long steel trestle. Far below, the normally placid stream was a surging mass of dull yellow froth beating against the stone piers.

"She's come up a lot since yesterday!" he called across the cab.

Fireman Sam Langill flicked a glance down at the flood reaching hungrily for the bridge, and nodded. "A lot higher!" he agreed.

Through the early afternoon they worked southward, the milk manifest growing longer at each trackside creamery. And with each addition, Engine 81 found it just a little harder to start the heavy train on the slick rails. LaParle used sand sparingly; he would need all of it in the dome by the time he crested Mount Holly for the long downgrade to the Boston & Maine at Bellows Falls. Number 88 was 15 minutes off the timecard when it rolled out of Leicester Junction, and there was scant hope for making any of it up in the remainder of the run. Water spurted from under every tie as the Pacific rolled her manifest, now 22 laden cars, southward at reduced speed. Visibility worsened with every mile; the slashing rain seemed like almost a solid wall parting over the headlight as the engine nosed into it. Placid brooks winding along the grade, where trout fishermen waved on summer afternoons, had now become sullen, menacing torrents.

At Proctor station the order board was up and LaParle ground his train to a stop. Normally, Train 88 highballed through Proctor, with No. 65, the

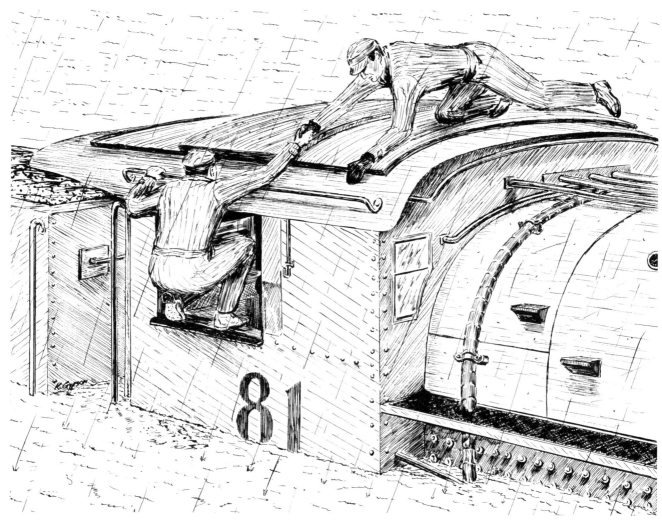

Fireman Sam Langill helps hogger Henry LaParle to the relative safety of the cab roof as flood water climbs higher and higher around the ill-fated milk train on Proctor siding. — *Ken Gypsom.*

Green Mountain Flyer, going into the hole on the passing track south of the station. Milk manifests got priority over everything on the Rutland, and in addition, all southbound trains had superior rights. Today, this procedure was to be reversed. The dispatcher at Rutland ordered Train 88 into the passing track to wait for the *Flyer,* reported late out of Rutland. The milk hotshot waited for two hours after it rolled off the high iron at 4:20; two hours while the torrent continued unabated. Water crept up to the ties, finally slid over the rails and began to rise around the quiet drivers. Roaring Otter Creek, now well over its banks, found a new and easier course down along the Rutland rails, plunging through the narrow overpass bridge at Proctor like a torrent through a millrace.

Two hours later, the drenched agent waded out to the combine and handed up copies of a new order; Number 88 was to back out of the passing track and up into the Proctor yard. The rear-end brakeman climbed forward over the slipping tops to deliver the head-end copy with the admonition, "Take it easy!" After what seemed like an eternity, his lantern waved the backup from the combine's platform. LaParle fed steam gently into the cylinders, then shut off quickly almost before the slack had bunched. To the rear, the bodiless lantern was waving a frantic washout. In this case it was no misnomer. Three cars ahead of the combine were weaving drunkenly above the flood; as the crew watched they settled lower in the brown water. There was no grade left under the ties and

Pacific No. 81 and her milk train are helplessly stranded just south of Proctor after the waters of Otter Creek have receded. With ballast washed away and tracks undermined, engine and cars sag drunkenly.

the middle cars of the train rested on suspended rails in the rushing, gnawing flood. Engine 26, performing switching duties at the Clarendon & Pittsford interchange at Florence, four miles up the line, was ordered down to help. By the time she chuffed into Proctor, water sloshed high up on her drivers and threatened to invade her firebox. Her headlight picked out two figures clinging to the rear railing on the coach, the rear-end crew hanging desperately to the shuddering, canting car. Ahead, several reefers hung shadow-like out over the water; the whole train was writhing like a tortured snake. Couplings touched for a brief moment, and the two soaked, shivering trainmen scrambled across to the engine's pilot and back over the running boards to the relative safety of the cab. Number 26 reversed quickly and snorted out. Nothing could be done for Train 88.

At the head end, the fire died in Engine 81 as the icy water hissed over the grates. For a minute a ghostly cloud of steam hung low beside the cab,

then wafted away into the darkness. Lights bobbed on the distant hillside that now marked the shoreline. LaParle and Langill huddled on their seatboxes as water crept up over the deck. When it threatened even those perches they climbed out on the running boards, then up over the cooling boiler to the cab roof. Behind the dead engine, cars teetered crazily, then one by one laid over into the flood like a row of dominos. The tender gave a sickening lurch that jolted the engine, began to slither to the left and then halted with the coupling intact. Water broke over it to lap at the tops of the cab windows, all that remained clear now was the rounded roof, a bit of the sand dome and the top of the stack.

A lantern glowed out on the water; the watchers on the bank had nailed together some timbers to form a crude raft, and now two volunteers rode the flimsy craft down the current as willing hands paid out rope. There was no controlling it, and there was no hauling it back against the current. The two would-be rescuers spent the night cling-

page 137

ing in a clump of trees and were rescued themselves in the morning.

Past midnight another craft, this time a rowboat, drifted down alongside the dead locomotive and LaParle and Langill clambered aboard. Their ordeal was over.

☆ ☆ ☆

The eastbound *Green Mountain Flyer* rolled out of the Rutland station at 2:26 P.M. into a wall of blinding rain. The standing slow order was superfluous; what little was moving on the Rutland line was creepingly regulated by the elements. Inside the glistening coaches it was warm and dry, though the handful of late luncheon customers in the diner commented acidly on the jolting series of stops and starts that slopped their coffee on the white linen cloths. Up ahead, visibility was nearly zero; the burning headlight beam was lost in the welter only a few yards ahead of the pilot. The train labored in an agonizingly slow climb into the grade up toward Mount Holly, the heavy consist

dragging like a dead weight on the straining engine. Down below, the passengers caught occasional glimpses of the flooding Otter Creek through the rain-sluiced windows. The *Flyer* crawled slowly on upward, through West Clarendon and Cuttingsville. Two hours later it labored into the little station at East Wallingford, 13 miles out of Rutland. Even in the coaches, the angry roar of Mill River, rampaging down the narrow mountain valley became an insistent, terrifying sound. Two trainmen, rain dripping in rivulets from their glistening black slickers, went through the cars with telegraph blanks.

"We may be here a while," they told the inquiring passengers with the unperturbed noncommittal manner that seems to be the hallmark of trainmen everywhere. A few, sensing that this would be no ordinary delay, scribbled out messages. The rest, glancing out into the gathering darkness placed their confidence in the competency of the men responsible for the train, and settled back with their magazines.

When the water had receded Proctor was still there, the worse for wear. The stone abutments of the overpass just above the station formed a sort of nozzle directing the rushing waters with a maximum of force to wash the ballast right out from under the tracks, with the results seen here. The rails gave way under the milk reefers of Train No. 88 on Proctor siding, awaiting the northbound *Flyer* which was never to arrive.

As for the train crew, confidence in themselves was being badly shaken. Below the tiny station, the little town of East Wallingford was a scene of carnage. The rampaging river had sliced the town in two, buildings disintegrating as they slammed down through the narrow valley. Of more concern to the railroadmen at the moment was the hungry gnawing of the raging water along the foot of the embankment on which the *Flyer* rested. The right of way was wet and spongy underfoot when one of them dropped off to slog his way to the station. Inside, the operator hunched down in the yellow light of the bay window, listening to the incessant chatter of the sounder. A sodden trackman huddled near the pot-bellied stove. "Guess we'll be here all night, watching things," he muttered disconsolately.

Another trackman slammed in out of the storm, wiping his dripping face. "Slide up the line. Track's covered!" he reported laconically. The operator cut in his key and rattled the message to the harassed dispatcher. In a moment the sounder clattered and the operator's pencil raced out the order on a 19 form: "Train 164 back with caution to Rutland". The waiting trainman picked up the flimsies and plunged out, pausing to hand a copy up to the cab before he swung aboard. In a moment he reappeared and ducked between the tender and the head-end car. There was the sharp report as the air hoses parted, and the engine eased forward, paused only long enough for the passing track switch to lock over, then clanked slowly back to the main and nosed against the Pullman at the rear end. Behind the tender, a trainman relined the switch for the main and started on down the track, lantern bobbing dimly through the murk. Air hissed in release and the *Flyer* inched backward at a bare crawl down the long grade, creeping slowly over the high bridge where Mill River raged in the darkness below, its angry roar booming up out of the narrow valley. Suddenly the bobbing lantern took on a definite pattern of motion — a frantic washout signal — and the train slammed to a jolting stop. Dimly, the lantern revealed a mass of mud and brush, oozed down from a side cut to completely obliterate the right of way. The *Flyer* certainly not living up to her name this night, was again perched on a fill.

Fifty feet below, water lapped at the base, seeping and cutting. The crew held a hurried consultation; this was obviously no place to sit for the night.

A few minutes before, they had crept down through the hamlet of Cuttingsville, and under the circumstances, that appeared to be the best spot for the *Flyer* to bed down for the night. Pushing upgrade the engine leaned into the pressing load. Heavy exhaust barked once, twice, then stuttered as the drivers spun on the greasy rails. Again and again the straining engine lost her footing until at last the string of varnish began to roll reluctantly up the grade. They tied her down at the Cuttingsville station, there to rest for an hour until another muttered conference shifted her cautiously back downgrade for a few hundred feet. No one told the passengers — no need for useless panic — that the rails were spreading as the roadbed evaporated under them. Down toward Rutland, where they were supposed to be rolling to safety, 200 feet of rail hung suspended in the air near East Clarendon.

Dawn found the marooned passengers and crew safe but hungry. The last remnants of food quickly disappeared from the diner, and the express agent checked his manifest. Oysters and haddock comprised a breakfast and lunch that constituted a limited but nourishing menu. A quick check revealed that the train was indeed marooned; the main highway up the valley was completely gone, and the country roads over the hills were impassable quagmires. During the early afternoon, volunteer forage parties of passengers and crewmen canvassed a few nearby farms, returning with enough food for a sketchy meal or two. By this time it was evident that there was no immediate danger to the train, and by Friday afternoon the deluge had slacked off. During Saturday afternoon, a work train chuffed cautiously up to the stalled train to take off passengers, and by Saturday evening the *Green Mountain Flyer*, dead engine coupled to the rear-end car, stood cold and empty on the hillside above the scene of raw desolation.

A scant half dozen miles to the east at the crest of Mount Holly, the westbound *Flyer*, from Boston, due into Rutland at 2:55 P.M. on Thursday, still reposed in solitude, her passengers removed by relays of automobiles laboring through the mud.

Washouts like these challenged Rutland repair crews all along the line. Stretches of track dangling over space, like the 225-foot section *(above)* two and a half miles north of Proctor and this other huge unsupported stretch just outside the same town were only two of the many grim sights in the wake of the deluge. — *Above: Collection of R. L. Church.*

Main Track

The Connecticut River, also on a rampage that fateful 1927 November, ripped through Bellows Falls, inundating the engine house and threatening to wash the nearby power canal bridge from its piers. Cars laden with dirt were spotted on it to weight it down. Waters swirled about the station in an alarming fashion. — *Above: Collection of R. L. Church.*

On Thursday afternoon at the first firm sign of impending disaster the dispatcher at Rutland had cancelled every train not already moving on the line. As reports began to pour in, it became increasingly evident that this was no local difficulty, all northern New England was in the throes of one of its worst calamities.

Every stream in the state was running wild, slashing through villages and sweeping up isolated farmhouses, carrying them down to smash out bridges with fiendish impartiality. By the time reports from stations all along the railroad had been gathered into the headquarters at Rutland, it was evident that nothing would move over the line for days to come. For that matter, hardly a wheel was turning on any railroad in the entire state of Vermont. As the flood roared out of the mountains into the Connecticut valley, that major river had risen rapidly, and the Boston & Maine went out of operation as its tracks and the Rutland terminal yards at Bellows Falls disappeared.

Receiver and General Superintendent L. G. Morphy took charge at the Rutland headquarters as soon as it became apparent that the situation was going out of control. General Manager French assumed responsibility on the Bellows Falls division, which was to suffer the worst damage of all. By Friday afternoon the deluge lessened and the harried executives could begin to assay some of the damage. Their findings were staggering. Out of 413 route miles on the railroad, 263 were useless. Three hundred and fifty-six separate washouts and slides had either carried away or buried more than 17 miles of right of way. The 450 foot, three-span truss bridge over the Winooski River north of Burlington had collapsed into a tangled mass of wreckage hundreds of feet downstream.

Down at Bellows Falls, the terminal yards were a twisted mass of undermined wreckage. A third of the roundhouse floor and a good portion of its walls were gone. The major bridge at Bellows Falls had been saved when French ordered a string of cars laden with coal and marble run out of the yard and spotted on it. Train 88 lay wrecked at Proctor where the passenger station and freight house were undermined. The east and west-bound *Green Mountain Flyers* were completely

marooned on Mount Holly. The Rutland yard was jammed with traffic held there when the line began to disintegrate. A score of bridges had been destroyed, damaged or weakened. It would cost more than $750,000 to put the line back in operation. (The estimated loss in revenue for 17 days was $285,000.)

As soon as the magnitude of the disaster became evident, the Rutland's managers swung into action. Every available man in the Maintenance of Way department was called out, and these were augmented by emergency recruits from the shops, freight houses and even the offices. Organized into work gangs, they were detailed to work out of Rutland toward Middlebury on the north and Bellows Falls and Chatham on the south. Other detached gangs started their seemingly hopeless job at Proctor, Brandon, Leicester and Middlebury, and from Summit down to Bellows Falls, doing what they could in the wake of the slowly receding water.

A call for help went out, and the New York Central dispatched two track gangs of one hundred men each, moving work trains as far as they could go, repairing the trouble spot, then moving ahead a few yards to repeat the process. Men from along the line volunteered and were quickly signed on. Within 24 hours, nearly 1,300 men and 22 work train crews were swarming out to do battle with the elements, laboring day and night to get their railroad back in operation. A New York Central pile driver moved onto the Chatham division, repaired the damage at Bridge 44 near Petersburgh Junction while crews heaped temporary fill and relined the twisted track to the north, and gradually worked up to Proctor by November 15.

North of Burlington, crews swung into action as the water dropped on November 6, working around the clock on temporary cribbing. In two weeks the temporary bridge was complete and the first train rolled over it on November 20.

As Thursday's flood receded, Rutland work trains used the little-damaged Clarendon & Pittsford tracks to bypass the wreck at Proctor, coming back on the Rutland line at Florence. The little C & P locomotives labored mightily; Rutland motive power being too big and heavy to negotiate the short line's light trackage.

By Tuesday following the flood, limited service was restored on the Burlington-Middlebury segment of the line, with a mixed train making the round trip every day. A work train started up the Bellows Falls division, working its way westward toward East Clarendon. The first night, it managed to make nine miles out of the 38 assigned to it.

While the Rutland struggled to get back into operation, the Delaware & Hudson stepped into the breach, handling passenger equipment and perishable manifests down from Rouses Point to Albany. On the 14th, the Delaware & Hudson moved the first freight into the city of Rutland over the old Rutland & Whitehall line, and a couple of hours later the Clarendon & Pittsford's little teakettles started to wrestle a total of sixty cars off the Rutland main above Proctor. On the same day, the repair gangs working south from Rutland and north from Bennington met, closing the

last gap on the Chatham division, and emergency freight began to move.

The road was still in trouble at East Clarendon, where a fill 425 feet long and seventy feet high had simply disappeared. Every available car was rushed to the monumental job of dumping more than 25,000 yards of new fill. The still-high river nibbled menacingly at the loose material; in desperation, Morphy issued new orders. Crews coupled on to a string of condemned cars in the Rutland yard and they crawled on their last trip up the grade toward Mount Holly, easing slowly out on the shaky fill. Waiting crews jacked them over and they crashed 70 feet into the river below, until 30 of them lay wrecked along the fill as an effective breakwall, protecting the road they had served so well for so long.

On the twentieth, a strange manifest pulled out of the Rutland yard and crept north via the Clarendon & Pittsford. Head-end cars and boxcars were loaded with an accumulation of mail, express and LCL freight; the Rutland was struggling back!

After the staggering work of reconstruction and clean-up, the *Flyer* continued to make its daily stop in Proctor. Here

Ten-Wheeler No. 78 slows down, the conductor waiting on the steps. The Rutland rolled once more. — *John Pickett.*

Floods were to hit the Rutland again, but caused much less damage in 1947 than they had 20 years before. East Creek, just out of Rutland, took out the railroad's two-track bridge and the adjacent highway structure. Here the Rut-land's hook, assisted by heavy equipment from Delaware & Hudson, places a new single-track deck girder over the creek to replace the old flood-wrecked span.— *Both: Rutland Railway.*

Even during the late 1930's, when the Rutland's future was badly clouded, an occasional double-header was required to move the spotty tonnage. Here Consolidations No. 23 and 26 team up to get a freight out of Rutland on a run to the north.

In the days of steam, Rutland terminal was a busy place, which sometimes seemed to be virtually an operating museum for old engines. The line-up in June 1949 wasn't too bad, though, with 4-6-0 No. 74, 2-8-2 No. 32 taking coal, 0-6-0 switcher No. 105, and Consolidation No. 31 all preparing for the day's work. — *Below: Robert F. Collins.*

Chapter 10

The Panama Canal Act was passed in 1915, legislation that in the stroke of a pen almost wrecked the Rutland, to the considerable benefit of the New York Central, after which the company slid into a gradual decline. Since the Central was the majority stockholder in the Rutland, it was legally interpreted that the New York Central, through its control of the Rutland Transportation Company, was operating shipping lines in direct competition with its own rails. The only recourse was to dispose of the little Ogdensburg-Chicago ships. New York Central happily took the added tonnage, left literally high and dry, to its own rails.

The Rutland's earnings immediately began to show a bad and worsening case of anemia. With only light on-line patronage, the Rutland had flourished on the volume of tonnage flowing east through Ogdensburg, and the return business destined for the Midwest out of New England, largely high-tariff manufactured goods.

The increase in traffic brought by World War I quickly concealed the general declining trend but was relatively short lived — a fortunate event for all, but not for the Rutland.

The change in the general economy, as it mushroomed in the postwar period, did not have the effect on the Rutland it had in other parts of the industrializing country. Revenues and traffic were up during this period by standards the Rutland had been accustomed to but again were all too short lived.

As the depression deepened following the crash of 1929, the Rutland managed to stave off disaster for a time. The road was in a strong finan-cial position at the turn of the decade in spite of the costly 1927 flood. Heavy previous investment in government bonds provided a financial backlog, and by drawing on this reserve the road was able to meet the interest payments on its indebtedness for six years. In the depression years following 1928 income hit the toboggan and crashed into a jumbled thicket of deficits.

By 1937, it was necessary to approach the first mortgage bondholders with the bad news that full payment of the interest charges was an impossibility, and to present to them a plan for reduced payments of interest over a period of years. The shadow of approaching insolvency loomed like a dark thunder cloud on the Rutland's horizon. Income had risen slightly in 1936 over the previous year's figure, making the deficit only half of that in 1935, but costs were rising and the prospects did not point to any increases that would eliminate the red ink from the ledgers.

The reduced interest payment plan was accepted, but in the face of steadily declining traffic and sharply reduced earnings, even the modified payment plan was doomed to quick failure. With the tenacity so typical of its state and its people, the road hung on desperately, trying every expedient to keep alive. Operating funds reached such a terrifying low that on many occasions if checks were presented for redemption on the date issued, there would be no money to cover them.

The inevitable was only delayed, not evaded; on May 5, 1938, at the order of U. S. District Judge Harland B. Howe of Burlington, the Rutland passed into receivership. George L. R. French, Vice Pres-

With severe winters the rule in Vermont and northern New York, the Rutland was obliged to take in stride its annual problems involving snow. The big snowplow in front of Consolidation No. 31, working north from Chatham on the "Corkscrew Division" waits in Stephentown while the crew thaws out over a cup of "joe" in the Stephentown House. — *Collection of F. Hewett.*

The first real storm of winter is blowing in off the lake this December day, 1949. Ten-Wheeler No. 73 with the six-car southbound *Flyer* is already hitting 35 m.p.h. at the south end of Burlington yard. — *Robert F. Collins.*

ident of the ailing road and veteran railroad man, was appointed Receiver. This action was taken only after the New England Coal and Coke Company of Boston filed a bill of complaint for the protection of itself and other creditors. The court also granted an injunction preventing any creditor from interfering with the operation of the road, and thereby jeopardize any chances of their eventually being paid. The Rutland's coffers were stuffed with bills but not greenbacks.

No time was wasted in reducing expenses. First, management payroll was drastically reduced by eliminating many positions, including president and his staff, general manager, assistant superintendent, claim agent, and more. Despite an almost forty percent decrease in management salaries, conditions were still critical, as the unofficial payroll remained unchanged. Wages were at an all time high as a result of a nine percent increase granted to all railroad employees in 1937. At the National Railway Wage Conference in Chicago, negotiations were under way for a fifteen percent cut, and Rutland officials were hoping relief would be forthcoming.

By early July Receiver Louis G. Morphy petitioned the court for permission to discontinue operations as revenues had become insufficient to continue. Receiver French had resigned and was replaced by Morphy, former chief engineer of the line.

At a public hearing held July 19 at the order of the court, general counsel Edwin C. Lawrence noted that $63,000 in taxes was owed to the state, $100,000 in other bills was outstanding, and there was no money available. Piled on this was a foreclosure petition from the trustees of the bondholders who would certainly junk the line and salvage what they could. Judge Howe pressed for an employee wage cut as the only solution to reduce expenses enough to continue operation.

The employees stood firm, feeling that management was trying to put something over on them, pointing out that the railroad's plight was none of their doing in the first place. They considered they had just grievances against poor management and absentee ownership. Judge Howe countered by cutting another $20,000 off the executive payroll that was practically a skeleton already.

At the close of the hearings, near the end of the month, Howe immediately notified the bondholders representatives to be ready to take over the Rutland in a few days. This would mean certain abandonment, for the bondholders had already said they would junk the line. Refusal of the employees to accept the pay cuts which would reduce expenses to a point where operating costs could be paid from revenues left no alternative but abandonment.

The court had ordered successor-Receiver Morphy to withhold fifteen percent of the employees' wages as the last hope of survival. This amount would temporarily build up as a lien against the property, second only to the unpaid taxes. The court stated that this amount would be paid back to the men when and if future conditions permitted. Judge Howe did not have the power to force such action but suggested that they voluntarily accept the plan as their share in helping to keep the company alive. August 4 would be the day the court would turn the line over to the bondholders, and oblivion would certainly follow.

The city of Rutland was stricken with gloom. The employees and their union had the fate of the line placed squarely in their laps. More than eight hundred men depended on the railroad for their living, and abandonment would mean permanent irreparable economic damage to the city and western Vermont in general. As the deadline approached everyone waited with bated breath.

The bold black headline on the Rutland *Herald's* August 4th edition must have brought many sighs of relief, if not actual exclamations of joy:

"RUTLAND RAILROAD SAVED FROM ABANDONMENT AS TRUCE IS REACHED IN WAGE DISPUTE."

The evening before, Receiver Morphy announced the union representatives had agreed under protest to accept the wage withholding plan and stick to their jobs.

The Rutland was saved! — at least for the present.

The problem of permanent rehabilitation could now be tackled with careful, deliberate planning. The major crisis was past, but a long pull remained

'Save the Rutland' Club

We are members of this Club and as members we are willing to cooperate and support a movement to make the citizens of Rutland and of the State of Vermont realize that we have a vital question before us. The following are our resolutions:

1. That we will wear the button of our club.

2. That we will talk about the railroad and thereby help to pass along the good word that our movement is going ahead to support the road.

3. That we will use the road whenever possible, but if we cannot do this we will help to recommend the use of the railroad to our friends.

4. That we will try to get other citizens of our city to join our club.

Supporters of the Rutland wore badges and signed pledges as tokens of their determined efforts to avert liquidation of the line which was threatened in the late 1930's.

ahead to enable the line to regain both its traffic and its earning power.

During the first half of the year, when it appeared more than likely the line would be abandoned, many businessmen and interested persons realized the gravity of the situation. The most logical way to keep the railroad going seemed to be with increased patronage that would ease the heavy financial burden. With this avowed intention, more than fifty men met on a hot July evening in the Rutland Chamber of Commerce and formed the Rutland Railroad Cooperating Traffic Association. To build enough highways adequately to fill the transportation gap created by abandonment of the Rutland would cost between ten and twelve million dollars. This would be reflected both in added shipping charges and in much higher taxes to the local businessmen.

After the August 4th triumph the organization, called the "Save the Rutland Club", began a vigorous campaign complete with pledges, membership buttons, parades, and advertising to solicit more business and actual donations to help the railroad back to its feet. One of the most effective pieces of promotion was a canvas-topped wagon pulled by a team of oxen displaying a sign "Shall we go back to this?" as it plodded about the streets of Rutland. Businessmen and citizens of western Vermont responded to the question by pledging over $12,000. Even the little city itself helped by subscribing $1000 in cash and forgiving a $2500 water bill the railroad had owed.

The Association's next step was to seek tax relief for the railroad, pointing out that it owed the State of Vermont $115,000 in back taxes and was technically faced with an additional one hundred dollars a day fine since April for non-payment. Almost a like amount, in addition, was owed in New York State.

Two alternatives were possible: either abate the taxes completely or cut the property valuation from 10 million to 1 million. The Traffic Association seemed to feel the second was the more practical and feasible and concentrated on that goal. After preliminary conferences with Governor Aiken and state tax officials, pointing out the still-critical financial status of the road, the Association, along with Chamber of Commerce and

Carload Service Chart

indicating day of arrival and delivery on minimum time schedules, but subject to change as conditions of operation warrant. The service indicated is based on most direct routes in connection with the Rutland Railroad.

From: Boston, Cambridge, Lawrence, Lowell, Watertown, Fitchburg, Springfield, Holyoke, Greenfield, Massachusetts; Nashua, Claremont and Keene, N. H.; Brattleboro, Springfield, Windsor, Vermont and many intermediate points.

To:

Rutland, Vt.	next A. M.	Birmingham, Ala.	6th A. M.
Burlington, Vt.	next noon	New Orleans, La.	6th A. M.
Detroit, Mich.	3rd noon	Little Rock, Ark.	6th A. M.
Toledo, Ohio	4th A. M.	Aberdeen, S. D.	6th A. M.
Columbus, Ohio	4th A. M.	Tulsa, Okla.	5th A. M.
Springfield, Ohio	4th A. M.	Oklahoma City, Okla.	6th A. M.
Cincinnati, Ohio	4th A. M.	Dallas, Texas	6th A. M.
Chicago, Ill.	4th A. M.	Galveston, Texas	7th A. M.
Indianapolis, Ind.	4th A. M.	El Paso, Texas	7th A. M.
St. Louis, Mo.	4th noon	Phoenix, Ariz.	8th A. M.
Louisville, Ky.	5th A. M.	Denver, Colo.	6th A. M.
Green Bay, Wis.	5th A. M.	Butte, Mont.	8th A. M.
Kansas City, Mo.	5th A. M.	Salt Lake City, Utah	7th A. M.
Omaha, Nebr.	5th A. M.	Spokane, Wash.	9th A. M.
St. Paul, Minn.	5th A. M.	Seattle, Wash.	9th A. M.
Minneapolis, Minn.	5th A. M.	Portland, Ore.	9th A. M.
Duluth, Minn.	5th A. M.	San Francisco, Calif.	9th A. M.
Memphis, Tenn.	5th A. M.	Los Angeles, Calif.	9th A. M.

Comparable Service to Many Additional Points

The time shown is not guaranteed and is subject to change without notice.

RUTLAND RAILROAD COMPANY
(L. G. Morphy, Receiver)
TRAFFIC DEPARTMENT AND AGENCIES

RUTLAND, VT.
Phone Rutland 1270
R. F. BOHMAN, Chief Traffic Officer, Rutland, Vt.
W. E. NAVIN, General Freight Agent, Rutland, Vt.
B. BIGELOW, Asst. General Freight Agent, Rutland, Vt.
J. A. PROCTOR, Asst. Gen'l Freight Agent, Rutland, Vt.
JOHN E. McGARRITY, General Freight Agent, Rutland, Vt.

BOSTON, MASS.
314 Old South Bldg. LIBerty 9178
W. M. Burrell, New England Agent
John M. Park, Traveling Agent
Albert L. Taylor, Traveling Agent

CHICAGO, ILL.
417 LaSalle St. Station Wabash 4200
O. L. Crawford, General Western Agent
Geo. A. Daley, Traveling Agent
Geo. W. Hanna, Traveling Agent

KANSAS CITY, MO.
912 Fairfax Bldg. Victor 6384-6385
L. M. Coffey, General Agent, Freight Dept.

MILWAUKEE, WIS.
Wisconsin-Broadway Bldg. Daly 5660-1-2
J. F. Scanlin, General Agent, Freight Dept.

MINNEAPOLIS, MINN.
805 Metropolitan Life Bldg. Atlantic 5281-2-3
A. W. Behrens, General Agent, Freight Dept.

ST. PAUL, MINN.
402 Pioneer Bldg. Garfield 5331
J. R. Tecsdale, General Agent, Freight Dept.

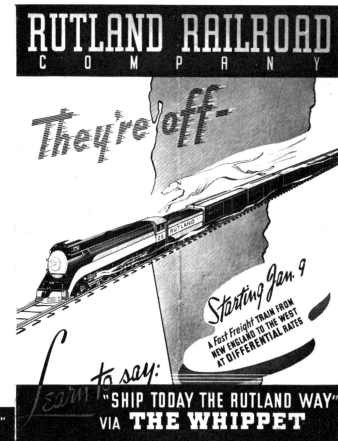

RUTLAND RAILROAD COMPANY

They're off—

Starting Jan. 9

A Fast Freight TRAIN FROM NEW ENGLAND TO THE WEST AT DIFFERENTIAL RATES

Learn to say:

We give you "THE WHIPPET"

A *Fast Freight* TRAIN FROM NEW ENGLAND TO THE WEST AT DIFFERENTIAL RATES

New England needs the Rutland Railroad—important differential route to the West. Another dramatic proof of what the Rutland means to New England is given by the "WHIPPET".

Fast freight service between New England and the West—speedy, safe, dependable service at differential rates—is a year-round need for many New England shippers and receivers.

The "WHIPPET" answers that need. This new fast freight will provide
—third noon delivery in Detroit
—fourth morning delivery in Chicago and Cincinnati
—fourth noon delivery in St. Louis
—swift service to other important points, *as per schedule on last page.*

For the friendly and enthusiastic cooperation of connecting carriers, the public and Rutland employes, who have made the "WHIPPET" possible, the management desires to express grateful appreciation.

The Rutland Railroad is engaged in a determined and resourceful "last stand" fight to save itself from liquidation. The Rutland must have more over-head traffic. The "WHIPPET" therefore is planned to serve a double purpose; to provide a new and needed service for New England, and to provide additional and needed tonnage for this important New England carrier.

Learn to say:

The PEOPLE OF WESTERN VERMONT *speak!*

IN an effort to assist in the preservation, for the benefit of the people of Western Vermont, of a medium of transportation vital for their welfare—the RUTLAND RAILROAD shippers and receivers of freight and other interested citizens organized the Rutland Railroad Traffic Association. The Association's primary purpose is to lend all possible assistance to the Railroad in its efforts to increase its business. One of the surest ways to secure and hold more and more business is through the improvement of service to the customer.

The installation of the "WHIPPET" fast freight service to the West is just that. We hope that shippers will use this fast service generously because it will serve them well and will be of immeasurable help in our fight to "SAVE THE RUTLAND" for the people of Western Vermont and for all who depend upon its service.

"SHIP TODAY THE RUTLAND WAY"
and
"KEEP THE RUTLAND ROLLING"

RUTLAND RAILROAD COOPERATING TRAFFIC ASSOCIATION

LEON S. GAY, President

business groups, moved to have all Vermont railroads partake of a twenty percent cut in assessed valuation. Early in January of 1939 this was effected resulting in a $25,000 reprieve for the Rutland alone. The plea to reduce the total valuation to the original figure of a million dollars was refused, but the tax commissioner said he was sympathetic and believed any further action should come from the legislature, thereby leaving hope for the possibility of further action on the tax relief endeavor.

Realizing the particular plight of the feeble Rutland a special five point bill was drawn up by State Senator Leon S. Gay, who also was President of the Rutland Traffic Association. When a public hearing on the bill was held late in February, the "Save the Rutland" campaign was carried into the legislative halls at Montpelier. The Rutland ran a special train, carrying two hundred representatives of shippers and Chambers of Commerce to air their feelings and the economic position of western Vermont before the state's lawmakers. Any one of the five factors could result in closing of the road: action by the bondholders, by the employees from whom over $200,000 in back wages was being withheld, by holders of equipment trust certificates, by the state collecting overdue taxes, or by the court.

The long-awaited final action came on St. Patrick's Day and would knock off two million more in the valuation of the Rutland's taxable property. With the previous twenty percent reduction, this cut the figure from ten million to just over six million dollars. The State of Vermont as well was doing its part to "Save the Rutland."

With this fifty percent reduction in the tax bill, followed by a similar move in New York State, as well as complete abatement of taxes for two years, the Rutland's tax problems were over for a while. Once the corporate life had been saved, efforts now could be directed at bringing the patient back to health.

The Traffic Association together with the railroad had already taken steps to improve revenues. With funds solicited from interested businessmen and other friends of the ailing line through the "Save the Rutland Club," a traffic expert, R. F. Bohman of the Heywood-Wakefield Company of Gardner, Massachusetts was temporarily hired. Economies in the overall handling of freight, pas-

sengers, maintenance, and office work were initiated, but the biggest single new item was THE WHIPPET.

The Rutland has always been a line with relatively little on-line industry, going almost from nowhere to nowhere in a rural area of two states. Industry couldn't immediately be increased appreciably, but perhaps bridge traffic could. If a fast freight train could get cars from Boston via Bellows Falls over the Rutland to Norwood in northern New York, and on to western points over the New York Central at a lower or differential rate, traffic would increase. It was also estimated that 15 carloads of LCL freight moved by highway from Boston to the Rutland area daily. With attractive rates and an equally attractive schedule it was hoped much of this business could be recovered.

The mechanical department pulled old No. 28, a 2-8-0 built by Alco in 1913, off the line, fixed her up with metal skirting, painted her black with silver trim, and proudly placed the rakish lettering THE WHIPPET on her tank. She was a living symbol of the Rutland itself, a tired old line giving a tired old engine a mediocre facelifting, hoping to gather new life into its system.

A 58-piece band played appropriate tunes through the open windows of Receiver Morphy's office (the outside temperature would have frozen the players to their instruments) as numerous speechmakers saw THE WHIPPET begin its rather short career on January 9, 1939.

Old No. 28, and several of her unstreamlined sisters, did an admirable job for a number of years racing from Bellows Falls in the early morning hours to Norwood and the New York Central connection for Syracuse and the West. *The Whippet* slogan was placed on many of the Rutland's old wooden boxcars and on all the cabooses, but No. 28 was the only engine to get the special uniform. It was probably burden enough to place the added skirting and trim on one engine with the road's finances what they were at the time.

Early in World War II the skirting was donated to the war effort as scrap, and old No. 28 faded anonymously back into the pool of tired dull engines on the Rutland's roster. *The Whippet* as a

The roundhouse in Rutland was the hub from which the Green Mountain line's colorful steam operations radiated.

Old No. 28, now named for the freight train, *The Whippet*, is dressed up in the height of 1939 style with black paint, silver trim, and skirts, yet! This was an effort to draw attention to the new time freight service and increase "bridge traffic" on the line. — *D. C. Wornom.*

time freight remained and proved to be a mildly successful venture.

As world tension mounted just prior to United States entry into World War II, traffic began to increase as well. The operating employees felt that they should be getting some of this apparent increased wealth in the form of back wages, being withheld since mid-1938. What they didn't realize was that expenses had been mounting, and deferred tax, maintenance, and equipment trust payments would soon be looming. If these were not met, wages would be no problem — there wouldn't be a railroad at all.

In an effort to cut expenses more, Morphy hoped to reduce wages further, but the unions and employees drew the line. Actually the road would continue to pay the men as much as they had been receiving, but there would be no technical obligation to pay back the withheld part of the wages. Many of the employees realized the overall situation and were willing to agree to the plan. They hadn't seen the money anyway and really had little hope of ever getting it.

Rumors about secret sums of money waiting to reorganize the road seemed to be entirely unfounded. The Rutland had no money, and as yet no plans had been definitely set up to secure new working capital.

The national unions balked, probably fearing that a precedent would be established that other lines would eventually use, since many were in almost as dire a state as the Rutland. The mediators got nowhere; a strike vote was taken and carried. The Rutland seemed certain to have the death blow struck at last, the first strike in its troubled history.

By mid-1940 things were getting pretty hot on the world's diplomatic fronts. The United States had pledged aid to England against her Nazi foe, and would soon be in the major conflict both in the East and in the West. President Franklin D. Roosevelt finally settled the question by voiding the embargo notices announcing shutdowns of railroad operations on the Rutland. All forms of negotiations had failed, but the Rutland was saved once again.

Seven months before Pearl Harbor, at a time when operating revenues were beginning to rise as a result of wartime movements, William E. Navin, general freight agent, stepped in to replace Morphy as receiver. Two years later the court which was technically running the line since receivership was effected in mid-1938, appointed Navin and Wallace M. Fay, as trustees. As President of the Vermont Marble Company, Fay represented the business community in the reorganization effort. Together with Navin, they would try to get the Rutland back on its feet.

The new management had few idle moments. In their desperate fight to reorganize the bankrupt line, they had few friends outside of the loyal shippers and loyal employees who had simply tightened their belts when meaningless paydays came and went. Trustees for the old Ogdensburg & Lake Champlain bonds, the company's first consolidated 4½ percent bonds, and Rutland-Canadian Railroad Company's claims moved in in a body. A petition filed in United States District Court in 1943, under which preferred stockholders requested permission to reorganize the company, was denied, though the following year the Court of Appeals reversed the decision and ordered that the various equity proceedings be set aside and that the Rutland be permitted to reorganize.

But the battle wasn't over. Not on the Rutland! A group of holders of the now badly-depreciated original stock, aware that business had improved a bit during the court shenanigans, and that the line now had some cash, petitioned that some of the old stock be permitted to participate in the new company. On May 11, 1944, a petition was filed in the Second Circuit Court of Appeals in New York, this time by the bondholders and the trustees, with the result that the case was transferred to Bankruptcy Court for reorganization.

With that, plans for the company's salvation began popping up like pussy willows in March. The company's plan called for recall of outstanding bonds to be replaced with new bonds and preferred stock; common stockholders in the old corporate structure would be disregarded.

A stockholders' group came forward with its own panacea, which was predicated on the issuing, for each outstanding $1,000 bond, $350 of income bonds, 2¼ shares of preferred stock, 8 shares of common, and $20 in cash. The plan proposed no

Ten-Wheeler No. 79 backs out of Canadian National's huge Turcot roundhouse on a cold Montreal morning in 1949. She will soon be speeding the *Flyer* back home toward Vermont.

At the north end of Victoria Bridge which crosses the St. Lawrence at Montreal, Ten-Wheeler No. 76 backs down to pick up the southbound *Flyer* which has been hauled out from Canadian National's Central Station by an electric locomotive. — *Both: E. L. Modeler.*

Pacific No. 83 was a familiar sight at the head of the *Flyer* south of Rutland for many years. In the 1932 photograph *(above)* she passes Ten-Wheeler No. 50 in the hole at Manchester with the Chatham wayfreight. The wartime picture *(below)* shows her speeding south out of Wallingford, toward New York, with four coachloads of revenue. When gasoline rationing is lifted, no doubt, the nearby highway will be more crowded, the train shorter. — *E. H. Brown.*

new money for the railroad, the proponents simply stating that since the Rutland now had some money, it didn't need more. In fact, the company had been able to scrape together enough to pay all back wages and retain $1,700,000. However, funded debt was $9,216,000 and unpaid interest had mounted to over three million.

The bond trustees came next with their plan, and the Interstate Commerce Commissioner, H. H. Kirby, had one of his own to submit.

The one that really got attention, at least in the public press, was that submitted by Lester P. Barlow, a cattleman from Shoreham in October of 1946. So revolutionary that it sent tremors through the rarified atmosphere of Wall Street, so radical in its concept that it might have more likely come out of the Granger country of the Midwest, the scheme gained wide consideration and much support.

In essence, what Barlow proposed was to set up a co-operative railroad. The idea was working well in farming circles, and since the Rutland was essentially a rural railroad, why not bring organizations like the Consumer Farmers Milk Co-operative and the National Farmers Union together to operate it?

More surprising than the radical elements of the idea was the source. Barlow was no garden variety ten-cow farmer. A top executive in the Glenn L. Martin Aviation Industries and an eminent consulting engineer, his worth was reputed to be well into the top half of the six-figure bracket. The Shoreham farm's feed lot could handle over a thousand prime beef cattle and covered 2,200 acres, which is a lot of Rutland territory.

Though the co-operative movement was well entrenched in agriculture, and consumer co-operatives had grown rapidly during the depression years, this was the first bold proposal to take over and operate a common carrier railroad.

The Interstate Commerce Commission looked at the proposal with a jaundiced eye. Something akin to this had been broached only a year earlier when a co-operative group had been formed to tap a line into a Kentucky coal field. The Interstate Commerce Commission pontificated that they could lay down a line all right, but the minute they carried

a pound of off-line cargo, they became subject to all the manifold rules and regulations of that body.

Much of the Rutland's right of way was acquired by land grant procedure with the government exercising its right of eminent domain. That precluded any possibility of operating the road as a private carrier. As a common carrier under the regulations of the Interstate Commerce Commission, the road would have to charge all co-operative members the same freight rates as any other shipper.

Another problem was the matter of salaries for the operating brotherhoods; the Rutland Crisis Committee, of which Barlow was a member, finally proposed a regular operating contract at standard wage rates. The thought of farmer-members at the throttles of Rutland locomotives was enough to strike terror into the heart of even the most confirmed co-operator!

Perhaps the most shaken individual concerned with the proposal was the tax collector. With the Rutland operating as a co-operative, it would, under the special government regulations which regard co-op profits as "savings," be exempt from taxation on such surplus earnings. Many an organization, struggling to stay alive and lure investment capital, would dearly love to operate under that rule.

Barlow disagreed violently with the plans proposed by the Rutland bond and stockholders for the reorganization of the road, charging that reorganization under any of the more conventional plans could never amount to more than a delay in the lingering death of the road.

The elements of his own plan, in essence, would revive the water-rail route that gave the Rutland its best years. He envisioned the establishment of a Rutland National Transportation Co-operative Corporation which would administer both the railroad and a shipping line. Following the charter of the corporation, trustees would be appointed by the courts to operate the system and arrange to pay off the original bonds — a prospect that did not entirely please the bondholders, in spite of the fact that the paper they held represented only about one one-hundredth of its face value in the actual market. There was a growing conviction among some that actual scrapping of the line would give them a greater return than continued operation under any plan. Many other bondholders abhorred the thought of not having a voice in the operation of the road; under the co-operative plan, they would be able to vote only the actual number of bonds held.

Yet another group bitterly opposing the Barlow plan was composed of private, independently owned businesses on the Rutland line, most of them shippers of greater or lesser substance. In addition to the operating transportation co-operative, the proposal called for the establishment of a local co-operative in each station town along the line which would both buy the farm produce and sell the needed feed, fertilizer, tools and other necessities to the farmers and their families. To put it bluntly, independent businessmen in Vermont and northern New York looked on the scheme as downright communistic.

Along with the formation of the co-operative organization, it was proposed to erect a monstrous mill for the manufacture of dairy and poultry feeds at Ogdensburg, adjacent to the old elevators, which could process grain directly off the group's own lake boats and trans-ship it out to the various "station-stores" by rail. The reinstitution of the water shipping line to the Midwest could increase the quantity of bulk material carried, at least part way over the Rutland's rails, on its inland journey from the ports of New York and Boston. Projecting the scheme a bit further, each local station community on the Rutland would have a local co-operative, presumably operating out of the railroad station (traffic being what it was, there was generally ample space) and administered by the station agent, who as a rule was not too heavily occupied with his scant railroad duties.

To round out the system, it was proposed that fertilizer ingredients, sugar and other bulk commodities could be brought into Lake Champlain via the New York Barge canal system and then rail-shipped from Larrabee's Point, terminus of the old Addison branch, or Burlington. Naturally these proposals brought forth evidence of displeasure from connecting and competing railroads and howls of anguish from the truckers who had been gleefully cutting into the Rutland's revenues for several years.

The Barlow plan was interesting; it may have had some concrete possibilities. It gained considerable support from many farmers in the region, particularly those who were members of the militant National Farmers Union, which maintained headquarters in the terminal city of Ogdensburg. The thing might even have worked to the eternal benefit of the great agricultural region and the distressed railroad serving it.

But when the Interstate Commerce Commission rendered its decision on a reorganization plan, it was not the one offered by Mr. Barlow.

In the plan that was accepted, equity holdings in the company were eliminated, and the capitalization was reduced from $18,298,300 to $10,992,450 composed entirely of stock. Bondholders and preferred stockholders in the Rutland Railroad Company received shares of common in the new organization. There were no fixed interest charges, although rental of the Addison Railroad remained at $15,000 a year.

After the courts and the Interstate Commerce Commission approved, a new charter was issued in mid-August. On the first day of November in 1950, the Rutland Rail*road* passed into oblivion after a long and lingering fiscal illness, and the Rutland Rail*way* came into being.

With the signing of the papers the Rutland had finally been saved — this time for sure.

The Rutland Railroad Company, whose preferred stock is represented by this certificate, ceased to exist after the reorganization of 1950. — *Collection of Robert Adams.*

Here are some passenger tickets, typical of the many issued down the years by the Rutland. A poignant reminder of the line's financial agonies can be found in the ticket issued by the "Trustees of Rutland Railroad." — *Collection of E. H. Brown.*

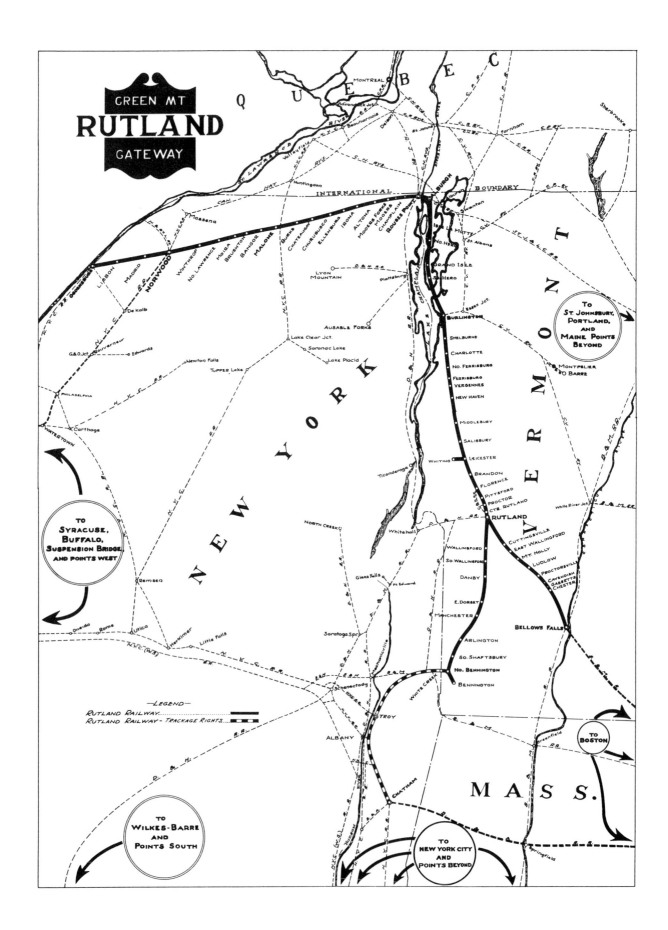

page 160

Chapter 11

~~~~~~ *The New Era*

The reorganized company, now the Rutland Railway, emerged in its fourth incarnation in a shaky condition but with a fighting chance for survival. It was evident to all concerned, however, that the reorganization had merely kept the road alive; only a combination of major surgery and a liberal dose of pep pills would restore it to health and give it a life expectancy to warrant any degree of confidence. It would require both able and energetic guidance if the necessary miracle was to be performed. The earlier and bitter experiences at the hands of absentee executives who knew little about the line and the territory, and at times appeared to care less, had been a lesson well learned.

Gardner A. Caverly, an apple-cheeked Vermonter and a member of the Boston stock exchange, was the unhappy owner of $100,000 worth of Rutland bonds. A hundred thousand in face value, but in 1941 they hit a low of five and one-half dollars on a thousand dollar face value.

Caverly figured there might be hidden potential in the Rutland. In that belief he was singularly alone; he was the only creditor to appear at the Interstate Commerce Commission hearings. His reasoning on the matter must have been convincing, for the trustees and the examiner named him to the temporary management committee. Under the reorganization plan he served briefly as a voting trustee, then went on the board of directors, and rapidly moved to a vice-presidency by 1951.

Long before he became President at the 1954 annual meeting, Caverly had been the motivating factor in the new Rutland. He didn't put much faith in Barlow's plan for reviving the line. As a

hard-headed businessman of considerable judgment, and not a railroader in the orthodox sense, it was his opinion the Rutland could and would survive through the simple expedient of making it the most efficient little railroad in the Northeast. He set out to do just that.

Gardner A. Caverly, president, Rutland Railway, 1954-57. – *New England Council.*

Here are two of the last steam engines ever purchased by Rutland; Mountain types from Alco in 1946. No. 90, painted green and trimmed in yellow, was placed on public display at the Rutland station when she arrived. No. 92 never looked more handsome than she did in May, 1952, almost at the end of her days, when she brought freight No. 120, latter-day successor to *The Whippet*, over Mount Holly with 30 cars from Bellows Falls. — *Below: Fred Sankoff.*

The basic ingredients for success were there: a fair right of way in reasonably good condition, a loyal group of employees, and the fierce determination of most Vermonters to make "their" railroad a going concern if it were humanly possible.

The court allowed the receiver to earmark enough cash to purchase four handsome 4-8-2's from Alco in 1946. These were quite similar to the Mountains that were turning in fine performances on the New York Central, but were somewhat lighter. With the exception of the new Alcos, the patched up engines that struggled over Rutland iron ran as much on prayer as steam. The roster of 58 locomotives that included Consolidations, Mikados, Ten-wheelers, Pacifics and Moguls (some nearing fifty years old) was a rolling museum of steam power.

Caverly's 407 miles of line included some impossible as well as unprofitable trackage. Not a swayback freight car on the line had been outshopped later than 1925. Half the train miles operated were accounted for by a passenger service that lost nearly $400,000 a year without any effort at all. To top it off, nearly 1100 people were on the payroll of this railroader's nightmare!

The first step was to replace the antiquated motive power with something less inclined to eat its figurative head off in operating costs. That was elementary; the problem was, how to pay for it. The reorganization provided for a capitalization of $11,000,000. With already pressing obligations, there was little ready cash and the American Locomotive Company, not without reason, seemed a little unwilling to extend unlimited credit to the Rutland. The ten mile, practically unused, Addison branch and fifteen miles of rusty sidings were scrapped. The ancient locomotive fleet, along with 180 of the worst freight cars, were pledged to the junkman, and the Rutland had its down payment on nine 1600 horsepower and six 1000 horsepower road switchers. Caverly convinced his board that these could be completely paid for out of improved operating efficiency and economy. Of necessity, the handsome new Mountains would go to the torch with the others. Four steamers amid a batch of new Diesels would hardly foster efficiency.

But Caverly was not a man made entirely of facts and figures. One evening at dusk, while driving over Mount Holly en route to his home in Ascutney, he met one of the 90-class Mountains struggling upgrade with northbound tonnage. The ground trembled, the setting sun was darkened with rising black smoke, and the white hot fire gleamed through the ashpan doors. He listened to the thunderous exhaust and the wail of her whistle echoing and re-echoing through the pine-clad hills. Never before had he been so deeply moved by the power and glory of steam. It was a subject fit for an artist, but Michelangelo himself could not have recorded the emotion that overwhelmed him. He was nearly brought to tears as the engineer waved for it was only the week before that he had signed the engine's death warrant.

The Rutland's rolling stock was in nearly as bad shape as the motive power. Not a new freight car had been purchased since the mid-twenties, and the ragtag line of sway-backed, splintered boxcars that overflowed the bad-order track was too discouraging to inspire much confidence in their life expectancy. Most would not be accepted by foreign lines. An order went out to Pullman-Standard for fifty new PS-1 freight cars, then 100 more, then another 100, and finally 200, making a total of 450 in all by 1957.

A contest had been held to create a fitting symbol which could be placed on the new equipment and serve as a co-operative image. An ornately shaped sign with large Rutland letters and the slogan "Green Mountain Gateway" was adopted and first appeared, six feet high, on the bright green and golden yellow boxcars. Seventy gondolas and 27 covered hoppers were also obtained, each having the new herald although not painted green and yellow.

An application to abandon the "corkscrew" Chatham branch met ICC approval in December of 1952. The 8500 tons of rail (some reusable elsewhere on the Rutland) 20 bridges, and tons of additional hardware would go a long way in helping to pay for the new equipment. The elimination of the operating expense and tax burden of this parasite branch alone would be substantially reflected in the balance sheet. The 57-mile branch had always been expensive to operate with its many grades and curves as well as its flood-susceptible

(Text continued on page 172)

The Rutland's covered bridge near Shoreham is the site for a sentimental stop by Ten-Wheeler No. 63, on the last run over the Addison Branch. A few of the faithful record the occasion for all time. A glaring white placard is tacked on the battered old station house at Leicester Junction, six miles east, giving Notice to the Public that service is to be abandoned on the branch after this date, May 21, 1951. Meanwhile No. 53 prepares to back

up for the car on the siding and then start on her last 13.4 mile run to Larrabee's Point. After service ceased on the branch, tracks were removed, time passed, and nature did its work. A few years later the right of way was nearly obliterated while old Shoreham depot and the covered bridge moldered in the Vermont sunshine. — *Top and left: James R. MacFarlane; right: Philip R. Hastings.*

Engineer Harry Wiggins oils around 4-6-0 No. 77 (above), stopped at Burlington April 14, 1948, on the last run of Train No. 46, an accommodation run which preceded the *Mount Royal* from Alburgh to Rutland, picking up mail and local passengers. — *Philip R. Hastings.*

The pathetic remnant of the once proud *Flyer* eases into its new terminus at Burlington in April 1952. Pacific No. 85 will uncouple here and go to the roundhouse instead of trailing her train on to the Canadian metropolis as in past years. — *Philip R. Hastings.*

Diesels No. 202 and 200 await assignment in Rutland terminal, shortly after their arrival in 1951. The steamers they will eventually replace are simmering in the background. — *Jim Shaughnessy.*

On one of her first runs after delivery, Diesel No. 202 has an easy time handling what is left of the *Flyer,* along the Connecticut River north of Bellows Falls. — *John Pickett.*

An old engineer realizes times have changed as he checks his watch prior to boarding Diesel No. 202 which will take the *Flyer* down to Bellows Falls from Rutland. — *Jim Shaughnessy.*

Only a week after arriving on the Rutland, Alco road switcher No. 201 helps Mike No. 33 across the Rouses Point trestle with manifest freight No. 119 for the New York Central connection at Norwood, N. Y. in the fall of 1951. — *Jim Shaughnessy.*

The "Corkscrew Division" went into history in 1953. Diesel hood unit No. 401 was assigned to haul the weekly local freight from Rutland during the last weeks of the Chatham branch. She is heading back to Rutland through the narrow Little Hoosic River valley near North Petersburgh N.Y. *(above)* a month before abandonment. She is coming north across the Boston & Maine tracks at Petersburgh Junction *(below)* the Wednesday before Easter that year. — *Both: Jim Shaughnessy.*

Wrecking crews were busy scrapping the remains of the Chatham branch during the summer of 1953. They were pictured at work near Center Berlin in July. While the junk contractor had his own power, Rutland crews hauled the heavy scrap trains north. With a string of gons, Diesel No. 403 drifts along the weed-covered line toward State Line crossing in June. After the wreckers had done their work only a faint evidence of rails remains amid the weeds and rotting ties. — *Top and left: Jim Shaughnessy; above: H. W. Towsley.*

page 171

location through the valley of the Little Hoosic River in eastern New York. Worst of all, and most significant, there was practically no business generated throughout its entire length.

Negotiations had been completed with the Boston & Maine and New York Central to re-route the Rutland train over their rails to maintain the traffic connection at Chatham. Rutland crews were qualified to operate over the foreign roads, and milk train No. 88, now almost entirely made up of through merchandise, completed the first trip over the new route on May 20, 1953. This left nothing in the path of the wreckers who reached Bennington on August 7, leaving only a weed covered line of rotting ties down the valley to Chatham. Old-timers may have shed a tear as they passed the abandoned frame stations, now used as hay sheds or hen coops, but the railroad they were dragging down was still living because of the sacrifice.

Labor troubles were not entirely over for the new Rutland, and some six hundred dissatisfied non-operating employees struck to enforce their demands for higher wages. The entire line was shut down on June 26, 1953, by the strike, the first in its 105-year history.

Twenty-one days later a settlement was made involving a 2½ cent an hour increase, retroactive to the previous September, and a current 1½ cent an hour addition.

The non-operating employees and their union inadvertently helped cure one of the Rutland's biggest headaches despite the increased expenses the settlement dictated. When the operating brotherhoods returned to their jobs, there was simply no passenger schedule to operate. The public protested, as did the Vermont Public Service Commission, but the Rutland had no other expedient if it were to continue to operate at all.

For a long time the passenger service had effectively wiped out what little profit the line could have generated. Up to its demise, the scantily patronized passenger service accounted for half the train miles and practically all of the road's losses. What's more, the creaking coaches were fast approaching the last stages of utter and complete collapse.

The through traffic from Boston, lured by more modern equipment, had largely gone over the Central Vermont anyway, while the New York traffic exhibited a preference for the Delaware & Hudson's route to Montreal. And the Rutland didn't own a single air-conditioned car.

To complicate matters further, subsidized air transportation had appeared in good quantity at the Rutland's only two major passenger traffic points, Burlington and Rutland. In the former city, Vermont's largest, rail traffic for Boston and New York was split with the Central Vermont. Buses had invaded these markets heavily too, leaving a very thin slice indeed of the passenger traffic pie for the Rutland.

Passenger losses had been mounting to astronomic figures, as high as $400,000 a year, even in the face of brave attempts to hide the obvious deficiencies of the *Green Mountain Flyer* and the *Mount Royal*. There were days when these trains operated with almost as many crewmen as passengers, and the inevitable was evident to nearly everyone before the events of early 1953 wrote finis to strings of varnish on the Green Mountain line.

Even the milk cars, a familiar and frequent sight on the Rutland for years, were noticeably absent toward the end of passenger operations. The revenue obtained from the transportation of milk slightly helped to offset the expense entailed by the empty seats in the cars that followed. But more and more milk was moving by truck, taking advantage of the faster, cheaper, and more efficient form of delivery now available with the expansion and improvement of the highways.

The disappearance of passenger service eliminated the need for many agency stations, and one by one they were closed. The great rambling brick station in Rutland was no longer needed, so the management made a deal with the city fathers, and down it came. A smooth parking lot went in on the site and helped solve a problem that sprang from the same basic source as the Rutland's passenger troubles — the horseless carriage and its successors.

Now the old coach shop at the north end of the yard was no longer needed. Company workmen replaced the giant doors with broad windows, tile went down over the service tracks on the worn concrete, sandblasting made the exterior brick look

(Text continued on page 180)

The last Rutland locomotive under steam was Pacific No. 81, used to heat shop buildings in Rutland while stationary boilers were under repair. The stack of locomotive tires in the foreground would never again ride the rails, for steam was finished, except for the leaking No. 81, when this picture was made in September, 1953. — *Philip R. Hastings.*

Along with her three Mountain type sisters, No. 92 waits in patient dignity for the recall to service that never came. After three years of waiting they all went to the torch in March 1955, graciously helping pay for the Diesels that replaced them. — *Jim Shaughnessy.*

No. 204 accelerates through Johnsonville, N.Y., where the Troy branch joins the main freight line of the Boston & Maine from Mechanicville. The agent waits to pick up the mail pouch which will be thrown off the northbound *Flyer,* in May 1953.

The next month, all 16 of the locomotives sat quietly in the Rutland yard for three weeks during the strike which prefaced the discontinuation of deficit-causing passenger service. Remnants of steam days are still to be seen. — *Both: Jim Shaughnessy.*

page 174

The Rutland took tremendous losses on its passenger service, as can be seen with the solitary patron riding into Burlington, which was as far as the *Flyer* went in its last months. The many empty seats in this car suggest that even the one coach on the train *(below)* may be superfluous. Here it is seen turning off the main line of the Boston & Maine from Troy at Hoosick Junction on to the North Bennington branch which will bring it to Rutland rails. — *Left: Philip R. Hastings; below: Jim Shaughnessy.*

Railway shops and yards dominate the air view of Rutland *(overleaf)*. The parking lot adjacent to the yard is on the former site of the station. The railway's office building is on the near side of the yard, in the massive building remodeled from the old coach shop. At upper right, the Howe Scale Company lies between the Bellows Falls line and the line which goes off to the right to Bennington. — *Bartlett Studio.*

Rejuvenation of the Rutland as an all-freight railway since 1953 brought many very noticeable changes to its properties in Rutland. The spacious parking lot was created to serve the needs of the city's downtown business, in place of the no-longer-needed passenger station and its little park. — *Rutland Railway*.

Nearby, under a large illuminated signboard proclaiming the business emphasis of the carrier, appear some of the 450 new green and yellow box cars emblazoned with the company's new herald, with the new switcher No. 500 hard at work. — *Rutland Railway*.

With no more coaches to repair, the old shop was remodeled to emerge as a general office building calculated to project the formidable image of the new status of the line. — *Rutland Railway*.

Caboose No. 46 gets an overhaul and the new green and yellow paint in the car section of the main shop in Rutland. The other end of the building houses the Diesel maintenance facility. The entire structure was once required for steam locomotive repair.

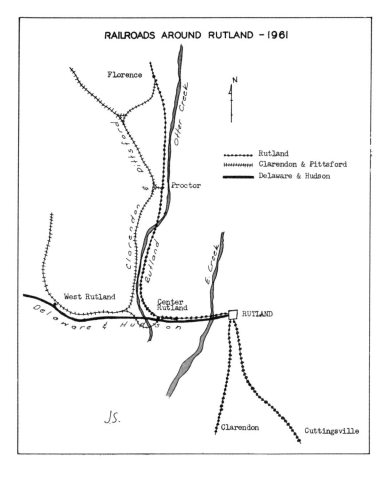

RAILROADS AROUND RUTLAND — 1961

Florence

Proctor

West Rutland

Center Rutland

RUTLAND

Clarendon   Cuttingsville

Otter Creek

Pittsford

Clarendon

Rutland

E. Creek

Delaware & Hudson

N

.... Rutland
HHHHHHH Clarendon & Pittsford
———— Delaware & Hudson

J.S.

like new, and bold aluminum letters which stood out in relief, proudly proclaiming "Rutland Railway" were placed across the front of the handsome building. The old transfer table pit was filled and covered with blacktop to serve as an employee parking lot. Finally, all operational and managerial offices of the resurgent company moved in from a half dozen locations around the city.

The old central steam plant was no longer needed. It was old, inefficient, and most of the buildings it served were gone now anyway. The steam generators that were in the Diesels for heating the passenger trains could now heat the few remaining buildings. There was no need for them on the road anymore. Two were rigged in a small annex outside the shop for heat and shop steam. The remaining two were placed in the maintenance of way shop and the office building.

Out along the line, coaling stations, water tanks, empty enginehouses, and unneeded way stations disappeared, being reflected in the local tax bills as they, too were whittled down to a reasonable size. Then came the hardest decision of all. The Rutland organization was top-heavy, with eleven hundred people on the payroll when reorganization

came in 1950. With stations closed, miles of branch line ripped up, less maintenance on new power and rolling stock, and no passenger service, the personnel roster had to be cut, and it was — down to half its former size. It was not a way to win popularity, but it was management's job to save the road.

The remaining 391 miles of line were still in reasonable shape, but still far from ideal for the type of running the vigorous new management visualized. The Maintenance of Way Department underwent a complete shakeup, and when the dust settled, each one of 13 section bosses had four men and 26 miles of track in his charge. Previously the Rutland was broken into forty sections, each with its own crew. The new gangs found that miraculously they had equipment to work with: modern tie tampers, spike pullers, Nordberg gandy cranes, power track wrenches, and right on down the line of new and efficient equipment. All that, and a fleet of new trucks to get men and materials to the right place at the right time would surely put the Rutland back in shape.

With the modernization of equipment came a modernization in the various other departments; the sales boys had something to sell now, and they went out and sold it. Solid volume of interline traffic began to ride the rails in increasing quantity as more and more shipping orders read "via Rutland." Freight schedules, with modern equipment, began to read as well as some of the passenger timecards of a decade earlier.

Even the Rutland's half million bushel grain elevator, spasmodically vacant since abandonment of the shipping line in 1915, was coming to life again. The Government was interested in storing surplus grain for national defense purposes, placing it in close proximity to New England and northern New York in case of emergency. In 1955 the directors voted to spend $150,000 to rehabilitate the elevator and dock facilities. A new building was built in 1956 to catch the overflow from the nation's record crop, and nearly a million bushels were in residence, the first in a number of years there on the banks of the St. Lawrence.

Given a reasonably free hand, the virtues of Yankee thrift and ingenuity came through. Since no other larger line wanted any part of the Rutland operation, the only alternative was to run it them-

The new Jordan spreader played an important part in the improvements which followed reorganization of the line in the early 1950s.

Rubber tires took to the Rutland's rails as new equipment arrived with the new era. — *Both: Rutland Railway.*

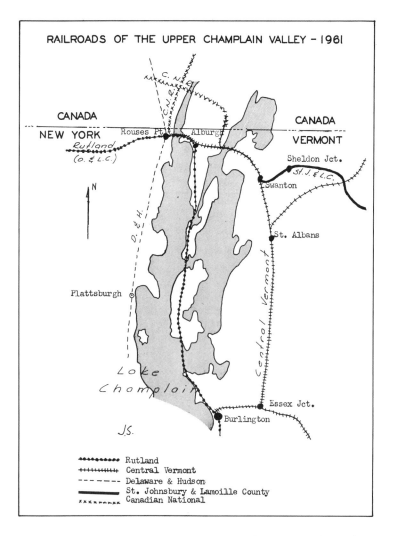

CANADA

NEW YORK

Rouses Pt. Alburg

CANADA

VERMONT

Sheldon Jct.

Swanton

St. Albans

Plattsburgh

Lake Champlain

Essex Jct.

Burlington

J.S.

••••••••• Rutland
+++++++++ Central Vermont
- - - - - - Delaware & Hudson
——————— St. Johnsbury & Lamoille County
xxxxxxxx Canadian National

selves and run it well. It has been said that adversity builds character. If that's true, and there is some evidence that it is, then Rutland people since the beginning have had fantastic quantities of both.

Caverly was no remote control executive. He rolled up his sleeves and went to work with the rest of the Rutland crew. He was everywhere on the line, inspecting improvements, checking the physical properties, talking to prospective shippers, trying to bolster the morale of employees whose pay checks amounted to only two-thirds of the standard wages for the industry. He was the youngest railroad president in the country when he stepped in as top "brass" on the Rutland in 1954.

The Rutland, through a century of history, had been fortunate in having men of decision and ability step forward when needed.

Caverly left the Rutland in 1957 to assume the executive vice-presidency of the New England Council, a group which seeks to stir new life in all Yankee industries. Alan T. Danver, who had moved up through the ranks to chief engineer, treasurer,

and finally executive assistant, took over the line. A practical operating man in addition to being a shrewd executive, Danver continued the efficient, aggressive practices of the line which now had 391 miles of first-class freight service, that brought it to the millennium.

During the troubled days of reorganization one holder of Rutland securities stated flatly that the line wouldn't pay a dividend until hell froze over, and probably not then either.

Hell must have frozen over in 1957, for the Rutland paid a dividend of $1.25 per preferred share. What's more, the only debts outstanding were the equipment notes issued when the moneymaking Diesels were purchased.

After six months Danver retired, having served the Rutland more than forty years. William I. Ginsburg, a Rutland merchant and chairman of the Democratic party in Vermont, was elected to the presidency. Previously, he had sat on the Rutland's board of directors as vice president in charge of industrial development.

Industrial development is what Vermont and the Rutland needed the most. Heavy industry is notably lacking along the Rutland line. Most of the heavy production is centered around the city for which the line is named, with the Howe Scale Company and the marble quarries around Proctor, to the northwest, accounting for the bulk of the tonnage. Burlington only originates and receives some traffic.

Over on the old O&LC line, the Aluminum Corporation of America's Massena works shipped quantities of the light, white metal out over the New York Central to interchange on to Rutland rails at Norwood. New plants following the opening of the St. Lawrence Seaway held promise for additional tonnage, and everyone hoped for a cement plant to be erected.

A slogan which appeared in the last public timetable issued before abandonment of the passenger services boasted, "Big enough to serve you — small enough to know you." This outlook was not dropped with the unused trains but was applied with increased vigor to the freight shippers. Vermonters have always felt that the Rutland was their railroad and they have fought hard and long to keep it alive.

The air view shows the Ogdensburg yards and half-million-bushel grain elevator on the banks of the St. Lawrence. The station is visible at the end of the track where wharf and car ferry slip are located. A car float and tug can be seen crossing just upstream from the dock.

Alco switcher No. 404, with 1000 horsepower, pushes a car down to the elevator past an extension built to store government surplus grain. — *Both: Rutland Railway.*

page 183

A big drop in railway business in Vermont made the Alco road switcher No. 400 surplus, so Rutland sold her. Here she emerges from the Rutland shop as Tennessee Railroad No.4. — *Gordon Cutler.*

With 3200 Alco horsepower ahead, Symbol Freight XR-1 with only seven cars, easily makes its way up the Williams River Valley past the covered bridge at Bartonsville in the summer of 1961. — *Jim Shaughnessy.*

Chapter 12

Prolonged periods of business prosperity or even general tranquility have been standout exceptions in the Rutland's troubled existence. If there were not natural disasters, there was mismanagement or financial exploitation. The record reads like The Perils of Pauline. Only through the shrewd maneuvering of John Page in 1870 did the line reap two decades of benefits from an absurdly high rental to its ancient enemy, the Vermont Central.

Perhaps in this mid-century there could be no excuse for the survival of a little line going literally from nowhere to nowhere, but the Rutland was doing it — and doing it well.

The fleet of 16 Diesels was completely paid for as was the large fleet of new freight cars. By all the rules of northeastern railroading in those troubled times, the 331 mile Green Mountain line should have been sinking for the third time in a pool of red ink, but it wasn't. Fact is, the Rutland made a little money during the late 'fifties, and even paid a modest dividend during two of those years. In 1955 an operating ratio of 84 was reached and a net income of more than $75,000 was reported.

Several factors contributed to the situation: the 58 aged steam locomotives were replaced by only 16 efficient Diesels; the work force was more than cut in half, from over 1200 down to about 400; deficit-producing passenger service was eliminated; an understanding state government had taken well-advised steps to ease the tax burden; a large fleet of money-making boxcars replaced the collection of junk other roads would not even accept; operating efficiency and red-ball handling that moved tonnage at passenger train speeds were instituted and the aggressive sales department got shipments to fill these trains.

In one giant step the Rutland had climbed above the continually rising level of costs and expenses into an area of profits. The debts were paid and there was even something left for the long forgotten stockholders. Many a larger railroad would have willingly changed places, lock, stock and crossties with the Green Mountain line. By industry standards the Rutland had it very good indeed during most of the 'fifties.

Since the last of the many reorganizations that had taken place in 1950, the men of the operating brotherhoods had worked for a bit less than the national pay standards as a means of keeping the road alive. Their cooperation helped the road over the difficult period when it made heroic efforts to bridge a half-century of obsolescence. Without a doubt, these men of the brotherhoods gave their full support to the transition and rebirth of their railroad.

When William I. Ginsburg assumed the presidency of the line in 1957 he brought with him a solid background as a successful businessman in the thriving little city of Rutland and wide respect as the state chairman of the Democratic Party in Vermont, in itself outstanding training in the field of unmitigated frustration in New England politics. Ginsburg acquired Rutland stock at less than its liquidation value. To him it was a sound business investment. Not that he intended to liquidate — no businessman worth his salt would deliberately wreck a going concern that could, and was, making money, especially one as important to the city and state in which he was a responsible leader.

The Rutland was a challenge, and Ginsburg set out to run it by the formulas that had spelled success in his other business enterprises. He began to apply to the Rutland the precepts he had learned as a merchant. First, that waste cuts profits and must be eliminated, and second, that the stockholders who risk their money to provide jobs are entitled to a fair return on their investment.

But the principles and conditions that exist in merchandising do not necessarily apply in railroad operation, as Ginsburg soon learned. Restrictive regulation was a new experience. Despite the fact that the Rutland road had obtained some measure of state tax relief, Federal tax money was being poured into a high-speed interstate highway that promised to siphon off a large part of the already meager on-line traffic originating in Burlington, the line's largest city.

A major point of contention between labor and management arose when it was proposed to consolidate the crew runs, breaking the railroad into two, rather than three operating subdivisions and to run a quantity of trains consistent with the demands of traffic. Crews operated between Rutland and Bellows Falls and/or Bennington; Rutland to Alburgh; and Alburgh to Ogdensburg. The new plan would make Burlington the midpoint of the operating subdivisions. This would reduce the number of crews needed and therefore place some crews on the extra list as well as requiring considerable commuting to Burlington, sixty miles from Rutland where most lived.

On occasion trains would only have a few cars and cancellation would save money. The loads could be handled on the next train. Management maintained that a hundred trains would be run if and when traffic warranted them.

Needless to say, these views were something less than popular with the crews out on the line. There was a new, younger crop of employees on the Rutland now; the old timers who remembered the hard times and realized the long range implications had mostly all retired anyway.

As the 'fifties drew to a close, that ever increasing tide of prices and expenses had caught up to the Rutland once again. With the St. Lawrence

Seaway project completed the temporary boom that construction materials brought to the Ogdensburg & Lake Champlain division was gone. The new business that was expected did not materialize as no cement plant appeared. Improving highways and different marketing theories removed more of the existing revenue possibilities.

Milk, once wheeled down the valley of Otter Creek in twenty-car hotshots, dwindled to a pitiful four or five cars a week on the Alburgh local, waybilled for Boston. The Federal regulators had cut western Vermont out of the New York milkshed in 1958 and with it went the fast manifest down over the old Lebanon Valley line, later over connecting routes, to a New York Central connection at Chatham. As better roads were built more trucks appeared, and the great flood of milk that once rode on the Rutland's rails was gone, and with it one of the biggest single sources of revenue.

The Rutland had looked very good when it jumped above the expense line on the economists' graphs with its extensive modernization program. There was little more that could be done after that drastic change had come about, and the road held rather constant as far as labor and plant were concerned. With revenue dropping further the rising expenses would once again submerge the road in deficit. Now there was nothing left to cut. The only place that more savings could be squeezed was from the work rules. Here the Rutland stood alone. Their basic problem was the same as that plaguing lines all over the country. The only difference was, the Rutland needed a solution immediately!

At a time when the rail brotherhoods were digging in all around the country for what would probably be one of the biggest battles in their entire existence, a concession in Vermont would be unheard of. Certainly no precedent was going to be set now, regardless of who wanted it or who benefited, labor or management.

For a hundred years Rutland crews had run across the Connecticut River at Bellows Falls to the Boston & Maine yards to deliver their trains. It was just something that was done. Now they began putting in for the extra pay that was spelled out under the rules. Other similar moves were initiated. Ginsburg firmly maintained that economies had to be effected if survival was expected. Grant-

Two new wide-cupola green-and-yellow cabooses No. 51 and No. 52 await their road's fate on a back track in Rutland. Built to Delaware & Hudson specifications, two were to be purchased a year to replace the aging fleet of wooden vans.

Thirteen of the line's 15 locomotives sleep away the months of inactivity in the silence of the once-bustling Rutland shop, while their future and that of their rails is being debated up and down the state, and in distant Washington. — *Both: Jim Shaughnessy.*

Rutland box cars jam the little yard at Bellows Falls in October, 1961, as they returned to their strike-bound line with no place to go. Later, all were leased to the Maine Central.

Grass grows tall in the once-busy yards at Rutland in July 1962, after almost a year of inactivity. — *Both: Jim Shaughnessy.*

ed, the road was ahead at the moment but it was frightfully clear that red ink was imminent if changes weren't made.

By September 15, 1960, after all attempts to work out a settlement had failed, things came to a head and the brotherhoods walked out.

A Federal Court injunction against the brotherhoods, served under the terms of the Railway Labor Act, ended the walkout 41 days later. A one year cooling off period during which formalized arbitration could possibly work out the grievances was begun. Some traffic fell away from the line as a result, but hard selling rebuilt it in a hurry; shippers liked the Rutland.

The question of wage rates and work rules still hung over the road like a dark cloud; an increase to national wage standards would wipe out the road's tenuous profits overnight. Negotiations continued while the trains kept running. Nothing had changed, the work rules would have to be changed and certainly no wage increase could be effected if survival was expected. President Ginsburg was adamant in his efforts to cut costs and increase operating efficiency through the elimination and combination of certain runs.

The situation remained deadlocked as the year-long cooling off period neared its conclusion, September 25, 1961. If anything, things were hotter! As the handsome fleet of green and yellow Diesels, followed by their identically clad buggies, rumbled home to the yard at Rutland on the 24th, the sounds of their chime horns seemed almost like the last chords of "Auld Lang Syne." Rust replaced trains on the rails of the dying old Rutland.

There was concern but not despair; the Rutland had been in this predicament before and pulled out. In fact, the similarity of the situation now and in 1938 was remarkable.

In those days of economic crisis before the war, traffic had seriously fallen away, and the brotherhoods were pressing for the back wages that a court-appointed receiver had withheld as a means of keeping the line alive. The cash received on any one day of business would be practically gone again at the end of the same day and there was nothing in reserve. Increasing costs and decreasing traffic volume had caught up with the inefficient old Rutland. Only the advent of World War II

which brought a presidential order stopping a strike and an increase in traffic postponed the problem for the moment. It returned again after the war but was solved for a time at least by the reorganization and modernization that took place in the early 'fifties.

This time, after two months of haggling in Rutland, the problem was brought to the office of Secretary of Labor Arthur J. Goldberg in Washington. As the leaders of the four striking brotherhoods bussed to the Federal City, the line's directors prepared to meet in Rutland.

After two days of conferences, Goldberg proposed the disputants submit the case to final and binding arbitration under the provisions of the Railway Labor Act. The National Arbitration Board was standing by to take over the case. Goldberg also recommended that the strike end immediately with all employees restored to service according to seniority and without reprisal; that the wage, vacation and cost-of-living issues and all pending grievances and time claims in dispute be submitted to the impartial arbitrators. To this the unions would agree!!

Ginsburg then wired Goldberg that the Secretary's proposals had been carefully considered by the Board of Directors but had been found unsatisfactory. As far as the Rutland was concerned, the recommendations provided no feasible means of reaching a workable settlement and would require resumption of losing operations for an indefinite period of time that insufficient funds could not justify. Protection of the corporation, its creditors and stockholders would make such a settlement impracticable.

Goldberg had invited the parties in dispute to the Washington meeting at the request of Congressional representatives and other Vermonters interested in a settlement. The office of the U. S. Secretary of Labor would, however, be the last place that the brotherhoods would be likely to relent in any way in respect to national standards and Goldberg was hardly in a position to ask it of them. It boiled down to the fact that any change in the present stand would have to take place in Rutland, not on a national level, and there was nothing that would indicate any softening on either side there.

Two years of disuse leave their mark on Vergennes station. The D.S. phone and train sheet repose in a dust-covered state of suspended animation, just as the agent left them when the strike began. Outside, the tracks slowly reappear from under the melting drifts which had been covering them before this March day, 1963. — *Both: Jim Shaughnessy.*

A comparatively weak, small railroad, the Rutland had struggled for years to meet national standards, but with declining revenue it could no longer pay the increases and survive. No one should have known it any better than its own employees.

Ginsburg knew it all too well; the company was in reasonably good financial shape but it couldn't be expected to continue if losing operations were to be carried on and the life blood drained away. He was obligated to the stockholders and to himself to keep the net value of the company as high as he could.

On the 4th of December, Ginsburg applied to the ICC for total and complete abandonment of the 331-mile line. It came like a bolt out of the blue Vermont sky, the whole State was shocked, especially the little city of Rutland.

Vermonters had come to think of the Rutland as part of the State and its heritage, as much a part as the stately elm trees or the granite hills. They would hear its trains pass in the stillness of the night and wave to its crews by day. It just seemed to be there, and gradually they began to take it for granted. It certainly had heritage, but what it needed was traffic.

Western Vermont in the 1840s was, and still is, a predominantly rural area; a continuing point of contention is the debatable subject of whether there are more cows than people in the State. Most years, the cows win. The Rutland serves the two largest cities, Burlington and Rutland; combined they amount to a scant 50,000 population. Heavy industry is almost non-existant, the major tonnage developing from the marble quarries around Proctor and a scale works in Rutland. The pipe lines have not yet reached Vermont, and a modest amount of petroleum products occasionally moves over the line.

Marble remained the most stable tonnage commodity handled by the Rutland over all its corporate life. Fed into the main by the busy little Clarendon & Pittsford road at West Rutland, Proctor and Florence, the white rock was a consistent source of revenue, probably the Gibraltar of the Rutland's balance sheets but most of that has now succumbed to the lure of the flat-bed truck. It was remarkable that the line had been able to attract the amount of differential or lower rate, non-rush bridge traffic that it did. This alone had provided a large part of the meager revenue but now even this was being routed over faster connections.

It is significant that the Rutland didn't have a single major source of on-line traffic that couldn't be served by another railroad. The city of Rutland itself could be served by the Whitehall branch of the Delaware & Hudson. Burlington could be served by the Central Vermont's branch from storied Essex Junction. The terminal city of Ogdensburg and the second largest northern New York community of Malone are served by the St. Lawrence division of the New York Central. And there you have it. There wasn't another major traffic point on the Rutland line except the little city of Bennington, and that could be neatly reached by the Boston & Maine with the acquisition of a couple of miles of Rutland trackage east of White Creek on the New York state line. Between them these carriers could handle ninety percent of all originating traffic and seventy-two percent of the Rutland's terminating traffic.

Abandonment hearings were scheduled by the Interstate Commerce Commission for late in March, and the various factions began to prepare their respective cases.

The State of Vermont vigorously opposed cessation of service, temporary or permanent, on the grounds it would jeopardize industrial growth in the already lean western part of the state and increase transportation costs to those who had used the railroad. It estimated that costs would run in excess of a half million dollars annually in added shipping charges alone. The New York industrial engineering firm of Coverdale & Colpitts was immediately retained by the State Public Service Commission to make a thorough analysis of the Rutland's situation.

U. S. Senator George Aiken petitioned the Department of Defense to investigate the role the line played in the nation's defense. The results were discouraging. Of a meager 97 government loads handled that year, 75 were just passing through and could have been easily rerouted. The bulk of the remaining 22 were military headstones from Vermont Marble's Proctor plant and could hardly qualify as strategic materials.

Idle Wallingford station and the Bennington Branch right of way lie under a blanket of snow on a winter's day in March, 1962.

That is where the milk traffic went. Trucks load milk at a Middlebury creamery beside the weed-covered sidings where once the busy milk reefers used to do the same job. — *Both: Jim Shaughnessy.*

A spark of the old days glowed again in the storm of protest that erupted in the form of an Emergency Committee to save the Rutland Railway. Made up of interested businessmen, it again tried to rally support and advanced two plans of action. It lacked the parading, button-wearing, banner-waving spirit of the old Save the Rutland Club of 1938, and now most people wouldn't be affected at all whether the Rutland was saved or whether it wasn't.

The brotherhoods, of course, had the most to say. Of the some 400 jobs at stake they represented about a quarter of them. They contended that the application for complete abandonment be denied on the grounds that there was no adequate financial justification for abandoning operations and that the losses shown were artificial because extended labor trouble, strikes, and legal expenses distorted the true picture. They claimed the road was making money for a period of time before the last strike and was using the abandonment action to by-pass the legal procedures for the settlement of labor disputes and to break a strike on its property. Abandonment would certainly break the strike, there would be no railroad to operate at all. Finally, the brotherhoods claimed that the general public and industry needed and required the rail service provided by the Rutland.

The Industrial Engineering consultants reported to its employer, the State, that Vermont commerce would be inconvenienced but not jeopardized by the road's demise. They also found that about ninety percent of the shippers who used the Rutland, but were now forced to make other arrangements, would return if and when service were resumed. Messrs. Coverdale and Colpitts noted, almost wistfully, that had the Rutland been operating during all of 1961, it would have shown an income of approximately $153,000 after fixed charges. In summary, they felt that certain sections of the existing Rutland trackage could be operated successfully by themselves if they were separated from the deficit-producing portions. These sections were from White Creek on the New York border to Shaftsbury and Bennington, Rutland to Burlington, and Bellows Falls to Gassetts. Whether the Rutland would retain these or other lines like the B&M, D&H, or CV acquire them as extensions to their

own systems was immaterial, they could support themselves with the traffic they could generate.

With this analysis as a basis, Governor F. Ray Keyser approached and effected an agreement with Ginsburg to allow the State to designate operators for these potentially profitable sections should the petition for total abandonment be approved. This agreement essentially provided that should the Rutland be allowed to abandon, or should it not choose to operate any of these sections itself, it would sell them to anyone who wanted them at a price somewhat below the net salvage value of that section, rather than junking it. The Rutland would give a credit of $190,000 toward the Rutland-Burlington section and $48,000 on the Bellows Falls-Gassetts stretch. In return the Rutland could retain rights to run a natural gas pipeline it had talked about along these portions and the State would no longer oppose the abandonment. The State would have this right of designation for a three month period ". . . after the date when a certificate of abandonment becomes effective."

The State, through Keyser, even offered to buy certain sections and operate them itself, made a firm offer, but was rejected by Ginsburg as being too low, only about half the actual scrap value.

This whole episode produced screams of "a deal" from certain factions of the opposition. What was apparently intended to be a means of restoring service to the State as soon as possible, was interpreted in different ways by different people. Despite everything, the agreement was signed and was to be a definite and binding consideration in the whole abandonment proceeding.

All through the winter while snow erased the roadbed from the picturesque countryside, a number of plans for operation were proposed, all requiring considerable money, and none providing it. Adjacent railroads refused to tread on Rutland rails, even for partial service, until a solution could be found to the existing labor conflict. Everyone wanted service, even temporary, but no one could figure a way to get it.

The little Clarendon & Pittsford Railroad, a subsidiary of the Vermont Marble Company, had stepped in to help the shippers of the Rutland area as much as it could. The C&P helped once before, in 1927, when it provided a connection for the

The busy junction between the Bellows Falls line, at the
left, and the Bennington branch, curving to the right, lies
snow-covered and unused as the melting snows of 1962
begin to reveal the rusty rails of the idle railway. Howe
Scale Company, Rutland's major industry, is obliged to find
other transportation for its products, for the duration. —
Jim Shaughnessy.

Rutland itself around a major washout that severed the main line in the Proctor area during the great flood. Now the C&P's little yard at Center Rutland, where it too connected with the D&H, was a beehive of activity. Freight was trucked to and from their team track by area shippers who normally received their cars over Rutland tracks.

Middlebury College, some thirty miles to the north, leased a tract of land on the north end of the C&P at Florence where it received, and eventually stockpiled, a hundred cars of coal during its heating season. Trucks then moved it to their powerhouse in Middlebury. The only loss to the little line was about six cars of raw marble block a day, brought up from a quarry on the Bennington branch of the Rutland at Danby. This was handled by a fleet of heavy trucks.

More cars were routed directly to Proctor, and the overall increase in traffic mushroomed so the C&P had to lease the single seventy-ton GE switcher its dying neighbor had used in its own yard at Rutland.

On March 22, 1962, the Interstate Commerce Commission examiners came to Vermont to hear the pros and cons on the Rutland's request to abandon the whole works. They set up shop in the State Armory and for nine days heard all who cared to comment on why the Rutland should not be allowed to quit. Two of these days were spent over on the old O&LC in Malone, getting the views of the northern York staters.

The general objection was based on the need by various shippers for the service the Rutland provided and how increased shipping charges would affect their business.

The New York Central requested that a 36-mile section between Norwood and Malone Junction in northern New York, over which it had trackage rights, be retained for their use.

The Rutland, as well, placed on the record its reasons for seeking the abandonment. The increased costs of operation due to the loss of business and the failure of efforts to curb the downward trend of revenue were the basic factors.

The Rutland maintained a number of freight soliciting offices around the country, had a reasonable physical plant and freight movement schedule, and even published piggyback rates on certain commodities it felt would be available. Its efforts to economize further by reducing the number of trains as well as the operating divisions, produced the problem it now had.

On April 4th, after hearing all the testimony, the examiners packed their transcript and returned to the Commission's Chambers in Washington to ponder the Rutland's fate. Deliberations of this type are never fast and a decision was not even expected until late in the year. Neither side in Rutland had budged an inch. All attempts by third parties to effect a compromise of any type, on either side, were rejected. The Rutland had been in bad trouble before, but someone had always saved it. If it pulled through this crisis it would certainly have the legendary nine lives of a cat.

Spring came and passed and as the summer wore on, weeds grew higher and higher, the drawbridges up through the islands of the lake rusted in their open position, and some road crossings were paved over to smooth the ride across. As the word from Washington was awaited, more plans to provide temporary service, until the decision was rendered, appeared and then disappeared.

The diabolical situation existed where nothing could be done until abandonment disposed of the present corporation and with it all its problems, or an agreement was reached. The latter now seemed beyond all hope.

The State realized this and had become more and more in favor of abandonment, primarily so a new organization could spring from the ruins of the old and provide the service it felt was so necessary to the local economy. No other railroad could buy, or even operate, the line while this dispute choked it off. Conferences were held and committees formed, but nothing came of them.

As fall approached it brought with it the State's gubernatorial elections and the numerous issues soon took shape. A big one this year was the Rutland situation and challenger Philip Hoff, a Democrat carrying the banner and endorsement of the State Committee of which Ginsburg was the chairman, charged that Keyser wasn't doing all he could to solve the problem. This seemed to be a logical claim, whether Keyser was or he wasn't. The weeds were now six feet high between the Rutland's rusty rails, the whole length of the State. Keyser, on the

Eight of the Rutland's nine 1600 h.p. road switchers wait on April 4, 1963 at the Delaware & Hudson spur near Temple Street crossing on the west side of their namesake city. They were leaving Rutland for the last time on their way to terminal switching jobs on the Louisville & Nashville. Their sister unit, No. 206, was moving government grain out of Ogdensburg elevator and was shipped directly from there. — *Rutland Herald*.

The last Rutland train on Bellows Falls branch picked up odds and ends of scrap on October 30, 1963. Here Diesel No. 405 pushes down the tall grass as she passes the old depot at Chester for the last time. — *Donald S. Robinson*.

other hand, was the goat for all the delays of bureaus, legal red tape, and lack of action, at least from a political viewpoint in the campaign. The passing of the "Buck" stopped with him.

In far away Washington on September 18, 1962 it was decided. The Rutland's death warrant was signed. It *could abandon* its historic little railroad.

The crux of ICC docket No. 21870 stated, ". . . it is our conclusion, that while there is a need for railroad service in the area, such railroad service and continued operation by the Rutland is not warranted." The report explained that a reduction of almost 100,000 carloads occurred in the line's freight volume during the past ten years. Much of this, 70,000 cars a year, was caused by business moving away without a corresponding increase from new or expanding operations in the area. More resulted in the loss to motor carriers, in the case of milk and cement, while still more to economic changes in consignee's operations, such as the conversion from coal to oil. The remaining 30,000 never showed up from other lines as bridge traffic. The Commission admitted that even a slight increase in wages would convert a small income to a deficit in view of these traffic losses. In prior cases, the Commission had not required carriers to continue running where their overall operations had been conducted at a system-wide deficit for a substantial period of time and where there was no reasonable prospect of conducting those operations at a profit in the foreseeable future.

The men in Washington did not agree with the brotherhoods' charge that the decline in traffic was the result of mismanagement or a change to a non-railroad president. Neither did they buy the charge that the "Ginsburg interests" bought in at a low price to realize face value upon liquidation. It was felt that a change of the presidency did not constitute a change in management and that every logical saving was effected wherever possible. The rearrangement and ultimate reduction in the number of trains operated was consistent with the traffic demands while still providing adequate service to its patrons. They noted that an abandonment proceeding is immaterial to the fact that the owners of a carrier may profit from the abandonment. In previous cases, as in this, "the matter of loss or gain from the salvage of a line is a matter entirely unrelated to the public convenience and necessity."

Finally, the Commission felt that a railroad could not reasonably be expected to operate a line at a loss in order to provide shippers with service for part of their traffic. The continued operation and maintenance of the line would impose an undue and unnecessary burden on the applicant and interstate commerce.

That was it! And so, in a 57-page document, 119 years of railroading came to an end.

The Rutland was dead.

Nothing could be done for ninety days after the effective date of October 26, 1962, during which time the management could entertain offers to buy all or part of the property. The portion of the Ogdensburg & Lake Champlain that the New York Central requested be exempt from the order was exempted but the Rutland's operations on that part were eliminated.

Ginsburg had his victory, if you could actually call abandonment a victory. It was what he must have wanted when he applied for it. The following month he had another. His man Hoff won the election and would be Governor in January. Whether the Rutland issue had any effect or not is hard to say, but Democratic Governors generally aren't that popular in Vermont.

As 1962 drew to a close the rail unions petitioned the ICC to reconsider the abandonment decision and after two tries got the Commission to delay the effective date of the abandonment order to January 29, 1963. Outgoing Governor Keyser asked the unions to withdraw their petition so abandonment could take place and allow service to be resumed by other railroads. The unions flatly refused, saying as far as they were concerned Keyser sided with management anyway and proved it when he signed the agreement with Ginsburg in March.

After almost 120 years of trouble it would certainly be out of place to have the Rutland die a quiet, painless death. Now that abandonment had been considered and a decision reached, events should have taken their normal, predetermined course — ah! but not on the Rutland. It had trouble living, and now it was having trouble dying.

The brotherhoods wanted the case heard by the full 11-member commission rather than the three-man sub-committee which handed down the ruling

Switcher No. 500, 70 tons, was purchased new from General Electric in 1951 for use in the yards at Rutland. When the line was hit by the 1962 strike, the neighboring Clarendon & Pittsford, a subsidiary of Vermont Marble Company, leased the No. 500 and later bought it. Two boys in Proctor, Vermont watch it pull a train of marble in from West Rutland. — *Both: Jim Shaughnessy.*

alleging that the matter was of general transportation importance. The ICC said it wasn't and refused to postpone the effective date any further.

In the final hours before the already extended effective date of the abandonment order would fall due, the Railway Labor Executives Association filed suit in the Federal District Court at Cleveland, Ohio, to obtain an injunction halting abandonment. They claimed errors existed in the ICC action, and asked that provisions be made for severance pay. Further, they requested that the abandonment order be suspended, enjoined, annulled, and set aside. Despite this action, the clock began ticking away the ninety-day period that would end April 29.

Newly installed Governor Hoff soon made good his election promise to get action on the Rutland situation by proposing a 3.5 million dollar measure in the State Legislature to purchase the whole line in Vermont. The measure would create a state transportation authority to acquire and operate the Rutland. This wasn't a new idea, Governor Keyser had made a similar proposal earlier, but after a year and a half of inactivity, the proposal seemed to have much more merit. Rumors constantly had other lines ready to move in at any time, but none had ever actually indicated a very serious interest.

By mid-March, two weeks of public hearings and numerous committee reports agreed something had to be done, but the proposed bill wasn't it. The Legislature was not at all warm to the idea of the State owning and running a railroad, especially in competition to tax-paying private enterprise. The 3.5 million was a lot of money and there was some confusion as to just what the State would have after paying out this sum — a functioning railroad or just a track with land under it.

Ginsburg told the lawmakers that the Rutland would have paid the increased wages in the beginning, provided they could have run the necessary number of trains and operated in a businesslike manner. Had management gone along with the union's demands, he said, they would be in the same position now anyway, only bankrupt.

The hearings on the appeal in Cleveland Federal Court were set for mid-April, and Governor Hoff went on record criticizing the union's delaying action and recommended that all efforts be made for speedy abandonment so other operations could begin. Hoff's representative tried to soothe labor, however, by saying the State had never been opposed to labor's claims for benefits, but was strongly opposed to continuing the proceedings. Time would run out for everyone on April 29; and the State neither had a bill to buy the line nor an outside buyer interested. In addition, Ginsburg stated dismantling operations would start within a week after the deadline. All nine of the 1600 HP road switchers had already been sold to the L&N Railway and departed Rutland early in April.

Now the State was nervous. If Ginsburg took up the tracks before a buyer came along, all would be lost. It set the legal machinery in motion to get an injunction and almost simultaneously such orders came from the Federal Court in Cleveland and the Superior Court in Vermont. In effect they would stop the Rutland from touching its tracks for an additional ninety days.

To add to all this confusion, the ICC took its own stand on the matter and postponed the effective date to May 20 ". . . to afford additional time for consideration of a motion by the Court for negotiation and sale of all or part of the line." In effect, this would give the State until August 20 to find a buyer.

Next, the Federal Court upheld the ruling by the ICC and the unions planned another appeal.

A revised bill which would allow the State to buy parts of the line but not operate it, came to the Legislature and highballed to victory by the end of May. This measure provided 2.7 million for the State to purchase the sections in question and either lease or sell them to interested operators it would designate.

A strange turn of events came in mid-June when it was announced the 21-month strike had been settled. This would have been a noteworthy move if it had taken place a year and a half before. Now it was largely academic. Governor Hoff acted as referee and the settlement was worked out between Ginsburg and the unions in Montpelier. Now the State could look for that long sought operator. Ginsburg said that he was definitely out of the railroad business for keeps. The unions would drop the suit against abandonment, the Rutland would drop its suit against the brotherhoods for their 1960 strike that was ended by an injunction, and an undisclosed cash settlement would be made to the four hundred employees.

All that remained now were the court orders prohibiting the Rutland from dismantling its tracks before the State could secure a buyer. All along, the State indicated that service would resume as soon as the present labor conflict was solved, by agreement or abandonment. The problem was solved now but no buyers were, or had ever been, seriously interested. The issue in the courts was whether the State's injunction prohibiting the dismantling of any facilities or tracks should be continued. The State argued "yes," but the Rutland said "no." Also, when did the actual ninety-day period agreed on by former Governor Keyser and Ginsburg actually begin? The Rutland said it coincided with the ICC's period, but the State argued that it didn't even start until that period ended and all pending legal action was disposed of.

Hoff and Ginsburg had another conference and came up with the compromise agreement that the now famous ninety day period would begin on August 6, giving the State until November 4 to exert its brokerage power to buy or designate operators.

The way seemed cleared at last for the Rutland to die. It had been trying now for almost two years.

In mid-August, 1963, the State purchased the Bennington to Burlington section, and later part of the Bellows Falls line, as it had secured interested operators. The Chatham had been gone for a decade, there was nothing but morning, noon, and night up through the islands north of Burlington, and no one wanted the old Ogdensburg & Lake Champlain.

It died as it was born and had lived — in conflict.

Down through the years able men like Follett, Page, Webb, Caverly and others had come in the hour of need. Now Fate had finally turned her back on the Rutland. This time no one came to save it.

Louisville & Nashville No. 256 transfers a cut of cars in DeCoursey yard, Covington, Kentucky, far from Vermont where, as Rutland No. 200, she had set the pace for modernization in the new era of her first line in the previous decade. — *Louisville & Nashville Railroad photo by C. Norman Beasley.*

L. & N. switcher No. 260 with a "Dixieland" box car in the yards at Louisville still wears the green and yellow color scheme which formerly brightened the Vermont landscape as Rutland No. 204. — *Louisville & Nashville Railroad photo by Charles B. Castner.*

L. & N.'s No. 257, formerly Rutland No. 201, swings through East Louisville with a Cincinnati local, the "old South" herald replacing the "Green Mt. Gateway" emblem under the cab window. — *John B. Fravert.*

The new, almost abstract, emblem of the Vermont Railway is placed on the red-painted side of onetime Rutland caboose No. 44 in the Rutland's old engine house at Burlington.

Until demands of traffic spelled out motive power requirements more definitely three of the Rutland's 400-class 1000 h.p. road switchers were leased by the Vermont Railway. Here No. 402 idles while the new railway's own General Electric 44T Diesel moves out of Rutland's old Burlington roundhouse, now Vermont Railway shops. — *Both: Jim Shaughnessy.*

Abandonment of all service by the Rutland left Western Vermont without rail service. Since transportation facilities were vital to the economy of this region, the state itself purchased the 130-mile section between Bennington and Burlington for 1.8 million dollars, leasing it to the Vermont Railway Corporation, under the direction of J. Wulfson, operator of the Middleton & New Jersey Railway in southern New York. Here Vermont Railway No. 1, bright red with white trim and lettering, switches cars in Burlington yard. — *D. Carol Shaughnessy.*

VERMONT RAILWAY

The new Vermont Railway began operations in midwinter, so it was immediately involved in problems of snow removal. Its second train, X-403, ran down to Bennington, January 14, 1964, the morning after a heavy storm. Road switcher No. 403, leased from Rutland, plows her way over hidden rails, south out of Manchester with the flanger, three empties, and caboose No. 1. On this page the train clears the track up Shaftsbury Hill south of Arlington, lifting the new snow into swirling clouds of crystalline whiteness. — *Both: Jim Shaughnessy.*

The first passenger train on Rutland rails since the summer of 1953 glides through the sun-drenched country south of Arlington on its way back to Rutland. The new operator, Vermont Railway Corporation, ran the excursion May 16, 1964 behind bright red No. 401, one of three Diesels leased from the old Rutland Company.

The Monadnock, Steamtown & Northern's excursion train glides through quaint green countryside just across from Bellows Falls on the Boston & Maine's Chesire Branch in July 1963. Her new home line will be the 26-mile stretch from Bellows Falls to Gassetts, and her owner, F. Nelson Blount, plans to use steam in common carrier service on this section he has leased from the state of Vermont, which had bought it from the Rutland in an effort to maintain service to the people in this region. — *Both: Jim Shaughnessy.*

Nelson Blount's Steamtown U.S.A. tourist train, in the 1964 season, with 2-8-0 No. 15, steams past the old covered bridge at Bartonsville, ten miles above Bellows Falls, on that section of former Rutland trackage he has leased from the state.

With Nelson Blount himself at the throttle, the No. 15 swings away from the Connecticut River valley through a deep cut into the Williams River valley toward Chester, 14 miles out of Bellows Falls. Rutland's Diesel No. 405 is at the back of the train because of the temporary absence of a siding on which to run the steamer around the train at the Bellows Falls end. — *Both: Jim Shaughnessy.*

EPILOGUE

A New Era,
But Not for the Rutland

e~~oe~~oe~~oe~~oe~~oe~~o

The Vermont Railway

The shock of the Rutland Railway's demise had hit hard in western Vermont. On several occasions through the years there had been threats, but someone or something had always come along to "Save the Rutland." Shippers and employees, already suffering the effects of long strikes, had been cast into an economic no-man's-land. Western Vermont was generally not that prosperous; earlier rail service, such as it was, had been poor; and complete lack of service certainly would not help. Prior to the actual abandonment a lot of heated discussion had been offered: purchase and/or operation of certain viable lines by adjacent railroads; acquisition by the State of Vermont and subsequent leasing to another operator; reorganization and operation of the old Rutland as before; and even, "Who needs it anyway?"

Even after official Interstate Commerce Commission abandonment as of October 26, 1962, court orders, injunctions, proposals, agreements, petitions, extensions and more rhetoric, thicker than the season's falling leaves, had flown through the cool Vermont air. In mid-August of 1963 the State of Vermont had bought the important Burlington to Bennington section and a portion of the Bellows Falls line for $1.8 million, net salvage value of these sections.

A report prepared for the State by the economic consulting firm of Coverdale & Colpitts found that 92 of 106 major shippers on the Vermont sections of the old Rutland would return to the rails if service were provided again. Acting on the strength of this study, Jay L. Wulfson, an officer of the Middletown & New Jersey Railroad — a downstate New York shortline — entered into a lease agreement with the Vermont State Transportation Authority. He agreed to operate 131 miles of track between Burlington and White Creek (the connection with the Boston & Maine) and the branch to Bennington for forty years in four ten-year renewable periods. The Bellows Falls line had little potential for traffic, compared to the Bennington-Burlington section, but its day would come. Rent was to be paid to the State on a sliding percentage scale in proportion to the railroad's gross operating revenues. In return the operators would receive control of the right-of-way and whatever lineside structures were spelled out in the purchase agreement with the Rutland, plus a good supply of rail hardware. Track maintenance and renewal were to be the responsibility of the operator.

To manage the rejuvenated line a privately owned common carrier was incorporated under the name of Vermont Railway in October 1963 and operations began on January 6, 1964. A Middleton & New Jersey GE 44-tonner was leased to become Vermont Railway No. 1 and was pressed into switching duties at Burlington until an estimate could be made of what the motive power requirements would be. Main line power fell to the able and venerable Alco RS-1's No. 401, 402 and 403, acquired on a lease-purchase agreement from the old Rutland. Two cabooses, a flanger and a pair of snowplows, also from the Rutland, made up the balance of the line's equipment. A grand new image for this equipment was presented in the form of bright red paint with white stripes and trim and featuring a stylistic logo of three overlapping mountain peaks in the form of an inverted "W." The Rutland heritage was carried on in the design by retaining the characteristic nose stripes of that road's units — along with its style of numbers — only with white on red, rather than yellow on green. Ironically, a group of 320 boxcars from the Rutland's own fleet of 40-foot cars, sold to Hudson Leasing Company of New York by the previous management, were leased, repainted dark green and given the new logo in white.

Despite the survey taken by the State of Vermont which had indicated that most of the shippers would return once rail operations had resumed, when it came time to do so, there was great hesitation. Many on-line shippers were convinced that the new company would not last a year. Traffic agents found it almost impossible to persuade new business to locate in western Vermont. In spite of this situation, a good level of service was established and maintained. In fact, in 16 years of operation the pattern has not changed significantly.

During the first year the VTR's gross income was $538,000. The road paid the State of Vermont $37,000 (seven percent of its gross) as rental. By 1973 revenues were about $1.5 million and the State received $130,000 — more than covering the interest and amortization of its investment in the project. Gradually, shipper confidence returned and traffic volumes increased. By the end of 1966 matters had improved to the extent that the line's first new locomotive could be obtained: a 1500 HP EMD switcher No. 501, which was capable of both switching and road duties.

A switch crew worked the Burlington area during the day and a road crew departed for Rutland and interchange with the Delaware & Hudson in the evening, making the round trip by the next morning, with road switching en route. In the morning another switch crew worked around Rutland and made the round trip to North Bennington and interchange with the B&M in the afternoon. This same crew handled local work in Bennington and interchange switching for the D&H at Rutland. Operations were — and still are — five days a week, with extra moves when required.

At present the vast majority of traffic originates or terminates on the western Vermont line, with about three quarters incoming and the balance outbound. It is made up mainly of dairy feed, fertilizers, agricultural products, fuel oil, coal, gasoline, road salt, propane, lumber, and miscellaneous loads coming in for the line's 150 or more customers. Outbound go marble and marble chips (used as a white pigment agent in paints and paper products), forest products, paper and random manufactured goods including maple syrup. Interchange of inbound and outbound traffic is about evenly divided between the B&M at North Bennington and the D&H at Rutland. Some volume is attributable to the Central Vermont at Burlington, with the smallest amount coming from the Green Mountain Railroad at Rutland.

Unfortunately, any bridge traffic potential was forfeited in the original purchase when the State elected not to include the portion of the line which ran up through the Islands to Rouses Point, New York. This exclusion seemed like a good idea at the time, considering maintenance costs of trestles, causeways, bridges and many miles of track with no shippers located on them. No one foresaw the great success of the Vermont Railway, thus today management wishes it had the line to interchange with the Canadian National and Canadian Pacific Railways for Canadian and Midwestern points. No doubt a good volume of overhead traffic would have been rolling over it out of New England. Such traffic had been the lifeblood of the old Rutland in its last years, but it was the state's intention when the Rutland line was salvaged that it serve Vermont customers, not make the lessee rich.

Some minor expansion of the VTR did occur in November 1972 when the 20-mile Clarendon and Pittsford Railway, wholly owned by the Vermont Marble Company, was acquired for $65,000. Corporate identity has remained separate on paper, although most officers of the VTR became officers of the new C&P. The marble company operated this line between Florence, Proctor and West Rutland for its own internal transportation needs as well as for common carrier purposes. This line, which parallels the Rutland trackage from Center Rutland to Florence, came into prominence after the great floods of 1927. The Rutland operated its through trains around the devastated Proctor area for a number of weeks over the little road's primitive tracks on unaffected higher ground between Center Rutland and Florence, bypassing immense washouts in and north of Proctor.

A red and white Alco S-4 switcher, purchased by VTR from the Chesapeake & Ohio and rented to the C&P, replaced the old line's two 44-ton center cab Whitcomb switchers. Five days a week at 7:00 A.M. the C&P job leaves the VTR engine-house in Rutland with a C&P crew for the day's work in Center Rutland, Proctor and Florence, where the marble and limestone operations of its former owner provide a good number of outgoing loads. Some finished marble is shipped, but mostly agricultural lime and white pigment agent for the paint-and-paper-making industries fill the cars. These traffic originating points are served from the old Rutland main line, but the bulk of the C&P's original trackage between West Rutland and Proctor and "over the hill" to Florence is unused.

Over the years motive power on the Vermont Railway has advanced from the original GE 44-tonner No. 1, through the three former Rutland RS-1's — plus an additional unit of this type acquired from the SOO line in 1967, to a fleet of Alco RS-3's, beginning with two ex-Lehigh and Hudson River units in 1970, with two more from the D&H added in 1972. New power began arriving in 1966 with EMD SW 1500 No. 501 and has reached the high point of two EMD GP 38-2's — one obtained in 1972, the other in 1974. The Alco locomotives have been well liked by the VTR and have given outstanding service. Initially they were inexpensive to purchase on the used locomotive market, but age and a growing scarcity of parts have curtailed long-range plans for them. Bowing to current production, advanced technology and higher horsepower EMD units, they are gradually being phased out.

The success of piggyback traffic throughout the country prompted the Vermont Railroad in the mid-1960's to acquire several hundred 40-foot trailers, again from Hudson Leasing Company, and establish loading terminals at North Bennington, Rutland and Burlington. Demand for off-line loadings in other commercial centers in New England and in the Midwest prompted the VTR to expand car-hire in the form of more than 5,000 piggyback trailers by the mid-1950's and to construct a terminal in East St. Louis, Illinois.

As business increased and more shippers located on the line, the need for additional boxcar capacity became apparent. To ease this shortage, almost all the 40-foot boxcars which made up the original Rutland's "new" fleet, and which were then leased by the VTR when it began operations, were stretched to 50 feet. This strategy helped, but these were merely old cars made longer. Heavier capacity trucks and cushioned underframes of the new generation of boxcars were needed to keep pace with increased demands placed on equipment in both home and foreign road service. By 1980, 950 big, new yellow boxcars carried the Green Mountain peak emblem and 510 more were acquired for the Clarendon & Pittsford. Throughout the country there is hardly a train which does not have in its consist either one of these boxcars or one of the 5,200 piggyback trailers.

The old Rutland roundhouse on the shore of Lake Champlain in Burlington serves as the railroad's main shop for maintenance of both locomotives and rolling stock. Here all repairs and painting of locomotives and cars are carried out, with only locomotive wheel-turning work being sent out to the D&H at Colonie, New York. All VTR dispatching is performed from Rutland by radio, with complete coverage achieved by an automatic repeater installation atop Killington Mountain. Much of the road's accounting is computerized and a third-generation installation went on line in April of 1974, giving management current information on a daily basis.

Under the terms of the Vermont State lease, track and roadbed maintenance are the lessee's responsibility and the Vermont Railway's management has done an excellent job. Contrary to popular belief, the physical plant of the Rutland was in reasonably good condition at the time of abandonment. During the course of the first dozen years of VTR operation, tie replacement was the only major item of expense in the maintenance budget. In the first four years of the 1970's over 100,000 ties were replaced and some 25,000 tons of stone ballast spread. To make the job more efficient, the company made heavy capital expenditures on mechanized maintenance-of-way equipment featuring electronic and automated operation. Several bridges have been reinforced and one span replaced to permit movement of heavier cars and allow faster train speeds. This whole program is in keeping with VTR's philosophy of providing service to shippers. Railroads in poor financial condition often allow their roadbeds to deteriorate because it is an easy way to save money in the short run. However, this practice ultimately leads to lower train speeds, derailments and undependable service.

For the VTR one of the most innovative directions which traffic promotion has taken has been in movement of petroleum products. During World War II much oil and gasoline had been moved nationally in solid trains, but in relatively small, individually loaded tank cars. In the mid-1970's General American Tank Car Leasing Corporation evolved its tank-train concept, whereby as many as 40 huge tank cars could be interconnected with flexible hoses for loading and unloading the entire string from only one connection. Like the unit coal and grain train concept, this new procedure changed the whole picture of railroad rate structures and made liquid bulk commodities again competitive on the rails.

The Vermont Railway immediately investigated this concept and worked out an arrangement with Mobil Oil to transfer all of the latter's heating oil and gasoline from the deep water port at Albany, New York, to its distribution center in Burlington — completely eliminating barge movements on Lake Champlain and the upper Hudson River Canal. In the first year, beginning January 1, 1978, 37.5 million gallons were shipped via the D&H/VTR routing, using only 20 cars. This service has continued to expand and by 1980 more cars had been put into service and additional customers were considering the service.

It is interesting to note that after only 10 years of operation, more on-line customers were shipping more tonnage on the VTR than had previously used the entire Rutland system before the 1961 strike. Despite the admonitions of consulting engineers, time has proved that the most profitable segment of the former 331-mile road had been wisely retained.

Recently at trackside lumber yards have located, feed mills have expanded, a beer distributor was built, a lime and marble business expanded and in Burlington a large bakery opened. In 1979, 503,422 tons were handled in 9,213 carloads. Of this total 6,579 loads came in and 2,634 departed — retaining the three-to-one inbound trend exhibited from the beginning of operations. All this activity resulted in a gross traffic revenue of $2,273,503, or more than four times that of the first year. Trailer and car leasing numbers are not reflected in these figures, but in good years they help strengthen the company's financial base and add to profits, of which a large amount is plowed back into maintenance.

There are several explanations for the successful operation of a route deemed in 1962 to be an unprofitable venture at best. A trim physical plant and a lean work force are two. More important, however, is personalized service. A prospective shipper can meet with the president or superintendent to work out problems — such as where and when sidings should be built — rather than having months of protracted negotiations and correspondence with a distant office or having requests fall upon deaf ears. Delays force shippers to look to other alternatives to meet their needs.

Labor problems that had troubled the old Rutland and finally led to its demise, have generally been avoided by the Vermont Railway, much to the approval of the State of Vermont, which had acquired the line to "get things going again." The 80 employees belong to no labor unions and there are no work rules other than the 12-hour federal work limitation for train crews. Each person must be qualified for his duties, but his work may not be restricted to one specific area. It was not uncommon to find Mr. Wulfson running the engine and his son serving as conductor, hauling a rush car to Middlebury on a weekend or spotting a load at a Burlington industry for early morning unloading.

President Wulfson and his staff had shown conclusively what can be accomplished, given a fair chance and a base from which to start. It is difficult to project what would have happened in terms of today's traffic and number of new on-line shippers had the old Rutland somehow continued functioning. Inefficiencies then existing would have continued and, given recent inflation cycles, would eventually have caught up with profits. The whole Vermont Railway story can serve as a model for many of the presently marginal operations around the country.

Thanks to VTR, the old Rutland still runs in Vermont — at least in spirit. On a quiet night one can still hear a far-off train whistle blowing for grade crossings, the sound echoing and reechoing off moonlit mountains.

☆   ☆   ☆

ROSTER OF VERMONT RAILWAY DIESEL LOCOMOTIVES †

Road Numbers	H.P.	Builder	Builders Model	Wheel Arrangement	Tractive Effort	Weight	Date Built	Serial Number	Note
1	380	GE	44-ton	B-B	22,000 lbs.	88,000 lbs.	1946	28467	1
5	600	EMD	SW-1	B-B	49,050 lbs.	196,200 lbs.	1940	1054	2
6	1000	Alco GE	S-1	B-B	57,500 lbs.	230,000 lbs.	1953	80631	3
10	380	GE	44-ton	B-B	22,000 lbs.	88,000 lbs.	1948	29967	4
250	1000	Alco GE	RS-1	B-B	60,600 lbs.	242,400 lbs.	1947	75557	5
401	1000	Alco GE	RS-1	B-B	60,600 lbs.	242,400 lbs.	1951	79350	6
402	1000	Alco GE	RS-1	B-B	60,600 lbs.	242,400 lbs.	1951	79572	7
403	1000	Alco GE	RS-1	B-B	60,600 lbs.	242,400 lbs.	1951	79573	8
404	1000	Alco GE	RS-1	B-B	60,600 lbs.	242,400 lbs.	1946	75215	9
501°	1500	EMD	SW 1500	B-B	64,330 lbs.	257,330 lbs.	1966	31990	10
601	1600	Alco GE	RS-3	B-B	56,500 lbs.	240,000 lbs.	1951	78926	11
602	1600	Alco GE	RS-3	B-B	56,500 lbs.	240,000 lbs.	1950	78071	12
603°	1600	Alco GE	RS-3	B-B	56,500 lbs.	240,000 lbs.	1952	80181	13
604	1600	Alco GE	RS-3	B-B	56,500 lbs.	240,000 lbs.	1952	80188	14
605°	1600	Alco GE	RS-3	B-B	56,500 lbs.	240,000 lbs.	1950	78369	15
606°	1600	Alco GE	RS-3	B-B	56,500 lbs.	240,000 lbs.	1950	78071	16
201°	2000	EMD	GP 38-2	B-B	65,000 lbs.	260,000 lbs.	1972	72665-1	
202°	2000	EMD	GP 38-2	B-B	65,000 lbs.	260,000 lbs.	1974	75603-1	
751°	1750	EMD	GP-9	B-B	56,500 lbs.	244,300 lbs.	1954	5340-2	17

° *Presently on Roster*

ROSTER NOTES

1. Orig. Middletown & N.J. No. 1; leased and returned to Middletown 1964.
2. Ex. Lackawanna No. 433; EL No. 355; purchased 1965 and sold to be used in Canada, October 1966.
3. Ex. C&O No. 5107; sold to Gulf Oil Chemicals Company, Pittsburg, Kansas, January 1980.
4. Ex. PRR No. 9334; purchased 1964; sold May 1965 Livonia Avon and Lakeville.
5. Ex. NYS&W No. 250; purchased November 1965; sold September 1966 EMD as trade-in on No. 501.
6. Ex. Rutland R.R. same numbers purchased January 1964; sold January 1967 Consumers Power Company.
7. & 8. Ex. Rutland R.R. same numbers purchased January 1964; sold June 1972 to Sabine River and Northern RR Company.
9. Ex. DSS&A No. 102, Ex. Soo No. 102; purchased March 1967; sold June 1972 to Sabine River & Northern RR Company.

10. Purchased new 1966; equipped with high speed flexicoil trucks and used in road service.
11. Ex. L&HR No. 12; purchased January 1970; retired for parts 1978.
12. Orig. L&HR No. 3; purchased November 1970; retired for parts 1978.
13. Orig. D&H No. 4091; purchased April 1972.
14. Orig. D&H No. 4098; purchased April 1972; sold to D&H December 1975.
15. Ex. L&HR No. 10; Ex. St. J&LC No. 205; Ex. M&B No. 10.
16. Orig. VTR No. 602; with parts from No. 601 and outside.
17. Originally Cleveland Union Terminal Co. No. 7301; purchased from them December 1980.

CLARENDON & PITTSFORD RAILROAD CO.

† *Data accurate as of 1981.*

Road Numbers	Builder	Builders Model	Serial Number	Date Built	Note
10	Whit.	44DE18A	60631	1945	1
11	Whit.	44DE18A	60632	1945	1
500	GE	70-ton	31175	1951	2

ROSTER NOTES

1. Sold for scrap to Rutland Waste & Metal Co., June 1973.
2. Sold to Kelley's Creek & Northwestern, April 1972.

Green Mountain Railroad

The rail line over the spine of the Green Mountains from Rutland down to Bellows Falls was pretty, but not prosperous — at least not since the milk plants at Chester, Gassetts, Ludlow and several more stations along the line had closed in the late 1940's. The line's function since then had been primarily as a link between the Boston & Maine and southern New England, for bridge traffic to the Ogdensburg line and for the Boston-Montreal passenger trains while they lasted. Originally the State of Vermont had considered buying only the southern end from Bellows Falls to Ludlow, since the only traffic-generating establishments were on this section. In Chester and Gassetts there were a few feed and fuel dealers, but most important in their need for rail service were two talc-producing plants — one in each town. Ludlow and Proctorsville might some day contribute traffic, but at present there was none between Ludlow and Rutland, just a lot of track and several big bridges to maintain.

When the matter of operating former Rutland trackage arose, one of the first people contacted by the State was F. Nelson Blount. He was well known in railroad circles as the operator of the two-foot-gauge Edaville Railroad in South Carver, Massachusetts, and as a collector and preserver of steam locomotives. His passion and, indeed, his historic contribution was the operation of steam locomotives in the grand manner, which he had been doing at several places around central New England for a few years. First he had displayed a number of steam locomotives during the summer of 1958 at Pleasure Island, a short-lived amusement park near Wakefield, Massachusetts. Then in 1961 he had run a steam-powered train on a section of the Concord & Claremont Railway near Sunapee, New Hampshire; on the B&M's Cheshire branch out of Keene, New Hampshire, the next season; and finally, on the north end of the Cheshire branch out of North Walpole in 1963.

Early in this period of operation Blount had purchased from the B&M the five-stall engine house in North Walpole, complete with turntable, coal tower and all facilities, to serve as a headquarters and shop for his growing endeavors and collection. The plant was also a museum of sorts, providing a view of what a small railroad terminal and shop were like at the turn of the century. Even better, it was now located right on his steam train operation site. The Monadnock, Steamtown and Northern Amusements, Inc. — better known as the MS&N Railroad — was formed to administer all these affairs which had previously been lumped into activities of and funding by the Edaville Corporation.

In the fall of 1962 Nelson Blount first approached Vermont's Governor F. Ray Keyser with the plan to shift his steam train operation to Rutland trackage. After abandonment was completed and the State had taken over the Rutland, Blount was a natural candidate for the operator. However, he wanted nothing to do with running a railroad throughout the entire state of Vermont. Running his steam train and possibly doing some freight business were his only interests. They did reach an agreement whereby he would run the southern end of the Bellows Falls subdivision for the 27 miles to Ludlow. This agreement went into effect shortly after the final fate of the Rutland had been decided and the Green Mountain Railroad Corporation had been formed to handle affairs.

The steam train moved to the Bellows Falls-Chester section of the line for the 1964 season. For Blount this arrangement had the added incentive of revenue which could be derived from serving existing and potential shippers on that section of the road and which would help offset costs of the passenger trains. It would also provide full time employment for his key people; give him the opportunity to run steam powered freight trains and even serve area shippers — a nice arrangement for everyone. A large tract of land two miles north of Bellows Falls and adjacent to the tracks was purchased as the future home for Blount's growing collection of steam locomotives and equipment. This location, now called Steamtown and/or Riverside, had once been considered by the Rutland for a new and expanded yard for the Bellows Falls region, but no action had been taken. Now, too, his shop facilities were located at the end of the line, although still separated from the station at Bellows Falls by a short section of B&M trackage of the Cheshire Division which ran across the stone arch bridge over the Connecticut River to North Walpole, New Hampshire. This short stretch of track would be a stumbling block between Blount and the B&M for several years. Finally, in February 1966, the logical step was taken to obtain free access to the engine house from the Vermont side.

All of these endeavors developed into a complex entanglement of corporations and agreements. First there was the Edaville Corporation, then the Monadnock, Steamtown & Northern Amusements, Inc., and later the Green Mountain Railroad Corporation, formed in 1964 to operate for the State of Vermont the lease of the Bellows Falls branch of the Rutland. Lastly, the non-profit Steamtown Foundation for the Preservation of Steam and Railroad Americana — commonly known as the Steamtown Foundation — was created to administer the new museum at Riverside and hold title to the equipment which had been preserved. While Blount's personal equipment was mixed in, such as ex-CPR 4-6-2 No. 1278 (numbered 127), management of everything was quite clearly under his control.

In June 1964 the new Steamtown Museum at Riverside opened and from it the steam excursion train departed for the 13-mile trip on the Green Mountain Railroad to Chester. There was an inter-mixing of crews and equipment between the Steamtown and Green Mountain enterprises, as essentially they all were under the same umbrella. Also during this period Nelson Blount was "saved" and became a Born-Again Christian. This conversion created problems for his staff and provided some interesting episodes. One might be button-holed by him while looking over the driving gear of the No. 89 or No. 127 or find a mini-revival meeting, complete with tent, at Summit — the congregation having been brought by a steam train driven by the preacher.

Business increased on the GMR as shippers saw that, as with the Vermont Railway, they could count on service being provided on a consistent basis. In early April 1965 freight operations got underway not with steam, but with recently purchased ex-Rutland RS-1 No. 405. In January of that year the State of Vermont had convinced the Green Mountain Railroad to lease the entire road

to Rutland, rather than only the 27 miles to Ludlow, thus opening the way for interchange at both ends and for possible future development along the northern part. The Rutland end of the Bellows Falls branch, which extended south out toward the Rutland town boundary, is still operated by the VTR. The latter commenced service 15 months before the GMR and the State was interested in arranging service as soon as possible on that section of track to shippers in Rutland.

Matters went well until August 1967. While flying from Riverside to his home in Dublin, New Hampshire, after a day at his beloved Steamtown, Nelson Blount was killed in the crash of his small plane. The executors of his estate were confronted with an incredible entanglement of business transactions intertwined with all the corporations he had created, in addition to his personal involvements. This accident would usher in a whole new era in the affairs of the Bellows Falls subdivision of the old Rutland.

The Green Mountain Railroad Corporation emerged as an independent employee-owned company with Robert W. Adams as chief executive officer. He had been terminal superintendent in Bellows Falls for the old Rutland and a key employee in the former Blount enterprises. The Steamtown Foundation assumed its own separate identity as a museum operator and became a lessee of trackage rights on the Green Mountain for the tourist steam train excursions from Riverside to Chester and occasional trips to Summit or Rutland. The GMR became exclusively a freight hauler and the several steam locomotives it owned were sold to Steamtown (ex-CPR No. 1246 and No. 1293) and to the Strasburg Railroad (ex-CNR 4-6-0 and No. 89). After all the Steamtown items were moved to the museum site at Riverside, the five-stall roundhouse at North Walpole became the main shop and headquarters for the Green Mountain. The station building at Chester became the business and freight office. In 1979 the old Railway Express building next to the Bellows Falls station was purchased for business and executive offices.

During 1973 the Green Mountain Railroad handled just under 120,000 tons, of which nearly 80 percent was originating traffic. Most interchange at present is with the Vermont Railway and the

Delaware & Hudson in Rutland, as there is a poor rate division with the Boston & Maine in Bellows Falls. As a result, loads must be lugged up the 1.8 percent grade northbound out of Ludlow to Summit and Mt. Holly. Southbound tonnage out of Rutland faces a similar upgrade trip to Summit. This grade is not an obstacle, since the six-cylinder 539 Alco engine can easily cope with this problem by means of doubling units on the road train. A single S-3 or RS-1 can handle about 18 loads over the hill, but a second unit is normally part of the power consist for 12 or more cars. This addition is made to increase train speed and reduce strain on the locomotives.

The Green Mountain has carried on the old Rutland tradition to an even greater degree than the Vermont Railway by adopting the exact green and yellow paint scheme. With old Rutland hands like Bob Adams in charge, this was a logical development. When the No. 405 was purchased from the Rutland the paint was in good condition, so only the name had to be changed.

The wisdom of keeping the line intact all the way to Rutland was demonstrated for a ten-day period in 1967 when the B&M had a wreck in the middle of the Hoosac Tunnel. During this time the B&M ran 26 freight trains — some with as many as 120 cars — over the Green Mountain tracks to Rutland, where they went down to North Bennington on the Vermont Railway to rejoin the B&M. Green Mountain and Vermont Railway pilots rode the trains, but B&M crews ran them.

Like other shortline railroads, the Green Mountain found it necessary to have its own boxcars in order to offset per diem charges of other lines' equipment on their road and to serve as an income-producing factor in the overall railroad market. Acquired on lease from the ITEL Corporation in 1976 were 100 50-foot boxcars. By 1980, 300 carried the green color and yellow herald of the little line and 100 covered hoppers had also been added. Covered hoppers were more efficient in handling talc in bulk rather than in bags loaded into boxcars.

The GMR usually runs five days a week with a three-man crew. Two track gangs keep the 50 miles of trackage in good condition, replacing ties and rails as needed, with an annual summer push to replace some of the original 80- and 90-pound rails with used 105-pound material. About 20 employees keep business moving regularly, with some seasonal people being added in the summer.

Having placed the Green Mountain Railroad on a steady course after its turbulent beginning in the Blount years, President Adams stepped down in 1978, but continues to remain active in the organization. Replacing him was Glen E. Davis, retired commander of the Vermont State Police, who had come up through the ranks in that organization and had been a student of railroads and their operations.

The success of the Green Mountain, like that of the Vermont Railway, can be attributed to the awareness of personnel in providing service to their customers. It is not unusual to see an official performing a job other than his normal corporate one. Continued attention to details has strengthened GMR's position in the region's transportation picture to the extent that two additional RS-1 locomotives were purchased from the Illinois Central Gulf Railroad in July 1976. Tonnage handled in 1979 had reached 204,027 — almost double that of only six years earlier. This volume took 3,528 cars in and out and produced gross operating revenues of $905,808. Rental payments to the State of Vermont were $26,800, approximately three percent of the gross.

Despite dependence on relatively few shippers, the GMR's future looks optimistic. The level and quality of service have been well established and thus are an encouragement to growth of regional business. Management is not some great, faceless corporation located miles away in the tower of a high rise, but is a small, close-knit enterprise doing business with neighbors. Vermonters like to deal with Vermonters. Since many GMR employees own stock in their company, there is a special outlook, compared to that of workers on larger lines. Each person at GMR can see the fruits of his labors, as, for example, a car delivered and a customer satisfied. Indeed, this section of the old Rutland was "saved," not only by the State of Vermont, but also by a modern-day version of the legendary "Green Mountain Boys," pulling coupling pins and throttles rather than musket triggers.

☆   ☆   ☆

ROSTER OF LOCOMOTIVES

Road Class	Road Number	H.P.	Builder	Builders Model	Wheel Arrange- ment	Tractive Effort	Weight	Date Built	Serial	Note
DES-1	302	1000	Alco GE	S-2	B-B	s = 69,420 c = 34,000	230,000	12/28/1948	76515	1
DES-2	303	1000	Alco GE	S-4	B-B	s = 69,420 c = 34,000	231,400	9/11/1950	78032	2
DES-2	305	1000	Alco GE	S-4	B-B	s = 69,420 c = 34,000	231,400	10/12/1950	78409	3
DRS-1	400	1000	Alco GE	RS-1	B-B	s = 72,900 c = 34,000	243,000	5/07/1948	75839	4
DRS-1	401	1000	Alco GE	RS-1	B-B	s = 73,000 c = 34,000	243,400	3/10/1950	77070	5
DRS-1	405	1000	Alco GE	RS-1	B-B	s = 72,000 c = 34,000	242,400	11/23/1951	79575	6

(Tractive Effort in Pounds — s = starting; c = continuous)

ROSTER NOTES

1. Ex. Delaware & Hudson 3026; GMRC 3026; GMRC 302. Bldrs. No. 76515, acquired 12/04/1969, held for making "slug" unit 10/1976.
2. Ex. Delaware & Hudson 3036; GMRC 3036; GMRC 303. Bldrs. No. 78032, acquired 5/02/1966, in service 10/1976.
3. Ex. Delaware & Hudson 3050; GMRC 305. Bldrs. No. 78409, acquired 12/04/1969, in service 10/1976.
4. Ex. Illinois Terminal 753; Illinois Terminal 1053; GM&O 1053; ICG 1053; GMRC 400. Bldrs. No. 75839, acquired 7/19/1976; mechanical rebuild; prime mover rebuild by ICG, Jackson, TN 7/1976; other work and paint by GMRC; in service 12/1976.
5. Ex. Illinois Terminal 756; Illinois Terminal 1056; GM&O 1052; ICG 1052; GMRC 401. Bldrs. No. 77070, acquired 7/19/1976; mechanical rebuild; prime mover rebuild by ICG, Jackson, TN 7/1976; other work and paint by GMRC; in service 12/1976.

6. Ex. Rutland Railway Corporation 405; GMRC 405. Bldrs. No. 79575, acquired 4/01/1965, in service 10/1976.

(*Note:* Although Ex. 1052 and 1053 appear in ICG renumbering lists, units were never actually renumbered by ICG and bore GM&O lettering when sold to GMRC.) (No diesel-electric locomotives owned by this carrier have been sold or disposed of since carrier commenced operations 4/01/65.)

Peter L. Read,
Officer in Charge — Locomotives
Green Mountain Railroad Corporation
Bellows Falls, Vermont

The Ogdensburg Bridge Port Authority and St. Lawrence Railroad

The northern New York section of the old Rutland — formerly the Ogdensburg & Lake Champlain Railroad, fondly referred to as the "Old & Late Coming" — had been prosperous in the old days, but not in recent times. A Rutland-owned steamship line had carried freight in and out of Ogdensburg and throughout the whole Great Lakes basin. The first railroad refrigerator cars to carry fresh butter to Boston had been constructed here. Once, a great flood of milk shipping started here, increasing in volume as it flowed all the way to Boston and New York. A change of milk marketing orders and technology dried up the milk traffic. After the St. Lawrence Seaway was completed, the short surge of traffic created by its construction ended also.

Only the meager flow of overhead, or bridge traffic, which moved at a slower, cheaper rate via this route and was turned over to the New York Central at Norwood, remained to fill out the once-a-day freight. When abandonment was proposed in 1963 there was only token opposition to track removal. This was easily accomplished except for a few industrial tracks around Malone which were taken over and served by the New York Central and the stretch from Norwood to the west end of the line at Ogdensburg. This 26-mile section was exempted from the dismantling order, since it was hoped that an operator might be secured for it. There was potential for business with a seaport facility being developed at a small site already owned by the Rutland and with several shippers, including the coal-burning New York State Mental Hospital in Ogdensburg. The line from Norwood to Malone Junction was also exempted from the abandonment order. The NYC had had trackage rights to reach Malone over that section since the time its line up through the Adirondacks had been cut back to Lake Clear Junction. This section, too, was finally removed when the NYC decided not to take over the trackage, but to serve Malone via the northern remnant of its Adirondack line down from Huntingdon, Quebec, Canada.

The Ogdensburg Bridge and Port Authority obtained a federal grant in 1966 of $410,000 to purchase the stretch of line out to Norwood from Ogdensburg. The associated real estate cost $350,000 and the balance was set aside for future rehabilitation projects. At that time the Port Authority operated a bridge over the St. Lawrence River, a now-defunct bus line over the bridge between Ogdensburg and Prescott, Ontario, and a small airport with the large name of Ogdensburg International Airport, which handled only a few commercial flights a day. Railroad operations were somewhat removed from OBPA's current endeavors, so they contacted Jay Wulfson of the Vermont Railway about the possibility of his operating the property for them. Already acknowledged as the very successful operator of the main section of the old Rutland, he was quite interested in the proposal, but backed out of a potential agreement when he learned that the State Hospital in Ogdensburg had converted from coal to natural gas. Supplying the hospital with coal would have been the only immediate, albeit seasonal, business on the little line. Until other sources of traffic or a seaport facility of some consequence could be developed, volume would be exceptionally lean.

Finally an agreement was reached with Herbert F. Heidt, a Middletown, New York restaurant owner and old friend of Wulfson's. Trains began running on the Ogdensburg & Norwood Railway in the spring of 1967. Motive power was provided by an ex-D&H S-4 1000 HP Alco switcher painted, ironically, in the Vermont Railway red-and-white color scheme, but lettered O&N No. 1. The old brick station in Ogdensburg, dating back to the 1850's, became the railroad's headquarters. A door was cut in the east end of the old structure to allow the freight house end to become the engine house.

Rutland trains had stopped running in September 1961. After such a period of non-service, rebuilding any volume of traffic would be quite difficult. Having tried for more than a year, Heidt embargoed the Ogdensburg & Norwood on November 1, 1968. It was then apparent that if the line was to be run at all, the Port Authority would have to do it. Therefore, an application was filed with the ICC to do so. It was eventually approved, with service resuming under OBPA direction in the fall of 1970. Business was not much better than before. Losses incurred in the rail operations had to be made up out of toll bridge receipts. Interestingly, the State Mental Hospital returned to burning coal after natural gas became scarce and expensive in the late 1960's. Its tonnage now makes up about half of the 300 to 400 cars handled per year.

In 1974 the St. Regis Paper Company approached James P. McGuiness, executive director of the Ogdensburg Bridge Port Authority, with a unique proposal — the gift of an entire railroad. The Norwood & St. Lawrence Railroad had been a prosperous adjunct to the paper company's business in the North Country since 1901, moving Quebec pulpwood from the St. Lawrence dock at Waddington to the company's plant at Deferiet, New York, near Watertown, via its own line to Norwood and for the remaining distance on the New York Central. However, the new St. Lawrence Seaway had made obsolete the old 14-foot draft boats that carried pulpwood to the river port of Waddington, so the sulphite pulp operation at Deferiet ended.

Thus, the Norwood & St. Lawrence Railway had become redundant and the St. Regis Paper Company offered the whole operation free to the OBPA, including all trackage, two G.E. 70-ton locomotives, shop facilities and engine house at

Norwood — and with a few lineside clients as well. This offer had some advantages for all concerned. The paper company got out from under a money-losing venture by writing off for tax purposes a $1,422,515 investment. The OBPA picked up some additional freight traffic, two locomotives, a fully equipped shop, more snow plow and work equipment, 22 acres of industrial land and another port facility on the St. Lawrence River at Waddington. To sweeten the deal the paper company even threw in $20,000 in cash.

In addition to taking over the Norwood & St. Lawrence, McGuiness convinced the Simplicity Pattern Company, the only major private customer on the line, to make an annual subsidy payment of $20,000 to ensure service, while the few remaining shippers on the N.&St.L. line agreed to pay a $30.00 surcharge per car to retain the service. This extra money, along with operating income, financed replacement in 1974 of 3,600 ties and other track maintenance on the road.

In 1976 the Port Authority participated with the New York State Department of Transportation in the "negotiated solution" to preserve service on the old New York Central's Ogdensburg secondary track running 20 miles from the NYC's St. Lawrence division at De Kalb Junction to Ogdensburg. This was one of many sections of the Penn Central not included in the final system plan at the formation of Conrail. Operation of this trackage under subsidy was initiated April 1 by the OBPA. During the course of the year the National Railway Utilization Corporation (NRUC) completed negotiations with the Port Authority to lease and operate all of the Authority's railroad properties, beginning April 1, 1977. This corporation, which already managed the Pickens Railway in South Carolina, was interested in establishing a fleet of boxcars for use throughout the country. Now, that company's blue boxcars with large white letters would appear with "St. Lawrence Railroad" on them, appropriately chosen for the area adjoining the great river.

A piggyback facility was built in Ogdensburg in 1978 under the leadership of the St. Lawrence Railroad, which further helped the Port Authority by making their bridge to Prescott, Ontario, a potentially important gateway between the United States and Canada. Part of the Rutland's grain elevator has been taken over by a molding sand producing company and a vast tract of land adjacent to the river offers promise of development.

Between 1976 and 1979 4,600 blue boxcars bearing the St. Lawrence Railroad's reporting marks appeared on the nation's rails. Two hundred of these cars were built in an assembly plant constructed in 1978 at Norfolk, New York. It also serves as a car repair depot, since demand for new boxcars slowed in late 1979. The St. Lawrence's 17 employees keep trains rolling three days a week, or as much as is required, as in the case of coal stockpiling at the Ogdensburg State Hospital. Closing of a paper mill late in 1978 halted operations on the De Kalb Junction-Ogdensburg segment, which reopened again in March 1980 under the name North County Railway — no longer affiliated with OBPA or the St. Lawrence Railroad. Traffic figures for that year showed 25,400 tons of freight handled, with 12,350 tons inbound and 13,050 outbound — an almost even balance, unusual for a small line.

This segment of the old Rutland, too, has survived through the action of a government agency — not the State, as in Vermont, but the Port Authority, a quasi governmental corporation which serves the needs of the area's taxpayers and shippers. Results here have not been as spectacular as in the case of the Vermont Railway, but there are not the industrial or population bases that exist in western Vermont. Great potential is present in the two seaway-fronting port properties at Ogdensburg and Waddington. All that is needed to bring a boom to the line is establishment of a container port or some other overseas trans-shipping activity. The Ogdensburg Bridge and Port Authority and its operator the St. Lawrence Railroad may indeed be on the brink of a new day. The Rutland's dream of a bustling seaport at Ogdensburg could come true — more than a century later.

☆   ☆   ☆

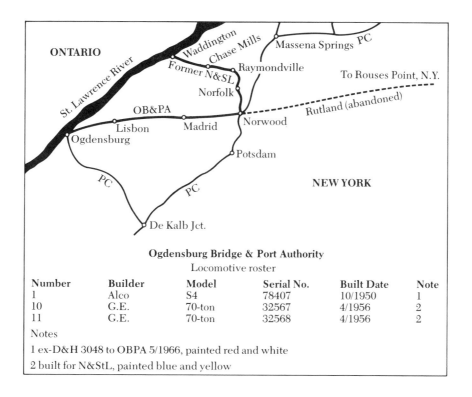

Ogdensburg Bridge & Port Authority
Locomotive roster

Number	Builder	Model	Serial No.	Built Date	Note
1	Alco	S4	78407	10/1950	1
10	G.E.	70-ton	32567	4/1956	2
11	G.E.	70-ton	32568	4/1956	2

Notes

1 ex-D&H 3048 to OBPA 5/1966, painted red and white

2 built for N&StL, painted blue and yellow

Conclusion

The concept of a state government owning and operating a railroad in competition with other forms of taxpaying transportation and theoretically using taxpayers' money to subsidize such an effort, was quite foreign to many, including Vermont legislators, at the time it was introduced. It was felt, however, that if the private sector could not accomplish this, then perhaps it was the time and place for government to attempt it. To Governor Keyser for proposing such a bold step forward and Governor Hoff for working out details to implement a workable plan must be given enormous credit for moving into uncharted political water. Their purpose was to retain rail service for all the residents of the communities involved. In the case of the old Rutland the attempt has succeeded so well that a number of other states, including New Hampshire, have embarked upon similar projects. Vermont itself has expanded the concept in the northern part of the state to the St. Johnsbury & Lamoille County Railroad (now the Lamoille Valley Railroad), which had given its last gasp under private ownership, and to the Washington County Railroad (formerly the Montpelier and Barre Railroad), in the Montpelier-Barre area. With the demise of the Penn Central, a number of marginal roads not included in the final system plan for Conrail have followed, the state-owned designated operator plan, essentially emulating Vermont's efforts of a decade before.

In addition to Vermont's return on the investment in the Rutland, there are benefits which far outweigh any rental income. In 1962, with the old Rutland completely shut down, a consultant's report had shown that on-line shippers were paying $700,000 annually in increased transportation costs. Such a drain on many of Vermont's hard-pressed industries and the negative impact which an absence of rail freight service had on industrial development in the region, affected the entire state and its residents. Accolades go to the State of Vermont for "Saving the Rutland" — at least in memory.

RUTLAND

ALBUM

Photographer Donald W. Furler caught this graceful Mikado with its busy train hustling through Otter Creek Valley in July 1949. The town of Proctor is nearby.

These three scenes provide a nostalgic glimpse of old-time railroading which brought few visible changes to the Rutland in forty years. The little Mogul on the opposite page was hauling its string of box cars and gondolas with a lone combination coach into Lebanon Springs in 1912. The carefully trimmed shrubbery and lawn suggest a resort setting of that period. Below that is a much more recent picture of an old Ten-Wheeler simmering beside battered man-powered coal facilities at Bennington. Only the trucks parked under the trees hint at the 1948 date of the North Bennington scene (*above*) dominated by the Ten-Wheeler with express and mail cars, the Chatham local headed by a bigger Consolidation and the old ball signal.—*Above: Donald S. Robinson; opposite above: Collection of Robert Lank; opposite below: Jim Shaughnessy.*

Fast handling of freight was a specialty of the Rutland. Speed is very evident in Philip R. Hastings' dramatic view on the opposite page of a Ten-Wheeler and Mikado teaming up to rush hot-shot freight No. 19 north along Burlington Bay. A similar pair of engines labor in the early morning mist near Center Rutland to swing 80 cars of northbound freight past an idle tall-stacked tractor which seems to mock their shape and vigor. The old slant-cylinder Consolidation works alone at Proctor switching the Vermont Marble Company's Clarendon & Pittsford Railroad interchange. — *This page: Robert F. Collins.*

Double heading of freight No. 19 was common practice during periods of good business. This train rolling through a grassy cut past Queen City Park, just south of Burlington, stretches far into the mist behind its Ten-Wheeler-Mikado team.

On the opposite page: In the flat country at the north end of Lake Champlain, a Mike handles westbound freight No. 9, coming past the signal guarding the Delaware & Hudson crossing near Rouses Point on an early morning in May, 1949. — *Both: Philip R. Hastings.*

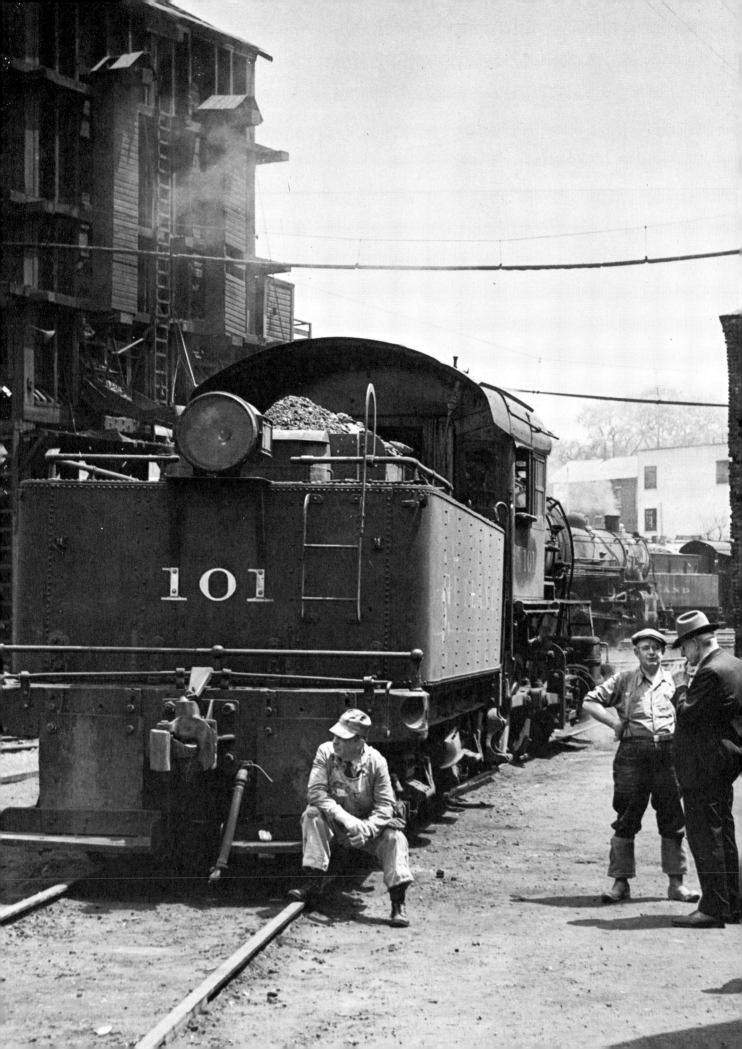

Faithful 0-6-0 switchers made up many a train for the Rutland. No. 101 provides a convenient seat for a trainman in Rutland yard, while two of his buddies talk the situation over. *Above:* Newly acquired from the dieselized Clarendon & Pittsford No. 107 reflects dignity, if not quite glamor, in the water at the south end of Burlington yard. By 1947, when this picture was made, the little drawbridge was seldom opened. From its signal bridge was taken the picture of the top side of No. 100. The fireman looks back, watching for the switchman's signal. — *Philip R. Hastings.*

Above left: The Consolidation engines saw plenty of freight service. Two brakemen enjoy the breeze on a hot August day, between unloading LCL, as No. 31 makes its leisurely way with the local across the pasture south of Proctor. *Left:* No. 23 takes a northbound extra out of Burlington, past the Central Vermont terminal, where a C.V. local is arriving from Essex Junction. No. 27 is in Alburgh roundhouse, awaiting its morning call as a helper west to Malone. The other engines in the background will handle milk and passenger trains for Ogdensburg. — *Above left: Robert F. Collins; others: Philip R. Hastings.*

page 231

Old steam engines kept hard at work during their last year, while the Diesels which would soon replace them were abuilding in Schenectady. Ten-Wheeler No. 76 takes on coal in Bellows Falls, near the old ball signal which protected the Rutland-Boston & Maine crossing. Soon she will take the Boston section of the *Green Mountain Flyer* over Mount Holly to Rutland. The veteran U.S.R.A. Consolidation No. 26 leads a Mikado at the head of the Norwood hot-shot from Bellows Falls through East Wallingford. With local freight X-26, the same engine waits in Rouses Point for the milk train to clear the Champlain bridge. — *Above: Fred Sankoff; others: Philip R. Hastings.*

Burlington yard was a busy place for old switcher No. 100 and Ten-Wheeler No. 50, one day in 1946. Soon to be replaced by another newer 0-6-0 from Rutland's neighbor, Clarendon & Pittsford, No. 100 will shove a cut of cars up a team track after the fireman finishes his talk with the switchman by the engine.
— *Philip R. Hastings.*

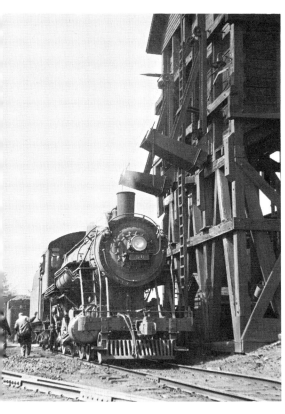

Before pulling out to the north with the local freight as shown in the opposite view, No. 50 had fueled up at the coal tower and backed onto the turntable on the engine house lead in preparation for the run. — *Philip R. Hastings.*

On the following pages: Burlington, the Queen City, suns herself on a beautiful afternoon in her inspiring site on the eastern shore of Lake Champlain, the Green Mountains rising in the distance. Here and there, graceful Colonial spires reach above the trees of Vermont's largest city. In the right foreground lie the Rutland's roundhouse and yards, with the station at left center. — *Rutland Railway.*

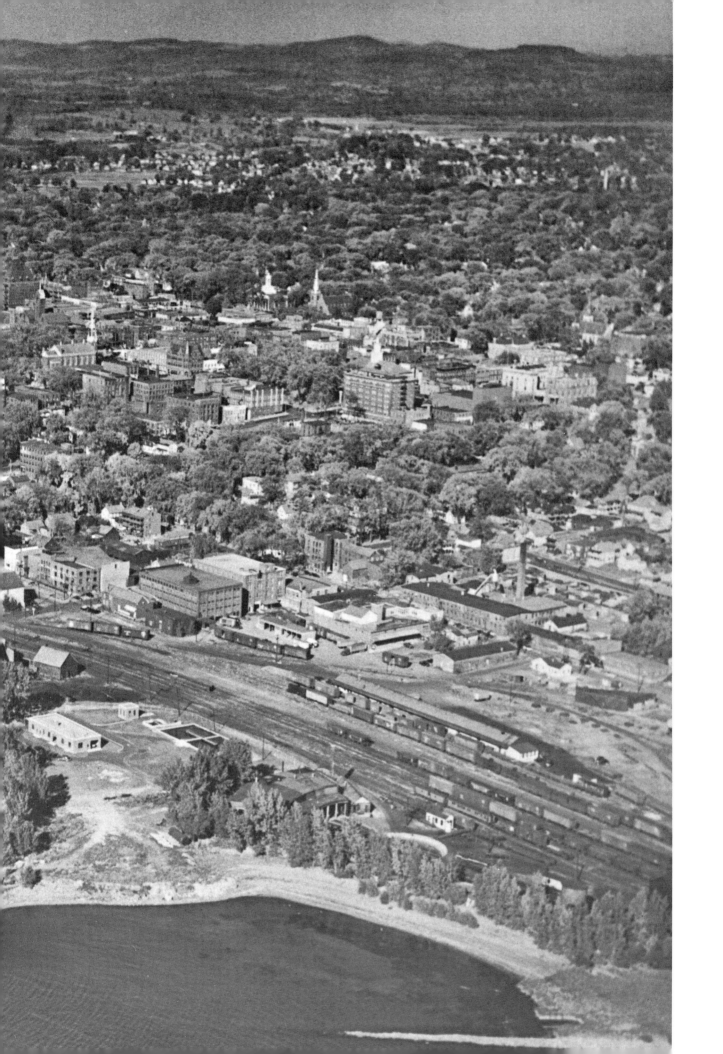

The fireman has really laid on the coal to give Consolidation No. 16 and its extra freight train a good start on its trip south out of Burlington where, in another part of the yard, the engineer of switcher No. 105 chats with a friend while No. 91 brings in freight No. 19 from Bellows Falls. The little 0-6-0, on a nearer track, looks deceptively large as compared with the huge Mountain engine, farther away. — *Philip R. Hastings.*

This frugal scene is likewise Burlington. A thrifty dowager from Battery Street gathers fuel for the home fires while a hostler trims the coal pile on the tender during the *Flyer's* 15-minute station stop. The contrast in tender sizes is overwhelming. — *Philip R. Hastings.*

Burlington's roundhouse on the shore turns its back on a magnificent panorama of Lake Champlain, but at night, when the engines are brought in for service, its interior provides a fantastic spectacle of its own, with the locomotives silhouetted against the glare of the work lights, — *Philip R. Hastings.*

Somebody was careless on the Canadian National the night of August 6, 1949. A caboose and gondola were left on the main line near St. John, Quebec, right in the path of the *Green Mountain Flyer,* coming south from Montreal. Pacific No. 85 made kindling of the caboose and climbed aboard the gondola. Unfortunately she was too heavy to ride home to Rutland just as she was and the C.N. wrecking crew had to ease the big engine out of the car. There were no human casualties. — *Collection of Gordon Cutler.*

Back in the Rutland Shop the big Pacific is being rebuilt after its mishap on C.N. rails. In the yard outside Rutland's own hook waits for a call to duty. In the background is the railway office building, once the coach shop. — *Jim Shaughnessy.*

Rutland's wrecker got a workout in more peaceful uses. In March 1951 it had to rescue sleepers of the northbound *Mount Royal* from the uncomfortable angle into which they were pitched when rain softened a fill south of Arlington. Nobody was hurt this time. *Above:* The hook frames a temporary trestle built in 1947 when floodwaters in East Creek outside Rutland carried away Rutland and Delaware & Hudson tracks. The Mikado engine brings a freight down from Norwood. Three years later a single track replaced this trestle. — *Philip R. Hastings; opposite, both: Jim Shaughnessy.*

The *Mount Royal*, overnight train out of Montreal, is due in a few minutes. Meanwhile the photographer, making like a baggage man, shoves aside snow to make way for the expected passengers on the platform. A two-wheeled mail cart is ready nearby. Further south, in Burlington, switcher No. 100 waits with a sleeper to add to the train. When the *Mount Royal* gets there, its 20-minute stop allows plenty of time for the Pullman to be hooked on, the conductor and engineer to discuss orders, and the coal passer—visible over the top of Pacific No. 85's cab—to trim the coal pile on the tender. — *Philip R. Hastings.*

Long, long freights were hauled across the Rutland trackage during the railway's prosperous years with Mikado engines often doing the honors. Load limitations on Rouses Point trestle oblige No. 32 to handle alone a westbound freight which fills almost the entire length of the bridge across the northern end of Lake Champlain. The same Mike, on another day, helps No. 36 work Bellows Falls-bound tonnage up Mount Holly near East Wallingford. — *Left: Philip R. Hastings; right: Robert F. Collins.*

The 46-year-old Ten-Wheeler ponders its future in the smoky depths of Alburgh roundhouse. The freight yard there with engine house and coaling ramp was busy this bright spring day in 1948. Engines No. 26 and 91 prepare to take freight No. 9 west to Norwood. The approach to Alburgh from the south over the islands is spectacular, as can be seen from these two tender-top views. Engineer Ray Haseltine brings No. 28 toward a slow board at Bow Arrow Point drawbridge on the smaller causeway connecting Grand Isle with North Hero Island. A few miles further on, at lonely North Hero station, the milk train gets a clear board to proceed toward Alburgh. The Pacific which usually handled these milk runs had broken down today, but Haseltine managed to make up 20 minutes with the old WHIPPET engine, more than accustomed to fast running in her day. — *Philip R. Hastings.*

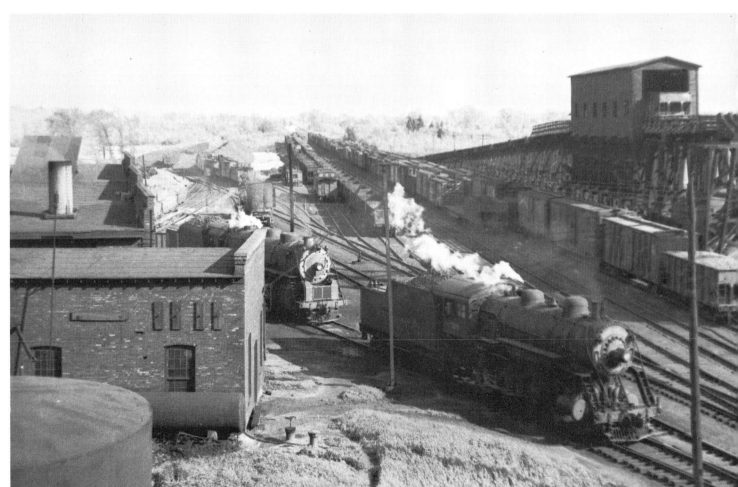

On the following pages: The milk train from Alburgh is clearing the Lake Champlain trestle to Rouses Point. Soon the Central Vermont local freight will move on to the east, while Ten-Wheeler No. 72 continues its run to Ogdensburg, dropping off empty milk cars on the way. — *Jim Shaughnessy.*

Western terminus of the milk runs, and of the Rutland, was Ogdensburg. In later years the yards were a ghostly and desolate reminder of the busy rail-water interchange here until 1915 when the line had to get out of the shipping business. This weedy yard with its closed roundhouse and almost deserted station is the destination of milk train No. 7, behind Ten-Wheeler No. 73, as it crosses Delaware and Hudson's main line west of Rouses Point. — *Philip R. Hastings.*

Milk trains accommodated passengers on the Ogdensburg subdivision, on a coach added at Alburgh. Empty track in front of the station is Central Vermont. The distant seesaw ball signal gives clear indication to enter the tracks used jointly by the two roads from here to Rouses Point. The old combine *(below)* has obviously seen better days as the train heads west from Rouses Point. Can shipments of milk were still handled as late as 1951. — *Above: Philip R. Hastings; below: Jim Shaughnessy.*

Ten-Wheeler No. 79 is pulling the *Green Mountain Flyer* out of Bellows Falls station, across Boston & Maine's Connecticut River line, and heading north past the old ball signal. On another less foggy day, her sister engine No. 76 takes on water outside the roundhouse, preparing to take a train on to the north, after it arrives from Boston. In the roundhouse at Rutland, Pacific No. 85 reposes in the shadowy depths of the old building, every ready to make the occasional run in a last gasp for glory before resigning herself to a cold, rusty end.
— *Left: Donald S. Robinson; right: Philip R. Hastings; below: Jim Shaughnessy.*

The weekly local on the Chatham branch has twelve miles to go to Bennington from Petersburgh Junction, where stands the old water tank, useless since the arrival of the Diesels. The little train rounding two of the many turns on the "Corkscrew Division" looks for all the world like a Colorado Narrow Gauge operation. — *Jim Shaughnessy.*

Consolidation No. 26 will team up with her sister, No. 27, just backing onto the Alburgh turntable, to take westbound freight No. 9 to Norwood. Mountain No. 91, behind the 26 in the picture, will help the train up the grade to Cherubusco. — *Philip R. Hastings.*

A pair of Mikados battle the grade over Mount Holly at Cuttingsville, Vermont, with Boston bound tonnage. — *Robert F. Collins.*

After nearly a half-century of faithful service, No. 52 is about ready for retirement as she brings a northbound local out of Center Rutland. The other Ten-Wheeler was built eight years later and, newly painted, presents a handsome sight as she takes a Bellows Falls extra out of Rutland yard during steam's glory days on the railroad. — *Above: Robert F. Collins; below: E. H. Brown.*

Lots of equipment was needed to keep the roadbed in repair. None was more ungainly than the strange contraption in front of Consolidation No. 15. It is a winch powered by steam from the locomotive. Its cable pulls a plow-like device through the string of ancient wooden side-dump ballast cars to push the fill out on the roadbed. Less spectacular is the useful motor speeder on which the Colchester section gang begins its day's work under a shroud of Lake Champlain fog, spring 1950. — *Above: Donald S. Robinson; below: Philip R. Hastings.*

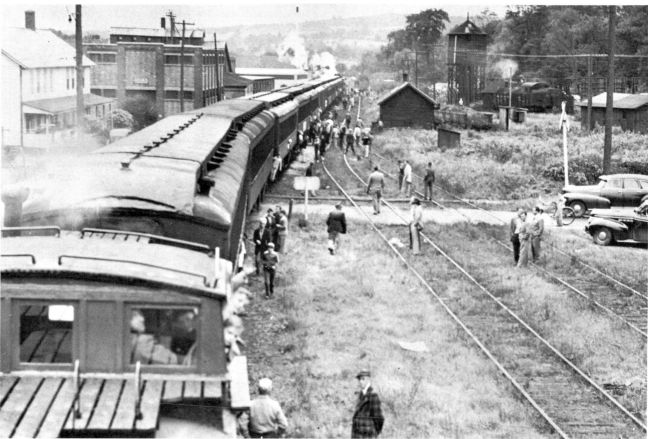

Exchange Club Special

Back in the 1940s the Chatham Exchange Club began its annual custom of a railroad excursion during the fall foliage season. These continued until the Rutland retired its old wooden passenger equipment in 1953. Author Jim Shaughnessy has pictured three of the final jaunts. Ten-Wheeler No. 77 brings the party into North Bennington in 1948. The 14-car special in 1950 stopped in Bennington to take on water while an old 4-6-0 lazily smokes by the water tank. Apparently the caboose was included in the consist for the benefit of small fry. The Chatham Branch was dieselized three months before the 1951 excursion and special arrangements were necessary to make it possible for elegant Mountain No. 93 to lead the way. She appears below at Berlin, N. Y.

The Tin Can

The local Burlington-Rutland freight was known to Vermonters as the *Tin Can.* During the late 1940s Philip Hastings photographed it repeatedly. Here he caught Ten-Wheeler No. 50 working it up the grade in snow-blanketed Queen City Park south of Burlington. On the other page Consolidation No. 14 takes the local past the depot at Charlotte on a warm summer day. Below is No. 50 again as she brings the *Tin Can* across the little drawbridge at the south end of Burlington yard. Lake Champlain and Burlington Bay sparkle in the background.

Milk Train

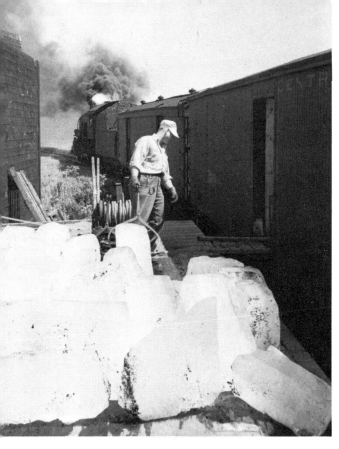

Here are three of Photographer Hastings' views of the milk train. Alburgh was an important stop on the day when the two pictures to the left were made. Switcher No. 109 removes the passenger car from the north-bound train while the reefers are being stocked with ice harvested from Lake Champlain the previous winter. While the cars are being cooled for the milk, the fireman is busy in Ten-Wheeler No. 73 getting up a good head of steam for the grade west of Rouses Point. From Bellows Falls to Alburgh the milk train carried mail cars. Below a warmly gloved trainman tosses a sack aboard the northbound train during a frigid stop at Shelburne.

Photographer Hastings has recorded an interesting action sequence of a meeting between southbound milk train No. 88 and a northbound local freight. *Opposite:* The milk train has stopped for the order board while two of its crew walk to the New Haven station house for orders. When they have the orders the board is cleared and Pacific No. 80 brings the train down the main as the opposing local eases into the passing track. *This page:* Once the northbound freight has cleared, No. 80 pours it on to accelerate her dozen cars on their way south to Rutland. Now Consolidation No. 14 drifts up the passing track in front of the Victorian gem of a depot to switch the sidings here at New Haven.

Milk trains No. 87 northbound and 88 southbound met at Burlington Union Station. *Opposite:* The Central Vermont yard extends north of the station. Here Ten-Wheeler No. 75 accelerates the northbound for its run across the islands to Alburgh. The actual meeting of the two trains is shown with Pacific No. 82 in from the north and 4-6-0 No. 79 from the south. *Above:*

The Rutland yard extends south from the station. The Pacific No. 80 in this wintry scene has just cleared the yard and is hauling its heavy load up the slight grade south of town. These were the days when a milk train was still a real train on the Rutland. Even in March 1950 it had 13 cars. — *Philip R. Hastings.*

Opposite: Here is another view of the afternoon meeting of the milk trains at Burlington's lakefront station. No. 79 is warming up for its run to the north as it sits beside a Pullman which will go out on train No. 46 in the evening. As the train gathers speed it passes Central Vermont's tank and engine house. *Above:* This time the milk train is led by Mountain type No. 90 as it heads toward the Champlain islands on its way to Alburgh and the west. — *Philip R. Hastings.* *Left:* Train No. 87 this time includes some freight along with the milk as it rolls into Alburgh behind the neat Ten-Wheeler. — *Jim Shaughnessy.*

page 273

Left: Two milk trains cross the watery miles of Lake Champlain. In the upper picture the train feels its cautious way across the shaky trestle from Rouses Point to solid Vermont ground and Alburgh. A prudent brakeman rides the combine platform ready for a hasty exit if need be. More substantial is the three-mile rock fill from the mainland to Allen's Point on South Hero Island. Pacific No. 80 brings train No. 87 to the island end of the Rutland's version of the water level route. New York State's Adirondacks rise behind the sparkling Champlain. — *Top: R. S. Ritchie; bottom: Philip R. Hastings.*

Above: Ten-Wheeler No. 79 is enveloped in steam as the last remnants of the clinkers which brought her milk train down from Alburgh are quenched in the ash pit at Rutland. — *Jim Shaughnessy.*

The Green Mountain Flyer

Here comes the *Flyer! Left:* Ten-Wheeler No. 78 brings the train down from Alburgh and Montreal through lonely North Hero, Vermont, while the crew of Pacific No. 80 look on, from the head of the northbound milk train waiting on the passing track. — *Philip R. Hastings.*

Train No. 64, the southbound *Flyer,* divided into two sections at Rutland. No. 64 went on to Bennington and Troy. No. 164 went to Bellows Falls and Boston. The Rutland connected with the Boston & Maine on each route and Rutland had trackage rights to Troy. A re-ciprocal arrangement between the two railroads equalized mileage by using engines and crews interchangeably over each other's tracks south of Rutland. Hence B. & M. locomotives were not infrequently to be seen in Rutland yards. *Above:* On adjacent tracks stand Rutland's Mountain No. 92 and B. & M.'s Pacific No. 3708 with the two halves of the southbound *Flyer.* The Pacific will head for Bellows Falls while the Mountain will be on its way to Bennington. *Below:* The B. & M. Pacific No. 3706 is on its way out of Rutland and heading for Bellows Falls. — *Above: Philip R. Hastings; below: John Pickett.*

Left: Well on her way out of Rutland the big Pacific brings the *Flyer* north through Center Rutland. — *John Pickett.*

Below: Bilingual signs are the rule at St. John (or St. Jean) Quebec where Ten-Wheeler No. 77 heads the southbound train for the border and Rouses Point.

Right: The engine crowds the 50 mph legal speed limit crossing Cold River bridge at North Clarendon on the way to Bellows Falls. — *Both: Philip R. Hastings.*

Opposite: The smoke from Ten-Wheeler No. 76 obscures most of the Boston-bound *Green Mountain Flyer* as it accelerates out of Rutland yard. 0-8-0 switcher No. 110 waits for a chance to switch a cut of cars. — *Philip R. Hastings.*

Left: Mountain type No. 93 drifts its wintry way under the covered bridge at 101st Street in Troy, N. Y. *Below:* B. & M.'s Pacific stops in North Bennington on its way from Rutland to Troy. The reciprocal arrangement between the lines eliminated changing power and crews at White Creek. — *Jim Shaughnessy.*

Opposite, top: The New York section of the *Flyer* carried milk cars in 1938 when photographer F. Stewart Graham pictured well groomed Pacific No. 83 at North Bennington.

Opposite, bottom: Ten-Wheeler No. 76 whistles for a crossing as she brings the Boston section through a beautiful autumn countryside at North Clarendon. Rutland is three miles ahead.

Above: The U. S. Customs inspector will board the southbound train when it stops at St. John, Quebec, after leaving the main line of Canadian National from Montreal. Between here and the border at Rouses Point he and the passengers in the four coaches will be busy with customs declarations. — *Left and above: Philip R. Hastings.*

Overleaf: Downtown Bennington looked like this from the air in 1963. It is interesting to compare this aerial view with the old engraving from 1887 reproduced on pages 96-97. — *Jim Shaughnessy.*

The many bridges added greatly to the expense of construction and maintenance on the Rutland. Here near Middlebury is the Brooksville trestle over a tributary of Otter Creek. The *Flyer* is about half way from Rutland to Burlington at this point. — *Philip R. Hastings.*

Double headed passenger operations were rare. 4-6-0 No. 77 and 4-8-2 No. 90 team up to start the train north from Burlington. The big Mountain was doubling north to handle National Guard troop movements west from Alburgh to Camp Drum, N. Y. — *John Pickett.*

Here is a Rutland engine on Boston & Maine tracks at Johnsonville, N. Y. The Pacific is approaching the junction with B. & M.'s freight line from Mechanicville which passes on the other side of the tower. — *William D. Middleton.*

Left: At Troy the *Green Mountain Flyer* was added to Delaware & Hudson's *Laurentian* for New York City. The flagman was on duty, but there seemed to be little traffic on the street in Troy crossing the tracks on which engine No. 92 arrived on its run from Rutland three days before the white Christmas of 1950. — *Jim Shaughnessy.*

Right: Mountain type No. 93 was still in its original green and yellow livery in January 1947 when photographed leaving Burlington. — *Robert F. Collins.*

Below: The whistle proclaims the spirit of Ten-Wheeler 76 as she speeds along at 55 mph two miles south of Burlington in mid-March 1950. — *Philip R. Hastings.*

Rutland's Ten-Wheeler No. 72 has just taken over from Boston & Maine's Pacific No. 3708 which brought the *Flyer* up from Boston. As soon as the mail is loaded the train will depart Bellows Falls for the north. — *Jim Shaughnessy Collection.*

Line and weather are clear ahead as the train speeds toward the U. S. border on C.N.R. tracks at Cantic, Quebec. Rutland's 4-6-0 No. 78 eagerly heads for home.

Right: Pacific No. 80 gathers speed as she approaches the drawbridge at the south end of Burlington yard. Soon she will have passed 0-6-0 switcher No. 107 and be on the way to Rutland. — *Below and right: Philip R. Hastings.*

The fireman waves to the 5x7 Speed Graphic of Donald W. Furler as the shiny black Ten-Wheeler leads the northbound *Flyer* through Center Rutland in 1949.

What more is needed to complete a scene of railroad yesterday? Here is a quaint depot, a manual block set to protect the train, a mailman with his dog, the agent coming out to greet the conductor, a Model A Ford parked nearby, and a small boy watching from the doorway as Ten-Wheeler No. 76 drifts in from Bellows Falls. Gassets is about half way to Rutland. — *Philip R. Hastings.*

Mountain type No. 93 brings the train from North Bennington on Boston & Maine tracks at Johnsonville, N. Y., past the tower controlling the junction where tracks to the left lead to Mechanicville. — *William D. Middleton.*

Passengers, mail, express, and order board at Danby are waiting for 4-8-2 No. 90 to bring in the New York section of the train. Two little girls watch from a safe vantage point on the unused baggage truck. — *Donald S. Robinson.*

Train No. 65, the northbound section of the *Flyer* from New York highballs past the little unused station at Clarendon behind Pacific No. 82, symbolizing the ultimate destiny of passenger service. Newly painted and trimmed Pacific No. 80 speeds along the lake shore north of Burlington. The armstrong speeder stood near the station house at Colchester. — *Philip R. Hastings.*

Opposite: The northbound train with a heavy load of mail and express cars makes its daily stop under the old ball signal at North Bennington. A private bus company provided a connection to Bennington five miles south. — *Jim Shaughnessy.*

Ten-Wheeler No. 79 swirls dust at the unused Bartonsville station, ten miles north of Bellows Falls, as she speeds the *Flyer* north to Rutland.

No. 77 will hurry the northbound train past the milk train which is waiting in the hole at Middlebury. Meanwhile the engineer of 2-8-0 No. 16 on the southbound local checks the running gear of the old engine which has now been running nearly forty years. — *This page: Donald S. Robinson.*

Right: Looking through the old ball signal, photographer Philip Hastings caught a dramatic 1946 view of the New York section of the *Flyer* coming into Rutland yard from Bennington behind Boston & Maine's Pacific No. 3656.

Opposite: 4-8-2 No. 92 brings the *Green Mountain Flyer* into a snowy North Bennington on the daily run to Troy and the New York Central connection. — *Jim Shaughnessy.*

Left: Diesels were soon to bump the majestic L-1 Mountain type engines into less glamorous roles. Here is No. 92 swinging the fast train into the Bennington branch just south of Rutland station in the fall of 1950. — *John Pickett.*

Below: Light Pacific No. 80 brings the southbound train into busy Middlebury station. The rider car of northbound milk train No. 87 waits in the clear to the left. — *Donald S. Robinson.*

The Mountain Type

These were the finest and ultimate expression of steam power on the Rutland. *Opposite:* No. 90 is seen from the Burlington coal tower by Philip R. Hastings. No. 93 is on Rutland turntable moving into position to doublehead with a Mikado on time freight No. 120 over the hill to Bellows Falls. Below, the author has caught No. 92 pensively waiting to have her fire cleaned on the Rutland ash pit.

On this page are two of Photographer Philip Hastings' views of No. 90 at work in Burlington. Here she dwarfs her Consolidation helper pulling 80 cars up the slight grade along Burlington Bay. Below she triumphantly enters the yard from the south.

Opposite: The author has portrayed an impressive profile featuring the solid brass number plate with figures and name in relief against a green painted background.

No. 92 presents a classic view for photographer Fred Sankoff at Alfrecha. She is rolling the Chatham freight south a few minutes out of Rutland on the Bennington line. Her first revenue run was on Norwood freight No. 19 in September 1946. Philip Hastings took her picture on this run in her shiny new green paint as she sped north out of Burlington.

Opposite: The Cuttingsville trestle across Mill River near East Wallingford presents a dramatic and resounding stage for Mountain No. 90 and Mikado No. 35 pulling up the grade out of Rutland with southbound freight No. 120. — *Philip R. Hastings.*

The Diesels

What the businesslike Diesels may have lacked in drama they made up in color. Their green-and-yellow painting is echoed on the caboose which conductor Robert Thurston boards at Florence after his Alburgh-bound local has set out cars at the Clarendon & Pittsford Railway interchange. They are also emblazoned on the box car behind Diesel No. 201. A perennial debate in Vermont is over the predominance of people or cows. Opposite, the brakeman and Diesel No. 202 patiently wait at the siding switch at Vergennes, so they can get their Alburgh local home to Rutland.— *Three Pictures, Jim Shaughnessy.*

Opposite: The local to Alburgh roars through Leicester Junction half way from Rutland to Burlington. Weedy track in foreground is the two-mile stub of the Addison branch which once crossed the shaky mid-lake trestle over Champlain to Ticonderoga, N. Y., but now ends at Whiting. Brandon station was the passing point of the Alburgh locals in 1958.

This Page: Toward the end of its operation the Chatham bound local crosses the Walloomsac River on Boston & Maine rails near the state line at White Creek, N. Y. This thrice-weekly run took the roundabout route via Troy and New York Central rails to Chatham following abandonment of the old "Corkscrew Division" tracks. The only Rutland engine ever to have two-way radio was the Alco road switcher shown here on the Burlington turntable. — *Four pictures: Jim Shaughnessy.*

The efficient new Diesels and the sparkling new box cars arrayed on Cuttingsville trestle bespeak a prosperous and progressive railway. With this testimony to the newest developments on railroading brought into a scene of immemorial natural beauty, one finds it hard to believe that the Rutland Railway was almost at the end of its career. In retrospect we know what happened. On this bright summer day it would not have been conceivable. — *Rutland Railway*.

Here is the Walloomsac bridge illuminated by 1.3 million flashbulb lumens. The thrice-weekly run of the Chatham bound RC-4 came this way on its round-about route via Troy and New York Central rails to Chatham following abandonment of the old "Corkscrew Division" tracks. — *Jim Shaughnessy.*

Brand new Diesel No. 204 pulls the milk train into the yard past Alburgh station in Fall 1951. North and south bound locals between Rutland and Alburgh pass at Brandon. Here northbound No. 201 holds the main line while the 207 eases past on the weedy siding. — *Jim Shaughnessy.*

Ray Haseltine chomps on his cigar holder as he gives two short blasts on the horn of Alco No. 401 before throttling out his green and yellow monster for the run from Chatham back to Rutland. Alcos No. 208 and 206 team up to head symbol freight XR-1 north toward Rutland down off Mount Holly near Cuttingsville. — *Jim Shaughnessy.*

Giant blocks of marble for the finishing plant at Proctor follow No. 206 from a quarry at Danby toward Rutland on the Bennington local. Symbol freight XR-1 slips downgrade into the home yard at Rutland from Bellows Falls. — *Jim Shaughnessy.*

The newly arrived local from Alburgh is being switched in Rutland yard. — *Jim Shaughnessy.*

Marble was the Gibraltar of the Rutland's balance sheets for over a century. The Bennington local picks it up from the Vermont Marble Company's quarry yard at Danby, 25 miles south of Rutland. With her full 2200 ton limit for the grade to Cherubusco No. 201 eases past Rouses Point station toward the Delaware & Hudson diamond with time freight No. 19 for the New York Central connection at Norwood. The L-1 class Mountains had only been rated for 1725 tons on this segment of the O. & L. C. division. — *Jim Shaughnessy.*

Opposite: Everything appeared neatly in place in Rutland yard when 1000 h.p. unit No. 402 spent a busy summer afternoon switching there. Quiet Proctor station shows little trace of the devastation wrought there by the 1927 flood. — *Jim Shaughnessy.*

Alco No. 201, handling the Rutland-Alburgh local sets out cars at the Florence interchange with the Clarendon & Pittsford, five miles north of Proctor. This Vermont Marble Company subsidiary contributed much tonnage to the Rutland. — *Jim Shaughnessy.*

The unusual was commonplace on the Rutland. Here the local to Alburgh is stopped to watch a steamboat crossing the track a mile from Lake Champlain at Shelburne. The sidewheeler was being moved to dry land exhibition at Shelburne Museum in spring 1955. — *Shelburne Museum, Inc. Staff Photographer Einars J. Mengis.*

Diesel No. 401 makes her leisurely way west near Champlain, N. Y., with the local for Malone. At the west end of the line Alco No. 403 has placed the caboose on the end of the train she has made up for Malone and Alburgh. Now she is ready for her night's rest. — *Jim Shaughnessy.*

The No. 403 crosses the Delaware & Hudson main line at Rouses Point with a vestigial milk train in the spring of 1952. Cars at the right are on the interchange track from the D. & H. yard. — *Jim Shaughnessy.*

Opposite: The hostler in Rutland pauses before putting the Rutland's original Diesel No. 200 away for the night. Train control unit on the 206 is used while running over Boston & Albany tracks to Chatham. Alco No. 206 takes on fuel in the glare of floodlights outside Rutland shop as the 208 and 200 wait for their morning assignments. — *Jim Shaughnessy.*

Above: General Electric switcher No. 500 gets her cooling system water checked before going to work on midnight shift switching in the home terminal yard at Rutland. — *Jim Shaughnessy.*

Engineer and fireman watch from the engine while LCL freight is being unloaded in Stephentown, N. Y., on the Chatham line. *Below:* The Alburgh local passes the little frame station at Florence several months before the memorable occasion when the southbound local drove a milk tank semitrailer into the little depot, demolishing both. Intact but dripping with milk, Diesel No. 401 had delivered a railroad reprisal against the trucks which had usurped the milk carrying business. *Right:* In a Christmas card setting, northbound CR-3 winds around Emerald Lake near North Dorset, March 1955. — *Three Pictures: Jim Shaughnessy.*

The train for Chatham sways under an old covered bridge over Boston & Maine tracks at North Troy on its roundabout route to the New York Central connection. The scene is as New England as franks and beans on Saturday night. And here is an engineer's-eye view of No. 206 from No. 203 as the Chatham-bound through freight approaches the B. & M. track at Hoosick Junction. — *Jim Shaughnessy.*

Right: The dwindled remnant of milk train No. 88 for Chatham, now symbol freight RC-2, eases through the weed-covered B. & M. main in Troy over its circuitous foreign trackage. Not a can of milk was handled since Vermont was cut from the New York milkshed by a federal marketing order in 1958. — *Jim Shaughnessy.*

A green and yellow caboose and a company box car follow Diesel No. 205 into the soft light of a Vermont evening, a lonely train at Vergennes. JX-2 moves in from Norwood behind Diesels No. 204 and 201 past the ball signal and over the Central Vermont-Boston & Maine line into Bellows Falls yard. *Opposite:* Rutland-bound freight XR-1 swings into the cut and away from the Connecticut River just above Bellows Falls on a gray February day in 1957. — *Three pictures: Jim Shaughnessy.*

VERMONT

In 1965 steam returned briefly to the Vermont Railway while it was privately owned. VTR-lettered 2-8-0 No. 97 (ex-Birmingham & Southeastern) was overhauled in Burlington and tested in service. In Burlington yard she builds steam pressure to take the daily road train down to Rutland.—*John Krause.*

ALBUM

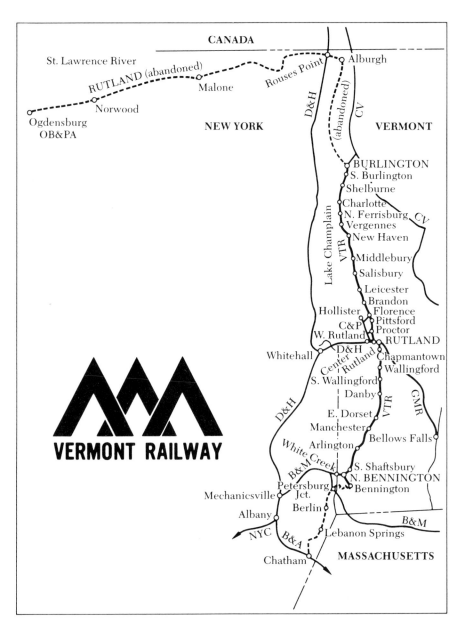

VERMONT RAILWAY

Shortly after operation of the Vermont Railway began, this steam-powered excursion pulls into North Bennington after departing Bennington for a day's round trip to Rutland on September 26, 1965. After several runs on the New Haven's Housatonic branch, No. 97's owners had brought the ex-Birmingham & Southern 2-8-0 to Burlington for repair work, during which time it made some break-in trips on VTR freight trains. It now operates on the Valley Railroad in Connecticut. —Jim Shaughnessy.

After running the train around the "Y" at North Bennington so that the open-windowed car would be at the rear of the train and away from the bulk of the cinders, No. 97 blasts north through Shaftsbury for Rutland on September 26, 1965.—*Jim Shaughnessy.*

Although employees of short line railroads do work other than their usual job on occasion, engine cleaning is not often done by the president. Jay Wulfson cleans the white running-board edge of switcher No. 501 shortly after its arrival in September 1966. Fate dealt an unfortunate blow when, on November 12, 1980, Mr. Wulfson passed away at age 49, leaving the legacy of being a pioneer in the concept of state support for short line railroads and their contributions to the community. Early in 1981, long-time management man John Pennington, former vice president, was named president by the board of directors.—*Jim Shaughnessy.*

EMD SW-1500 No. 501, the first new locomotive purchased by the VTR, switches at the south end of the yard in Burlington in July 1967.—*Jim Shaughnessy.*

President Jay Wulfson and the first of the "new" power obtained by his road after beginning operation. In the Burlington yard on August 5, 1970, he stands in front of ex-Lehigh & Hudson River RS-3 No. 12 in her new Vermont Railway dress.—*Jim Shaughnessy.*

The former Rutland roundhouse on the shore of Lake Champlain in Burlington serves as the Vermont Railway's maintenance shop for both cars and locomotives. New GP-38-2 No. 201 is eased out of the shop stall for the evening Burlington-Rutland train in June 1973. At the right, a recently purchased ex-C&O Alco S-4 sits awaiting repairs before serving as No. 6 on the Clarendon & Pittsford. — *Jim Shaughnessy.*

One General Motors product helps another. A Chevrolet pickup pulls the Burlington turntable, turning EMD No. 201 while the electric motor which normally powers the structure is out for repairs, on June 23, 1973.—*Jim Shaughnessy.*

The Whiting Company in Burlington is representative of new business that has located on the old Rutland line since the Vermont Railway's take-over. Here No. 201 spots a bulk commodity car by the firm's modern plant.—*Jim Shaughnessy.*

The Burlington engine house that once housed Rutland ten-wheelers is today the main repair shop for the Vermont Railway and where, on May 25, 1974, RS-3 No. 604 and GP-38-2 No. 201 rest in the modernized interior.—*Jim Shaughnessy.*

Burlington yard is the real operating center of the VTR, even though Rutland has more volume and is the location of the dispatcher. Ex-Rutland RS-1's No. 401 and No. 402 have just caboosed the daily freight for Rutland and are about to get on the head end on July 25, 1967.—*Jim Shaughnessy.*

Ex-Rutland 1000 HP RS-1 No. 403 pulls out of the old Rutland round-house in Burlington. This building is the VTR's main shop, handling all types of work on boxcars, maintenance-of-way equipment and locomotives.—*Jim Shaughnessy.*

One of the late active RS-1's, No. 404 teams up with new EMD SW 1500 No. 501 in an unusual combination to power the southbound out of Burlington in June 1969. No. 404 was not one of the ex-Rutland engines of that type, but was obtained from the Soo Line in 1967.—*Jim Shaughnessy.*

The 6:00 P.M. departure time is at hand in Burlington on May 16, 1979. The engineer and head-end brakeman look back toward the caboose to be sure the conductor gets on board before they start for Rutland with their dozen assorted cars.—*Jim Shaughnessy.*

The train northbound for Burlington rolls across Brooksville trestle over the New Haven River four miles north of Middlebury, while teenagers frolic in the water on a beautiful August 9, 1971.—*Jim Shaughnessy.*

VERMONT RAILWAY

Alco No. 603 moves on Clarendon & Pittsford Railway trackage into the
plant area of the agricultural lime-producing plant in Florence, Vermont,
to gather outbound loads.—*Jim Shaughnessy.*

The Rutland engine house doors frame (on the left) No. 501 making up the afternoon train for Bennington and (on the right) No. 202, which will return north on the Burlington train later in the evening.—*Jim Shaughnessy.*

In August 1979 the unit oil train rolls along Otter Creek near Rutland as two boys wave while fishing in the clear waters. This special service was initiated in January 1978 to bring petroleum products from the deep water terminal in Albany, New York, via D&H to Rutland and on to Mobil Oil's terminal in Burlington — at better rates than the previous barge-canal-lake routing. About 35 cars make two round trips a week.—*Jim Shaughnessy.*

Winter in the upper valley of Otter Creek, near Danby, south of Rutland, finds RS-3's No. 404 and No. 402 rolling south toward Bennington under cold blue skies on the last day of February in 1969.—*Jim Shaughnessy.*

The Bennington train behind Alcos No. 404 and No. 402 rolls south over the Mill River Bridge at Clarendon on February 28, 1969.—*Jim Shaughnessy.*

VERMONT RAILWAY

In May 1976 the train down to Bennington from Rutland rolls through budding hillsides near North Dorset and Emerald Lake, with Mt. Tabor in the distance (right).—*Jim Shaughnessy.*

The afternoon freight for Bennington departs Rutland with GP-38-2 No. 202 leading a mixed consist, including piggyback trailers bound for interchange to the B&M. The two-stall engine house and office at right are Vermont Railway's Rutland headquarters and contain the offices of the dispatcher and the freight agent handling all Rutland, C&P and D&H interchange matters.—*Jim Shaughnessy.*

The downbound freight from Rutland to Bennington passes well-kept farm buildings south of Arlington as it heads for the B&M connection behind EMD No. 202.—*Jim Shaughnessy.*

A typical scene on the Vermont Railway—a new locomotive pulling a string of modern cars through a picturesque rural setting. The Bennington train rolls south through Shaftsbury in the spring of 1976.—*Jim Shaughnessy.*

In June of 1967 four South Shaftsbury children wave as the Bennington train rolls past the location of the old station, now marked by only a sign.—*Jim Shaughnessy.*

The afternoon freight down from Rutland arrives in North Bennington behind EMD No. 202. The grand old Victorian station there, dating from Bennington & Rutland Railroad times in the 1950s, fell into disrepair after Rutland passenger service ended in 1953. It remained in that condition until the town acquired it in the early 1970s. With the help of an architect whose offices are now on the second floor, they completely restored the old structure for use as town offices.—*Jim Shaughnessy.*

The interchange scene at North Bennington is similar each day, but with different cast members. In July of 1965 the B&M's unit of the day, up from Mechanicville, New York, is GP-9 No. 1715, while the Vermont Railway's RS-1 No. 401 moves off the freight house track.—*Jim Shaughnessy.*

In July 1964 North Bennington yard—with the now-vanished Rutland water tank—receives No. 401, pulling in from Rutland with the day's business for the B&M connection. This tonnage makes up a little less than half of the road's interchange volume.—*Jim Shaughnessy.*

The interchange meet in North Bennington finds ex-Rutland No. 402 in the yard spotting its train for the B&M, while that road's GP-9 No. 1730 waits on the Bennington branch of the "Y" in July 1966.—*Jim Shaughnessy.*

On this December day in 1967, before the B&M gets in from Mechanicville, the relatively new EMD SW 1500 No. 501 arrives in the empty North Bennington yard and sets its train over on a yard track, leaving its caboose clear of the main track by the old freight house now serving as the freight's agent's office.—*Jim Shaughnessy.*

With a single car, the south end train behind Alco RS-1 No. 401 departs North Bennington on the Bennington branch past the local swimming hole (just east of the station) in July 1964.—*Jim Shaughnessy.*

The Bennington branch is served via the north leg of the "Y" at North Bennington. On July 15, 1964, No. 401 heads south with one car.—*Jim Shaughnessy.*

A string of piggyback cars with EMD No. 501 in charge rounds the Bennington leg of the "Y" at North Bennington to be spotted for unloading at the new North Bennington trailer ramp, in March of 1970.—*Jim Shaughnessy.*

At least once a year, an inspection trip is made over the line with state and business leaders on board to view the progress being made and to point out business opportunities and locations. Rounding the north leg of the "Y" at North Bennington, No. 401 leads leased D&H director's car No. 200 toward Bennington on July 17, 1964.—*Jim Shaughnessy.*

Like the annual inspection of the line by state officials, periodic industrial development efforts are made to attract new shippers. On May 21, 1968, EMD No. 501 heads an old Rutland wooden coach, refurbished inside as a lounge and inspection car, toward Bennington at Sunderland.—*Jim Shaughnessy.*

During the Bicentennial Year, 1976, the State of Vermont sponsored a series of daily steam-powered excursions from Bennington to Burlington on the Vermont Railway, with several stops en route where patrons could board and depart. Steamtown equipment and Pacific No. 1293 were leased for service. On September 6 and 7 the year before, an experimental run on the route was made with Pacifics No. 1278 and No. 1246, shown here at New Haven, Vermont, returning from Burlington on the second day (see pages 268 and 269).—*Jim Shaughnessy.*

VERMONT RAILWAY

GREEN MOUNTAIN ALBUM

Ex-CPR Pacific No. 1278, shown here as MS&N No. 127, was owned personally by Nelson Blount. On a Sunday afternoon in the fall of 1966, at Summit, Vermont, Blount stands in the cab doorway with Fred Richardson (his longtime friend and associate in railroading affairs) on the fireman's seat.—*Jim Shaughnessy.*

Aboard rented D&H business car No. 500, Governor Philip Hoff takes to the Vermont campaign trail in the grand manner of past presidential whistle-stop tours. Shown here as a special pulled by an ex-CPR Pacific, it leaves Steamtown on October 8, 1966. Governor Hoff was primarily responsible for trains running here and on the Vermont Railway, as it was he who implemented the State of Vermont's purchase of those several segments of the Rutland that remain today. He was unsuccessful at his attempts for reelection.—*Jim Shaughnessy.*

On October 8, 1966, Steamtown No. 127 hauls Governor Hoff's campaign special north of Gassetts along the Williams River toward Duttonsville Gap, Summit and Rutland. The special will continue on to Burlington behind Vermont Railway diesel No. 501.—*Jim Shaughnessy.*

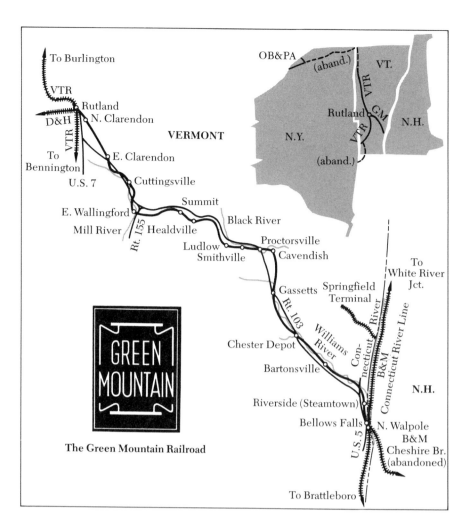

The Green Mountain Railroad

Steam excursions were not uncommon after the Vermont Railway began operation. On April 23, 1967, Green Mountain Railroad's ex-CNR 2-6-0 No. 89 rolls south through Danby toward Bennington with equipment leased from the Steamtown and Green Mountain Railroads.—*Jim Shaughnessy.*

Classic Cuttingsville trestle over the Mill River receives Green Mountain 2-6-0 No. 89 (ex-CNR), blasting upgrade with open-windowed Steamtown (ex-B&M) coaches on an excursion from Rutland to Bellows Falls on May 1, 1965 (see page 305 and cover).—*Jim Shaughnessy.*

Little ex-CNR 2-6-0 No. 89 presents a pretty picture as she rolls two coaches across the deck bridge over the Williams River Gorge at Brockways Mills on May 30, 1967.—*Jim Shaughnessy.*

On April 30, 1966, Green Mountain Railroad ex-CNR 2-6-0 No. 89 (sold to Strasburg Railway in 1972), down from Rutland with an excursion of five cars, rolls south toward Bellows Falls past the Bartonsville covered bridge.—*Jim Shaughnessy.*

Some of the more spectacular steam exhibitions occur in the fall as Steamtown hosts its annual railfan weekend and runs several special excursions over the Green Mountain Railroad, with one usually going all the way to Summit or Rutland. Three ex-CPR G-5 class Pacifics accelerate out of Bellows Falls after having backed down from Riverside for a photo run on October 30, 1976.—*Jim Shaughnessy.*

GMR Pacific No. 1246, named the "F. Nelson Blount" and now owned by the Steamtown Foundation, rolls the last train of the operating season across the Williams River trestle at Rockingham on October 26, 1964.—*Jim Shaughnessy.*

Steamtown's ex-CPR Pacifics No. 1293 and No. 1246 roll north over the high bridge in Ludlow toward Summit with a Steamtown railfan weekend excursion on October 21, 1979.—*Jim Shaughnessy.*

The Williams River and the covered bridge at Bartonsville witness the early morning arrival, on October 21, 1979, of a Steamtown doubleheader with No. 1293 and No. 1246 in charge.—*Jim Shaughnessy.*

During the railfan weekend of October 29-30, 1976, the first tripleheader was operated from Bellows Falls to Chester. On Saturday afternoon the three G-5 class Canadian Pacific 4-6-2's pose on the bridge over the Williams River Gorge at Brockways Mills.—*Jim Shaughnessy.*

Glenn E. Davis, president of the Green Mountain Railroad, with No. 401 at the North Walpole (New Hampshire) engine terminal, on July 9, 1980.—*Jim Shaughnessy.*

Monadnock Northern steamer No. 15 backs out of the ex-B&M engine house at North Walpole in July of 1963 to run the day's excursion train for Steamtown, on the north end of B&M's Cheshire branch. During the following year there were excursions on the old Rutland line across the river in Vermont. The round house finally became the home of the Green Mountain Railroad. Shown in the background are some of Steamtown's locomotives which were later moved to the Riverside museum site), including ex-N&P No. 759 before it made its famous comeback to main line operations.—*Jim Shaughnessy.*

North Walpole engine terminal and yard of the Green Mountain Railroad, where, on July 9, 1980, RS-1's No. 401 and No. 405 are being inspected and washed down prior to departure on daily freight XR-1 to Rutland and back. In the distance is the former B&M engine house that was headquarters for the Monadnock, Steamtown & Northern, which became the Green Mountain after Nelson Blount's death.—*Jim Shaughnessy.*

Cuttingsville trestle is an ideal location on the Bellows Falls branch of the old Rutland, providing over the years many exciting photographs of both steam and diesel power (see page 305 and cover).—*Jim Shaughnessy.*

Green Mountain Railroad train XR-1 pulls into Rutland to set its train out in the interchange yard by the venerable buildings of the Howe Scale Company. Tracks to the left are those of the Vermont Railway's Bennington line. The Bellows Falls track of the old Rutland, on which the Green Mountain train is running here, also belongs to the VTR for about a mile (to where the GMR's trackage begins). See pages 194, 297 and 314 for this same scene under other conditions.—*Jim Shaughnessy.*

With RS-1 No. 401 in the lead and four of the new covered hoppers in the consist, train RX-2 at East Clarendon climbs toward Summit. This same scene, but with Rutland steam power, is seen on page 259.—*Jim Shaughnessy*.

In a less conventional view Green Mountain train
XR-1 rumbles north across the photogenic Cuttingsville trestle.—*Jim Shaughnessy.*

The old Rutland depot at Ludlow, Vermont, has been taken over by the town and restored to a chamber of commerce office and a visitors' center. In July 1980, train XR-1 waits until track maintenance gangs working up toward Summit finish their day's work and clear the main line so that the trip to Rutland can be completed.—*Jim Shaughnessy.*

Just west of the station in Ludlow, the small overpass bridge still has the words "Rutland R.R." in faded letters. In this July 1980 view of the Green Mountain Railroad's Rutland-bound freight XR-1, the engineman engages in the time-honored custom of waving to lineside children.—*Jim Shaughnessy.*

One of the main talc loading points is at Smithville, just south of Ludlow. This large new plant of Windsor Minerals, Inc., replaces one tucked tightly in the gorge of the Williams River near Gassetts. About an hour is spent spotting empties for loading and picking up loads. One of the 100 new covered hoppers of the Green Mountain Railroad is seen in the loading shed at left.—*Jim Saughnessy.*

En route to Cavendish, Rutland-bound freight XR-1
climbs along the Williams River toward the narrow
Duttonsville Gulf. In the left distance is the old talc
plant of Windsor Minerals, Inc., which now operates from its new, larger plant in Smithville.—*Jim
Shaughnessy.*

The former Rutland depot at Chester, Vermont, now serves as the GMR traffic and freight agents' office. Behind the station, train XR-1 switches a Green Mountain boxcar on the track used by Steamtown's steam locomotive to run around its excursion train at the upper end of the trip.—*Jim Shaughnessy.*

Green Mountain northbound XR-1 rumbles across the B&M diamond at Bellows Falls station. The old Railway Express building behind the station has been purchased recently by GMR and now houses the line's general office. The large bells on the ends of the Green Mountain diesels came off CPR steam engines that were scrapped or were in Steamtown's collection at the time that all of Nelson Blount's rail operations were consolidated.—*Jim Shaughnessy.*

The old covered bridge at Bartonsville is beginning to sag, but still sees Steamtown's steam locomotives pass daily in summer. Green Mountain train XR-1 rolls by with chime horns blaring (see also pages 184, 207 and 296).—*Jim Shaughnessy.*

Recently obtained bay-window caboose No. 51 (from the B&LE) clatters across the B&M diamond in Bellows Falls as XR-1 begins its trip for the day up to Rutland.—*Jim Shaughnessy.*

Green Mountain train XR-1 crosses the classic stone arch bridge over the Connecticut River between North Walpole, New Hampshire, and Bellows Falls, Vermont, as it starts its journey north to Rutland. —*Jim Shaughnessy.*

This 1980 view of the once-busy yard and station area in Rutland, as seen from the River Street Bridge, shows Green Mountain Railroad train XR-1 arriving to back its train onto the interchange track. In the background is the vast new shopping center which has taken the place of Rutland tracks. Note (at center right) the tall building which appears in earlier views (see pages 32, 188, 315 and 317). —*Jim Shaughnessy.*

The Green Mountain Railroad

THE OBPA

ALBUM

The old Rutland station at Ogdensburg, dating back to the 1850s and the days of the Northern Railroad of New York, was converted into the general offices and engine house of the Ogdensburg & Norwood Railway after the Port Authority first acquired that section of the old Rutland. Behind the ex-CPR caboose and station, the St. Lawrence River and part of Canada can be seen. Headquarters are now located in the old Norwood and St. Lawrence buildings in Norfolk.—*E. H. Blabey II, courtesy* Railfan Magazine.

Ogdensburg Bridge & Port Authority Alco S-1 No. 1 switches hoppers at the New York State Hospital's coal stockpile in July of 1975. The hospital was the principal source of traffic on the old Rutland line, but converted to natural gas, only to reconvert at a later date. Its conversion from coal was the reason the first lessor, the Ogdensburg & Norwood Railway, had to give up the operation and return it to the Port Authority to run.—*Tom Trencansky, courtesy* Railfan Magazine.

St. Lawrence Railroad No. 10, formerly of the Norwood &
St. Lawrence, a GE 70-tonner in red, white, and blue
color scheme, was conveyed to the Port Authority in 1974
and was rebuilt by United Railway Supply Corporation in
Montreal.—*Bruce Curry.*

Ex-Delaware & Hudson S-1, lettered "Ogdensburg &
Norwood," works the Norwood yard; but by November 1,
1968, it had reverted to the OBPA, as the O&N could not
make a go of the operation.—*Collection of Jim
Shaughnessy.*

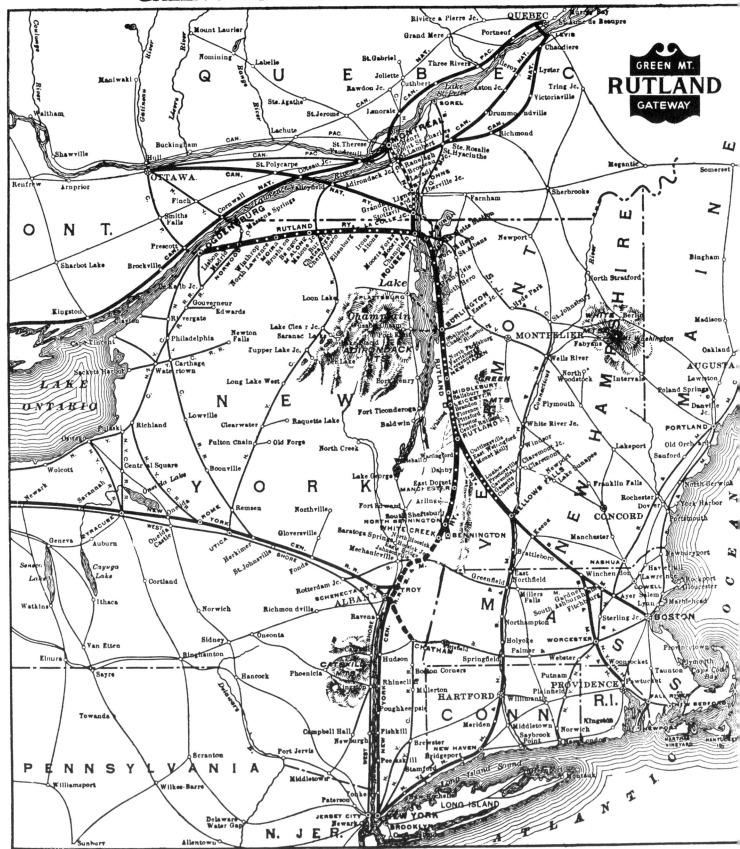

Map made after 1953. The Chatham branch has been omitted and the dotted lines indicate trackage rights route.

APPENDIX

Locomotives of the Rutland Railroad

⟡⟡⟡⟡⟡⟡⟡⟡⟡⟡ *and Its Subsidiary Lines*

and of the Adirondack & St. Lawrence
and St. Lawrence & Adirondack Railroads

The dredging up of facts in connection with early locomotives is a difficult job at best. With Rutland and all its combinations, acquisitions, leases, and outside interests, it was almost impossible.

F. Steward Graham of Bennington has shown fantastic dedication and completeness in compiling this complicated roster of the Rutland's locomotives. Different numberings under various management as well as the integration of acquired lines' power into the whole fleet has made the roster even hard to read, to say nothing of its fabrication by Mr. Graham.

This excellent record is available here through the courtesy of President Charles E. Fisher of the Railway and Locomotive Historical Society for whose bulletin #90 Mr. Graham first prepared this work.

JIM SHAUGHNESSY

LOCOMOTIVES OF THE RUTLAND COMPANIES

Rutland & Burlington R. R.	1843-1867
Rutland Railroad	1867-1951
Rutland Railway Company	1951-1963

The history of the locomotives of the Rutland Railroad is quite as complicated as that of the road itself. The financial affairs and many changes in management, ownership and operation, as well as its leases of smaller lines and its own leasing to the Central Vermont, are all matters of record and have been fully described by various writers.

The records of the locomotives, however, which came under control of the Rutland System and should be accounted for in any history of that company's motive power, have not been so carefully preserved and, as a result of the frequent changes in corporate set-up, present a problem that is both interesting and difficult.

To systematically record and account for the locomotives that at one time or another were the property of the Rutland it seems advisable to consider them by groups, following the chronological management "eras" of the road's career in somewhat of the following order:

1. The locomotives from the road's beginning, in 1843, to the time it was leased to the Central Vermont, December 30th, 1870, including engines of the roads under lease to the Rutland, such as the Vermont Valley, Montreal & Plattsburg, and others, if any. Roster I accounts for these and the Rutland's locomotives under the C. V. lease, which existed from 1870 to May, 1896. Of the engines turned over to the C. V. under this rental agreement, a number were scrapped and some new ones added to the Rutland's roster. The Rutland engines were eventually renumbered into the C. V. 200 series, but, perhaps, not until about 1886. This date is indicated by the fact that locomotives built in that year by Baldwin, for the O. & L. C., were numbered in the 300's. This series had been assigned to O. & L. C. engines, that road having been leased by the C. V. at about the same time as was the Rutland. The Rutland engines were re-lettered, with "C. V. R. R." painted on the tenders, and, in smaller letters, the words "Rutland Division."

During each of the foregoing periods there was a great deal of re-naming, re-numbering, and re-assignment of locomotives and here again is much conflicting information concerning these changes.

2. Another group, which is really the beginning of the current series, is composed in part of the locomotives returned to the Rutland, upon cancellation of the C. V. lease, in May, 1896, and which retained their 200 series numbers until 1901. To these must be added engines acquired by purchase and by absorption of the O. & L. C., in 1899, the Bennington & Rutland Ry., in 1900, and the Chatham & Lebanon Valley, in 1901.

3. The locomotives of the 1901 series, including many of the foregoing, to which were added a number of new ones. Of this group, 77 were renumbered into the N. Y. C. series, in 1905, when that road "took over" the Rutland. Some incidental renumbering took place in this series.

4. The final number series of the Rutland was adopted in 1913, when the N. Y. C. released the Rut-

land locomotives from their numbering system, and they were changed into a new series, Nos. 10 to 155, except thirteen shown elsewhere, which retained the N. Y. C. numbers.

During the years 1865 to 1871, the Rutland leased the following small roads: The Addison R. R., Montreal & Plattsburg, Vermont & Massachusetts, Vermont Valley, and Whitehall & Plattsburg Railroad.

The leases for these roads were transferred to the Vermont Central, at about the same time that the Rutland was leased to that company, and, of these roads, the V. V. and the M. & P. were the only ones whose motive power appears in the Rutland's locomotive history.

The M. & P. was a reorganization, in 1868, of the bankrupt Plattsburg & Montreal Railroad. In 1869, it acquired lease of the Whitehall & Plattsburg. Both roads were leased to the Rutland on January 23rd, 1871, and the lease was transferred to the Vermont Central and Vermont & Canada Railroads, on January 14th, 1873. On February 25th, of that year, control of the lines was purchased and they were merged with the New York & Canada, now part of the D. & H. The line extended from Plattsburg to Mooer's Jct., and it was by means of this road that Rutland freight was handled between Burlington and the O. & L. C. R. R., after being transported across Lake Champlain by steamer. The M. & P. eventually became part of the D. & H.

THE M. & P. LOCOMOTIVES

Rec'd	Name	Builder	C/N	Date	Type	Cyls.	DD	Remarks
1852	Clinton	Amoskeag	61	1852	4-4-0	14x20	60	Disposition unknown.
1852	Plattsburg	Taunton	106	1852	4-4-0	14x20	66	Renamed Saranac.
1852	Mooers	Taunton	112	1852	4-4-0	14x20	66	Disposition unknown.
1853	West Chazy	Taunton	144	1853	4-4-0	14x20	66	
1863	Saranac	Taunton	37	1849	4-4-0	16x20	54	ex-Rutland 3, "Vergennes."
1863	Col. Williams	Taunton	87	1851	4-4-0	14x20	66	ex-Rutland & Washington.
1863	Chazy	Hinkley	47	1845	4-2-0	11½x20	60	From Northern (N. Y.) R. R.
1869	Plattsburg	Taunton	32	1849	4-4-0	15x18	60	ex-Rutland 9, "Rutland."
1869	Cavendish	Taunton	77	1851	4-4-0	15x18	60	ex-Rutland 14, "Cavendish."
1871	Ticonderoga	Taunton	116	1852	4-4-0	14x20	55	Ret'd to Rutland. Sc 1880.

(The above roster was supplied by Mr. Robert R. Brown, Lachine, P. Q.)

"Plattsburg," No. 106, was sold, by 1863, to the Watertown & Rome R. R., where it was renamed "Antwerp."

"Mooers," No. 112, was repaired by Taunton, October, 1857, and renamed "S. F. Vilas."

"West Chazy,, was sold in 1853 to the Providence & Worcester R. R., and renamed "Providence." Probably was never on the M. & P.

"Chazy" was originally Old Colony R. R. "Mayflower."

"Plattsburg," No. 32, went to the D. & H.

THE VERMONT VALLEY R. R.

Incorporation of the Vermont Valley R. R. was authorized on Nov. 8th, 1848, under the laws of the State of Vermont, and, on May 12th, 1865, the road was leased to the Trustees of the Rutland & Burlington, this lease being assigned to the Vermont Central and the Vermont & Canada Railroads, on Jan. 23rd, 1871. The road extended from Bellows Falls to Brattleboro, where it connected with the Vermont & Massachusetts R. R., to eventually form part of the through line from

Bellows Falls to Long Island Sound. At the time of the lease, the V. V. had four locomotives, as shown herewith, which were renumbered to Rutland Nos. 36 to 39, according to the Engineer's Report of 1873. Shortly thereafter, they were replaced by a second group bearing the same numbers, one of which was the V. V. engine numbered 39, changed to No. 40, and one was M. & P. No. 3, changed from No. 42 to No. 39.

A partial V. V. locomotive roster follows.

No.	Name	Builder	C/N	Date	Type	Cyls.	DD	Reb.	Rut.#
1	Putney	Rogers	267	7-2-51	4-4-0	14x20	66	1869	36
2	Dummerston	Rogers	264	6-17-51	4-4-0	14x20	66	1870	37
3	Westminster	Rogers	276	8-27-51	4-4-0	14x20	60		38
4	Brattleboro	Rogers	461	1-31-54	4-4-0	15x22	60	1869	39-40

There is photographic record of a V. V. No. 4, named "G. Morris," which appears to be a Danforth engine of the 1870's, but there is no evidence that this engine operated under Rutland control.

Lease of the V. V. was cancelled in 1892.

In connection with the numerous renumberings to which the Rutland's locomotives have been subjected, it might be well to keep in mind the following items, which may help to explain some of the apparent irregularities which appear in the following rosters, or which may be encountered elsewhere.

The renumbering into the C. V. 200 series took place no earlier than 1886, and perhaps was not completed until about 1891. After being returned from C. V. control, the engines retained these 200 series numbers until late in 1901. It appears that the change of numbers to the 1901 series was made as the engines were shopped, although this statement cannot be confirmed. The renumbering into the N. Y. C. Lines series in 1904-05, appears to have been done all at one time.

The N. Y. C. purchased control of the Rutland in 1904, and sold a one-half interest to the New Haven in 1911. This sale released the Rutland locomotives from the N. Y. C. number system, and the tenders of these engines were almost immediately re-lettered "Rutland." New locomotives, purchased in 1912, were so lettered, although the actual renumbering to the final (1913) series did not take place until 1914, or perhaps as late as 1915, the engines carrying their N. Y. C. Lines numbers in the interim. A former employee of the Rutland recalls that this change of numbers took place within a period of "two weeks or so."

The unusual set-up used in Roster IV, showing the current equipment from 1913 to 1951, was made necessary in order to show the origin and record of each engine thereon, with the various numbers in chronological order. To do this necessitated showing the dimensions separately.

ROSTER I

This roster lists the engines of the Rutland & Burlington and Rutland Railroads, from 1847 to December 30th, 1870, when the Rutland was leased to the Vermont Central. It also includes the locomotives of lines under lease to the Rutland, the leases for which were eventually transferred to the Vermont Central. Some Rutland engines were disposed of prior to the lease and, therefore, did not pass into C. V. control. These are marked with an "X".

The roster further includes locomotives transferred to the Rutland Division, so-called, by the C. V., and shows the renumbering of the Rutland engines into the C. V. 200 series, which took place no earlier than 1886, and may have extended over several years.

The locomotives are arranged in the following order:

Nos. 1 to 35, from the Rutland Railroad.
Nos. 36 to 39, 1st series, from the Vermont Valley.
Nos. 40 to 42, 1st series, from Montreal & Plattsburg.
2nd Nos. 1, 9, 17 and 3rd No. 9, from the Central Vermont.
2nd Nos. 36 to 42, mostly from the Central Vermont.
2nd No. 211 and Nos. 231 to 235 *by* the Central Vermont, former A. & St. L. motive power.

(°) Indicates further data in the Roster Notes.

No.	Name	Builder	C/N	Date	Type	Cyls.	DD	Disp.	CV #
	Nantucket°	Hinkley	2	1841	4-2-0	10½x20	60	Sc 1855	X
	Vulcan°	R. Norris		1840				Sc 1855	X
1	Burlington	Taunton	33	1849	4-4-0	15x18	60	Sc 1887	
2	Charlotte°	Taunton	50	1850	4-4-0	16x20	54	Sc 1878	
3	Vergennes°	Taunton	37	1849	4-4-0	16x20	54	Sc 1887	
4	New Haven	J. Souther		1851	4-4-0	16x20	60	Unknown	
5	Middlebury°	Taunton	35	1849	4-4-0	15x18	60	Sold 1866	X
5	Middlebury	L. B. Tyng		1865	4-4-0	15x24	60	Sc 1892-5	202
6	Whiting°	Hinkley	6	1842	0-4-0	13½x20	48	Sc 1865	X
6	Benslide	Taunton	402	1867	0-4-0	15x22	44	Sc 1900	203
7	Brandon°	Taunton	45	1850	4-4-0	16x20	54	Sc 1886	
8	Pittsford°	Taunton	49	1850	4-4-0	16x20	54	So 1881	
9	Rutland°	Taunton	32	1849	4-4-0	15x18	60	To M&P	
10	Clarendon	Taunton	66	1851	4-4-0	15x18	60	Sc 1874	
11	Cuttingsville°	Bal'vale		1849	4-4-0			Sc 1868	X
11	Gov'r Page°	Taunton	447	1868	4-4-0	16x24	60		205
12	Mt. Holly°	Taunton	36	1849	4-4-0	16x20	54	So B&LM	
13	Ludlow°	Taunton	52	1850	4-4-0	15x18	60	So after 1878	
14	Cavendish°	Taunton	77	1851	4-4-0	15x18	60	Unknown	
15	Chester°	Taunton	48	1850	4-4-0	15x18	60	Sc 1892	206
16	Rockingham°	Bal'vale		1849	4-4-0			Sc 1868	X
16	Moosalamoo	Taunton	448	1868	4-4-0	16x24	60	Sc 1900	207
17	Bellows Falls°	Taunton	34	1849	4-4-0	15x18	60	Wr 1876	

No.	Name	Builder	C/N	Date	Type	Cyls.	DD	Disp.	CV #
18	Otter Creek*	Hinkley	548	1854	4-4-0	15x24	60	Sc 1892	209
19	Ethan Allen*	Hinkley	552	1854	4-4-0	15x24	60	Sc 1893	210
20	Gen'l Strong*	Taunton	78	1851	4-4-0	16x20	60	Sc 1891	211
21	Nathan Rice*	Amoskeag	50	1852	4-6-0	16x22	54		212
22	John Howe*	Amoskeag	51	1852	4-6-0	16x20	60	Sc 1890	
23	Tim. Follette*	Amoskeag	72	1853	4-4-0	16x22	60	Sc 1890	213
24	Sam'l Henshaw	Amoskeag	73	1853	4-6-0	15x20	60	Sc 1868	X
24	N. L. Davis	Taunton	426	1868	4-4-0	15x22	60	Sc 1900	214
25	Lake Dunmore*	Hinkley	546	1854	4-4-0	15x24	60	Sc 1893	215
26	Know Nothing*	Hinkley	549	1854	4-4-0	15x24	60	Sc 1893	216
27	Killington*	Taunton	355	1865	4-4-0	16x24	60		217
28	Addison*	Taunton	356	1865	4-4-0	16x24	60		218
29	Gov. Underwood*	Taunton	366	1865	4-4-0	16x22	66		219
30	Peter Butler*	Taunton	480	1869	4-4-0	16x24	60		220
31	John Simonds*	Taunton	483	1869	4-4-0	16x24	60		221
32	J. M. Haven	Rutland		1870	4-4-0	16x22	66	Sc 1900	222
33	Geo. B. Chase*	Taunton	509	1870	4-4-0	16x24	60		223
34	J. H. Williams	Taunton	512	1870	4-4-0	16x22	60	Sc 1900	224
35	Lawrence Barnes	Taunton	514	1870	4-4-0	16x24	60	Sc 1899	225
36	VV#1 Putney	Rogers	267	1851	4-4-0	14x20	66		
37	VV#2 Dummerston	Rogers	264	1851	4-4-0	14x20	66		
38	VV#3 Westminster	Rogers	276	1851	4-4-0	14x20	60		
39	VV#4 Brattleboro	Rogers	461	1854	4-4-0	15x22	60	To 2nd #40	
40	M&P Plattsburg	Taunton	32	1849	4-4-0	15x18	57	To D&H	
41	M&P Saranac	Taunton	37	1849	4-4-0	15x20	62	Sc 1887	
42	M&P Ticonderoga	Taunton	116	1852	4-4-0	14x20	55	To 2nd #39	

The following locomotives were added to the Rutland Division, by the C. V., either as additional equipment or to replace engines that had been disposed of.

No.	Name	Builder	C/N	Date	Type	Cyls.	DD	Disp.	CV #
1	Burlington*	St. Albans		1872	4-4-0	17x24	68		201
9	Oswegatchie*	Hinkley	260	1850	4-4-0	15x18	66	Sc-1872-3	
9	Rutland*	St. Albans		1872	4-4-0	16x24	60		204
17	Chas. Clement*	St. Albans		1873	4-4-0	16x24	66		208
36	J. Burdette*	Taunton	466	1869	4-4-0	16x24	66	Fr #38	226
37	Shelburne*	Taunton	464	1869	4-4-0	16x24	66		227
38	J. Burdette*	Taunton	466	1869	4-4-0	16x24	66	To #36	
38	America*	Baldwin	2454	1871	2-6-0	17x24	54		228
39	Ticonderoga*	Taunton	116	1852	4-4-0	15x20	66	Sc 1880	
40	Brattleboro*	Rogers	461	1854	4-4-0	15x22	60	Fr 1st #39	
41	Salisbury*	Hinkley	403	1852	4-4-0	15x24	60	Reb. TLW 1873	
	Salisbury	Taunton (Reb)		1873	4-4-0	15x24	63		229
42	Rockingham*	Hinkley	194	1848	4-4-0	15x24	60		230
211*		Schenect	3510	1891	0-4-0	16x24	50		211
231*		Mason	583	1877	4-4-0	17x24	63		231
232*		Schenect	3511	1891	4-4-0	18x24	69		232
233*		Schenect	3512	1891	4-4-0	18x24	69		233
234*		Schenect	3506	1891	4-6-0	18x24	56		234
235*		Schenect	3505	1891	4-6-0	18x24	56		235

ADDITIONAL DATA. ROSTER I

These items are arranged in the same order as the locomotives appear in the foregoing roster.

"Nantucket" was bought from the New Bedford & Taunton R. R. by Chamberlain, Strong & Co., the contractors who built the road. "Vulcan" was bought from the Boston & Worcester R. R., and was placed in service on Nov. 22nd, 1850. These two engines appear in the 1855 inventory, but were scrapped shortly thereafter. It is doubtful that they were ever numbered.

1. "Burlington" rebuilt at Rutland, October, 1865.
2. "Charlotte" rebuilt at Rutland, October, 1863.
3. "Vergennes" rebuilt at Rutland October, 1863. Sent to the M. & P. as the "Saranac." Returned to the Rutland on December 25th, 1873.
5. "Middlebury" wrecked at Pittsfield in November, 1864. After being rebuilt by Taunton, it was sold to the Fitchburg & Worcester, in 1866.
5. "Middlebury" rebuilt from a second hand engine, by L. B. Tyng, at Northfield Shops, October, 1865, and sold to the Rutland. Rebuilt at Rutland, 1870. Said to have been built for the U. S. M. R. R.
6. "Whiting" bought from the Boston & Worcester R. R., ex-Tiger, 1842.
7. "Brandon" rebuilt at Rutland in 1866 and 1871.
8. "Pittsford" rebuilt at Rutland in 1867. Sold to D. C. Linsley in June 1881. Renamed "Glengarry."
9. "Rutland" rebuilt at Rutland in 1869. Transferred to the M. & P. as the "Plattsburg," and went to the D. & H.
11. "Cuttingsville," ex-"Red Bird."
11. "Governor Page" renamed "L. E. Roys."
12. "Mt. Holly" rebuilt at Rutland, 1866. Sold to D. C. Linsley, of the Burlington & LaMoille R. R., as "William Hale."
13. "Ludlow" was running between Brattleboro and Bellows Falls on Nov. 15th, 1878.
14. "Cavendish" rebuilt at Rutland, 1865.
15. "Chester" rebuilt at Rutland, 1868.
16. "Rockingham," ex-"Brown Bird."
17. "Bellows Falls" rebuilt at Rutland, 1865. Wrecked on the Addison R. R., Oct. 31, 1876.
18. "Otter Creek" rebuilt 1871.
19. "Ethen Allen" renamed "Green Mountain" in 1855; "Wide Awake" in 1862; rebuilt at Rutland in 1867 and renamed "Pico."
20. "General Strong" rebuilt at Rutland in 1873.
21. "Nathan Rice" renamed "E. A. Birchard" in 1864, and rebuilt to 4-4-0, 16x24-60.
22. "John Howe" renamed "H. E. Chamberlain" in 1869, and rebuilt to 4-4-0, 16x20-60.
23. "Timothy Follette" renamed "Col. Merrill." Rebuilt in 1866 and 1875.
25. "Lake Dunmore" renamed "Dunmore." Rebuilt in 1868.
26. "Know Nothing" renamed "J. A. Conant" in 1855; "Ethan Allen" in 1862.
27. "Killington" rebuilt at Rutland, 1874.
28. "Addison" rebuilt at Rutland, 1878.
29. "Governor Underwood" renamed "J. Burdette." Rebuilt in 1877.
30. "Peter Butler" rebuilt in 1874.
31. "John Simonds" rebuilt in 1874.
33. "George B. Chase" received as "Geo. M. Barnard" and renamed at once.
1. "Burlington" ex-C. V. "Stowe," No. 63. Rebuilt 16x24.
9. "Oswegatchie" came from the Northern (NY) R. R.
9. "Rutland" sold to Manchester, Dorset & Granville No. 1.
17. "Charles Clement" ex-C. V. "Pacific," No. 24.
36. "J. Burdette" ex-C. V. "W. C. Smith," No. 71. Renamed "E. W. Horner."
37. "Shelburne" ex-C. V. "St. Albans," No. 2.
38. "America" ex-C. V. "Pacific," No. 81.
39. "Ticonderoga" ex-C. V. "Stranger," No. 34.
40. "Brattleboro" ex-C. V. "Brattleboro." Scrapped before 1-1-76.
41. "Salisbury" ex-C. V. "Richford" No. 35.
42. "Rockingham" ex-C. V. "Missisco," No. 25.
211. Ex-A. & St. L. No. 1.
231. Ex-B. & L. M. "Burlington."
232. Ex-A. & St. L. No. 11.
233. Ex-A. & St. L. No. 12.
234. Ex-A. & St. L. No. 32.
235. Ex-A. & St. L. No. 31.

Engine No. 8, the PITTSFORD, was one of the original engines to run in Vermont. It was built for Rutland & Burlington by Taunton in 1850.

ROSTER II

This roster contains the record of Rutland locomotives, which were numbered in the C. V. 200 series, plus those added to this series after cancellation of the C. V. lease in May, 1896, and prior to the renumbering in 1901. It includes the 300 series engines received from the Ogdensburg & Lake Champlain R. R. in 1899.

Although the locomotives of the Bennington & Rutland Railway and the Chatham & Lebanon Valley R. R. were acquired during this period, they are not included in the roster, as they are accounted for in separate rosters of those roads.

(°) Indicates further data in the Roster Notes.

Engines' names can be found by referring to Roster I.

CV No.	Old No.	Builder	C/N	Date	Type	Cyls.	DD	Weights	Disp'n	1901
201	1	St. Albans		1872	4-4-0	17x24	68	72550		62
202	5	Northfield		1866	4-4-0	15x24	60	58300	Sc 1892-5	
203	6	Taunton	402	1867	0-4-0	15x22	54	48500	Sc 1900	
204	9	St. Albans		1872	4-4-0	16x24	60	74300	So. MD&G 1	
204	37	Taunton	464	1869	4-4-0	16x24	63	68100	Fr. 227	63
205	11	Taunton	447	1868	4-4-0	16x24	60	68100		64
206	15	Taunton	48	1850	4-4-0	15x20	60	58200		
207	16	Taunton	448	1868	4-4-0	16x24	60	68100	Sc 1900	
208	17	St. Albans		1873	4-4-0	16x24	66	72550		65
209	18	Hinkley	548	1854	4-4-0	15x24	60	Reb '71	Sc 1892	
210	19	Hinkley	552	1854	4-4-0	15x24	60	55450	Sc 1893	
211	20	Taunton	78	1851	4-4-0	16x20	60		Sc 1891	
211	—	Schenect	3510	1891	0-4-0	16x24	60	64800		80
212	21	Amoskeag	50	1852	4-4-0	16x24	60	68300		66
213	23	Amoskeag	72	1853	4-4-0	16x22	60	67000	Sc 1890	
214	24	Taunton	426	1868	4-4-0	15x22	66	67600	Sc 1900	
215	25	Hinkley	546	1854	4-4-0	15x24	60	57700	Sc 1893	
216	26	Hinkley	549	1854	4-4-0	15x24	60		Sc 1893	
217	27	Taunton	355	1865	4-4-0	16x24	60	62300		67
218	28	Taunton	356	1865	4-4-0	16x24	60	62300		68
219	29	Taunton	366	1865	4-4-0	16x22	66	67600		69

The SALISBURY was built by Hinkley in 1852. It appears with Central Vermont No. 229 on her boiler front. — *Collection of C. H. Nash.*

CV No.	Old No.	Builder	C/N	Date	Type	Cyls.	DD	Weights	Disp'n	1901
220	30	Taunton	480	1869	4-4-0	16x24	60	68100		70
221	31	Taunton	483	1869	4-4-0	16x24	60	68300		71
222	32	Rutland		1870	4-4-0	16x22	66	67600	Sc 1900	
223	33	Taunton	509	1870	4-4-0	16x24	60	68100		72
224	34	Taunton	512	1870	4-4-0	16x24	60	68100	Sc 1900	
225	35	Taunton	514	1870	4-4-0	16x24	60	68300	Sc 1899	
226	36	Taunton	466	1869	4-4-0	16x24	66	67500	Unknown	
227	37	Taunton	464	1869	4-4-0	16x24	63	68100	To 204	
228	38	Baldwin	2454	1871	2-6-0	17x24	54	74350		370
229	41	Hinkley	403	1852	4-4-0	15x24	60	52885	Sc 1897	
230	42	Hinkley	194	1848	4-4-0	15x24	60	51200	Unknown	
231	—	Mason	583	1877	4-4-0	17x24	63	73275		73
232	—	Schenect	3511	1891	4-4-0	18x24	69	100300		182
233	—	Schenect	3512	1891	4-4-0	18x24	69	105500		183
234	—	Schenect	3506	1891	4-6-0	18x24	56	115800		480
235	—	Schenect	3505	1891	4-6-0	18x24	56	115800		481
236	—	Schenect	4550	1897	4-4-0	18x24	69	110000		184
237	—	Schenect	4551	1897	4-4-0	18x24	69	110000		185
238*	—	Manchester	445	1872	4-4-0	15x22	66	66000		79
239	—	Schenect	5009	1899	2-6-0	19x26	57	121000		386
240	—	Schenect	5010	1899	2-6-0	19x26	57	121000		387
241	—	Schenect	5109	1899	4-4-0	18x24	69	110000		186
242	—	Schenect	5110	1899	4-4-0	18x24	69	110000		187
243*	—	Schenect	5545	1900	4-4-0	18½x26	68	127000	So 1902	188
244*	—	Brooks	3448	1900	4-4-0	18½x26	68	127000	So 1902	189
245	—	Schenect	5405	1900	2-6-0	19x26	57	121000		388
246	—	Schenect	5404	1900	2-6-0	19x26	57	121000		389
247	—	Schenect	5406	1900	2-6-0	19x26	57	121000		390
248	—	Schenect	5407	1900	2-6-0	19x26	57	121000		391
249*	—	Brooks	2772	1897	4-4-0	19x26*	68	126500		190
250*	—	Brooks	2774	1897	4-4-0	19x26*	68	126500		191
251*	—	Schenect	4932	1898	4-6-0	20x28	61	161000		420
252*	—	Schenect	4933	1898	4-6-0	20x28	61	161000		421
68*	—	Rome		1889	4-6-0	18x24	64	99600		192
69*	—	Schenect	2765	1889	4-6-0	18x24	64	99600		193

The following locomotives were placed on the Rutland, upon acquisition of the O. & L. C. in 1899, and retained their 300 series numbers until the renumbering of 1901.

303		Taunton	435	1868	4-4-0	16x24	60	62500	Sc 1900	
306		Mason	286	1868	4-4-0	16x24	60	62500		74
309		McKay & Aldus		1867	4-4-0	16x24	60	66000		
310		Malone		1865	4-4-0	15x24	60	60000		
313		Malone		1862	4-4-0	15x20	54	55000		75
314		Baldwin	8309	1886	2-6-0	19x24	54	93000		392
317		Portland	456	1882	2-6-0	18x24	54	81800		382
318		Baldwin	10638	1890	2-6-0	19x26	54	107000		393
319		Portland	457	1882	2-6-0	18x24	54	81800		383
320		Baldwin	10914	1890	2-6-0	19x26	54	107000		394
321		Baldwin	8310	1886	2-6-0	19x24	54	93000		395
322		Baldwin	10916	1890	2-6-0	19x26	54	107000		396
323		Baldwin	10917	1890	2-6-0	19x26	54	107000		397

CV No.	Builder	C/N	Date	Type	Cyls.	DD	Weights	Disp'n	1901
324	Baldwin	10924	1890	4-4-0	17x24	66	86000		172
326	Baldwin	10925	1890	4-4-0	17x24	66	86000		173
327	Malone		1872	4-4-0	16x24	54	66200		76
329	Rh. Is'd	1584	1885	2-6-0	19x24	54	100000		398
330	Rh. Is'd	1585	1885	2-6-0	19x24	54	100000		399
331	Malone		1870	4-4-0	16x24	60	73500	Sc 1900	
336*	Rh. Is'd	2983	1894	4-6-0	19x24	56	112000		490
337*	Rh. Is'd	2984	1894	4-6-0	19x24	56	112000		491
338*	Rh. Is'd	2985	1894	4-6-0	19x24	56	112000		492
339*	Schenect	4645	1897	2-8-0	22&34x28	54	153000		550
340*	Schenect	4646	1897	2-8-0	22&34x28	54	153000		551
341*	Schenect	4647	1897	2-8-0	22&34x28	54	153000		552
342*	Baldwin	4392	1878	2-8-0	19x24	51			519

ADDITIONAL DATA. ROSTER II

238. Present information indicates that this engine was originally New London Northern No. 20; later C. V. No. 170 and transferred by the C. V. to St. L. & A. No. 1, after which it became Rutland No. 238 and finally No. 79.

243. Sold to the Canadian Pacific, their Nos. 2nd 180, 298 and 198.

244. Ordered as B. & R. No. 16. Delivered as Rutland No. 244. Sold to the Canadian Pacific, their Nos. 2nd 181, 299 and 199.

249-250. Ex-St. L. & A. Nos. 5 and 7. Cylinders changed to 18"x26".

251-252. Ex-St. L. & A. Nos. 8 and 9.

68. Ex-N. Y. C. No. 691.

69. Ex-N. Y. C. No. 698.

336-338. Ordered by Smith & Hanfield, Contractors, as Nos. 61, 62 and 63. Delivered as O. & L. C. Nos. 336, 337 and 338.

339-341. Received as cross-compounds. Changed to simple, 19"x28".

342. Built as B. N. Y. & P. No. 151 and was sold or transferred to the Western New York & Pennsylvania R. R., and was later sold to the O. & L. C. in 1897.

Rutland No. 16, the MOSSALAMOO, was built by Taunton in 1868. — *Collection of C. H. Nash.*

THE LOCOMOTIVES, 1896 to 1951

The lease of the Rutland Railroad to the Central Vermont was cancelled on May 7th, 1896, and there appears to be no authentic record of the locomotives returned at that time, by the Central Vermont. The report of the Vermont Railroad Commission for the year 1898 credits the Rutland with 29 locomotives, whose exact identity is a matter of some speculation, but available information indicates that they may have been those marked (*) in the following roster.

These engines had been numbered in the C. V. 200 series and retained the same numbers on the Rutland until the 1901 renumbering. Since it is reported that the C. V. had 139 locomotives in 1896, and 111 in 1897, it would appear that the C. V. returned 28 to the Rutland, and it is assumed herein that all of the 28 engines on the Rutland Division roster (C. V. 200 series) were returned, leaving the 29th engine in doubt. Of these 29 only 19 survived until the 1901 renumbering, and the other 10 are listed in a separate, short roster.

The Rutland added at least 56 more engines to its roster before this renumbering, some of these coming by purchase of new power, others from acquired roads, viz., O. & L. C., Bennington & Rutland Ry. and Chatham & Lebanon Valley R. R. Five of the original 29 Rutland engines were former A. & St. L. power that had been assigned to the Rutland Division.

During 1902, twenty-one new locomotives were purchased, bringing to 106 the number of engines owned by the Rutland, between the cancellation of the C. V. lease, in 1896, and the renumbering of Rutland motive power into the N. Y. C. series, in 1905. Due to sales and other disposition only 77 were changed into that series.

In 1913, the N. Y. C. released the Rutland locomotives from its numbering system, and the Rutland instituted its own system, in most cases by merely dropping the first two digits of the N. Y. C. numbers. Because of duplication this was not possible in all cases, and a few of the older engines continued to carry the N. Y. C. numbers until scrapped.

These 13 were Nos. 50, 793, 794, 796, 797, 1060, 1063, 1880, 1881, 1892, 1893, 1898 and 1899. A few others were given new numbers which bore no relation at all to the old ones.

Record of the company's engines from this change in 1913 up to the present time (1951) is shown in Roster IV.

The year 1950 witnessed the first use of Diesel power on the Rutland. Trials were made with an ALCo 1600 H.P. road switcher, No. 1601, and concurrently with an EMD diesel, Bangor & Aroostook No. 568. The first train service run was made on trains 88 and 83, between Rutland and Chatham, on December 19th, 1950, with the No. 1601. This machine was subsequently purchased as part of an order for five similar, and was numbered 200, the others being 201 to 204, and were placed in service during the first half of 1951. Six 1000 H.P. Diesels, Nos. 400 to 405, were later ordered from the American Locomotive Company, the first of which were placed in service late in 1951.

Use of steam power on the Chatham Branch (the former C. & L. V. R. R.) was discontinued on June 30th, 1951, when the engine shed and coaling station at Chatham, N. Y. were permanently closed. However, arrangements were made to handle the annual Exchange Club excursion, Chatham to Rutland, with steam power, on September 30th, 1951.

Painting the engines of the 90 class a bright green, when they were built, caused much favorable comment, and gave the locomotives a fine appearance, when the paint was new, but, with lack of proper care, they soon took on a grimy coat, which could hardly be distinguished from black paint, and the green coat was soon discarded. Because of their fine coloring and "snappy" performance, these handsome 4-8-2's were known as the "Green Hornets."

ROSTER III

Rutland Locomotives. Series 1896-1901 and 1901-1905.
Original 29 marked*

1901 Series No.	Prior Rd or 1896 #		Builder	C/N	Date	Type	Cyls.	DD	Wt.	Series 1905 NYC#	Series 1913 No.
·60	B&R	8	Schenect	563	1869	4-4-0	16x24	69	77000	1060	1060
61	B&R	9	Schenect	564	1869	4-4-0	16x24	69	77000	1061	——
62*		201	St. Albans		1872	4-4-0	16x24	68	72550	——	——
63*	(a)	204	Taunton	464	1869	4-4-0	16x24	63	68100	——	——
64*		205	Taunton	447	1868	4-4-0	16x24	60	68100	1064	——
65*		208	St. Albans		1873	4-4-0	16x24	66	72550	1058	——
66*		212	Amoskeag	50	1852	4-4-0	16x24	60	68300	——	——
67*		217	Taunton	355	1865	4-4-0	16x24	60	62300	——	——
68*		218	Taunton	356	1865	4-4-0	16x24	60	62300	——	——
69*		219	Taunton	366	1865	4-4-0	16x24	66	67600	——	——
70*		220	Taunton	480	1869	4-4-0	16x24	60	68100	——	——
71*		221	Taunton	483	1869	4-4-0	16x24	60	68300	——	——

1901 Series No.	Prior Rd or 1896 #		Builder	C/N	Date	Type	Cyls.	DD	Wt.	Series 1905 NYC#	Series 1913 No.
72*		223	Taunton	509	1870	4-4-0	16x24	60	68100	---	---
73*	(b)	231	Mason	583	1877	4-4-0	17x24	60	73275	---	---
74	O&LC	306	Mason	286	1868	4-4-0	16x24	60	62500	---	---
75	O&LC	313	Malone		1862	4-4-0	15x20	54	55000	---	---
76	O&LC	327	Malone		1872	4-4-0	16x24	54	66200	1059	---
77	C&LV	3	D. C. & Co.		1854	4-4-0	15x20	60		---	---
78	C&LV	5	Brooks	910	1883	4-4-0	14x22	56		---	---
79		238	Manch'r	445	1872	4-4-0	15x22	66	66000	---	---
80*		211	Schenect	3510	1891	0-4-0	16x24	51	64800	50	50
81			Manch'r	26419	1902	0-6-0	18x24	51	101700	447	102
82			Manch'r	26420	1902	0-6-0	18x24	51	101700	448	103
83			Manch'r	26421	1902	0-6-0	18x24	51	101700	449	104
100	(c)NYC	49	Schenect	4401	1896	4-4-0	14x22	63	78700	33	99
170	B&R	11	Schenect	1918	1884	4-4-0	17x24	64	84500	793	793
171	B&R	12	Schenect	1919	1884	4-4-0	17x24	64	84500	794	794
172	O&LC	324	Baldwin	10924	1890	4-4-0	17x24	69	87900	795	---
173	O&LC	326	Baldwin	10925	1890	4-4-0	17x24	69	87900	796	796
174	C&LV	6	Baldwin	10841	1890	4-4-0	17x24	63		797	797
175	C&LV	9	Baldwin	10849	1890	4-4-0	17x24	63		798	---
176	(d)NYC	471	Schenect	1713	1883	4-4-0	17x24	64	79800	---	---
177	NYC	1076	N. Y. C.		1872	4-4-0	17x24	70	81300	1062	---
180	B&R	14	Schenect	4199	1894	4-4-0	18x24	64		864	84
181	B&R	15	Schenect	4200	1894	4-4-0	18x24	64		865	85
182*	(e)	232	Schenect	3511	1891	4-4-0	18x24	69	103000	862	82
183*	(f)	233	Schenect	3512	1891	4-4-0	18x24	69	103000	863	83
184		236	Schenect	4550	1897	4-4-0	18x24	69	110000	866	86
185		237	Schenect	4551	1897	4-4-0	18x24	69	110000	867	87
186		241	Schenect	5109	1899	4-4-0	18x24	69	110000	868	88
187		242	Schenect	5110	1899	4-4-0	18x24	69	110000	869	89
188	(g)	243	Schenect	5545	1900	4-4-0	18½x26	69	127000	---	---
189	(h)	244	Brooks	3448	1900	4-4-0	18½x26	69	127000	---	---
190	SL&A	5	Brooks	2772	1897	4-4-0	18x26	68	126000	1000	80
191	SL&A	7	Brooks	2774	1897	4-4-0	18x26	68	126000	1001	81
192	(p)	68	Rome		1889	4-4-0	18x24	64	99600	---	---
193	(p)	69	Schenect	2765	1889	4-4-0	18x24	64	99600	1063	1063
200			Schenect	26413	1902	4-6-0	20x26	69	154000	2040	40
201			Schenect	26414	1902	4-6-0	20x26	69	154000	2041	41
202			Manch'r	26415	1902	4-6-0	20x26	69	154000	2042	42
203			Manch'r	26416	1902	4-6-0	20x26	69	154000	2043	43
204			Manch'r	26417	1902	4-6-0	20x26	69	154000	2044	44
205			Manch'r	26418	1902	4-6-0	20x26	69	154000	2045	45
206			Schenect	26574	1902	4-6-0	20x26	69	154000	2046	46
207			Schenect	26575	1902	4-6-0	20x26	69	154000	2047	47
210			Schenect	26833	1902	4-6-0	20x26	69	158000	2048	48
211			Schenect	26834	1902	4-6-0	20x26	69	158000	2049	49
212			Schenect	26626	1902	4-6-0	21x26	63	168000	2050	50
213			Schenect	26627	1902	4-6-0	21x26	63	168000	2051	51
320	SL&A	3	Schenect	5591	1900	2-6-0	20x28	57	155200	1884	144
321	SL&A	4	Schenect	5592	1900	2-6-0	20x28	57	155200	1885	145
370*		228	Baldwin	2454	1871	2-6-0	17x24	54	74350	1879	---
380	B&R	5	Schenect	3351	1891	2-6-0	18x24	55	104000	1880	1880
381	B&R	6	Schenect	3352	1891	2-6-0	18x24	55	104000	1881	1881
382	O&LC	317	Portland	456	1882	2-6-0	18x24	54	81000	1882	---
383	O&LC	319	Portland	457	1882	2-6-0	18x24	54	81000	1883	---
386		239	Schenect	5009	1899	2-6-0	19x26	57	121000	1886	146

387		240	Schenect	5010	1899	2-6-0	19x26	57	121000	1887		147
388		245	Schenect	5405	1900	2-6-0	19x26	57	121000	1888		148
389		246	Schenect	5404	1900	2-6-0	19x26	57	121000	1889		149
390		247	Schenect	5406	1900	2-6-0	19x26	57	121000	1890		150
391		248	Schenect	5407	1900	2-6-0	19x26	57	121000	1891		151
392	O&LC	314	Baldwin	8309	1886	2-6-0	19x24	57	98600	1892		1892
393	O&LC	318	Baldwin	10638	1890	2-6-0	19x24	57	110000	1895		153
394	O&LC	320	Baldwin	10914	1890	2-6-0	19x24	57	110000	1894		152
395	O&LC	321	Baldwin	8310	1886	2-6-0	19x24	57	98600	1893		1893
396	O&LC	322	Baldwin	10916	1890	2-6-0	19x24	57	110000	1896		154
397	O&LC	323	Baldwin	10917	1890	2-6-0	19x24	57	110000	1897		155
398	O&LC	329	R. I.	1584	1885	2-6-0	19x24	58	100700	1898		1898
399	O&LC	330	R. I.	1585	1885	2-6-0	19x24	58	100700	1899		1899
420	(i)	251	Schenect	4932	1898	4-6-0	20x28	61	161000	2153		
										Re	2063	63
421	(j)	252	Schenect	4933	1898	4-6-0	20x28	61	161000	2154		
										Re	2064	64
422			Schenect	26576	1902	4-6-0	21x26	63	165000	2052		52
423			Schenect	26577	1902	4-6-0	21x26	63	165000	2053		53
480*	(k)	234	Schenect	3506	1891	4-6-0	18x24	57	116000	2155		
										Re	2061	61
481*	(l)	235	Schenect	3505	1891	4-6-0	18x24	57	116000	2156		
										Re	2062	62
482			Schenect	26628	1902	4-6-0	21x26	63	165000	2054		54
483			Schenect	26629	1902	4-6-0	21x26	63	165000	2055		55
484			Schenect	26630	1902	4-6-0	21x26	63	165000	2056		56
485			Schenect	26631	1902	4-6-0	21x26	63	165000	2057		57
490	(m)O&LC	336	R. I.	2983	1893	4-6-0	19x24	57	112000	2157		
										Re	2060	60
491	(m)O&LC	337	R. I.	2984	1893	4-6-0	19x24	57	112000	2158		
										Re	2058	58
492	(m)O&LC	338	R. I.	2985	1893	4-6-0	19x24	57	112000	2159		
										Re	2059	59
519	(n)O&LC	342	Baldwin	4392	1878	2-8-0	19x24	51	108200	2265		—
550	(o)O&LC	339	Schenect	4645	1897	2-8-0	19x28	55	153000	2424		
										Re	2401	10
551	(o)O&LC	340	Schenect	4646	1897	2-8-0	19x28	55	153000	2425		
										Re	2402	11
552	(o)O&LC	341	Schenect	4647	1897	2-8-0	19x28	55	153000	2426		
										Re	2403	12

Of the "original" 28 locomotives returned by the C. V. to the Rutland, the following 10 were disposed of prior to the 1901 renumbering, and have not been included in the above roster.

C. V. Series No.	Builder	C/N	Date	Type	Cyls.	DD	Disp'n	
203*	Taunton	402	1867	0-4-0	15x22	44	Sc 1900	
204*	St. Albans		1872	4-4-0	16x24	68	So 1902	(MD&G)
207*	Taunton	448	1868	4-4-0	16x24	60	Sc 1900	
214*	Taunton	426	1868	4-4-0	16x22	66	Sc 1900	
222*	Rutland		1870	4-4-0	16x22	66	Sc 1900	
224*	Taunton	512	1870	4-4-0	16x22	60	Sc 1900	
225*	Taunton	514	1870	4-4-0	16x24	60	Sc 1899	
226*	Taunton	466	1869	4-4-0	16x24	66	Sc ?	
229*	Hinkley	403	1852	4-4-0	15x24	60	Sc 1897	
230*	Hinkley	194	1848	4-4-0	15x24	60	Sc ?	

ADDITIONAL DATA. ROSTER III

a. ex-227.
b. ex-Burlington & La Moille "Burlington."
c. Inspection engine "Ne-Ha-Sa-Ne." Ex-StL&A No. 10; NYC&HR No. 49; Rutland No. 100; NYC Lines No. 33; Rutland No. 99.
d. N. Y. C. No. 532 to No. 471.
e. ex-A. & St. L. No. 11.
f. ex-A. & St. L. No. 12.
g. Sold 1902. C. P. R. 2nd No. 180-298-198.
h. Sold 1902. C. P. R. 2nd No. 181-299-199.
i. ex-St. L. & A. No. 8.
j. ex-St. L. & A. No. 9.
k. ex-A. & St. L. No. 31.
l. ex-A. & St. L. No. 32.
m. Ordered by Smith & Hanfield, Contractors. Delivered to O. & L. C.
n. Built as Buffalo, New York & Philadelphia No. 1. Was sold or transferred to the Western New York & Pennsylvania, and later sold to the O. & L. C.
o. Built as cross-compounds, cylinders 22″ & 34″x28″. Changed to simple, 19″x28″.
p. Nos. 68 and 69, ex-NYC Nos. 691 and 698, respectively.

LOCOMOTIVES SCRAPPED. 1901 and 1905 Series

1901 No.	1905 No.	Date Scrapped
61	1061	8-1906
64	1064	2-1908
65	1058	5-1909
76	1059	8-1906
80	50	ab 1914
172	795	5-1910
175	798	9-1912*
177	1076	5-1908
370	1879	6-1909
382	1882	7-1911
383	1883	11-1909
519	2265	12-1911

* Totally demolished in wreck with Milk Train pulled by #2044, at Soldiers' Home Crossing, Bennington, Vt., Sept. 7th, 1912.

Modern-looking American No. 67 was built by Schenectady in 1891 as Adirondack & St. Lawrence No. 11. It had a long history of rebuilds and served its last days as a switcher in Bennington. — *F. Stewart Graham.*

Nos. 1913	NYC Nos. 1905	1901 1905 Nos.	Nos. 1896 1901	Prior Road & No.		Builder	C/N	Date	Type		Ret'd.
10	2424	550		OLC	339	Schenect	4645	1897	2-8-0		6-1934
re	2401										
11	2425	551		OLC	340	Schenect	4646	1897	2-8-0		1-1934
re	2402										
12	2426	552		OLC	341	Schenect	4647	1897	2-8-0		1-1934
re	2403										
14	2414					Schenect	48011	1910	2-8-0		5-1951
15	2415					Schenect	48012	1910	2-8-0		3-1951
16	2416					Schenect	48013	1910	2-8-0		8-1951
17	2417					Schenect	48014	1910	2-8-0		4-1948
18	2418					Schenect	43037	1907	2-8-0		5-1948
19	2419					Schenect	43038	1907	2-8-0		9-1947
20	2420					Schenect	43039	1907	2-8-0		10-1949
21	2421					Schenect	43040	1907	2-8-0		12-1949
22	2422					Schenect	43041	1907	2-8-0		10-1939
23	2423					Schenect	43042	1907	2-8-0		11-1951
24	2424					Schenect	50150	1911	2-8-0		12-1950
25	2425					Schenect	50151	1911	2-8-0		4-1951
26	2426					Schenect	53280	1913	2-8-0		1-1952
27	2427					Schenect	53281	1913	2-8-0		6-1951
28	2428					Schenect	53282	1913	2-8-0		8-1951
29	2429					Schenect	53283	1913	2-8-0		9-1952
30	2430					Schenect	53284	1913	2-8-0		12-1951
31	2431					Schenect	53285	1913	2-8-0		1-1952
32						Schenect	59609	1918	2-8-2		11-1951
33						Schenect	59610	1918	2-8-2		8-1951
34						Schenect	59611	1918	2-8-2		8-1952
35						Schenect	59612	1918	2-8-2		12-1951
36						Schenect	59613	1918	2-8-2		10-1951
37						Schenect	59614	1918	2-8-2		11-1951
38	2038					Schenect	47310	1910	4-6-0	To #72	
39	2039					Schenect	47311	1910	4-6-0	To #73	
40	2040	200				Schenect	26413	1902	4-6-0		4-1951
41	2041	201				Schenect	26414	1902	4-6-0		4-1935
42	2042	202				M'chester	26415	1902	4-6-0		1-1935
43	2043	203				M'chester	26416	1902	4-6-0		11-1939
44	2044	204				M'chester	26417	1902	4-6-0		8-1939
45	2045	205				M'chester	26418	1902	4-6-0		12-1950
46	2046	206				Schenect	26574	1902	4-6-0		1-1932
47	2047	207				Schenect	26575	1902	4-6-0		1-1934
48	2048	210				Schenect	26833	1902	4-6-0		7-1946
49	2049	211				Schenect	26834	1902	4-6-0		2-1951
50	50	80	211	ASL	1	Schenect	3510	1891	0-4-0		ab 1915
50	2050	212 (see note)				Schenect	26626	1902	4-6-0		4-1951
51	2051	213				Schenect	26627	1902	4-6-0		12-1951
52	2052	422				Schenect	26576	1902	4-6-0		9-1951
53	2053	423				Schenect	26577	1902	4-6-0		11-1951
54	2054	482				Schenect	26628	1902	4-6-0		10-1946
55	2055	483				Schenect	26629	1902	4-6-0		4-1948
56	2056	484				Schenect	26630	1902	4-6-0		4-1948

Nos. 1913	NYC Nos. 1905	1901 1905 Nos.	Nos. 1896 1901	Prior Road & No.		Builder	C/N	Date	Type		Ret'd.
57	2057	485				Schenect	26631	1902	4-6-0		6-1950
58	2158	491		OLC	337	Rh. Island	2984	1893	4-6-0		12-1921
re	2058										
59	2159	492		OLC	338	Rh. Island	2985	1893	4-6-0		12-1921
re	2059										
60	2157	490		OLC	336	Rh. Island	2983	1893	4-6-0		1-1919
re	2060										
61	2155	480	234	ASL	31	Schenect	3506	1891	4-6-0		12-1926
re	2061										
62	2156	481	235	ASL	32	Schenect	3505	1891	4-6-0		12-1918
re	2062										
63	2153	420	251	SLA	8	Schenect	4932	1898	4-6-0		6-1939
re	2063										
64	2154	421	252	SLA	9	Schenect	4933	1898	4-6-0		6-1939
re	2064										
65	1000	190	249	SLA	5	Brooks	2772	1897	4-4-0	Fr #80	12-1935
66	1001	191	250	SLA	7	Brooks	2774	1897	4-4-0	Fr #81	9-1926
67	862	182	232	ASL	11	Schenect	3511	1891	4-4-0	Fr #82	1-1932
70	2036					Schenect	47308	1910	4-6-0		9-1951
re	2070										
71	2037					Schenect	47309	1910	4-6-0		10-1951
re	2071										
72	2038					Schenect	47310	1910	4-6-0	Fr #38	10-1951
73	2039					Schenect	47311	1910	4-6-0	Fr #39	1-1952
74	2074					Schenect	51564	1912	4-6-0		8-1953
75	2075					Schenect	51565	1912	4-6-0		11-1951
76	2076					Schenect	51566	1912	4-6-0		8-1952
77	2077					Schenect	51567	1912	4-6-0		10-1951
78	2078					Schenect	51568	1912	4-6-0		11-1951
79	2079					Schenect	51569	1912	4-6-0		12-1951
80	1000	190	249	SLA	5	Brooks	2772	1897	4-4-0	To #65	12-1935
80						Schenect	66327	1925	4-6-2		
81	1001	191	250	SLA	7	Brooks	2774	1897	4-4-0	To #66	9-1926
81						Schenect	66328	1925	4-6-2		
82	862	182	232	ASL	11	Schenect	3511	1891	4-4-0	To #67	1-1932
82						Schenect	66329	1925	4-6-2		8-1952
83	863	183	233	ASL	12	Schenect	3512	1891	4-4-0		So 10-1920
83						Schenect	68052	1929	4-6-2		9-1952
84	864	180				Schenect	4199	1894	4-4-0		So 10-1920
84						Schenect	68053	1929	4-6-2		12-1951
85	865	181		B&R	15	Schenect	4200	1894	4-4-0		So 10-1920
85						Schenect	68054	1929	4-6-2		1-1953
86	866	184	236			Schenect	4550	1897	4-4-0		1-1932
87	867	185	237			Schenect	4551	1897	4-4-0		1-1932
88	868	186	241			Schenect	5109	1899	4-4-0		2-1936
89	869	187	242			Schenect	5110	1899	4-4-0		Sc 1-1932
90						Schenect	74376	1946	4-8-2		3-1955
91						Schenect	74377	1946	4-8-2		3-1955
92						Schenect	74378	1946	4-8-2		3-1955
93						Schenect	74379	1946	4-8-2		3-1955
99	33	100	NYC 49	SLA	10	Schenect	4401	1896	4-4-0	Obs'n	5-1936
100	445					Cooke	43035	1907	0-6-0		9-1952
101	446					Cooke	43036	1907	0-6-0		1-1951
102	447	81				M'chester	26419	1902	0-6-0		7-1945

103	448	82				M'chester	26420	1902	0-6-0	8-1946
104	449	83				M'chester	26421	1902	0-6-0	8-1946
105	450					M'chester	53286	1913	0-6-0	12-1951
106	451					Schenect	54887	1914	0-6-0	9-1953
107	(Bought 3-29-46)			C&P	9	Schenect	66084	1924	0-6-0	9-1953
109						Pittsburg	60158	1918	0-8-0	11-1951
110						Pittsburg	60159	1918	0-8-0	12-1951
144	1884	320		SLA	3	Schenect	5591	1900	2-6-0	7-1946
145	1885	321		SLA	4	Schenect	5592	1900	2-6-0	7-1946
146	1886	386	239			Schenect	5009	1899	2-6-0	6-1934
147	1887	387	240			Schenect	5010	1899	2-6-0	1-1934
148	1888	388	245			Schenect	5405	1900	2-6-0	5-1936
149	1889	389	246			Schenect	5404	1900	2-6-0	8-1936
150	1890	390	247			Schenect	5406	1900	2-6-0	10-1940
151	1891	391	248			Schenect	5407	1900	2-6-0	12-1928
152	1894	394	320	OLC	320	Baldwin	10914	1890	2-6-0	7-1923
153	1895	393	318	OLC	318	Baldwin	10638	1890	2-6-0	7-1927
154	1896	396	322	OLC	322	Baldwin	10916	1890	2-6-0	3-1921
155	1897	397	323	OLC	323	Baldwin	10917	1890	2-6-0	7-1923
793	793	170		B&R	11	Schenect	1918	1884	4-4-0	1-1919
794	794	171		B&R	12	Schenect	1919	1884	4-4-0	11-1926
796	796	173	326	OLC	326	Baldwin	10925	1890	4-4-0	5-1916
797	797	714		C&LV	6	Baldwin	10841	1890	4-4-0	11-1915
1060	1060	60		B&R	8	Schenect	563	1869	4-4-0	7-1914
1063	1063	193		NYC	698	Schenect	2765	1889	4-4-0	1-1919
1880	1880	380		B&R	5	Schenect	3351	1891	2-6-0	7-1918
1881	1881	381		B&R	6	Schenect	3352	1891	2-6-0	12-1920
1892	1892	392	314	OLC	314	Baldwin	8309	1886	2-6-0	11-1915
1893	1893	395	321	OLC	321	Baldwin	8310	1886	2-6-0	5-1913
1898	1898	398	329	OLC	329	Rh. Island	1584	1885	2-6-0	9-1913
1899	1899	399	330	OLC	330	Rh. Island	1585	1885	2-6-0	12-1914

1st Nos. 83, 84 and 85 were sold to the Fort Smith & Western, becoming Nos. 4, 6 and 5, respectively, on that road.

Abbreviations Used:

ASL	Adirondack & St. Lawrence R. R.	OLC	Ogdensburg & Lake Champlain R. R.
B&R	Bennington & Rutland Ry.	SLA	St. Lawrence & Adirondack R. R.
C&LV	Chatham & Lebanon Valley R. R.		
C&P	Clarendon & Pittsford R. R.		
	(Vermont Marble Company)		

No. 50. This number was used concurrently on the 0-4-0 and the 4-6-0 for a short time, until the former was sold.

Nos.	Cyls.	DD	Valves	Valve Gear	Weights		
					OD	Total	
10-12	19x28	54	Slide	Stephenson	135500	153000	
14-17	22x30	63	Piston	Stephenson	187000	211000	To 22½x30, #17
18-23	22x30	63	Piston	Stephenson	186000	209000	To 22½x30, all
24-25	22½x30	63	Piston	Stephenson	188000	213000	
26-31	22½x30	63	Piston	Stephenson	188000	213000	
32-37	26x30	63	Piston	Walschaert	220000	292000	
40-47	20x26	69	Piston	Stephenson	115000	154000	
48-49	20x26	69	Piston	Stephenson	117000	158000	
50-55	21x26	63	Piston	Stephenson	132000	168000	
56-57	21x26	63	Piston	Stephenson	130000	165000	
58-60	19x24	57	Slide	Stephenson	82000	112000	
61-62	18x24	57	Slide	Stephenson	91000	116000	
63-64	20x28	61	Slide	Stephenson	123000	161000	

	Nos.	Cyls.	DD	Valves	Valve Gear	Weights OD	Total	
	65	18x26	68	Piston	Stephenson	84000	126000	
	66	18x26	68	Slide	Stephenson	84000	126000	
	67	18x24	69	Slide	Stephenson	70000	106000	
	70-71	22x26	69	Piston	St. to Wals	159000	204000	To 22½x26
	72-73	22x26	69	Piston	St. to Wals	148000	198000	To 22½x26
	74-79	22½x26	69	Piston	Walschaert	155000	211000	
1st	80-81	18x26*	68	Piston**	Stephenson	84000	126000	To 65-66
1st	82-83	18x24	69	Slide	Stephenson	70000	106000	82 to 67
1st	84-85	18x24	70	Slide	Stephenson	70000	106000	
2nd	80-82	25x28	69	Piston	Walschaert		278000	
2nd	83-85	25x28	73	Piston	Walschaert	175800	292500	
	86-89	18x24	69	Slide	Stephenson	70000	110000	
	90-93	26x30	73	Piston	Walschaert	232000	348000	
	99	14x22	63	Slide	Stephenson	49700	78700	
	100-101	19x26	51	Slide	Stephenson	136000	136000	
	102-104	18x24	51	Slide	Stephenson	101000	101000	
	105	19x26	51	Slide	Stephenson	139000	139000	
	106	20x26	51	Piston	Walschaert	144000	144000	
	107	21x28	57	Piston	Walschaert	168000	168000	
	109-110	25x28	51	Piston	Baker	214000	214000	
	144-145	20x28	57	Slide	Stephenson	135000	155000	
	146-151	19x26	57	Slide	Stephenson	103000	121000	
	152-155	19x26	57	Slide	Stephenson	91000	110000	
	793-794	17x24	64	Slide	Stephenson	60000	84000	
	796	17x24	66	Slide	Stephenson		86000	
	797	17x24	63	Slide	Stephenson		80000	
	1060	16x24	69	Slide	Stephenson		77000	
	1063	18x24	64	Slide	Stephenson	64000	99600	
	1880-81	18x24	55	Slide	Stephenson	88800	104000	
	1892-93	19x24	54	Slide	Stephenson		93000	
	1898-99	19x24	54	Slide	Stephenson		100000	

*1st #80, cylinders changed to 19x26, when superheated in June, 1916.

**1st #81, Piston valve cylinders replaced by slide valves.

Walschaert valve gear applied to #70 in Feb. 1917; #71, Nov. 1917; #72, Feb. 1920; #73, Aug. 1920.
Superheaters applied to #70 in Aug. 1913; #71, June 1914; #72, Feb. 1920; #73, Aug. 1920.

Ten-Wheeler No. 203 became 2043 under New York Central, finally ending her days as Rutland No. 43. It was built by Manchester in 1902.

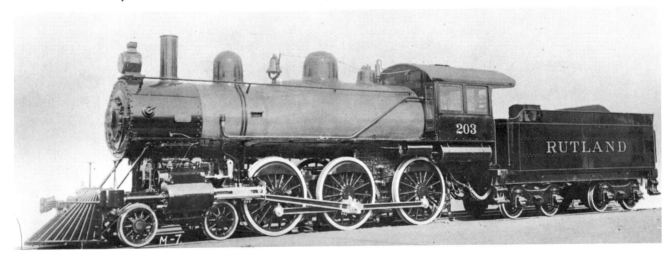

RUTLAND LOCOMOTIVE CLASSIFICATION 1913 Series

	Nos.	Class	To Class			Nos.	Class	To Class		Nos.	Class	To Class
	10-12	G-14				61-62	F-14			106	B-2-c	
	14-17	G-34b				63-64	F-13			107	B-3	
	18-23	G-34a				70-73	F-2-h	F-2-k		109-110	U-3	
	24-25	G-34c				74-79	F-2-j			144-145	E-1-d	
	26-31	G-34d		1st		80-81	C-2			146-151	E-14	
	32-37	H-6-a		1st		82-83	C-1			152-155	E-17	
	40	F-12	F-12a	1st		84-85	C-1-a			793-794	C-25	
	41	F-12				86-89	C-1-b			796	C-28	(NYC)
	42-43	F-12	F-12a	2nd		80-82	K-1			797	C-29	(NYC)
	44	F-12		2nd		83-85	K-2			1000-1001	C-2	
	45	F-12	F-12a			90-93	L-1			1060-1063	C-X	(NYC)
	46-47	F-12				99	Pony			1880-1881	E-12	
	48-49	F-12	F-12a			100-101	B-2-a			1892-1893	E-15	(NYC)
	50-57	F-11	F-11a			102-104	B-9			1898-1899	E-16	(NYC)
	58-60	F-15				105	B-2-b					

SUPERHEATERS

Engine Nos.	Installed	Engine Nos.	Installed	Engine Nos.	Installed
14	1-1926	40	8-1919	56	4-1928
15	1-1925	42	8-1918	57	5-1927
16	2-1924	43	4-1916	70	8-1913
17	2-1919	45 (Cole)	4-1910	71	6-1914
18	5-1915	48	7-1915	72	2-2-20
19	9-1915	49	7-1913	73	8-24-20
20	12-1914	50	4-1915	74 to 79	when built
21	10-1914	51	8-1912	1st 80	6-1916
22	6-1917	52	9-1912	2nd 80 to 85	when built
23	2-1918	53	1-1916	90 to 93	when built
24 to 31	when built	54	10-1913	106 to 107	when built
32 to 37	when built	55	10-1914	109 to 110	when built

The first superheater used was installed on No. 45. This was a Cole Superheater. All others were Schmidt type.

Consolidation No. 25, from Schenectady in 1911, class G-34c, has a modern air pump mounted up front. — *John Pickett.*

ROSTER OF RUTLAND RAILWAY DIESEL LOCOMOTIVES

1600 HP Road Switchers

No.	Class	Builder	Number	Drivers	Drivers	Weight	Tractive Force
200*	DRS-6a	Alco-GE	78252	1950	40	248000	52500
201	DRS-6a	Alco-GE	78594	1951	40	248000	52500
202	DRS-6b	Alco-GE	78880	1951	40	248000	52500
203	DRS-6b	Alco-GE	78881	1951	40	248000	52500
204	DRS-6b	Alco-GE	78882	1951	40	248000	52500
205	DRS-6c	Alco-GE	80155	1952	40	248000	52500
206	DRS-6c	Alco-GE	80156	1952	40	248000	52500
207	DRS-6c	Alco-GE	80157	1952	40	248000	52500
208	DRS-6c	Alco-GE	80158	1952	40	248000	52500

All sold to L&N in April, 1963

1000 HP Road Switchers

No.	Class	Builder	Number	Drivers	Drivers	Weight	Tractive Force
400	DRS-1	Alco-GE	79349	1951	40	242400	34000
401	DRS-1	Alco-GE	79350	1951	40	242400	34000
402	DRS-1	Alco-GE	79572	1951	40	242400	34000
403	DRS-1	Alco-GE	79573	1951	40	242400	34000
404	DRS-1	Alco-GE	79574	1951	40	242400	34000
405	DRS-1	Alco-GE	79575	1951	40	242400	34000

No. 400 Sold to Tenn. Railroad Sept. 1956
Nos. 401-403 Leased to Vt. Ry. Corp. Jan. 1964

No. 404 Sold to Norwood & St. Lawrence 1964
No. 405 Leased by Nelson Blount on his leased section of Bellows Falls Div.

600 HP Switcher

No.	Class	Builder	Number	Drivers	Drivers	Weight	Tractive Force
500	DES-2	GE	31175	1951	36	137600	23600

No. 500 sold to Clarendon & Pittsford in Aug. 1962

*No. 200 originally Alco. No. 1601

Shown at the north end of the old Burlington depot in 1910, Ten-Wheeler No. 2044 sports her N. Y. Central number. Manchester built her for Rutland in 1902 as No. 44.

Engine No. 75, above, was built in 1849 as the CHATEAUGAY. After more than 50 years of running, her lead truck wheels didn't match. Switcher No. 447 later became No. 102. Engine No. 2043, at the bottom, is a Ten-Wheeler, class F-12a from Manchester, 1902, originally numbered 203.

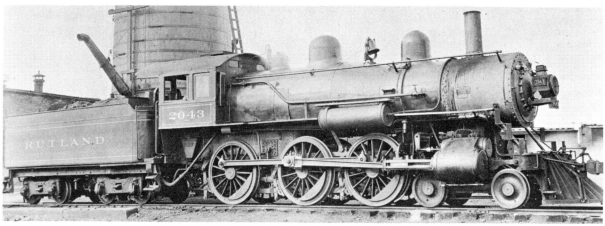

The SHELBURNE (*top*) No. 37 came to Rutland a year after Taunton built her for Vermont Central in 1869. The RIDEAU was originally ST. REGIS No. 23 on North-ern Railway. Light Ten-Wheeler No. 49, Class F-12a, Alco '02, has Fox patent trucks on her tender. — *Top: Collection of C. H. Nash; below: John Pickett.*

Queens of the fleet were the L-1 class Mountains. No.
93, last steamer ever to come to the Rutland, was delivered in 1946. The six U.S.R.A. Mikado class H-6a
engines served the Rutland well from 1918 to 1952. —
Both: Jim Shaughnessy.

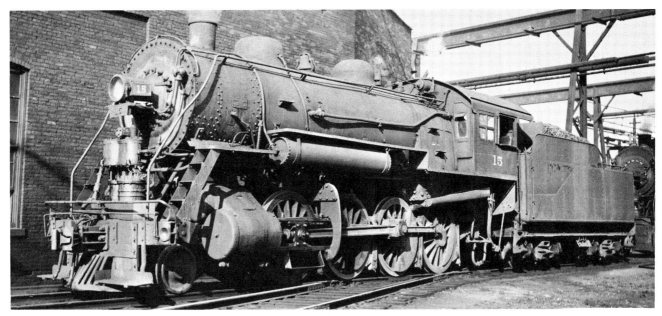

Opposite: No. 15 was one of the four 1910, class G-34d Consolidations. Under her picture is another Consolidation, 1913, class G-34a. At the bottom, clean painted, is a class F-11a Ten-Wheeler with Stephenson valve gear but piston valves. — *Top: John Pickett; Middle: Robert F. Collins.*

On this page are two 0-6-0 switchers of different vintage. No. 106 was the only one in class B-2c, 1914. No. 107 was purchased for $500 from Clarendon & Pittsford when that nearby marble line dieselized in 1946. This bargain switched the Burlington yards for the next seven years. — *Above: Jim Shaughnessy; below: Donald W. Furler.*

The Ten-Wheelers above were both from Alco. No. 72 was class F-2k, 1910; No. 74 was F-2j, 1912. Also from Alco was light Pacific No. 80, class K-1, 1925. — *Top to bottom: Jim Shaughnessy, Robert F. Collins, Donald W. Furler.*

In order to have any appreciation of the O&LC power it should be first considered in its entirety. During the half century of the road's independent existence the motive power was constantly undergoing changes. When the locomotives that were acquired by the Rutland show up in the Vermont road's listing, their sequence in retrospect is destroyed. The Malone shops turned out some new locomotives, but they consisted mostly of parts from older ones with the exception of the boilers in many cases. When the Vermont Central leased the Northern New York line in 1870, the O&LC's equipment was renumbered in the 300 series. To complicate matters further, additional power was added by the leasing road. Finally, upon purchase of the line by the Rutland in 1899, much of the power was renumbered again and appears in subsequent Rutland listings.

No.	Name	Builder	Build. No.	Date	Type	Cyls.	DD
1	Sorel	Amoskeag	#16	4-10-1851	4-4-0	16x20	72
1	J. C. Pratt	Malone			4-4-0	15x20	60
301	W. J. Rust		Sc 1892				
2	Richelieu	Taunton	#62	12-25-1850	4-4-0	15x20	66
2	G. M. Barnard	Taunton	#471	8-12-1869	4-4-0	16x24	60
302	W. L. Frost		Sc 1895				
3	Rideau	Essex Co.		12- -1851	4-4-0	16x20	66
3	J. W. Pierce	Taunton	#435	6-30-1868	4-4-0	16x24	60
303	J. W. Pierce		Sc				
4	Oswegatchie	Hinkley & Drury	#260	4- 8-1850	4-4-0	15x18	66
	Sold to Rutland & Burlington R. R. 1-23-1872						
4	J. C. Pratt	Taunton	#431	4-30-1868	4-4-0	16x24	60
	Renamed—H. A. Church						
304	H. A. Church		Sc 1895				
5	Deer	Kirk		5- -1850	4-4-0	16x20	68
5	DeWitt C. Brown	Mason	#282	6-11-1868	4-4-0	16x24	60
305	DeWitt C. Brown		Sc 1895				
6	Trent	Essex Co.		8- -1851	4-4-0	15x18	60
6	Abraham Klohs	Mason	#286	8-24-1868	4-4-0	16x24	60
306	A. Klohs		R. #74				
7	Welland	Essex Co.		7- -1851	4-4-0	15x18	60
7	J. S. Farlow	Malone			4-4-0	15x24	60
307	J. S. Farlow		Sc 1895				
8	Ottawa	Taunton	#25	11-22-1848	4-4-0	15x18	60
	Purchased from Norfolk Co. R. R.—"Waterford"						
8	Malone	McKay & Aldus		1867	4-4-0	16x24	60
308	Malone		Sc 1895				
9	Ontario	Souther		10- -1850	4-4-0	15x20	60
9	Ogdensburg	McKay & Aldus		1867	4-4-0	16x24	60
309	W. A. Short		Sc				
10	Ausable	Hinkley & Drury	#277	9-30-1850	4-4-0	15x20	60
10	Stag	Malone		1865	4-4-0	15x24	60
310	Gen. Grant		Sc				
11	Saranac	Hinkley & Drury	#270	8- 6-1850	4-4-0	15x18	60
11	Fawn	Malone		1866	4-4-0	15x24	60
311	Gen. Sherman	(renamed 1872)	Sc 1895				
12	La Grasse	Hinkley & Drury	#276	9-19-1850	4-4-0	15x20	60
12	Welland	Malone (reb.)			4-4-0	15x20	54
312	Welland		Sc 1891				
13	Chateaugay	Hinkley & Drury	#234	4-26-1849	4-4-0	14x18	60
13	St. Lawrence	Malone		1862	4-4-0	15x20	54
313	St. Lawrence		R. #75				
14	Niagara	Essex Co.		2- -1852	4-4-0	15x24	54
14	Champlain	Malone		1864	4-4-0	15x20	54
314	Champlain		Sc 1886				

No.	Name	Builder	Build. No.	Date	Type	Cyls.	DD
314	Not Named	Baldwin	#8309 R. #392	12- -1886	2-6-0	19x24	54
15	Michigan	Essex Co.		3- -1852	4-4-0	15x24	54
15	Fawn	Malone		1872	4-4-0	14x20	60
315	Fawn		Sc 1891				
16	Racquette	Hinkley & Drury	#300	4- 2-1851	4-4-0	16x20	54
16	Stag	Malone			4-4-0	14x20	60
316	Stag		Sc				
17	Erie	Hinkley & Drury	#299	4- 1-1851	4-4-0	16x20	54
	Renamed—Ontario—rebuilt				0-4-0	12x20	60
317	Economy	Portland	#456 R. #382	6-20-1882	2-6-0	18x24	54
18	Superior	Souther Rebuilt & Renamed		5- -1851	4-4-0	16x20	54
	Richelieu	Malone			4-4-0	14x20	60
18	Not Named	Baldwin	#10229	9- -1889	4-6-0	19x24	54
	Ex. C. V. #91. Returned to C. V. re 250—sold N. L. N.							
318	Not Named	Baldwin	#10638 R. #393-153	5- -1890	2-6-0	19x26	54
19	Genesee	Essex Co.		5- -1851	4-4-0	15x20	54
19	Economy	Malone (re 31)			0-4-0	12x20	60
319	Energy	Portland	#457 R. #383	7-18-1882	2-6-0	18x24	54
20	St. Clair	Essex Co.		8- -1851	4-4-0	15x20	54
20	Turtle	Malone			0-4-0	11x20	40
20	Not Named	Baldwin	#10242	9- -1889	4-6-0	19x24	54
	Ex. C. V. #33. Returned to C. V. re 220—sold N. L. N.							
320	Not Named	Baldwin	#10914 R. #394-152	5- -1890	2-6-0	19x26	54
21	Huron	Essex Co.	Sc—1876	8- -1851	4-4-0	15x20	54
321	Not Named	Baldwin	#8310	12- -1886	2-6-0	19x24	54
22	St. Lawrence	Hinkley & Drury	#248	10- 8-1849	4-4-0	16x20	54
22	Not Named	Baldwin	#10236	9- -1889	4-6-0	19x24	54
	Ex. C. V. #92. Returned to C. V. re 222—sold to N. L. N.							
322	Not Named	Baldwin	#10916 R. #396-154	5- -1890	2-6-0	19x26	54
23	St. Regis	Hinkley & Drury	#281	10-22-1850	4-4-0	16x20	54
23	Rideau	Malone (rebuilt)			4-4-0	16x20	60
323	Not Named	Baldwin	#10917 R. #397-155	5- -1890	2-6-0	19x26	54

The Genesee was built for Ogdensburg & Lake Champlain in 1851. During the Central Vermont lease she had C.V. lettering with a small "O.& L.C." between the two words.

One of the last new locomotives to come to the O.& L.C. while under lease was Baldwin 2-6-0 No. 320 and carried no name. Here she is with the Vermont parent's name on her tank. The ECONOMY, a beautifully decorated Mogul, stands on the banks of the St. Lawrence at Ogdensburg. The W. J. RUST, shown at Malone station, was rebuilt at the shops there some years after its 1851 birthday at the Amoskeag works. *Below:* Built for Vermont Central as the RICHMOND, this American was renamed WARREN K. BLODGETT by O.&L.C. The story of its ownership and operation under lease can be inferred from the lettering on the tender. — *Bottom: Collection of Lawrence Doherty.*

No.	Name	Builder	Build. No.	Date	Type	Cyls.	DD
24	Champlain	Hinkley & Drury	#236	5-23-1849	4-4-0	15x20	54
24	Superior	Malone (rebuilt)			4-4-0	15x20	54
324	Not Named	Baldwin	#10924	1890	4-4-0	17x24	66
			R. #172				
25	Salmon	Hinkley & Drury	#261	5- 1-1850	4-4-0	13½x20	48
25	Huron	Taunton	#62	12-25-1850	4-4-0	15x20	66
325	Orginially "Richelieu" #2		Sc—1891				
26	Little Salmon	Hinkley & Drury	#255	11-26-1849	4-4-0	11½x20	48
26	St. Clair	Malone			4-4-0	15x20	54
326	Not Named	Baldwin	#10925	1890	4-4-0	17x24	66
			R. #173				
27	Little Trout	Hinkley & Drury	#262	5- 2-1850	4-4-0	11½x20	48
27	Sorel	Malone		1872	4-4-0	16x24	54
327			R. #76				
28	Chazy	Hinkley & Drury	#47	8- 1-1845	4-2-0	11½x20	60
	From Old Colony R. R.—"Mayflower"—Sent to Montreal & Plattsburgh R. R.						
28	Ottawa	Malone (May have been #8 reblt)			4-4-0	14x18	60
328	Ottawa		Sc				
29	La Grasse	Hinkley & Drury	#276	9-19-1850	4-4-0	15x20	60
	Formerly #12—		Sc 1876				
329	S. A. Carlton	Rhode Island	#1584	1885	2-6-0	19x24	54
			R. #398				
30	Salmon	Hinkley & Drury	#261	5- 1-1850	4-4-0	13½x20	48
	Formerly #25		Sc—1876				
330	D. W. Lawrence	Rhode Island	#1585	1885	2-6-0	19x24	54
			R. #399				
31	Genesee	Essex Co.		5- -1851	4-4-0	16x24	54
	Originally #19—rebuilt		Sc—1870				
331	Hoyle	Malone		1870	4-4-0	16x24	60
			Sc				
332	Chateaugay	Mason	#291	10-12-1868	4-4-0	16x24	54
	Formerly C. V. "Braintree"		Sc—1895				
333	W. J. Averill	Mason	#296	11-18-1868	4-4-0	16x24	54
	Formerly C. V. "Fairfax"		Sc—1895				
334	W. K. Blodgett	Mason	#297	11-30-1868	4-4-0	16x22	66
	Formerly C. V. "Richmond"		Sc—1895				
335	W. A. Haskell	Mason	#295	12-11-1868	4-4-0	16x22	66
	Formerly C. V. "Stowe"		Sc—1895				
336	Not Named	Rhode Island	#2985	1-18-1894	4-6-0	19x24	56
	Formerly S. & H. #63		R. #493-60				
337	Not Named	Rhode Island	#2983	1-19-1894	4-6-0	19x24	56
	Formerly S. & H. #61		R. 491-58				
338	Not Named	Rhode Island	#2984	1-19-1894	4-6-0	19x24	56
	Formerly S. & H. #62		R. #492-59				
339	Not Named	Schenectady	#4645	1897	2-8-0	22&34x28	51
			R. #550-10				
340	Not Named	Schenectady	#4646	1897	2-8-0	22&34x28	51
			R. #551-11				
341	Not Named	Schenectady	#4647	1897	2-8-0	22&34x28	51
			R. #552-12				
342	Not Named	Baldwin	#4392	1879	4-6-0	19x24	51
	Formerly B. N. Y. & P. #1		R. #519				

Nos. 336-338 were built for and used by Messrs. Smith & Hanfield, contractors who built the Van Cortland cut-off on the Putnam Div. of the New York Central. No. 342 was originally built for the Buffalo, New York & Philadelphia R. R., their #1 and sold or transferred to the Western New York & Pennsylvania and then sold to the O. & L. C.

(O&LC tabulation by Lawrence Doherty)

Consolidation No. 12 was a rebuild of Ogdensburg & Lake Champlain compound No. 341. She came to the Rutland when her original line was acquired, as did American No. 324, an 1890 Baldwin product, which retained its C.V. number until all Rutland power was renumbered in 1901. The compound Consolidation at the bottom of the page was one of three acquired by O.&L.C. just before becoming a Rutland subdivision.

The history of the earliest motive power of the B. & R. begins with a group of eight engines built for the Western Vermont R. R., predecessor of the Bennington & Rutland. Of these, seven came from Hinkley, in the years 1851-2-3, and one from the Lowell Machine Shop, in 1854. There is some question as to whether all of these were delivered to the W. V., and it is possible that the "Danby" became the "Cayuga," on the New York & Harlem, although the New York State Report of 1856 shows the latter as having 15"x 18" cylinders, while the "Danby's" were 16"x20".

Eliminating this one engine leaves seven, which, by coincidence, is the number of Troy & Boston engines said to have been seized by the B. & R., at the time that the lease of the W. V. to the T. & B. was abandoned. The final disposition of the original seven W. V. engines is unknown. However, if these engines were allowed to deteriorate, while in possession of the T. & B., as claimed by the B. & R. in thir suit against that company, it may readily be assumed that, after thirteen to sixteen years of service and neglect, they were unfit for anything other than scrapping.

The following roster of the B. & R. is believed to be fairly accurate, but it is possible that there may have been more changes in the names of the locomotives than are recorded here. There are at this time (1950) men who remember the B. & R. engines, but it is difficult to get them to agree, in all respects, as to the names on them. Mr. George McMaster, of Rutland, who worked for the B. & R. and the Rutland, from June 26th, 1882, until 1938, has been the most reliable source of information, and the roster was made up partly from his recollections.

Much of the motive power on the Lebanon Springs R. R. was supplied by the B. & R., which had leased that road, prior to its opening in the middle of 1869. The first excursion train on the L. S. R. R. was run from Bennington to New Lebanon, on July 21st, 1869, and was pulled by the new B. & R. engine, "Mountain Girl." The B. & R. also furnished locomotives to move freight up and down the Bennington & Glastenbury R. R., after that road had been electrified for passenger service only.

An item of interest, which may or may not be generally known, was brought out in the compilation of the data on the B. & R. locomotives. Photographs of second No. 7 and of No. 10 showed engines bearing the well known Rogers characteristics, but with "Brooks" on the steam chest casing. Inquiry brought forth the following explanation from your Editor.

"Horatio G. Brooks, founder of the Brooks Works, left the employ of the Erie to start the locomotive building company bearing his name. He had run, worked on and with Rogers engines, and he admired them. His first locomotives followed very closely their pattern, even to the fluted steam and sand dome (coffee pot, some call them) castings. In addition to the name being stamped on the steam chests, you can always tell them because the sand domes were not as high as the Rogers, but a hasty glance would lead one to believe that they might be Rogers engines. Later, Brooks introduced his smoother outlined castings and his unmistakable cabs, but his first engines are frequently confused with those of Rogers."

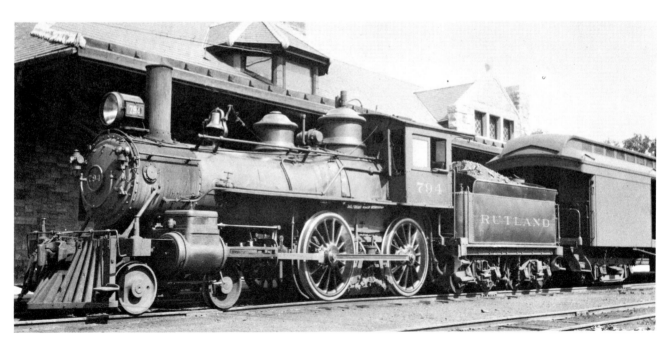

Bennington & Rutland called No. 794, shown at Bennington Station on the opposite page, the TRENOR L. PARK when it came from the Schenectady works in 1884. B. & R.'s No. 8 was named the MOUNTAIN BOY, *above*. Rutland would later assign her the number 60. *Below:* The venerable M. S. COLBURN was B. & R.'s second No. 7, received from Brooks in 1873. — *Opposite: F. Stewart Graham; others from his collection.*

LOCOMOTIVES OF THE WESTERN VERMONT R. R.
All 4-4-0 Type

Name	Builder	Date	C/N	Cyls.	DD
Martin E. Denny	Hinkley	11- 4-1851	339	14x20	66
Wallingford	Hinkley	12-29-1851	350	16x20	60
Bennington	Hinkley	6-21-1852	377	14x20	66
Danby	Hinkley	8-28-1852	393	16x20	60
Manchester	Hinkley	10-16-1852	405	14x20	66
Shaftsbury	Hinkley	1-10-1853	420	16x20	54
No name	Hinkley	1-21-1853	421	16x20	54
Falcon	Lowell M.S.	1854		14x20	66

BENNINGTON & RUTLAND RAILWAY

No.	Name	Builder	C/N	Date	Type	Cyls.	DD	Remarks
1	Hiland Hall	Mason	241	1866	4-4-0	15x22	66	
2	Luther Park	Baldwin	1520	1866	4-4-0	14x20	60	Sc 1894
3	A. L. Miner	Baldwin	1527	1866	4-4-0	14x20	60	
3		Rogers	1910	1871	4-4-0	15x22	54	
4	C. G. Lincoln	Baldwin	1529	1866	4-4-0	14x20	60	
5	Lebanon	NRR (NH)		1862	4-4-0	14x24	60	
5	Trenor W. Park	Schenect.	3351	1891	2-6-0	18x24	55	To Rut. 380-1880
6	Manchester	Rogers	765	1857	4-4-0	14x20	66	
6	H. P. McCullough	Schenect.	3352	1891	2-6-0	18x24	55	To Rut. 381-1881
7	G. F. Carman	Rogers	166	1849	4-4-0	14x20	66	
7	M. S. Colburn	Brooks	189	1873	4-4-0	16x24	60	From #11
8	Mountain Boy	Schenect.	563	1869	4-4-0	16x24	66	To Rut. 60-1060
9	Mountain Girl	Schenect.	564	1869	4-4-0	16x24	66	To Rut. 61-1061
10	C. E. Houghton	Brooks	185	1873	4-4-0	16x24	60	
11	M. S. Colburn	Brooks	189	1873	4-4-0	16x24	60	Ren'd #7
11	M. S. Colburn	Schenect.	1918	1884	4-4-0	17x24	63	To Rut. 170-793
12	Trenor L. Park	Schenect.	1919	1884	4-4-0	17x24	63	To Rut. 171-794
13	No engine							
14	J. G. McCullough	Schenect.	4199	1894	4-4-0	18x24	64	To Rut. 180-864-84
15	F. B. Jennings	Schenect.	4200	1894	4-4-0	18x24	64	To Rut. 181-865-85
16	Not named	Brooks	3448	1900	4-4-0	18½x26	68	Received as Rut. #244

ROSTER NOTES

2nd 3. Ex. S. L. & N. No. 3. Purchased from Bennington & Glastenbury R. R., about 1889. Destroyed in wreck, at South Shaftsbury, 1-15-1894.

1st 5. Ex. "James Sedgley," L. I. R. R. Received August 1869.

1st 6. Ex. "Pacific," L. I. R. R. Received August 1869.

1st 7. Ex. "Albany" No. 27, N. Y. & Harlem; Sold by NY&H to L. I. R. R. and renamed "G. F. Carman." Received August 1869.

2nd 7. Reb. Taunton 5/1882. Later renamed " H. W. Spafford."

8. Renamed "Frank C. White." Renamed "E. D. Bennett."

9. Renamed "C. J. McMaster."

10. Ex. N. Y. B. & M. No. 1.

1st 11. Ex. N. Y. B. & M. No. 3.

14. Sold to Ft. Smith & Western No. 6, October, 1920.

15. Sold to Ft. Smith & Western No. 5, October, 1920.

16. Sold, 1902, to C. P. R. Nos. 181-299-199.

Bennington & Rutland's No. 15 lost her name, F. B. Jennings, and was rebuilt before appearing in the picture above as Rutland's American No. 865. The big Mogul No. 1881 in the snowy picture at the right also had a name, H. P. McCullough when she served B. & R. as No. 6. Newest of the B. & R. engines when the Rutland bought that line in 1901 was American No. 244 with its unusual Belpaire firebox.

A rather thorough search failed to locate or even suspect the existence of any official records of the locomotives of the L. S. and C. & L. V. Railroads. What data are available are for the most part from recollections and from records of other roads, whose motive power eventually found its way to the Lebanon Valley lines. With the exception of the two eight-wheelers received from Baldwin in 1890, every one of the engines of these companies had seen service on one or more other roads. There are also indications that locomotives were leased from time to time, probably from the N. Y. C. & H. R. and the B. & R. Records of the Rome Locomotive Works show that, on January 6th, 1886, Lackawanna & Pittsburg No. 208 was delivered to the L. S. R. R. for trial, but was not accepted and was returned. It was subsequently sold to the New York, Rutland & Montreal, together with L. & P. No. 210. Since the N. Y. R. & M. was one of the operators of the Lebanon Springs road (1885 to 1888), it is possible that these engines were used on that road, although they do not appear in the appended rosters, and their ultimate disposition is not known.

Apparently none of the L. S. engines bore names, which is unusual, in view of the period in which the railroad operated. From what material is available, it appears that there were two renumberings of the locomotives, the scheme of the first one being something to wonder about, where No. 1 became No. 12, No. 3 was changed to No. 233, No. 4 to 69, and No. 5 remained unchanged. The date of this renumbering is not certain, but it was probably about 1890, and was done primarily to make room for new Nos. 1 and 2, received that year. Later on the 1890's, Nos. 1 and 2 were changed to Nos. 6 and 9 respectively, and No. 233 was changed back to No. 3. An interesting story is told about the former change and accounts for the absence of numbers 7 and 8 on the final C. & L. V. roster.

These engines, Nos. 1 and 2, were scheduled to be renumbered to Nos. 6 and 7, when some one located a brass plate bearing the number "66" cast thereon.

This plate was cut in half and one "6" was placed on the number plate of No. 1. The other "6" was inverted, becoming "9", and was placed on the No. 2. Hence, Nos. 1 and 2 became Nos. 6 and 9, and the use of numbers 7 and 8 was by-passed. It would appear that this masterpiece of economy took place in Vermont, rather than in New York!

After the C. & L. V. took over the Lebanon Springs road, it purchased two second hand locomotives, viz., the No. 4, an 0-6-0 (often erroneously identified as a former Lehigh Valley engine), and the No. 5, a 4-4-0, the latter purchased from the Rhode Island Locomotive Works.

Only four engines from the C. & L. V. went to the Rutland: Nos. 3, 5, 6 and 9. The No. 9 became Rutland No. 175 and, later, No. 798. It was while carrying this number that she was in a collision with Rutland No. 2044, pulling a south-bound milk train, near the Soldiers' Home Crossing, in Bennington, on September 7th, 1912. The No. 798 was so badly damaged that she was never repaired.

An account of the Lebanon Springs locomotives, in the Central Vermont Bulletin, of the R. & L. H. Society, states that, according to Mr. George J. McMaster, Master Mechanic on the old Bennington & Rutland Railway, the Lebanon Springs started out with three second-hand locomotives—the "Chazy," "Mad Tom" and "King Phillip." The first came from the O. & L. C., by way of the Rutland & Burlington; the second may have been the "Romulus," Norris, 1839, on the Seaboard & Roanoke, purchased from the U. S. Military R. R., and the "King Phillip" was probably the engine of the same name from the Boston & Providence R. R., Locks & Canals, 1839. These locomotives were all scrapped at Rutland, Vt., during the early seventies. This being the case, and records indicating that the next engine purchased was from the D. & H., in 1878, it would seem that the road's operations were carried on, during this period, with leased power.

The other known locomotives appear in the following rosters.

LEBANON SPRINGS RAILROAD LOCOMOTIVES TO 1890

No.	Ren'd	Builder	C/N	Date	Type	Cyls.	DD	Rec'd
1	12	Taunton	162	1855	4-4-0	16x22	54	10-1880
2		R. K. & G.	303	1852	4-4-0	14x20	54	10-1880
3	233	D. C. & Co.		1854	4-4-0	15x20	60	5-1881
4	69	Br. & Kn'd		1859	4-4-0	15x20	60	5-1881
5	5	Br. & Kn'd		1857	4-4-0			- 1878

1. Built for the Rutland & Washington R. R. named "Chamberlain." Renamed "Merrit Clark," prior to 1867. Became D. & H. #114. To L. S. in 1878.
2. Built as New York & Harlem #10, "Troy."
3. Built as New York & Harlem #11, "George L. Schuyler."
4. Built as New York & Harlem 2nd #3, "United States."
5. Built as New York & Harlem #23, "Island Belle."

1890-1899

No.	Ren'd	Builder	C/N	Date	Type	Cyls.	DD	Rec'd
1		Baldwin	10841	1890	4-4-0	17x24	63	Ren. C&LV #6
2		Baldwin	10849	1890	4-4-0	17x24	63	Ren. C&LV #9
5	(x-5)	Br. & Kn'd		1857	4-4-0			Scrapped 1897
12	(x-1)	Taunton	162	1855	4-4-0	16x22	54	Scrapped 1897
69	(x-4)	Br. & Kn'd		1859	4-4-0	15x20	60	Scrapped 1897
233	(x-3)	D. C. & Co.		1854	4-4-0	15x20	60	Ren. C&LV #3

CHATHAM & LEBANON VALLEY R. R.

No.	Builder	C/N	Date	Type	Cyls.	DD	
3	D. C. & Co.		1854	4-4-0	15x20	60	To Rutland #77
4	?		?	0-6-0	15x20	60	
5	Brooks	910	1883	4-4-0	14x22	56	To Rutland #78
6	Baldwin	10841	1890	4-4-0	17x24	63	To Rutland #174-797
9	Baldwin	10849	1890	4-4-0	17x24	63	To Rutland #175-798

No. 5 was ex-Narragansett Pier #3, bought from R. I. Locomotive Works.

The topheavy-appearing 0-6-0 switcher on the opposite page had a mysterious history and lineage, but was obviously not brand new when photographed in 1900 at Chatham. Chatham & Lebanon Valley No. 5 was an American dating from 1883. She had unmatching lead wheels by the time her picture was taken outside the Chatham engine house.

Because a number of engines from the A. & St. L. and the St. L. & A. railroads eventually reached the Rutland, mention should be made of these roads in connection with Rutland motive power.

The Herkimer, Newport & Poland R. R., forming the southern end of the A. & St. L., was chartered on June 29, 1880, and opened to traffic in 1881-2. Its gauge was 42", and the line extended from Herkimer, east of Utica on the Mohawk River, in a northwesterly direction to Poland, N. Y. In 1892 the track gauge was changed to standard. At about this time, the N. H. & P. was continued to Remsen, 11 miles, through construction of the H. N. & P. Extension R. R.

In 1891-2, the A. & St. L. was built from the Remsen terminus to Malone, N. Y., and became part of the Mohawk & Malone R. R., by consolidation, in 1893, the M. & M. being a consolidation of the above three lines. The M. & M. was leased to the N. Y. C. & H. R., and was operated as part of that road's Mohawk Division. During its existence, the A. & St. L. had forty or more locomotives, on the tenders of which was lettered the road's name, and was painted the road's symbol, a "fleur-de-lis." Many of these locomotives were acquired by the Central Vermont, which assigned at least five of them to the Rutland Division, so-called, then under lease to the C. V.

For some time after the formation of the M. & M., tenders were lettered Adirondack & St. Lawrence *Line*, by which name the road was known. First Nos. 1, 2 and 3 of the A. & St. L. were originally the narrow gauge engines of the H. N. & P., which were rebuilt to standard gauge, and later Nos. 1 and 3 became C. V. Nos. 9 and 12.

In order to complete a rail route from Malone to Montreal, the Malone & St. Lawrence R. R. was built from Malone to the Canadian Line, where it connected with the St. Lawrence & Adirondack R. R., extending from there to Valleyfield, P. Q., and which was completed on January 11th, 1892. Dr. W. S. Webb acquired this line in June, 1892, and turned it over to the Central Vermont for operation, for a few years. Connection was made at Valleyfield to Ottawa, and, at Coteau, to Montreal via the Grand Trunk.

The line was returned to Dr. Webb, who (1) leased part of the Grand Trunk line from Valleyfield to Beauharnois, (2) built the Southwestern R. R. (chartered in Canada on Sept. 10th, 1891) from Beauharnois to Caughnawaga Jct. (now Adirondack Jct.), and (3) obtained trackage rights from there to Montreal, nine miles, over the Canadian Pacific. The St. L. & A., the M. & St. L., and the Southwestern Railroads were consolidated in 1896, to form a new St. L. & A., which was leased to the N. Y. C. & H. R. R. R. from June 1st, 1898, to January 1st, 1905, when the N. Y. C. bought all of the stock of the St. L. & A.

The St. L. & A. owned at least 30 locomotives, of which eight were acquired by the Rutland, and the others by the New York Central. Tenders of some of the engines were lettered with the road's full name, but, in later years, the single word "Adirondack" was painted instead.

To add to the confusion caused by the similarity of names of these two roads, there was another road bearing the name Adirondack & St. Lawrence. This was a short line (3.61 miles) in western New York, extending from Hermon village to DeKalb Jct., on the New York Central, and on which operations were suspended on February 12th, 1921. This road had three locomotives at the time of abandonment.

THE LOCOMOTIVES OF THE ADIRONDACK & ST. LAWRENCE R. R.

No.	Builder	C/N	Date	Type	Cyls.	DD	Date	Disposition To
1	Baldwin	5627	1881	4-4-0	10x16	42		ex-HN&P 1. To CV 9. Sc 1899 "Edward W. Burnes"
2	Mason		1874	2-4-4T	12x16	36		ex-HN&P 2; ex-New Brunswick Ry. "Henry W. Dexter"
3	Baldwin	4286	1878	2-6-0	14x18	42		ex-HN&P 3; ex-Georgia Land & Lbr. Co. "J. C. Anderson". To CV 12-4
1	Schenectady	3510	1891	0-4-0	16x24	51	1891	CV 211; Rut 80; NCYL 50; Rut 50
2	Schenectady	3515	1891	0-4-0	16x24	51	1891	CV 20-49
4	Rh. Island	710	1878	2-4-4	11x16	42		ex-N. Y. Elevated Ry. 45. To 99
6	Schenectady	828	1872	4-4-0	16x24	63		ex-NYC 224; ex-361; To CV 13-42
7	No data						1897	Scrapped W. Albany
11	Schenectady	3511	1891	4-4-0	18x24	69	1891	CV 232; Rut 182; NYCL 862; Rut 82-67
11	Schenectady	3593	1892	4-4-0	17x24	63	1892	CV 30-50
12	Schenectady	3512	1891	4-4-0	18x24	69	1891	CV 233; Rut 183; NYCL 863; Rut 83
12	Schenectady	3594	1892	4-4-0	17x24	63	1892	CV 31-51

page 422

13	Schenectady	3513	1891	4-4-0	18x24	69	1891	CV 107-102
14	Schenectady	3514	1891	4-4-0	18x24	69	1891	CV 108-103
15	Schenectady	3754	1892	4-6-0	20/30x26	70		NYC 993-2025
16	Schenectady	3755	1892	4-6-0	20/30x26	70		NYC 994-2026
17	Schenectady	3825	1892	4-6-0	20/30x26	70		NYC 995-2027
30	Schenectady	3706	1892	4-6-0	19x24	62	2/94	LV 707-1125
31	Schenectady	3506	1891	4-6-0	18x24	56	1892	CV 234; Rut 480; NYCL 2061; Rut 61
31	Schenectady	3707	1892	4-6-0	19x24	64	2/94	LV 706-1124
32	Schenectady	3505	1891	4-6-0	18x24	56	1892	CV 235; Rut 481; NYCL 2062; Rut 62
32	Schenectady	3722	1892	4-6-0	19x24	63	1892	CV 116-209
33	Schenectady	3723	1892	4-6-0	19x24	63	1892	CV 117-210
34	Rh. Island	2730	1892	4-6-0	19x24	56		Ren. 113. 1892, to CV 113-206
35	Rh. Island	2727	1892	4-6-0	19x24	56		Ren. 114. 1892, to CV 114-207
38	Rh. Island	2726	1892	4-6-0	19x24	56		Ren. 112. 1892, to CV 112-205
39	Rh. Island	2762	1892	4-6-0	19x24	56		Ren. 115. 1892, to CV 115-208
50	Schenectady	3686	1892	2-6-0	20/30x26	57		NYC 842-1813
51	Schenectady	3687	1892	2-6-0	20/30x26	57		NYC 843-1814
52	Schenectady	3826	1892	2-6-0	20/30x26	57		NYC 844-1815
60	Schenectady	4055	1893	2-8-0	22/33x26	51		NYC 996-2210
61	Schenectady	4056	1893	2-8-0	22/32x26	51		NYC 997-2211
80	Schenectady	3879	1892	4-6-0	19/28x24	69		NYC 998-2186
81	Schenectady	3880	1892	4-6-0	19/28x24	69		NYC 1000-2187
82	Schenectady	3883	1892	4-6-0	19/28x24	69		NYC 1001-2188
83	Schenectady	3884	1892	4-6-0	19/28x24	69		NYC 1002-2189
84	Schenectady	3885	1892	4-6-0	19/28x24	69		NYC 1003-2190
99	Schenectady	3639	1892	2-4-6	16x22	61		"St. Lawrence" To CV 109
99	Rh. Island	710	1878	2-4-4	11x16	42		From #4. Inspection engine
101	Schenectady	3878	1892	4-4-0	19x24	69	1892	CV 129-106
110	Rh. Island	2760	1892	4-6-0	19x24	56	1892	CV 110-203
111	Rh. Island	2761	1892	4-6-0	19x24	56	1892	CV 111-204
112	Rh. Island	2726	1892	4-6-0	19x24	56	1892	From 38. To CV 112-205
113	Rh. Island	2730	1892	4-6-0	19x24	56	1892	From 34. To CV 113-206

American No. 1000 with Belpaire firebox, was built by Brooks in 1897 for St. Lawrence & Adirondack.

No.	Builder	C/N	Date	Type	Cyls.	DD	Date	Disposition To
114	Rh. Island	2727	1892	4-6-0	19x24	56	1892	From 35. To CV 114-207
115	Rh. Island	2762	1892	4-6-0	19x24	56	1892	From 39. To CV 115-208
116	Schenectady	4114	1893	2-6-0	19x26	57	1893	CV 130-336
117	Schenectady	4115	1893	2-6-0	19x26	57	1893	CV 131-337
118	Schenectady	4116	1893	2-6-0	19x26	57	1893	CV 132-338
119	Schenectady	4117	1893	2-6-0	19x26	57	1893	CV 133-339
120	Schenectady	4118	1893	2-6-0	19x26	57	1893	CV 134-340
—	Schenectady	4144	1893	4-4-0	18x24	74	11/93	Sold to C. R. R. of Pa. #6. Named "Ne-Ha-Sa-Ne." No A&StL number.

Note: #99, Schenectady #3639, was sold to the Central Vermont, where it was rebuilt to a 4-4-0, an inspection engine, retaining its name "St. Lawrence."
#99, Rhode Island #710, was rebuilt from a former N. Y. Elevated Railway locomotive.
The above record, showing Schenectady Nos. 3706 and 3707 as going to L. V. Nos. 707 and 706, respectively, concurs with the L. V. records. Schenectady records show that Nos. 3706 and 3707 became L. V. Nos. 706 and 707, respectively.
Nos. 116 through 120 were probably ordered by the A. & St. L., but were probably delivered to the C. V. without ever seeing service on the A. & St. L.

LOCOMOTIVES OF THE ST. LAWRENCE & ADIRONDACK R. R.

(Names shown at end of roster)

No.	Builder	C/N	Date	Type	Cyls.	DD	Date	Disposition To
1	Schenectady	4130	1893	2-6-0	19x26	57		NYC 784-1687
1	Schenectady	4437	1896	4-4-0	18x24	67	1897	CAR 24-628; GTR 1331-2240; CN 311
1	Manchester	445	1872	4-4-0	15x22	66	1898	ex-CV 170; ex-NLN 20. To Rut 238-79
1	Schenectady	1655	1882	4-4-0	17x24	64		From #11; ex-NYC 452, ex-256. Received 12-1898
2	Schenectady	4393	1895	2-6-0	19x26	64		NYC 785-1688
2	Brooks	2677	1896	4-6-0	20x26	57		Ren'd 4
2	Schenectady	4438	1896	4-4-0	20x24	67		CCC&StL 203; NYCL 7143
2	Schenectady	2221	1886	4-4-0	17x24	64		From #12; ex-NYC 494, ex-267, ex-489, ex-276. Rec'd 4-1900
3	Brooks	2678	1896	4-6-0	20x26	57		NYC 2028
3	Schenectady	4394	1895	4-4-0	20x24	73		From #13; to CCC&StL 202; NYCL 7142
3	Schenectady	5591	1900	2-6-0	20x28	57	1900	Rut 320; NYCL 1884; Rut 144
4	Schenectady	4439	1896	4-6-0	20x26	57	1896	MC 452-8180
4	Brooks	2677	1896	4-6-0	20x26	57		From #2; To NYCL 2029
4	Schenectady	5592	1900	2-6-0	20x28	57	1900	Rut 321; NYCL 1885; Rut 145
5	Schenectady	4334	1895	4-6-0	20x26	64	1896	MC 453-8181
5	Brooks	2772	1897	4-4-0	18x26	64	1900	Rut 249-190; NYCL 1000; Rut 80-65
6	Brooks	2668	1896	4-6-0	18x26	69	1896	LS&MS 602-544-5019
6	Brooks	2773	1897	4-4-0	18x26	64		NYCL 1002 (1903-4)
7	Brooks	2669	1896	4-6-0	18x26	69	1896	LS&MS 603-545-5017
7	Brooks	2774	1897	4-4-0	18x26	64	1900	Rut 250-191; NYCL 1001; Rut 81-66
8	Brooks	2670	1896	4-6-0	18x26	69	1896	LS&MS 604-546-5018
8	Schenectady	4932	1898	4-6-0	20x28	61	1900	Rut 251-420; NYCL 2153-2063; Rut 63
9	Schenectady	4933	1898	4-6-0	20x28	61	1900	Rut 252-421; NYCL 2154-2064; Rut 64
10	Schenectady	4401	1896	4-4-0	14x22	63	1900	NYC&HR 49; Rut 100; NYCL 33; Rut 99

10	Schenectady	6128	1901	4-4-2	19x26	69	1901	NYCL 2900-2800-3800-800
10	Schenectady	5181	1899	4-6-0	20x28	70		ex-NYCL 2002; ex-2028; ex-NYC 950. To NYCL 2002 again, 1903-4
11	Schenectady	1655	1882	4-4-0	17x24	64		ex-NYC 452; ex-256; To 4th #1
11	Schenectady	6136	1901	4-4-2	19x26	69	1901	NYCL 2901-2801-3801-801
11	Schenectady	5182	1899	4-6-0	20x28	70		ex-NYCL 2003; ex-2029; ex-NYC 951. Back to NYCL 2003, 1903-4
12	Schenectady	2221	1886	4-4-0	17x24	64		ex-NYC 494; ex-267; ex-489; ex-276. To 4th #2
12	Schenectady	6137	1901	4-4-2	19x26	69	1901	NYCL 2902-2802-3802-802
12	Schenectady	5184	1899	4-6-0	20x28	70		ex-NYCL 2005; ex-2031; ex-NYC 953. Back to NYCL 2005, 1903-4
13	Schenectady	4394	1896	4-4-0	20x24	73		To 2nd #3, etc.
15	Brooks	2667	1896	4-8-0	21x26	55	1896	BR&P 139. To Cumberland & Manchester #56

LOCOMOTIVE NAMES

Road No.		C/N	Name
1		4437	Beauharnois
2	(4)	2677	Kushaqua
3		2678	Cascapedia
4	(2)	2677	Kushaqua
6		2668	Mattawa
7		2669	Mirimichi
8		2670	Madawaska
10		4401	Ne-Ha-Sa-Ne
15		2667	Manitou

St. Lawrence & Adirondack's third No. 1, shown here at Ellenburg, became Rutland No. 79 after the shuffling of the northern New York Railroads in the early 1900's, when Dr. Webb became involved in the Vermont line's affairs.

CHRONOLOGY OF THE RUTLAND RAILROAD

Compiled by: DAVID W. MESSER

1843	Nov. 1:	Champlain & Connecticut River Railroad Company chartered
1845	May 14:	Northern Railroad Company incorporated
1845	Nov. 5:	Western Vermont Railroad incorporated
1847	Nov. 6:	Champlain & Connecticut River Railroad changed to Rutland & Burlington Railroad Company
1847		Rutland & Washington Railroad chartered
1848	Nov. 8:	Vermont Valley R. R. incorporated
1848	Nov. 13:	Rutland & Whitehall Railroad chartered to build a line parallel to Rutland & Washington to Castleton
1849		Vermont & Canada leased to Vermont Central
1849	Dec. 18:	First train runs over Rutland & Burlington on Bellows Falls-Burlington line
1850	Sept. 20:	Northern Railroad of N. Y. opened for traffic
1851		First refrigerator car in the U. S. placed in operation on Northern R. R. of N. Y.
1852	Mar. 25:	Organization of Lebanon Springs Railroad
1852	Aug. 31:	Champlain Transportation Co. purchased by Rutland & Burlington, service initiated to Rouses Point and Plattsburgh
1853	Nov. 19:	Control of Rutland & Burlington transferred to Mortgage Trustees
1855	Jan.:	Champlain Transportation Co. sold, later being purchased by Rensselaer & Saratoga
1857	Nov. 1:	Western Vermont R. R. leased to Troy & Boston
1864	June 18:	Incorporation of Ogdensburg & Lake Champlain Railroad Company
1865	May 12:	Vermont Valley R. R. leased by Rutland & Burlington
1865	July:	Through freight service provided between Rutland and Burlington and Rensselaer and Saratoga
1865	Aug. 1:	Formation of first Bennington & Rutland Railroad Company from Western Vermont R.R.
1866	June:	First Fenian campaign (O&LC R.R.)
1867	June 25:	Rutland & Burlington reorganized to form the first Rutland Railroad Company, effective July 9, 1867
1867	Nov. 21:	Organization of Addison Railroad Company
1867	Jan. 15-16:	Termination of Bennington & Rutland lease by Troy & Boston; leased by John Page and J. Gregory Smith
1868		John Page becomes president of the Rutland
1870	Jan. 1:	Bennington & Rutland and Lebanon Springs R. R. consolidated into Harlem Extension R. R.
1870	Mar. 1:	O&LC leased to Vermont Central R. R.
1870	May 26:	Second Fenian encampment
1870	Sept. 26:	Whitehall & Plattsburgh R. R. from Ticonderoga to Port Henry leased to Rutland R.R.
1870	Dec. 1:	Vermont & Massachusetts leased to Rutland R. R.
1870	Dec. 7:	Addison Railroad leased to Rutland R. R. for 99 years
1870	Dec. 30:	Rutland Railroad Company leased to Vermont Central Railroad Company for 20 years from January 1, 1871
1871	Jan. 23:	Montreal and Plattsburgh R. R. leased to Rutland
1877		Central Vermont R. R. terminates lease of Bennington and Rutland

1884		Charles Clement takes over presidency of the Rutland
1888		Percival Clement takes over presidency from his son Charles
1890	Dec. 31:	Rutland Railroad Company leased to Central Vermont Railway Company for 99 years from January 1, 1891 (renewal of former 20-year lease to V. C.)
1896	May 7:	Central Vermont in receivership; Rutland returned to owners
1899	July 1:	Rutland-Canadian R. R. leased to Rutland R. R.
1901	Jan. 21:	Second Rutland Railroad Company formed by consolidation with Rutland-Canadian Railroad
1901	Sept. 6:	Third Rutland Railroad Company formed by consolidation with Bennington & Rutland R. R.
1901	Oct. 26-28:	Fourth Rutland Railroad Company formed by consolidation with Ogensburg and Lake Champlain R. R.
1901	Dec. 23-24:	Fifth Rutland Railroad Company formed by consolidation with Chatham and Lebanon Valley R. R.
1902	May 1:	W. Seward Webb assumes presidency of the Rutland
1904-1905		Controlling interest in the Rutland obtained by New York Central & Hudson River R. R.
1911	Feb.:	Half of New York Central's Rutland stock sold to the New Haven R. R.
1914	July 1:	Panama Canal Act passed forcing Rutland to cease water transportation and sell its steamers
1917	Dec. 28:	Control of Rutland assumed by United States Railroad Administration
1920	Mar. 1:	Government control of Rutland terminated
1925	Nov. 5:	Incorporation of Rutland Transportation Co.
1927	Nov. 3-5:	The "Great Flood" devastates the Rutland
1932	June 25:	Passenger train service terminated on Chatham Division
1938	May 5:	Rutland Railroad passes into receivership
1938	July:	"Save the Rutland" Club formed
1939	Jan. 9:	Inaugural run of *The Whippet*
1941		Both New York Central and New Haven railroads sell remaining Rutland stock to private investors
1950	Nov. 1:	Reorganization of Rutland Rail*road* into Rutland Rail*way*
1953	May 20:	ICC grants permission to abandon Chatham branch
1953	June 26:	Rutland hit by three week strike, first in its history. All passenger service eliminated
1960	Sept. 16:	Rutland hit by first of two major strikes, lasting 41 days until November 1, 1960
1961	Sept. 25:	Second major strike — last Rutland train
1961	Dec. 4:	Rutland applies to ICC for abandonment
1962	Mar.-Apr.:	ICC abandonment hearings — seven days in Rutland and two days in Malone
1962	Sept. 18:	ICC approves application for abandonment, effective January 29, 1963
1963	Jan. 28:	Railway Labor Executive Council obtains U. S. District Court injunction in Cleveland blocking abandonment
1963	Jan. 29:	Abandonment effective date postponed to May 20, 1963, to allow State of Vermont to secure buyers
1963	May 29:	Vermont Legislature passes $2.7 million bill allowing State to purchase certain sections of Rutland for subsequent lease to operators
1963	Nov. 4:	Rutland Railway Company free to dispose of property as it sees fit—State of Vermont's power to designate operators ends

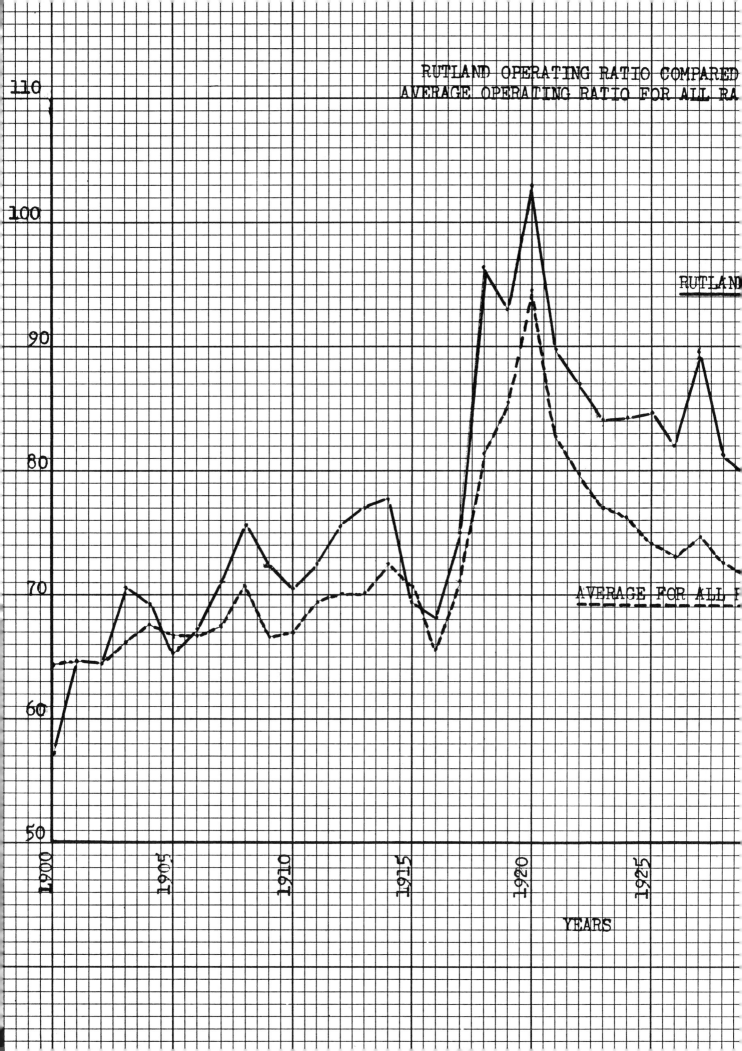

RUTLAND OPERATING RATIO COMPARED
AVERAGE OPERATING RATIO FOR ALL RA

RUTLAND

AVERAGE FOR ALL

110

100

90

80

70

60

50

1900   1905   1910   1915   1920   1925

YEARS

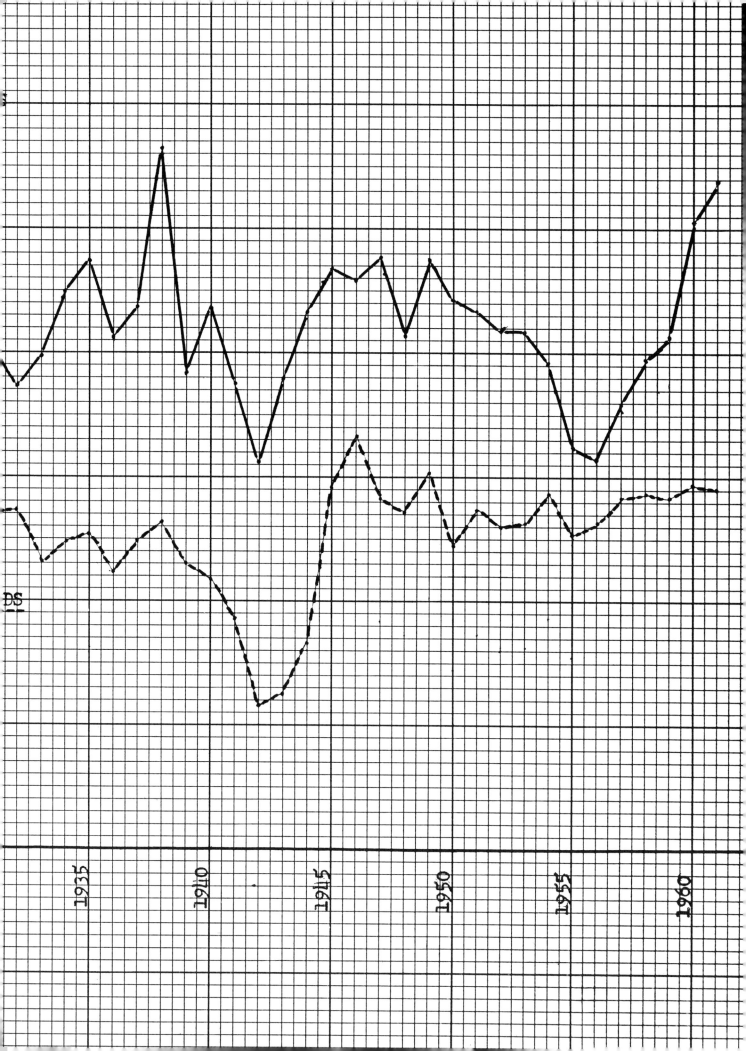

1935   1940   1945   1950   1955   1960

POPULATION OF MAJOR TOWNS, 1960

Alburg	426	Danby	250	Mount Holly	70
Altona	350	E. Dorset	140	N. Bennington	1,437
Arlington	1,111	E. Wallingford	150	N. Ferrisburg	200
Bellows Falls	3,831	Ellenburg Dpt.	300	N. Hero	50
Bennington	8,023	Ferrisburg	170	N. Lawrence	400
(Berlin)*	800	Florence	80	Norwood	2,200
Brandon	1,675	Grand Isle	65	Ogdensburg	16,122
Brushton	553	Leicester Jct.	100	Proctor	1,978
Burlington	35,531	Lisbon	280	Proctorsville	476
Cavendish	250	Ludlow	1,658	Rouses Pt.	2,160
Cen. Rutland	125	Madrid	800	Rutland	18,325
Champlain	1,549	Malone	8,737	Salisbury	130
Charlotte	160	Manchester	875	Shelburne	250
Chateaugay	1,097	Middlebury	3,688	S. Hero	55
(Chatham)*	2,426	Moira	500	S. Shaftsbury	600
Chester	923	Mooers	543	Vergennes	1,921
				Wallingford	900

*On Chatham Branch abandoned 1953

BIBLIOGRAPHY

Baker, George P., *Formation of the New England Railroad Systems,* Cambridge, Mass., Harvard Univ. Press, 1949.

Harlow, Alvin F., *Steelways of New England,* 1st edition, New York, Creative Age Press, 1946.

Haynes, Rutherford, *Troy and Rensselaer County,* New York, 1925

————, *Historical Sketch of Rutland R.R. Co.,* 2nd edition, December, 1949.

Laut, Agnes C., *The Romance of the Rails,* 2nd edition, New York, Tudor Publishing Co., 1936.

Lewis, Robert G., *Handbook of American Railroads,* 2nd edition, New York, Simmons-Boardman Pub. Co., 1956.

Pletz, Wm., *History of Rutland Ry.,* 1958.

Shaughnessy, Jim, *Delaware & Hudson,* San Diego, Ca., Howell-North Books, 1967.

Articles in Periodicals

Berry, Watson B., "The First Refrigerator Car," *Railroad Magazine,* XXIII, No. 3, Feb. 1938, P. 67.

Blabey, E. H., III, "Rutland Revival, Part III — Ogdensburg Bridge & Port Authority," *Railfan Magazine,* Vol. 1, No. 4, Fall 1975, p. 30.

Curry, Bruce, "Rutland Revival, Part I — The Vermont Railway," *Railfan Mag.,* Vol. 1, No. 3, Summer 1975, p. 18.

————, "Vermont: Small Investment, Big Return," *Railway Age,* Vol. 175, No. 1, Jan. 1974, p. 10.

————, and Donald Valentine, Jr., "Rutland Revival — Part II — Green Mountain Railroad," *Railfan Magazine,* Vol. 1, No. 4, Fall 1975, p. 23.

Doherty, Lawrence, "General History of the Ogdensburg & Lake Champlain Railroad," *Bulletin,* Railway and Locomotive Historical Society, Aug. 1942, pp. 91-95.

Graham, F. Stewart, "Locomotives of the Rutland and Its Subsidiary Lines," *Bulletin No. 90,* Railway & Locomotive Historical Society, May, 1954, pp. 83-111.

Gross, H. H., "The Barlow Plan," *Railroad Magazine,* XLI, No. 4, Jan. 1947, pp. 11, 16.

Huban, George H., "That Little Train That Could," *Vermont Life,* XI, No. 1, Autumn, 1956, pp. 3, 4, 6, 7.

Hungerford, Edward, "Vermont Central-Central Vermont — A Study in Human Effort," *Bulletin,* Railway and Locomotive Historical Society, Aug., 1942, pp. 13, 40.

————, "Locomotives of the Rutland R. R.," *Railroad Stories,* XII, No. 4, Nov., 1933, pp. 130-131.

Navin, William E., "The Founding of the Rutland Railroad," *Vermont Quarterly,* XIV, No. 3, July, 1946, pp. 91-94.

————, "O. & L. C. Division of C.V. Locomotives," *Bulletin,* Railway & Locomotive Historical Society, Aug. 1942, pp. 60, 61, 96-98.

————, "Rutland Builds Modern Plant," *Modern Railroads,* X, No. 10, Oct. 1955, pp. 69-74.

————, "Rutland Locomotives," *Bulletin,* Railway and Locomotive Historical Society, Aug. 1942, #90.

————, "Rutland to Store Grain for U.S. at Ogdensburg," *Modern Railroads,* X, No. 10, Oct. 1955, P. 64.

Sargent, D. W., "The Rutland R. R.," *Bulletin,* Railway and Locomotive Historical Society, Aug. 1942, pp. 74-81.

Shedd, Tom, "Green Mountain Miracle," *Modern Railroads,* X, No. 10, Oct. 1955, pp. 57-59, 61, 62.

Thorne, Frederick C., "The Green Mountain Route," *Trains,* VI, No. 5, March, 1946, pp. 28, 31-35.

Wilson, Charles M., "Green Mountain Gateway," *Railroad Magazine,* LXVIII, No. 4, June, 1957, pp. 19, 20, 24.